Organizational Culture

FOUNDATIONS FOR ORGANIZATIONAL SCIENCE
A Sage Publications Series

Series Editor
David Whetten, *Brigham Young University*

Editors
Peter J. Frost, *University of British Columbia*
Anne S. Huff, *University of Colorado* and *Cranfield University* (UK)
Benjamin Schneider, *University of Maryland*
M. Susan Taylor, *University of Maryland*
Andrew Van de Ven, *University of Minnesota*

The FOUNDATIONS FOR ORGANIZATIONAL SCIENCE series supports the development of students, faculty, and prospective organizational science professionals through the publication of texts authored by leading organizational scientists. Each volume provides a highly personal, hands-on introduction to a core topic or theory and challenges the reader toÿ20explore promising avenues for future theory development and empirical application.

Books in This Series

PUBLISHING IN THE ORGANIZATIONAL SCIENCES, 2nd Edition
Edited by L. L. Cummings and Peter J. Frost

SENSEMAKING IN ORGANIZATIONS
Karl E. Welck

INSTITUTIONS AND ORGANIZATIONS
W. Richard Scott

RHYTHMS OF ACADEMIC LIFE
Peter J. Frost and M. Susan Taylor

RESEARCHERS HOOKED ON TEACHING:
Noted Scholars Discuss the Synergies of Teaching and Research
Rae Andr, and Peter J. Frost

THE PSYCHOLOGY OF DECISION MAKING: People in Organizations
Lee Roy Beach

ORGANIZATIONAL JUSTICE AND HUMAN RESOURCE MANAGEMENT
Robert Folger and Russell Cropanzano

RECRUITING EMPLOYEES: Individual and Organizational Perspectives
Alison E. Barber

ATTITUDES IN AND AROUND ORGANIZATIONS
Arthur P. Brief

IDENTITY IN ORGANIZATIONS: Building Theory Through Conversations
Edited by David Whetten and Paul Godfrey

PERSONNEL SELECTION: A Theoretical Approach
Neal Schmitt and David Chan

BUILDING STRATEGY FROM THE MIDDLE: Reconceptualizing Strategy Process
Steven W. Floyd and Bill Wooldridge

MISSING ORGANIZATIONAL LINKAGES: Tools for Cross-Level Research
Paul S. Goodman

THE CONTINGENCY THEORY OF ORGANIZATIONS
Lex Donaldson

ORGANIZATIONAL STRESS: A Review and Critique of Theory, Research, and Applications
Cary L. Cooper, Philip J. Dewe, and Michael P. O'Driscoll

INSTITUTIONS AND ORGANIZATIONS, Second Edition
W. Richard Scott

ORGANIZATIONAL CULTURE: Mapping the Terrain
Joanne Martin

Joanne Martin
Stanford University

Organizational Culture

Mapping the Terrain

Foundations for
Organizational
Science
A Sage Publications Series

Sage Publications
International Educational and Professional Publisher
Thousand Oaks ▪ London ▪ New Delhi

For information:

Sage Publications, Inc.
2455 Teller Road
Thousand Oaks, California 91320
E-mail: order@sagepub.com

Sage Publications Ltd.
6 Bonhill Street
London EC2A 4PU
United Kingdom

Sage Publications India Pvt. Ltd.
M-32 Market
Greater Kailash I
New Delhi 110 048 India

Printed in the United States of America

Library of Congress Cataloging-in-Publication Data

Martin, Joanne.
  Organizational culture: Mapping the terrain / by Joanne Martin.
     p. cm. — (Foundations for organizational science)
  Includes bibliographical references and index.
  ISBN 0-8039-7294-6 (C: alk. paper) — ISBN 0-8039-7295-4 (P: alk. paper)
  I. Title. II. Series.
  HM791 .M37 2001
  302.3´5—dc21

                                                       2001001020

02   03   04   05   06   07   08   7   6   5   4   3

Acquiring Editor:	Marquita Flemming
Editorial Assistant:	MaryAnn Vail
Production Editor:	Diana E. Axelsen
Editorial Assistant:	Cindy Bear
Copy Editor:	Dan Hays
Typesetter/Designer:	Christina M. Hill
Indexer:	Jeanne Busemeyer
Cover Designer:	Michelle Lee

Contents

List of Tables and Figures

Introduction to the Series

The title of this series, **Foundations for Organizational Science** (FOS), denotes a distinctive focus. FOS books are educational aids for mastering the core theories, essential tools, and emerging perspectives that constitute the field of organizational science (broadly conceived to include organizational behavior, organizational theory, human resource management, and business strategy). Our ambitious goal is to assemble the "essential library" for members of our professional community.

The vision for the series emerged from conversations with several colleagues, including Peter Frost, Anne Huff, Rick Mowday, Benjamin Schneider, Susan Taylor, and Andy Van de Ven. Many common interests emerged from these sympathetic encounters, including enhancing the quality of doctoral education by providing broader access to the master teachers in our field, "bottling" the experience and insights of some of the founding scholars in our field before they retire, and providing professional development opportunities for colleagues seeking to broaden their understanding of the rapidly expanding subfields within organizational science.

Our unique learning objectives are reflected in an unusual set of instructions to FOS authors. They are encouraged to (a) "write the way they teach," framing their book as an extension of their teaching notes rather than as the expansion of a handbook chapter; (b) pass on their "craft knowledge" to the next generation of scholars, making them wiser and not just smarter; (c) share with their "virtual students and colleagues" the insider tips and best bets for research that are normally reserved for one-on-one mentoring sessions; and (d) make the complexity of their subject matter comprehensible to nonexperts so that readers can share their puzzlement, fascination, and intrigue.

We are proud of the group of highly qualified authors who have embraced the unique educational perspective of our "Foundations" series. We encourage your suggestions for how these books can better satisfy your learning needs—as a newcomer to the field preparing for prelims or developing a dissertation proposal or as an established scholar seeking to broaden your knowledge and proficiency.

DAVID A. WHETTEN
SERIES EDITOR

Acknowledgments

Any lengthy book gets written with much help. An exceptionally generous group of friends and anonymous reviewers undertook the gargantuan task of critiquing an early draft of the manuscript. Peter Frost offered, as always, a mix of support and keen insight. Dave Whetton, the editor of the **Foundations for Organizational Science** series, did as I asked and challenged my assumptions and assertions as hard as he could. He did so with panache and cogency, and even after my greatest efforts to respond fully, his arguments continue to ring in my ears. Ralph Stablein and Walter Nord helped me to maintain a critical perspective and sharpened my discussion of qualitative methods. Gideon Kunda spent hours reading and arguing about the ideas in this book, increasing my awareness, and making it very difficult for me to settle for easy answers to tough problems. Deb Meyerson, coauthor of articles that were the genesis of the three-perspective view of culture, was again a partner in this endeavor. She found what I had not said, what I should have said, and what I should not say. A second group of helpful friends gave detailed critiques of chapters in their areas of expertise: Mary Jo Hatch, Hazel Markus, Michael Morris, Denise Rousseau, and Majken Schultz. The diversity of views that these critics offered made this a much better book, although perhaps to their credit they might disown some of the views I express.

This book was also written with the help of people who never saw the manuscript but whose intellectual ghosts sat on my shoulders as I wrote. Linda Smircich and Marta Calás, through their work and through memories of the long talks we have had throughout the years, constantly pulled me toward more radical theories and methods. This was exceptionally valuable because I am usually surrounded by more conservative intellectual influences. John Van Maanen's work has taught me that it is essential that a cultural portrait capture the complex diversity of views held by lower-level employees. John also writes like an angel, albeit an angel with an eye for irony, an ear for what is not said, and a voice unlike any other. Although I did not attain his grace with words, his work encouraged me to try. Ed Schein, one of the fathers of organizational culture research, has taught me with patience and persistence to honor his ideas with the depth of understanding they deserve. In addition to these guiding ghosts, I thank the doctoral student-collaborators who worked with me on the studies that form the empirical backbone of the cultural theory presented in this book: Alan Wilkins, who first introduced me to the topic of culture; Caren Siehl, Melanie Powers, Michael Boehm, Sim Sitkin, Martha Feldman, Mary Jo Hatch, Kathy Knopoff, and Christine Beckman; and Deb Meyerson, my most frequent coauthor, co-conspirator, and friend. These people have been my teachers.

The references section at the end of this volume is long enough to be a book in itself. Lea Richards, my faculty assistant, spent long days tracking down disappearing citations and doing all the unrewarding, picky work involved in constructing such a reference list. Linda Bethel typed and drew the most difficult figures and tables and also gave Lea much needed help when the references needed proofing. The Graduate School of Business at Stanford University has been consistently generous in its support of my research and writing, not in the least by attracting such fine doctoral students.

On a more personal note, I have two Beaux to thank. The younger one, Beau M. Sheil, is my son. His love of life and fine sense of humor are a pleasure and a reminder of what is important. For decades, my husband, the other Beau Sheil, has been a constant source of love and encouragement (including much appreciated computer expertise and proofreading for this manuscript). He is the rock that supports all else in my life, including this book. Thank you all.

To Beau A. Sheil, my husband,
and Beau M. Sheil, my son,
who constantly remind me of what is important.

I

Mapping the Cultural Terrain

1   Introduction and Overview

When organizations are examined from a cultural viewpoint, attention is drawn to aspects of organizational life that historically
have often been ignored or understudied, such as the stories people tell
to newcomers to explain "how things are done around here," the ways in
which offices are arranged and personal items are or are not displayed,
jokes people tell, the working atmosphere (hushed and luxurious or
dirty and noisy), the relations among people (affectionate in some areas
of an office and obviously angry and perhaps competitive in another
place), and so on. Cultural observers also often attend to aspects of
working life that other researchers study, such as the organization's official policies, the amounts of money different employees earn, reporting
relationships, and so on. A cultural observer is interested in the surfaces
of these cultural manifestations because details can be informative, but
he or she also seeks an in-depth understanding of the patterns of meanings that link these manifestations together, sometimes in harmony,
sometimes in bitter conflicts between groups, and sometimes in webs of
ambiguity, paradox, and contradiction.

Culture as a Metaphor and Culture as a Variable

The long-winded definition of culture in the prior paragraph takes positions on some of the issues that divide cultural researchers. One of the most important is Smircich's (1983a) distinction between studies of culture as a metaphor for organizational life and studies of culture as a variable. Studies that assume culture can be treated as a variable are usually assuming a functionalist viewpoint. Functionalist studies of culture offer the promise, to the delight of many managers, that a "strong" culture (one that generates much consensus among employees of an organization) will lead to outcomes most top executives desire to maximize, such as greater productivity and profitability. Functionalist studies bring a kind of cultural research into the mainstream of organizational behavior, where research streams that fail to establish a causal link to performance-related outcomes have seldom managed to achieve long-term prominence. Critics of functional cultural research react with dismay at the intrusion of mainstream preoccupations into "their" cultural domain. For example, Calás and Smircich (1987) declared that cultural research had, by the end of the 1980s, become "dominant, but dead." Although this death knell was premature, many cultural researchers continue to oppose a functionalist approach to the study of culture. Cultural studies that eschew functionalism generally prefer a symbolic approach (Alvesson & Berg, 1992; Pondy, Frost, Morgan, & Dandridge, 1983; Schultz & Hatch, 1996), focusing on the symbolic meanings associated with cultural forms such as rituals and physical arrangements (Schultz, 1995). Although functional approaches often treat culture as a variable, used to predict outcomes, symbolic approaches tend to view culture as a lens for studying organizational life (Smircich, 1983b).

The definition I previously offered assumes that culture is a metaphor, a lens for examining organizational life. That does not mean that culture encompasses and eclipses all other ways of studying organizations. It does mean that, along with many others, I believe a cultural study should include detailed accounts of a wide range of familiar and unfamiliar aspects of organizational life in a "thick description" (a phrase coined by Geertz [1973] that means an account full of detailed observations). What distinguishes a cultural study from an inventory, however, is a willingness to look beneath the surface, to gain an in-depth understanding of how people interpret the meanings of these manifestations and how these interpretations form patterns of clarity, inconsistency, and ambiguity that can be used to characterize understandings of working lives.

In this book, I also include cultural studies that define culture differently—as a variable that can be conceptually distinguished and measured separately from other more familiar organizational variables. Culture-as-a-variable studies usually focus on a single cultural manifestation, such as top executives' espoused values or employees' self-reports of the informal norms. As will be shown, these different approaches to defining culture—as a metaphor for organizational life and as a variable—are only the first of a long list of issues about which cultural researchers vehemently disagree.

Focus of the Book:
Cultures in Organizations as a Vortex

When culture is defined as a way of studying everyday life in organizations, the question of scope quickly arises. What is not culture? Is culture just another word for organization? Does cultural theory and research encompass all organizational theory and research? The scope of cultural studies of organizations is much narrower than these questions imply. Cultural theory and research is just one of many organizational domains, and it certainly does not encompass all the others. People cannot learn all they need to know about organizations by studying culture. Simultaneously, however, cultural theory and research is a broad area of organizational inquiry. The field has become a vortex, drawing in people who are studying culture for very different reasons and working from very different scholarly assumptions.

Some people have been drawn to the study of culture in organizations because they find noncultural studies of organizations—for example, those that focus on variables such as size, structure, technology, and demography—dry and narrowly focused. These researchers revel in the kinds of topics—rituals, symbolic meanings, and humor—that some cultural studies examine. Some researchers have been drawn to cultural studies because this domain has been open to qualitative methods, such as long-term participant observation, discourse analysis, and textual deconstruction, that have not readily been accepted in many mainstream organizational topic domains. These qualitative methods seemed to offer particularly useful ways to deepen understanding of cultural phenomena. For some, cultural research fills a void—offering the promise of clarity and unity in a confusing and ambiguous world. For others, culture offers a way to capture and express complexities central to everyday life in organizations. Many applied researchers have been excited by the potential of culture research to provide some solutions for managers searching for new ways to motivate and control employees, using values to generate commitment and increase productivity and perhaps even profitability. These are not the only reasons for studying culture, but they are representative.

Because of the range of reasons why organizational researchers have been drawn to cultural studies, the major controversies that have polarized and sometimes revolutionized disciplines in the humanities and other social sciences are represented within the field of organizational culture studies as well. Neopositivist cultural research (like much of mainstream organizational research) uses the scientific method to develop and test theory, working from deductively derived hypotheses that can be empirically tested and potentially proven false. Therefore, a neopositivist cultural study's empirically based conclusions are usually described as objectively true ("Our study demonstrated that . . ."), with the goal of developing generalizable theory. In contrast, interpretive studies of culture describe a context in great detail, usually seeking to develop context-specific understandings rather than generalizable theory. Interpretive studies focus on socially constructed knowledge—how people interpret what happens to them. Some interpretive studies frame their conclusions in terms that implicitly claim to be the best available or even an objectively true representation of the culture studied. Other interpretive studies of culture, including those written from a postmodern position, implicitly or explicitly challenge any objective truth claim, explaining that other subjective interpretations are always possible. Postmodern cultural studies, for example, use deconstruction to show how a study's textual rhetoric hides its own inevitable weaknesses if it attempts to claim an inviolable place from which objective truth can be presented. Such postmodern analysis attempts to show that literally any argument contains the seeds of its own destruction. Intellectual traditions, such as neopositivism, interpretive approaches, and postmodernism, all have contributed to cultural studies of organizations and to other domains of organizational research.

Because of the range of scholarly assumptions these researchers hold, the body of literature that focuses on organizational culture is large and diverse, crossing disciplinary and methodological barriers. Also, given that the field of organizational culture research has become a vortex, drawing in scholars who take differing positions on the controversies that have polarized the humanities and social sciences during the past few decades, it can sometimes be difficult to discern which disputes pertain only to the study of culture and which pertain, more broadly, to the study of organizations. Therefore, readers familiar with other volumes in this **Foundations for Organizational Science** series will find that the domain of this book is necessarily broader.

In this book, my focus, unless stated otherwise, is on cultural issues at the organizational level of analysis. (Many of these ideas will also be of relevance to work group and national cultures, and when this relevance becomes salient I discuss it usually in footnotes.) When I discuss broader issues that have application to all organizational studies, not just studies of cultures in organizations, I signal this change of focus. For example, Chapter 2 examines a range of epistemological, methodological, and theoretical issues that are of particular interest to cultural researchers but that have applicability to all organizational theory and research.

**Managerial Fads,
Seductive Promises, and Where I Stand**

Given the range of reasons for studying culture, and the range of intellectual traditions represented in organizational culture research, it is no wonder that there is little agreement about what culture is, what it is not, how to study it, and what we know and do not know about it. In this book, my goal is to represent the complexity of this body of literature, capturing the range of conflicting assumptions about what theories, political interests, methods, and styles of writing are most appropriate for studying cultures in organizations. Before proceeding, however, it is important to acknowledge that although I attempt to offer a balanced portrait of opposing views, my opinions and biases will come through, whether I want them to or not. Although I am more comfortable with the usual impersonal academic writing style, I believe it will help you as a reader to distinguish what I believe from what others believe if I am honest and explicit about where I stand on some of these issues. I do this here, and again whenever I view it as necessary. This kind of discussion of the preferences and opinions of an author is *reflexivity,* and it is particularly important in cultural studies, in which so many divergent assumptions are often left unsaid or asserted as truth.

Beginning in the early 1980s, when I first began to do cultural research, some cultural studies offered companies a soothing promise: Organizations could supposedly develop "strong" cultures, becoming havens of harmony in which employees shared their leader's beliefs, assumptions, and vision for the company. Sometimes, this "strong" culture argument went one step further, offering the holy grail: If an organization could build a sufficiently "strong" culture, improved productivity and profitability would result. This was a seductive promise for managers, particularly those who held high-ranking positions in large, internally diverse organizations. It offered a leader-focused way to achieve agreement, on issues where it mattered most, in organizational domains that seemed riddled with misunderstanding, confusion, unspoken dissent, and, sometimes, overt conflict. Not surprisingly, many organizations invested considerable sums of money trying to build a "strong" culture (seeking organizational consensus regarding values and goals of top executives) and capture the competitive advantages of this new route to profitability.

Unfortunately, many of these cultural claims were oversimplified— yet another managerial fad that failed to deliver on its promises. For example, many of the "strong" culture companies of the early 1980s encountered severe financial problems shortly after their praises had been sung. Eager advocates of cultural solutions suddenly began asking culture researchers pointed questions about missing control and comparison groups: Were there equally profitable companies that lacked "strong" cultures? Did other "strong" culture organizations have troubled financial histories? Organizational consensus, across hierarchical ranks and functional divisions, is very difficult to achieve except with regard to values and goals (such as "quality" or "customer satisfaction") that are relatively abstract and as controversial as apple pie. Many practitioners who had invested time and money in cultural change interventions became disillusioned. "Strong" culture claims had been oversimplified and ultimately were less than useful—an expensive mistake for many companies.

Despite these failings, the promise of a leader-centered, unified culture as a key to financial performance has kept its allure, particularly but not exclusively in the United States. This is a Lazarus of an idea; it appears to die and then is resurrected. In every decade, organizations face new problems and become enamored of what appear to be new solutions. In the 1990s, hierarchies were flattened, downsizing and restructuring thinned managerial and other ranks, and boundaries between functional divisions ("silos") were breached. Also, as women and other underrepresented groups have entered the labor market in unprecedented numbers and attempted to rise through the ranks, discord and complaint have often ensued because rules designed by and for members of one group may place others at a subtle, or not so subtle, disadvantage. The Internet has revolutionized, at least temporarily, presumptions about finance, marketing, labor markets, and compensation. A global economy, new organizational forms, the Internet, and a more diverse workforce have left complex problems and unanswered questions in their wake. The new cultural answers to these dilemmas are too often variants of the old: With the right corporate vision, mission statement, or leader, an organization can build a highly committed, unified culture that fosters productivity and profitability.

I have no fondness for this Lazarus of a cultural "theory." For reasons I discuss later, I believe that the evidence on balance does not support these contentions. Furthermore, the purpose of a social science theory is not to comfort managers with promises of relatively easy solutions but to capture and perhaps even construct organizational experiences, in all their discomforting complexity, conflict, ambiguity, and flux. I believe that only a small part of an organization's culture consists of issues and perceptions that people see clearly and agree on. The rest is characterized by incompletely understood conflicts between groups; inconsistencies between, for example, what people say they value and what they do; ambiguities about what frequently used phrases and goal statements actually mean; and irreconcilable paradoxes and contradictions. An oversimplified theory, however comforting and appealing, is not likely to be useful if it ignores important complexities in the world it attempts, imperfectly, to represent. Application of an oversimplified theory is not only a potential waste of organizational resources; it can also undermine society's shaky commitments to the academic enterprises of education and research.

Fortunately, cultural theory and research have more to offer than easy promises of culture as a key to profitability. For example, offering an understanding of a culture, or cultures, is a worthy goal in its own right. Studies of organizational culture have proliferated in the past two decades. At first, this literature seems to offer a confusing morass of

conflicting findings. This book dissects and sifts through cultural studies based on very different intellectual traditions and shows how, taken
in combination, these cultural studies reveal insights not available from
other types of organizational research. The key to this argument is the
phrase "taken in combination." If cultural studies are to offer more than
easy answers that do not live up to their promise, cultural researchers
will need to learn to understand, value, and use highly divergent approaches to the study of culture.

Occam's Razor:
The Case for and Against Simple Theories

To understand culture using divergent approaches taken in combination will inevitably produce complexity. It is tempting, therefore, to
offer an overarching, highly abstract scheme that combines these divergent approaches in some integrative theoretical model, ideally one that
permits (as in the usual review of a body of literature) a linear tale of
progress toward enlightenment to be told. Major differences cannot be
ignored, however, if the various approaches to culture are to be fully understood and their potential contributions fully valued. For this reason,
the phrase "taken in combination" is a difficult project. It does not entail
a flight to unifying abstraction or a "blender" approach that pulverizes
difference. Instead, the field of cultural studies requires that participants learn to evaluate, knowledgeably and open-mindedly, studies that
are based on theories, political assumptions, methods, and epistemologies that are vastly different from each other. Only then can we make
sense of the morass of contradictory empirical results and theoretical
conclusions that characterizes the organizational culture literature.

At this point, some will say, "Stop. This sounds unnecessarily or un-
desirably complicated. What happened to Occam's razor?" William of
Occam was the fourteenth-century English philosopher who argued
that the best theory is the one that makes no more assumptions than
necessary. Occam's razor, then, pares away all that is extraneous, leaving
behind a theory that is elegant because it is parsimonious.[1] The danger,
however, lies in going too far in the direction of parsimony, leaving a
theory that is so oversimplified that it distorts or misrepresents the phenomenon it is trying to explain. The theoretical approach taken in this
book is complex, reluctantly, because simpler theories do not suffice. A

certain amount of complexity (or requisite variety) is necessary to capture the scope of the contributions that cultural approaches can offer to organizational studies.

Is this theoretical hair-splitting of interest only to ivory tower academics? Not if a theory needs complexity to acknowledge and explain important aspects of cultural dynamics, essential for understanding culture and for taking action in organizations. For example, if people experience their lives in organizations as ambiguous, paradoxical, ironic, or in constant flux, then any theory of culture that ignores these complexities is incomplete and oversimplified. Lewin's famous dictum "There is nothing so useful as a good theory" also implies that a bad theory may be useless—or worse.

Complex ideas, in contrast, may be quite useful. For example, suppose that in one company managers want to encourage employees to increase productivity. From the viewpoints of those employees called on to produce more, this call to productivity may seem to be unfair exploitation of those who are already working hard. A theory that includes these silenced or softer voices is more complex than a theory that includes only the views of top management, but it may be more useful than a simpler vision of culture because it permits people to anticipate who will resist the productivity initiative and why. Indeed, I agree with Rousseau (personal communication, July 26, 1999) that one of the most critical contributions of cultural research has been to give voice to the perceptions and opinions of those who are less powerful or marginalized. When research includes the subjective experiences that mainstream organizational research has underemphasized, that research shakes loose our preconceptions, expands the categories we use to think about organizations, and offers new alternatives for action. This is, after all, what theories are supposed to do.

It is difficult to move from an intellectual acknowledgment of the value of theoretical complexity to an active appreciation of it. Researchers are usually exposed to a limited number of theoretical and methodological approaches, even in the best of universities. By the time a doctoral student picks a thesis topic and a committee of faculty readers, he or she is usually urged to use the one "right way" or "best way" to approach that topic. In contrast, this book and the work it cites require that we attempt to understand studies based on political assumptions, epistemologies, methods, and/or theoretical orientations markedly different from our own. Cultural work that is initially the most unfamiliar can become the most illuminating.

This does not mean cultural researchers have to adopt unfamiliar approaches in our own research, although this may happen. We do, however, have to make a commitment to learn enough about unfamiliar approaches to theory building and research so that we can understand what these scholars are attempting to do. Without this commitment to understanding the unfamiliar, we run the risk of dismissing insights that would otherwise be inaccessible. For example, cultural researchers often have strong preferences for either qualitative or quantitative research. Thus, whole bodies of cultural research are dismissed as unworthy: for example, "That's an ethnography—just anecdotes about a single organization. A journalist could have written it. For example is no proof" or, equally dismissive, "No one can capture the complexity and richness of a culture in a sequence of numbers." This kind of dogmatism in the cultural arena severely limits the range of studies that are viewed as able to contribute to understanding. This can be seen, for example, in the narrow body of culture studies cited in most journal articles; authors cite (and maybe even read) primarily those studies that agree with their own theoretical and methodological preconceptions. I would know writing this book had achieved one of its purposes if, after reading it, researchers and teachers appreciated, drew on, assigned, and cited a broader variety of cultural studies. This is not the only goal of this book, so a discussion of the audience and objectives of this book might be useful at this point.

Goals of the Book

I wrote this book primarily for graduate students, junior scholars, and maybe even some seasoned researchers who wish to grapple with the body of literature that explores cultures in organizations. Some readers will simply want a guided tour of this literature; others will contribute to it. Because this body of literature requires learning about approaches to scholarship and methods not generally used in mainstream organizational research, this book might be useful even for those whose interests lie in theoretical domains other than culture. For example, the discussion of rationales behind various quantitative and qualitative methods in Chapter 2 might make useful reading for a methods course for sociological or organizational doctoral students. This is not a "how-to" book for professionals, such as managers and consultants, who do cultural work in organizations, and discussion of applied issues is minimal. Anyone, however, might find ideas that can spark interesting cultural research or applied cultural diagnosis or change projects.

The primary goal of the book is to open readers' minds about new ways to think about and study cultures so that culture can be understood in different and deeper ways. Ultimately, I hope that a book such as this might help improve the range and quality of cultural research that is done by organizational scholars. For readers new to the study of culture, I hope to introduce various ways of approaching this topic, in clear terms, so that it is understandable why people disagree so vehemently about these issues. I discuss these disagreements frankly, while explaining, in a contagious way, my enthusiasm for this domain of scholarly work so I do not discourage others who are thinking of entering the fray. I hope to entice readers to learn from the work of researchers whose premises they do not share. Being open to the potential contributions of unfamiliar approaches is not the same as suspending judgments of quality. For example, there are good and bad ethnographies and good and bad quantitative studies. We have to learn a fair amount about an alternative approach to scholarship before we are knowledgeable enough to make such quality assessments. This book aims to be helpful in that regard so that readers feel able to draw their own conclusions about the benefits and demerits of a wide variety of theoretical and methodological viewpoints.

On a more pragmatic level, I discuss, openly and honestly, the practical and political issues that influence the publication of cultural work, particularly in peer-reviewed journals. I will be frank about how some approaches to cultural research, particularly unfamiliar epistemologies and methods, have been misinterpreted and devalued, hampering the development of cultural studies and hurting the careers of some scholars. Finally—and this may be relevant to those who are not contemplating becoming cultural researchers themselves—I highlight the ways in which choosing a research topic and a method involves taking a position regarding the political interests your research will serve, the methods of persuasion you will use to get your views across to readers, and the boundaries of the phenomenon you wish to explain. These are ambitious goals for any one book, so let's begin.

Dragons and Dilemmas

This book offers a summary of what we know, and would like to know, about cultures in organizations. It is a bit like those old-fashioned maps of the world, drawn by hand long before the days of Mercator projections and satellite photographs. The center of those old maps usually contains the known world, drawn with highly detailed outlines and clear borderlines. Travel routes cross, diverge, and, as they move away from the center of the map, eventually fade and disappear. In the corners of those old maps, borderlines become fuzzy, signposts appear, and unexplored territories are marked with phrases such as "Terra Incognita" and "Dragons Lurk Here." This book presents a map of the terrain of cultures in organizations, complete with borders, pathways, forks in the road, and signposts to unexplored territories, some of which may contain intellectual gold and others, more likely, the career equivalent of dragons.

There are many ways to map a terrain. I have chosen to do it by discussing several dilemmas that face any cultural researcher as he or she works on a cultural research project. Each of these dilemmas consists of a series of related questions that a cultural researcher must answer. These questions pose a dilemma because they have no single right answer. Unfortunately, too often we resolve these dilemmas automatically, giving accustomed or easy answers. My objective in this book is to problematize each of these dilemmas by laying out a variety of plausible solutions and showing how each solves some problems while creating others. Any choice entails not choosing other alternatives. What we exclude often determines what we can see and what conclusions we therefore draw.

These dilemmas are not meant to be mutually exclusive categories. They overlap and intersect. Each dilemma creates a need to rethink or to have a deeper understanding of the dilemmas discussed previously. Some issues resurface, again and again, appearing in a different light as the argument proceeds. Single preferred resolutions to these dilemmas will not be forthcoming. This is why they are labeled dilemmas. By the end of this book, however, the implications of choices, and nonchoices, will seem more complex, and each dilemma should be more fully understood so that more informed choices can be made.

These are not the only dilemmas that are relevant to the study of culture. Other authors undoubtedly would draw the map, and choose dilemmas, differently. Although there are other ways to summarize what explorers of this territory have learned, these particular dilemmas do trigger discussion of a wide range of problems and, together, offer one way to think through the options and, ultimately, make informed choices of your own. In the following, each of the dilemmas is introduced with enough detail so you can understand why each is important. Because these dilemmas are discussed in separate chapters, the following sections of this chapter provide an overview of the book.

Part I:
Mapping the Cultural Terrain

Chapter 1: Introduction and Overview

The first part of the book consists of Chapters 1 through 6. These chapters introduce the book and offer an overview of its contents; outline several important disputes that have polarized the humanities and social sciences, with particular relevance for cultural studies; offer various approaches to defining the contents of organizational cultures; explore the relationship of three of the most prominent theories of culture; and examine power questions that surface in cultural studies, asking "In whose interest is this research done?"

Dilemma: Why do cultural researchers disagree
so vehemently with each other? Where do I stand
with regard to these disputes?

Chapter 2: The Culture Wars

Some of the fiercest and most intractable intellectual disputes in the humanities and social sciences have surfaced, relatively recently, in the interdisciplinary field of organizational studies. Within this field, some have reacted to these differences of opinion with antagonism, arguing that the field should focus its efforts and resources on just a few research topics. Others argue that creativity and insight flourish best when "a thousand flowers bloom," while still others claim that these differences are "an empirical question" that can be settled definitively by fine research. Although these intellectual disputes about fundamental matters are not unique to studies of organizational culture, these fights have been particularly acute in the cultural domain, leading some to find a new meaning for the term *culture wars*. For this reason, understanding the assumptions that underlie these disputes is essential for anyone who wants to understand the body of cultural literature that has emerged in the past few decades. These disputes sustain some of the most important debates about the appropriate or "best" approaches to studying cultures in organizations.

Chapter 2 reframes these disputes as a difference of opinion regarding five questions as they pertain to cultural research: Is culture an objective or subjective phenomenon? Should a culture be understood from an insider (emic) or outsider (etic) point of view? Are generalizations from a cultural study possible and desirable or should cultural understanding be context specific? Must a broad variety of cultural manifestations be studied or can a narrow focus offer sufficient insight into the whole? and Is depth of interpretation the most important indicator of a study's quality or can this criterion be sacrificed to increase the numbers of cultures studied?

There are alternative, plausible answers to these questions. Disentangling these arguments, separating the actual differences from the misunderstandings, is a complex task. Each of these fundamental intellectual disputes affects what cultural theories a researcher chooses to examine, what interests that research serves, what methods are used, what writing style is used to present the results, and how that research is therefore received and evaluated. These issues are discussed, with an exclusive focus on organizational culture research, in the next few chapters of the book.

Dilemma: What is culture and what is not culture?

Chapter 3: Pieces of the Puzzle:
What Is Culture? What Is Not Culture?

Any cultural study needs to be based on a definition of culture, but there are no commonly agreed on definitions. At first glance, organizational culture researchers seem to agree with each other: Culture is usually defined as that which cultural members share. The common use of the word "shared," however, masks profound disagreement about exactly what is shared. Analysis of a wide range of definitions of culture shows that cultural researchers do not agree about what culture is, about what should be excluded from the concept of culture, and whether their perceptions and opinions are indeed shared.

To complicate matters further, researchers' definitions of culture often bear little relationship to what they actually study when they claim to be studying culture; cultural definitions and operationalizations (how culture is measured in a given study) are often only loosely coupled. For example, although cultural researchers usually define culture as that which is shared, often their data include hints or overt statements that some things are not shared. Furthermore, studies that do focus on the shared often do so because they have tautologically justified excluding, via their definition of culture, any aspect of their data that is not shared by many or most people studied. Also, although the focus of these studies is often "organizational" culture, most studies stop far short of studying a full range of organizational employees—usually stopping at the managerial and professional ranks. For all these reasons, theoretical definitions of culture should be regarded with a great deal of skepticism.

Chapter 3 addresses the dilemma regarding how culture is defined by (a) examining the content of what researchers actually study when they claim to be studying culture (their "operational" definitions of culture) and then (b) analyzing the theoretical implications of these choices, explaining the advantages and limitations associated with a range of common choices. Because each way of operationally defining culture limits what a study can conclude and what it cannot see or say, this first dilemma (like the others discussed later) has no single correct resolution. A range of ways to define culture, operationally, are offered and analyzed so the reader can make an informed choice. It is important to make definitions and operationalizations of culture consistent within a single study so that it is clear what theoretical conclusions can and cannot be drawn. In the process of discussing the limitations associated with various ways of defining culture, examples of a wide range of cultural manifestations, such as stories and rituals, are presented, illustrated, and interpreted. In this way, researchers will be exposed to vivid examples drawn from a wide range of cultural studies and will see what can be learned from studying each of a wide range of cultural manifestations.

Dilemma: Which theoretical perspectives
should be used to study culture?

Chapter 4: Single-Perspective Theories of Culture

Cultural theories disagree about fundamental principles, making the choice of a theoretical perspective an important and difficult dilemma. Chapter 4 distinguishes three theories of culture that have dominated organizational culture research to date. I call these theories the integration, differentiation, and fragmentation perspectives. Most of this research has used only one, or at most two, of these perspectives in a single study. Historically, advocates of these three cultural theories have either been antagonistic to or ignored each other's work. To illustrate how and why advocates of these three perspectives disagree strongly with each other regarding what culture is, I present these theoretical conflicts as a vehement argument among three hypothetical scholars. The issues that generate discord in this hypothetical argument have created misunderstandings and conflicts in the cultural literature. Although there is little about which these theoretical perspectives agree, each has generated an impressive body of empirical support, suggesting (to those of a neopositivist persuasion) that none of these three perspectives can be easily dismissed. Chapter 4 provides a review of contemporary cultural research, showing what studies, using each of these single perspectives, have concluded. These theoretical distinctions are also used to show how organizational culture is distinguishable from related concepts, such as organizational climate, identity, and image.

Chapter 5: A Three-Perspective Theory of Culture

Chapter 5 advocates using the three divergent theoretical points of view, introduced in Chapter 4, to study a single culture. To explain why this three-perspective approach is preferable, at least in my view, this chapter begins with an example—a description of an academic culture, written to illustrate a single theoretical perspective. Deeper analysis reveals that two other cultural perspectives illuminate aspects of this academic culture that are not salient from the first point of view. I then argue that if a context is studied using all three perspectives in some sequence, such a three-perspective study will give a more complex and fuller view of a culture. Many studies supporting this contention are summarized and cited.

Such a three-perspective view of culture is controversial in that it defines culture as including not only that which is shared in an organization-wide consensus but also "the patterns of meanings that link these manifestations together, sometimes in harmony, sometimes in bitter conflicts between groups, and sometimes in webs of ambiguity, paradox, and contradiction" (page 3, this volume). This three-perspective view is also controversial because it takes a subjective approach, arguing that any culture can be usefully viewed, from all three perspectives, at any point in time. Thus, it is not the case that one perspective provides an objectively more accurate description of a given culture at a given point in time; all three perspectives will be useful at any point in time. These controversies are critical to the study of culture. Many find it difficult to abandon the conviction that culture consists of that which is shared. Also, many mainstream organizational researchers are neopositivists who find it difficult to see phenomena from a subjective rather than objective vantage point. For these reasons, these two controversies are explored in-depth so that readers are exposed to strong arguments on both sides of both issues.

Dilemma: Whose interests are served by this research study?
In whose interests do I want to write?

Chapter 6: Interests and Claims of Neutrality

Chapter 6 takes on the issue of power—specifically the interests served by different kinds of cultural research. A theory or an empirical paper might, at first, seem to be apolitical—an objective portrayal of research results. Many researchers assume that an empirically based social science is "value free" or "value neutral"—that differences in ideology can and should have no impact on empirical results or their interpretation. As a result, normative differences in orientation to power are often elided, minimized, or ignored in cultural research. Chapter 6 argues that power is often, perhaps always, implicit in cultural research, even if it is not explicitly discussed. To try to ignore the political implications of a cultural study is to be blind to the workings of power in that research. This chapter examines how power-related interests are explicitly examined in various kinds of cultural research. It also follows implicit hints, reading silences (what is not said and who is not studied) to reveal blind spots in theory and omissions in empirical work that express or favor the interests of one group over another. In this way, Chapter 6 shows how to access a study's assumptions about where power lies and, normatively, what can be done about it.

Chapter 6 includes an argument among the three hypothetical researchers who disagreed so vehemently about theoretical issues in Chapter 4. In this chapter, they focus on the question of whose interests should be served by cultural work, and again their views conflict. When the issues underlying this argument are analyzed, three different approaches to power are distinguished. Some research is clearly done in the managerial interest. Other research is critical and focuses on the interests of groups of people with less power, such as labor, minorities, or women. Finally, some studies seem to be purely descriptive, with no evident (although it may be hidden) commitment to furthering the interests of either the powerful or the powerless

After reading Chapters 4 through 6, the reasons for clashes of theoretical assumptions, and sometimes hidden orientations toward questions of power, should be easier to understand and anticipate. The reader is left with a dilemma: What is my own normative orientation toward power in organizations? How does it affect my research? What theoretical and normative blind spots, then, can I anticipate in my own thinking about culture? Do I want to learn from the cultural research conducted within each of these traditions now that its normative power orientation is revealed? How might I reinterpret the findings of a given study to take into account its normative orientation? Some readers will decide to refrain from examining the work in some of these traditions because their personal normative preferences are different. At least the normative implications of that choice, and the theoretical blind spots that are likely to result, will have been clearly and consciously considered.

Part II:
Doing Cultural Research

The second part of the book consists of three chapters that address issues that any cultural researcher must face: "What methods should I use?" "How will the quality of this research be evaluated?" and "What writing style will best describe what I found?"

Dilemma: What are the premises, strengths, and weaknesses of the various methods used to study culture? Which methods do I prefer and what are the implications of that decision?

Chapter 7: To Count or Not to Count?

Cultural researchers have vehement methodological disputes. Quantitative culture researchers often disdain qualitative studies and vice versa. Quantitative researchers also dispute among themselves, arguing, for example, about the kinds of inferences that can be drawn from correlations between cultural variables and measures of firm profitability. Qualitative researchers also quarrel among themselves, usually about whether a researcher has spent enough time to gain a deep understanding of a culture.

Chapter 7 takes these arguments seriously and reviews some of the most important debates that create and sustain disagreements about the appropriate or "best" methods for studying culture. This chapter reframes these arguments as differences of opinion regarding the five intellectual disputes introduced in Chapter 2: Is culture an objective or subjective phenomenon? Should a culture be understood from an insider (emic) or outsider (etic) point of view? Are generalizations from a cultural study possible and desirable or should cultural understanding be context specific? Is the breadth of cultural manifestations studied unimportant or essential? Is depth of interpretation the most important indicator of a study's quality or are other criteria (such as studying a large number of cultures) more important? To ground this discussion, I show how these debates could affect the choice of methods to study a particular question (whether a multinational company should adapt to local cultural contexts or impose standardized policies and practices from headquarters).

These five intellectual disputes are used as a framework to discuss a range of quantitative and qualitative methods that have been used to study culture. I also discuss and illustrate the strengths and weaknesses of hybrid methods that bridge the qualitative-quantitative divide.

Correlations among methods choices, theoretical perspectives, and interests are outlined. These correlations create blind spots—types of contexts that are never studied, theoretical questions that are never addressed, and so on. To alleviate this shortcoming, I argue that cultural research would benefit from the use of a wider range of theoretical, ideological, and method combinations. Such a varied approach, however, does not mean that questions of methodological adequacy should be sidelined. Chapter 7 outlines (different) criteria for assessing the quality of quantitative, qualitative, and hybrid study designs.

Although Chapter 7 is addressed to those who simply want to read cultural literature, it also should be useful for cultural researchers who repeatedly must answer the following kinds of questions: Do I want to maximize objectivity or subjectivity in my own cultural research? Do I want an insider or outsider approach to the culture? How many of a given study's results are context specific? Do I believe generalization is appropriate or desirable? If so, does my study design permit that kind of generalization? How important is it, from my perspective, to understand a given culture in-depth? What criteria are appropriate for evaluating the method I have chosen? and Looking ahead, what set of methods skills do I need to develop, given the kinds of cultural issues I want to understand? In raising these questions, and delineating the strengths and limitations of a wide range of methods, Chapter 7 should help cultural researchers and readers assess inherent limitations and theoretical implications associated with the choice of any method.

Dilemma: Can I anticipate how a cultural study will be evaluated? What criteria will I use when I evaluate my own or others' cultural research?

**Chapter 8: Putting It All Together:
Reviews of Sample Studies**

Criticisms of cultural studies often have a shrill and intolerant tone, particularly in informal conversations and blind peer reviews for journal publication. Researchers new to the cultural domain may not be prepared for the intensity of these critiques, especially when it is their own work that is being criticized. As the previous chapters show, in the cultural domain assumptions about theoretical perspectives, interests, and methods differ profoundly. Although such assumptions often remain tacit in published work, they do surface in reviews of refereed journal articles. Particularly when those reviews are blind (i.e., unsigned), a reviewer's theoretical and methodological preferences may implicitly or explicitly affect how a manuscript is evaluated. Such assumptions can determine whether a paper is accepted, whether a study or body of cultural work is generally respected, or whether a given researcher gets promoted. Although problems in the reviewing process arise in all fields, the vehement disagreements among organizational culture researchers can make this process particularly difficult.

To help researchers anticipate the reactions of colleagues, and to make the material presented in prior chapters come to life in a situation that is both concrete and important, Chapter 8 offers hypothetical reviews of several actual studies. The studies reviewed represent many of the theories and interests discussed in Chapters 3 through 6 and include a variety of the methods discussed in Chapter 7. These "reviews" are brief and oversimplified, usually taking either a strongly positive or strongly negative position. After each set of reviews, I offer my opinion, tying it into the material presented in earlier chapters. Chapter 8 brings together many of the issues raised earlier in the book and encourages the reader to anticipate how he or she might use these ideas during the revision process. The hypothetical reviews should help a researcher anticipate what kinds of criticisms of a particular method are likely to be made and, of these, which are appropriate and which can and should be disputed. Some desensitization to criticism, especially criticism that might seem unfair, may also be useful so that cultural researchers do not become discouraged during the review process, but researchers must enter it with a well-honed sense of the strengths, as well as the inevitable limitations, of the choices they have made.

Dilemma: Why are new ways of writing about culture
being adopted and which, if any, of these approaches
might enrich my own work?

Chapter 9: Writing About Cultures:
A Crisis of Representation?

In an empirical study, the researcher is faced with a dilemma: how to write a description of a culture or cultures. At first, this seems an easy problem to resolve. Most study authors simply follow journal norms that usually require the scientific writing style favored by quantitative researchers, in which a literature review and hypotheses precede data presentation. In contrast, qualitative researchers often prefer to let theory emerge from data in what is called "grounded theory" development. This requires a different writing style. Usually, qualitative researchers choose a style that implies that the cultural description is accurate, realistic, factual, and certain. This writing style is what Van Maanen (1991) labeled a *realistic tale*. Recently, the use of such scientific or realistic writing styles has been challenged, creating what some have called a crisis regarding representation. A brief discussion of the reasons for this alarmist language shows why cultural writing poses a dilemma for which there are no longer any easy answers.

An author has to do more than self-consciously choose a writing style if the difficulties inherent in writing about culture are to be grappled with. These difficulties are particularly salient for qualitative culture researchers. To glimpse these difficulties, consider the problems associated with the word "represent." It matters whose eye is doing the beholding, whose voice is allowed to speak in quotations on the page, and whose mind is selecting which words to quote. The researcher, like a filmmaker, directs his or her eye toward some things and therefore away from other things that are happening at the same time, perhaps eliminating some things so as not to overwhelm the story line. To what extent can an individual author or informant claim to represent others? Even if two people are looking at the same thing, what one person sees, and the meaning he or she attaches to that perception, may not be the same as what another might see. Furthermore, when an author makes editorial decisions about what to include or exclude in a text, he or she is engaging in a complex power game that draws attention to some viewpoints while silencing others. Therefore, to what extent can the words in a paragraph of prose, or a clip of videotape, be considered an "accurate" representation of what was perceived? Once questions such as these are raised, the comforting certainties of a realist tale seem to evade fundamental difficulties that merit serious consideration. How can one write about a culture and include, without textual incoherence, the complex relationship between what is perceived and the perceiver? How can a culture be described if members and researchers each may view events and experiences in that culture differently? How can one or many (how selected?) perceivers represent a culture? How should the quotations from informants, and the observations of the author, be selected for inclusion and exclusion? How can disagreements, uncertainties, and ambiguities, not to mention the layered effects of cultural change, be represented in linear prose? Should the author ever adopt a realistic style? What are the alternatives?

Chapter 9 summarizes critiques of realistic cultural descriptions. A variety of alternative styles of writing about culture are illustrated, with citations to exemplars for those who wish to read about or try an alternative approach. For example, the author can confess his or her own reactions to the culture, as the process of socialization and, it is hoped, cultural acceptance proceeds. Alternatively, the author can offer dynamic and vivid "snapshot tales" that capture what it was like to be a participant-observer in a particular culture. Or, instead of the author speaking for (less powerful) informants, the informants can author parts or all of a cultural description. Multivocal accounts, written by researcher and informant coauthors, can represent different views from inside and outside a culture. Quotations from informants can represent different groups' views of a culture, with the author joining the conversation as an equal, or less than equal, participant. Each of these writing styles has produced cultural accounts that are exceptionally informative in ways that could not be achieved using traditional scientific or realistic approaches. No matter how an individual researcher resolves the writing dilemma in a given study, self-conscious consideration of the issues raised by the process of writing about culture in Chapter 9 should deepen awareness of the complexity inherent in studying cultures. For cultural researchers, these new writing styles present an opportunity to have fun experimenting, with serious intent.

Part III:
Exploring the Edges of Cultural Theory

Chapters 10 and 11 focus on the future of cultural research. Chapter 10 focuses exclusively on the issue of how cultural boundaries have been defined, suggesting that a more sophisticated approach to boundary drawing would require that we rethink many of the basic premises of cultural theory and research in intriguing ways. Chapter 11 outlines several important—but as yet undone—research projects.

Dilemma: Should we reassess the ways in which we
have drawn cultural boundaries? Would this suggest
we should reevaluate some of the premises of cultural theory?

Chapter 10: Cultural Boundaries: Moveable,
Fluctuating, Permeable, Blurred, and Dangerous

What defines what is inside or outside a culture? At first, this seems an easy question to answer. Most studies pick a context to study and simply assume that all people in that context are members of the culture. Consider all the assumptions that are implicit in this approach, however: Individuals embody, or carry, a culture, or culture is carried by job or task assignments, so that all members of a particular job classification are assumed to share a culture. Such an approach implies that people in a given set of jobs might be replaced and the culture would still remain intact. Furthermore, if a culture is carried in physical bodies or in job or task assignments, the physical or legal boundaries of a context constitute the edges of its culture. In such a conceptualization, boundaries are firm, clearly understood, and impermeable. Either one is in the culture or one is out.

Now, consider variations on these assumptions about boundaries. For example, allow for variations in intensity of membership in a culture so that some bodies are more fully members than others. To further complicate matters, what if culture is defined in ideational rather than material terms so that culture is seen as consisting of ideas and meanings rather than particular people or jobs? In ideational conceptions of culture, borders become permeable because ideas or interpersonal contacts can be imported or exported from the larger society or surrounding community into or out of an organizational context. Now the idea that a context, such as an organization, can have a unique culture seems less likely because at least some parts of a culture are likely to be shared with a surrounding cultural context. Where, then, are the boundaries of an "organizational" culture? Once intensity of membership in a culture is a possibility, culture can more easily be seen as a subjectively rather than an objectively defined concept. An organizational member can refrain from being a member of its culture or can be less of a member than another employee with the same job assignment. Even boundaries—what is in and out of the culture—can be seen as a subjectively created product of culture; edges can be socially constructed and those social constructions can change. Furthermore, if cultural membership is a subjective phenomenon, it lies in the eye of the beholder. One cultural member may view boundaries (and other cultural products) differently than another; researchers may also differ, even regarding the same cultural context.

As these examples indicate, decisions about where to draw boundaries pose tough questions with fundamental theoretical implications. There are no easy answers to these boundary-defining dilemmas. Dealing with these complexities requires a new language for talking about culture, one that does not assume that membership in the context being studied is the same as membership in a culture. Here, the map analogy can be helpful. On those old maps of the world, boundaries sometimes are fuzzy or dissolve into dotted lines. Cultural researchers need a map drawer's ability to allow boundaries to be uncertain in their location, permeable, fluctuating, and ambiguous, to allow for the possibility that cultural membership may not be conferred automatically by physical location, a paycheck, or a job assignment. Dragons lurk at the edges of a cultural map, raising fundamental theoretical questions. It is in this sense that boundaries are dangerous. Where a boundary is drawn reflects how a study is defining culture and what assumptions about power are explicitly or tacitly being made. Revisiting these issues, in the context of deciding where the edges of a culture lie, reveals the inescapable difficulties of assessing what is, and what is not, culture in a given context. Chapter 10 problematizes the boundary issue, making it clear that where edges are drawn must be congruent with what theoretical position is chosen and what normative position on questions of power is preferred.

Dilemma: Of all the possible cultural studies to be performed, which might be the most important?

Chapter 11: Terra Incognita:
Ideas for Future Research

Chapter 11 offers several ideas for future research. These research projects can be thought of, in terms of the map of the cultural terrain, as spots where the map is marked "terra incognita." It is my hope that, in a few cases, intellectual treasure might be buried here. In other cases, these research ideas might serve as a stimulus for brainstorming ideas I have not thought of so that, in another decade, our understanding of cultures in organizations may be enriched in unexpected ways. We begin, then, at the well-explored center of the map of the terrain of culture and end, in Chapter 11, at its less explored edges.

Note

1. I am indebted to Bill Starbuck, who first raised the issue of Occam and the value of theoretical simplicity and parsimony in the book jacket notes of my first book about culture (Martin, 1992a). What he thinks of this volume remains to be seen.

2   The Culture Wars

To see a world in a grain of sand,
And a heaven in a wild flower,
Hold infinity in the palm of your hand,
And eternity in an hour.
            —Blake (1863/2000, p. 285)

Some researchers choose to study a single cultural context in great detail and depth, in effect seeing the world in a grain of sand—that is, they study culture with a sample size of one cultural context. Other researchers react with disdain to such case studies and prefer to study many cultures, even if that means understanding less about each one. Such differences in methods choices occur because cultural researchers make radically different assumptions regarding fundamental issues. To further complicate matters, some cultural researchers (myself included) have changed their positions on these issues as they have become familiar with opposing points of view. To understand the contemporary state of cultural theory and research, it is necessary to grapple with some of the major intellectual disputes that have swept through the humanities and social sciences in recent years. Although these disputes may be familiar to some readers, for others this introduction may be a first exposure.

Here, a few of these disputes, of particular importance to cultural studies, are discussed. These disputes concern objectivity and subjectivity, etic (outsider) and emic (insider) research, generalizable and context-specific research, focus and breadth, and level of depth. These five issues are introduced here in terms relevant to all organizational studies; their particular application to cultural studies is then discussed in this and subsequent chapters. These disputes are struggles between opposing terms—dichotomies such as "objectivity and subjectivity" and "etic and emic." I use the word "and" between these opposing terms to signal that these dichotomies are overdrawn, exaggerating differences at the expense of understanding the ways in which these oppositions blur and merge.

Ontology and Epistemology: Background

As a prelude to discussing objective and subjective approaches to studying culture, a very brief and simplified introduction to ontology and epistemology may be useful for some readers. In this brief introduction, I draw heavily on the work of Chia (1996) because his clear and cogent introduction to these issues is of particular usefulness to cultural researchers. *Ontology* is a set of assumptions about the nature of reality—how things are. In contrast, *epistemology* concerns theories about how we know about the nature of reality—that is, how we know about how things are. Of course, epistemology entails some assumptions about the nature of reality, making it difficult to disentangle it from ontology. Chia usefully distinguishes two kinds of ontology that he calls being-realism and becoming-realism, both of which will be helpful in framing the material in this book.

Being-Realism

Chia (1996) argues that in being-realism,

There is a fundamental split between the *word* and the *world* [italics added] (Harré, 1986) and that the world is made up of discrete and identifiable material and social entities (Whitehead, 1926/1985, p. 58) which can be faithfully documented using precise literal concepts and categories. . . . To *know* means to be able to represent accurately in our minds using linguistic or visual forms what the world "out there" is really like. . . . Combinations of words, from which theories are built, somehow match up with pieces of the "real" world. (p. 36)

According to being-realism, reality "preexists independently of obser-vation" (Chia, 1996, p. 33), enabling organizational scientists to treat ideas, such as "organizations" or "cultures," as unproblematic objects of analysis—as if "their ontological status were not a critical issue in its own right" (p. 33).

Unlike some other researchers discussed later, Chia believes that on-tology and epistemology are tightly coupled. He argues that being-realism is congruent with representational epistemologies so that lan-guage can be used, unproblematically, to represent reality, accurately communicating what is "out there." For example, whenever we write about culture, our language is related to our representational epis-temology. Chia (1996) explains it as follows:

> The grammatical structures of language organize our consciousness and thought processes, making it then possible for us to think about our experi-ences retrospectively in a discrete, differentiated, linear and sequential man-ner. As an epistemological posture, therefore, representationalism entails the systematic filtration of our concrete experiences into the precast mould-ing of the grammatical logic of language. In this abstractive manner, we selectively reduce and make more comprehensively manageable our lived experiences in the very act of recounting them. (p. 39)

Representational epistemology is invoked, implicitly, when a critic observes that a particular study "reifies culture." *Reification* means writ-ing about culture as if it could be accurately known and as if that knowl-edge could be represented in language, unproblematically. For example, this book has sometimes described culture research supporting the three theoretical perspectives in being-realism terms. In Chapter 1, I stated, "Although there is little that these three theoretical perspectives agree about, each has generated an impressive body of empirical sup-port, suggesting (to those of a neopositivist persuasion) that none of these three perspectives can be easily dismissed." If and only if one disregards the parenthetical remark alluding to neopositivism, this "being-realism" language treats the three theoretical perspectives as if they were reified things "out there," whose existence could not be challenged because of the volume of empirical evidence that supports their existence. In contrast, as described in the following section, a becoming-realism ontology would ask how these concepts came to be created as categories, perhaps drawing attention to what other conceptual approaches represent—"paths not taken" that could have been used.

Becoming-Realism

Becoming-realism focuses on the process of becoming so that how things come to be, defines what they are. According to Chia (1996, p. 34), becoming-realism directs the attention of organizational researchers to processes: how we order, codify, frame, and classify our perceptions, our data, and our theoretical abstractions. These processes create *apparently* stable and reified ideas, such as truth claims about what is known about abstractions such as "individuals," "organizations," and "cultures." Thus, processes of ordering and classifying, and so on are intimately intertwined with the ways we use language in our texts to summarize data and build theories about how reality is socially structured. Chia is an advocate of becoming-realism. He argues that the problem with being-realism ontology and representational epistemologies is that they gloss over important shortcomings in our knowledge base— shortcomings that are inescapably tied to the inherent limitations of language and the ways those limitations shape our perceptions and conceptualizations. As Chia explains,

> As an academic ideology for directing research and inquiry, [representationalism] suppresses the problematical nature of its own truth claims by unreflexively concentrating attention onto the "outcomes" of research, thereby ignoring the philosophical problems underpinning its own epistemological stance. In so doing it conveniently ignores the paradoxes and contradictions surrounding its knowledge claims. (p. 39)

Chia (1996) argues that we can know only what we can put into language, but if we use representational writing strategies we are not expressing awareness of the ways language is shaping what we can think. Thus, whether we want to or not, when researchers write or speak about culture, we use words, categories, and concepts to alter meanings, hide ambiguities, and circumvent problematic contradictions and uncertainties. As discussed in Chapter 9, there are ways to highlight the inevitable uncertainties of the conceptualization and writing processes, in accord with becoming-realism, to better capture the ambiguities inherent in the study and representation of cultural material.

Some challenges to Chia's arguments are relevant here. Chia views ontology and epistemology (and methods choices and writing strategies) as tightly coupled. (Among the many books available, Burrell and Morgan [1979] provide an overview of these issues, one that also views epistemological and methodological choices as correlated.) Others (including myself) view methods and epistemology as being much more loosely coupled. Some take the position that the problem for cultural research lies not in being-realism but in representational epistemologies. From this point of view, one can accept the being-realism view of reality but endorse epistemologies that eschew representationalism. For example, assuming we are all limitedly rational knowers, we may construct knowledge within the constraints of language and do so in a way that captures elements of differing viewpoints. Cultural descriptions written in this manner can eschew, to some extent, representational epistemologies, as discussed in Chapter 9. Despite these differences of opinion, Chia's ideas, particularly regarding representational epistemology, will be useful background for the material that follows.

Objectivity and Subjectivity

Much of the organizational literature, like most fields of social science, reads as if scholars could discover and accurately represent the objectively "true" nature of the empirical world, in accord with being-realism and representational epistemology. Certainly, this is the writing style expected in most mainstream organizational journals. In accord with this emphasis on objectivity, many social science doctoral students are taught to do research according to the scientific method, using deduction and induction to prove or falsify hypotheses. Most researchers, however, when pressed, would agree that purist claims of objectivity (sometimes labeled "naïve realism") are overblown (e.g., Bogdan & Taylor, 1975; Cook & Reichardt, 1979; Gephart, 1988; Van Maanen, 1979). As H. Markus (personal communication, August, 2000) notes, "Counting pond scum or stars requires categorization, and is therefore subjective and problematic."

This modesty about objectivity is appropriate. Philosophers of science have repeatedly undermined claims of objectivity, challenging the logical foundations of the fundamentals of the scientific method, such as induction, deduction, and falsification (for accessible introductions, see Chalmers, 1982; Nord & Connell, 1998). Even "hard" scientists such as physicists struggle with the implications of data suggesting that the act of perceiving or measuring transforms whatever is being assessed. In addition, what may seem objectively true at one time is subject to revision as it changes and as apparent understandings change. What may seem to be objective fact, such as an experience or a body of data, is subjectively perceived by humans and processed by human sense making. For example, even an apparently objective stimulus, such as the set of sounds in a language, may be heard differently by speakers of different languages because their preconceptions influence the sound distinctions they can perceive (Boas, 1901). In a psychological experiment, subjects identified slides of ordinary playing cards; the addition of anomalous cards, such as red spades or black hearts, was misperceived to fit subjects' preconceptions (Bruner, Goodnow, & Austin, 1956). For similar reasons, eyewitness testimony is notoriously unreliable because different people observing the same event recall it differently (e.g., Yarmey & Yarmey, 1997).

This brief and simplified discussion of objectivity and subjectivity has implications for cultural research. Some cultural researchers treat culture as a reified object, a "thing" "out there" that can be objectively perceived and measured, the same way, by anyone who views it. This is, in part, what is meant by the criticism that a study "reifies" culture, in accord with being-realism and representational epistemologies. In contrast, most cultural researchers argue, in accord with becoming-realism, that researchers and cultural members subjectively interpret and represent what they observe rather than perceiving an objective reality. For example, the taste of some foods, such as dog meat, is not objectively determined. There is considerable variation in people's subjective reactions: Americans deem dogs inedible and esteem beef, whereas some Indians refuse to eat beef and some Africans consider dog meat a delicacy (Sahlins, 1995). As these examples indicate, the same material conditions can produce a variety of perceived and enacted cultural "realities." Indeed, Sahlins advocates a strong version of the subjective position, arguing that the cultural cannot be derived directly from experience or event because experiences occur in a world already symbolized, and thus meanings are always arbitrary in relation to the object being signified.

Many cultural researchers do not go so far as Sahlins (1995), preferring instead to view perceptions as constrained by what is being perceived. As Stablein (1996) argues, subjectivity does not mean "anything goes." Subjectivity is constrained by aspects of the stimulus being perceived, and this process of perception, memory, and interpretation is not just an individual phenomenon. Observation occurs in a collective, social context in which the social construction of reality (Berger & Luckmann, 1967) constrains and influences judgments. If reality is subjectively constructed even in this limited way, then a cultural researcher must focus attention on the subjective frameworks of cultural members in addition to the apparently objective "facts" and material conditions of their lives.

Although some of the studies cited in this book take a purely objectivist or subjectivist approach, I view culture as both objectively and subjectively constrained. This approach implies that cultural descriptions should include physical manifestations of a culture, such as dress norms and the noise and dirt or the quiet and luxury of a workplace, as well as observable formal practices and structures, such as the amounts of money different employees earn or to whom they report. In addition, the subjective meanings associated with these observable manifestations must be gathered and interpreted. In other words, I believe that culture has both material and ideational aspects, and both must be studied. It is important to note that subjectivity does not imply consensus. Interpretations need not be consensual because the same manifestation may carry different meanings for different perceivers. For example, if an oil company gives women managers a 9% pay raise, the management may believe that this pay increase is quite generous, whereas the women managers may be discontent because comparable male managers still earn considerably more money (Martin, Brickman, & Murray, 1984). A ritualized event, such as an award banquet, a company junket, or a planned change intervention, may be perceived differently by different participants, who may react variously with skepticism, ambivalence, or enthusiastic endorsement (e.g., Bartunek & Moch, 1991; Rosen, 1991; Van Maanen & Kunda, 1989). When cultural studies include meanings and interpretations of material or observable cultural manifestations, their authors are tacitly or explicitly assuming that the social meanings of an object, event, or experience are subjectively experienced and interpreted and cannot be inferred directly from their material or physical characteristics.

Etic (Outsider) and Emic (Insider) Research

To explore the relevance of the objective and subjective distinctions to cultural research, the etic versus emic distinction will be helpful (for an introduction to this concept and to anthropological methods, see Agar, 1986; Morris, Leung, Ames, & Lickel, 1999). Most organizational research outside the cultural arena takes an etic stance, assuming that a researcher can adequately, and perhaps even accurately, decide what categories and questions are appropriate for investigating a particular context or set of theoretical questions. Usually, in etic research, categories are deduced from prior theory and research, not from material gathered during a study.

To give a quantitative example of an etic approach used in cultural studies, a researcher might decide (drawing on prior research) which dimensions are important aspects of culture in organizations. This researcher might then construct a questionnaire, asking respondents to report cultural norms along these dimensions. For example, members might be asked to rate, on a 9-point Likert scale, whether their group is cooperative or competitive, individualist or collective, or autocratic or participative. These kinds of self-report data are etic in that the researcher who chooses the dimension categories does so while maintaining an outsider position with regard to the cultures being studied. Responses to these kinds of questionnaires can be factor analyzed. Here, too, the researcher etically determines the labels assigned to those factors, naming the relevant dimensions of cultural comparison. A good example of this kind of research is Hofstede's multidimensional classification of national cultures in terms of power distance, masculinity-femininity, individualism-collectivism, and so on (see also dimensional studies of organizational culture by Kilmann, Saxton, Serpa, & Associates [1985] and Rousseau [1990b]). Etic cultural research includes any study, quantitative or qualitative, in which the conceptual categories are imposed by the researcher rather than initiated by the cultural member who is being studied. The key, for an etic study, is to explain cogently why these particular concepts and operationalizations were chosen, usually with reference to both reliability and validity.

In contrast, most organizational studies of culture follow the lead of many sociocultural anthropologists who have argued with great conviction that it is essential that a researcher learn, as far as is humanly possible, to view things from an emic or insider point of view. One of the first to articulate this approach was Malinowski (1922, 1961, p. 25), who claimed (although he also kept scandalous, racist research diaries) that he sought to "grasp the native's point of view, his relation to life, to realize his vision of his world." Geertz (1983, p. 58) described the emic approach in more colloquial language: "The trick is to figure out what the devil they think they are up to." The emic approach is particularly useful when a researcher is trying to understand cultural practices, such as headhunting or mass layoffs, that may be quite unfamiliar to the researcher. For example, Evans-Pritchard (1937, p. 69) studied Azande beliefs in witchcraft: "A group of people were sitting beneath a granary which, unknown to them, had been weakened by termites. The granary collapsed, causing injury, and witchcraft was blamed." As Hatch (1973) rephrases Evans-Pritchard's observations,

> The Azande were aware that the natural cause of the granary's collapse was the action of termites, but to the people this merely explained how, and not why, the structure fell. Why was it *this* granary which happened to collapse, and why did it do so precisely when these persons were beneath it? (p. 249)

To reach the level of understanding required to phrase the question in this way, especially when trying to understand an unfamiliar or distasteful cultural practice, a researcher needs to learn enough about a culture to get inside the minds of cultural members—to "think like a native." Among anthropologists, Boas is sometimes given credit for being among the first to pack his bag, pitch his tent in the middle of a village, and attempt to get "behind the veil" that stood between him and the thoughts of the people he wished to understand. How does a researcher achieve this kind of empathetic understanding? Boas (1901) advised,

> The student must endeavor to divest himself entirely of opinions and emotions based on the peculiar social environment into which he [*sic*] is born. He must adapt his own mind, so far as it is feasible, to that of the people whom he is studying. The more successful he is in freeing himself from the bias based on the group of ideas that constitute the civilization in which he

lives, the more successful he will be in interpreting the beliefs and actions of man [*sic*]. (p. 1)

This is an idealized description, implying that a cultural researcher must have a corner on the empathy market—"some sort of extraordinary sensitivity, an almost preternatural capacity to think, feel, and perceive like a native . . . some unique form of psychological closeness, a sort of transcultural identification" (Geertz, 1983, p. 56). Instead, Geertz offers a more attainable vision of the process of developing emic understanding: "Understanding the form and pressure of . . . natives' inner lives is more like grasping a proverb, catching an allusion, seeing a joke—or . . . reading a poem—than it is like achieving communion" (p. 70). Geertz describes the anthropologist's task as that of a translator (rather than being an empathizer) from the native's emic into the translator's community's etic, blurring boundaries between emic and etic:

> "Translation," here, is not a simple recasting of others' ways of putting things in terms of our own ways of putting them (that is the kind in which things get lost), but displaying the logic of their ways of putting them in the locutions of ours; a conception which again brings it rather close to what a critic does to illumine a poem than what an astronomer does to account for a star. (p. 10)

Implicitly, Geertz's (1983) description of research as a translation task draws attention to the difficulty of making a clear distinction between the etic and emic approaches, a point explored in more depth in critiques of social science research (Clifford & Marcus, 1986). Emic analysis inevitably incorporates the etic (and vice versa), at least insofar as the researcher's emic perspective is etic to the situation being studied. Geertz (1973, p. 9) describes this problem in simpler terms: "What we call our data are really our own constructions of other people's constructions of what they and their compatriots are up to." For example, Boas (1901) refers, in the quotation cited previously, to the researcher as "he" and the subject of study as "man." This language choice prefigures the criticisms of feminist anthropologists, who have found that male anthropologists mostly study men, in part because it is easier for male anthropologists to establish close relationships and build emic understandings of members of their own sex. To the extent that male and female experiences of a culture differ, such studies are incomplete (e.g., Rosaldo & Lamphere, 1974).

There are many different versions of what it means to adopt an emic perspective, but most acknowledge that the identity of the ethnographer inevitably creates an objectifying distance between researcher and informants. In contrast, reflexive ethnography seeks to characterize the relationship between the ethnographer and the informant in more equal terms (Bruni & Gherardi, in press):

> A relation of reciprocal implication and participation: While the researcher observes, s/he is observed, so that ethnography can be viewed as the result of a textual collaboration, as the outcome of this dual hermeneutic process. The ethnographer is considered to be engaged in a symmetrical reflective exercise (Linstead, 1993) and, far from being an "alien," the ethnographer conveys cultural assumptions and preconceptions, and enjoys an active presence which makes his/her role different from that of the "professional stranger" (Agar, 1980) as an "uncontaminated expert" (Tedlock, 1991; Van Maanen, 1988).

Acknowledging the difficulty of attaining an emic position uncontaminated by etic distancing, Geertz (1973) suggests a more modest goal—that the researcher's task is to find a balance between emic and etic vantage points

> so as to produce an interpretation of the way a people lives which is neither imprisoned within their own mental horizons, an ethnography of witchcraft written by a witch, nor systematically deaf to the distinctive tonalities of their existence, an ethnography of witchcraft written by a geometer.[1] (p. 57)

Organizational researchers who seek an emic-etic balance have an extremely difficult task to perform because they do not study tribes living on isolated Pacific islands or deep in the jungles of Brazil. In most cases, the cultures we study are microcosms of the cultures we live in or, if not, they are at least more familiar to us than the witches of Azande were to Evans-Pritchard. The difficulty of finding an etic-emic balance is exacerbated for those of us who do "halfie research"—that is "research conducted by a researcher who comes from the culture she studies, but who, during the work, is a member of another culture, that 'commissioned' the research project" (Czarniawska, 1998, p. 4). This kind of study is more common now as anthropologists return home from exotic islands to study their own cultures and immigrants study the cultures of their origins. In such circumstances, as Czarniawska (p. 5) notes, researchers and actors in the field keep alternating between "She is like us/I am like them" and "She is . . . /I am different," making misunderstandings multiply.

For many organizational researchers, whether or not we are "halfies," it is as difficult to maintain sufficient distance from what we observe— to free ourselves from strong preconceptions—as it is to translate "what the devil they think they are up to" with sufficient empathy. The illusion that we may have attained an emic view may come too easily to us, un- less we deliberately select organizations that seem, at first, to be odd, distasteful, or simply unusual. Also, if the sites we study are outliers in some way, then how can we think about moving from our data to some kind of generalizable theory? Of course, as outlined in the next section, many cultural researchers do not seek to build generalizable theory—a stance that is inconceivable to many researchers trained in the quantita- tive tradition.

Generalizable and Context-Specific Knowledge

Geertz's (1973, p. 57) words, quoted previously, reveal an important assumption: The task of an anthropologist is to produce "*an* [italics added] interpretation of the way *a* [italics added] people lives." Geertz is assuming that the task of a cultural researcher is to study a singular way of life and not to produce abstractions that can be used to generalize across cultures. He seeks to describe a single culture, richly and deeply (Geertz, 1973) or to contrast a very small number of cultures, mostly to highlight their differences (Geertz, 1983), or both. Many ethnographers and other researchers share Geertz's focus on the concrete details of particular contexts. For example, Van Maanen and Barley (1985) state their distrust of theoretical abstractions quite openly:

> Theorists of the social world deal with the most ephemeral, delicate, and elu- sive of matters. It is easy to slip away and start granting theoretical entities (like culture, rules, deviants, organizations, etc.) status as iconic significa- tions. They are always metaphoric. From my perspective, the only effective antidote for the air sickness caused by theoretical flight is periodic returns to the field. (p. 35)

One reason given for preferring to avoid generalization is the assumption that every culture is unique. Boas (1901) explained this viewpoint by arguing that historical accidents, such as a hostile attack from a neighboring tribe, produce a singular cultural configuration, much as a boulder tumbling down a mountainside produces an erosion pattern unmatched anywhere else. Particularly if people place great value on individual distinctiveness (which is less often the case in collectivist societies such as China) (e.g., Markus & Kitayama, 1991, 1994; Morris & Peng, 1994), it may be socially desirable to belong to a collectivity that is (objectively) or that views itself (subjectively) as unique. Organizations often seek to define themselves as unique to have a distinctive niche in a market or to attract and retain employees. Some—but by no means all—organizational studies of culture assume cultural uniqueness. Others make a softer claim: that specific kinds of knowledge may be context specific, such as when copier repair technicians give advice in the form of context-specific recommendations rather than general, abstract rules (Brown & Duguid, 1991).

Another way to justify the study of a unique, or at least single, culture is to argue that any one culture is not the only one conceivable in a particular context. The same circumstances could have led to a multiplicity of possible outcomes (e.g., Sahlins, 1985; Sebag, 1964, pp. 166-167). From this point of view, the study of a single case is possible; the study of generalizable principles is a dead-end road. The objective of a single case study, then, is an appreciation of contextually specific knowledge rather than an understanding that emerges from the process of abstraction and generalization across cases. Geertz (1983, p. 232) admits that this approach is "rather entranced with the diversity of things." He (1973) concludes that

> the notion that the essence of what it means to be human is most clearly revealed in those features of human culture that are universal, rather than those that are distinctive to this people or that, is a prejudice that we are not necessarily obligated to share. (p. 43)

For other researchers, trained to appreciate large sample sizes, random sampling procedures, reliability and validity measures, and statistical tests, a disdain for generalization is difficult to comprehend: Isn't building theory, they ask, the goal of empirical research? What use is a study unless the goal is to understand what causes a phenomenon and to use that knowledge to predict, under appropriate conditions, what effects will occur? At the very least, shouldn't one seek multiple, systematic comparisons to build generalizations within and across case studies of culture? Such concerns for generalization, for example, led Hodson (1998) to code organizational and workplace characteristics (approximate indicators of culture) in 108 English-language ethnographic case studies, seeking generalizations.

In contrast, ethnographers argue that their goal is to understand a context deeply and to provide an interpretative frame for its understanding. They do not seek to make predictions, discover generalizable laws, or build theories of causality:

> A characteristic of scientific explanation is that it allows predictions, since it attempts to supply the causal factors behind a phenomenon so that when appropriate conditions exist, the phenomenon can be expected. By contrast, [ethnography] attempts to make a phenomenon intelligible, and the issue of prediction does not arise. (Hatch, 1973, p. 336)

> Conceptualization [in ethnography] is directed toward the task of generating interpretations of matters already in hand, not toward projecting outcomes of experimental manipulations or deducing future states of a determined system. (Geertz, 1973, p. 26)

This disagreement, regarding contextually specific versus generalizable knowledge, underlies a conflict in the cultural literature. Studies that treat culture as a variable and seek to predict outcomes (such as commitment or profitability) usually are trying to build generalizations, whereas studies that define culture as a metaphor, a way of looking at life within a collectivity, usually focus on context-specific knowledge (Smircich, 1983b) and eschew most generalizations.

If ethnographies do not seek to build generalizable theories, then what is the purpose of ethnography? Is there any role for abstraction or for theory in context-specific cultural research? Geertz (1973) addresses this issue:

> The major theoretical contributions not only lie in specific studies—that is true in any field—but they are very difficult to abstract from and integrate into anything one might call "culture theory" as such. Theoretical formulations hover so low over the interpretations they govern that they don't make much sense or hold much interest apart from them. . . . The essential task of

theory building here is not to codify abstract regularities but to make thick description, not to generalize across cases but to generalize within them.
[Cultural theory is] inseparable from the immediacies thick description presents. . . . What generality it contrives to achieve grows out of the delicacy of its distinctions, not the sweep of its abstractions. (pp. 25-26)

Thick descriptions are richly detailed accounts of single cultures. Echoing the quotation from the poet Blake (1863/2000), with which this chapter began, such case descriptions give readers an ability to "see a world in a grain of sand"—that is, to see an entire culture in a single, sharply focused description. Such a description is based on information from multiple informants and other sources of information, such as conversational analysis (Tulin, 1997). The objective of such accounts is not to build generalizations from a sample size of one (context). From this point of view, an abhorrence of generalization or abstraction is more comprehensible because these conceptual activities gloss over the richly textured detail that is the content and the goal of ethnographies. For example, Alvesson (1998) challenges Hofstede's classification of national cultures according to power distance, drawing on ethnographic evidence that suggests such categories are misleading. Alvesson concludes,

> The rich interpretive capacities of culture can only be utilized if the study is open-minded, careful, locally oriented, and close to social practices and meanings in organizations. This is then the opposite from questionnaire-based, generalization-oriented research, which cannot go beyond "thin description" (to reverse Geertz's concept of thick description). (p. 15)

This debate about the desirability of generalizability echoes the old dispute between ideographic research (interpretation of a single case) and nomothetic research (developing generalizable laws from the study of many cases) (see Morrill & Fine, 1997). Nomothetic researchers, such as experimental psychologists and quantitative sociologists, often disdain the ideographic approaches of their case study-oriented forebears, echoing the old Talmudic saying, "For example is no proof." In contrast, ideographic researchers, such as those who do ethnographic case studies, are also often disdainful of abstraction. They are especially critical of those who would develop an abstract theory from a single case study, as can be seen in Geertz's (1973, p. 21) dismissal of the

"Jonesville-is-the-USA microcosmic model" or "the Easter-Island-is-a-testing-case 'natural experiment' model."

Such expressions of disdain for opposing points of view regarding generalization should be regarded with some skepticism. It is a rare ethnographer who does not fall into some kind of generalizing language. Even Geertz (1983) argued that he did not study the culture of a village; rather, he studied the culture of a larger collectivity *in* a village. His claim can be seen as a variant of the whole/part fallacy—generalizing about a whole culture from the study of a smaller unit within it. Thus, the dichotomies evident in any discussion of generalizability tend to mask a more complex reality (Weick, 1999). In any discussion of methodology, rhetoric is often more dichotomous than what people actually do, at least when they study cultures.

Focus and Breadth

Cultural research shows great variation in what is studied, when researchers claim to be studying culture. Some studies focus narrowly on one or more cultural manifestations. Thus, for example, O'Reilly, Chatman, and Caldwell (1991), using a Q-sort task, asked study participants to sort cards, with each card containing an adjective, into piles of words that did and did not describe the cultures of the organizations in which they worked. Kilmann et al. (1985) and Rousseau (1990b) used questionnaires, much like those described previously as etic research, to get study participants to report the behavioral norms of their organizational cultures. These are narrowly focused or specialist studies of culture. They use one kind of cultural manifestation, such as self-reports of behavioral norms, to operationally define a culture. Implicitly, narrowly focused studies assume that it is sufficient to study a single cultural manifestation or a very few manifestations because if a wider range of manifestations were studied, the results would be largely the same. Implicitly, then, such studies assume that study participants' answers would be consistent across manifestations.

In contrast, other cultural studies emphasize breadth by examining a variety of cultural manifestations. In these studies, researchers need not assume that interpretations of these manifestations are consistent with each other. For example, Botti's (1995) study of a Japanese-Italian effort at collaboration in a manufacturing plant, Kondo's (1990) examination of a family-owned food-processing company in Japan, and Kunda's

(1992) ethnography of a U.S. engineering company all include interpretations of formal policies, structures, informal practices, rituals, and organizational stories, as well as extensive descriptions of the physical environments in which people worked. In Geertz's terms, these are thick descriptions. This breadth in the range of cultural manifestations studied is characteristic of ethnographic research and is more difficult to achieve when quantitative measures are used. Because it takes time to build a rich understanding of the relationships among a wide variety of cultural manifestations, breadth is achieved at the cost of being able to study only one or a very few cultural contexts, thus making generalization across contexts, even if it were desired, very difficult to attain. Thus, trade-offs between focus and breadth constrain the kinds of theoretical conclusions that can be drawn from a study. This dichotomy between focus and breadth, like many of the other dichotomies discussed in this chapter, is overdrawn. Just how much breadth is enough? Isn't any study, to some extent, a narrowly focused view?

Level of Depth

Sociocultural anthropologists advocate that researchers learn the language of cultural members and then spend 1 or 2 years as a participant-observer, living and working with the people being studied. Eventually, it is hoped, the researcher will come to be accepted as a cultural member. In ideal circumstances, the researcher might even be invited to undergo a formal, ritualized initiation into membership status. This is a first step toward emic understanding, which is predicated on the researcher being able to "penetrate the front" of public, polite behavior and gain the insights that come when people relax the constraints expected in interactions with outsiders. Psychologists make similar points when they argue that social desirability concerns affect how people behave, for example, when they try to control the impression they make on others. Only when facades are penetrated can a researcher hope to gain depth of understanding.

Recent ethnographic accounts are often skeptical about the difficulties of a researcher ever being accepted as an insider or ever being able to see a culture from an emic perspective. On the cover of Clifford and Marcus's (1986) book, which critiques such claims of privileged cultural acceptance, a photograph shows an ethnographer. He is pictured bent over his notes, with a cloth over his head shielding him from the sun and blinding him to his surroundings. "Natives" stand in the shadows watching with various indecipherable expressions. Granted, this ethnographer's notes may contain deeply empathetic, emic understanding of the natives, but the photograph suggests otherwise. Even skeptical views regarding the ability of ethnographers to develop emic understandings, such as those in Clifford and Marcus's book, retain the conviction that the insights available from a long-term participant observation study offer greater depth of understanding than other, more superficial approaches to understanding, such as the use of quantitative survey instruments.

Schein (1985, 1996, 1999) and Rousseau (1990a) stress the theoretical importance of depth of understanding. Schein (1985) distinguished three levels of depth in cultures, beginning with the most superficial: artifacts such as stories, rituals, dress, and décor; values (attitudes that can be articulated with relative ease); and basic assumptions (that are usually tacit and difficult to determine because they are taken for granted). According to Schein (1987), the best method for gaining an in-depth understanding of a culture is to enter a discussion (with therapeutic undertones) with cultural members, using the interview goals and techniques of a clinical psychologist to tap unconscious and preconscious assumptions. Schein argued that within a collectivity such as an organization, if a researcher attains in-depth understanding, he or she can ascertain if most members of the collectivity share the same assumptions. Basic assumptions tend to be quite abstract, such as whether people can be trusted or whether concerns about an organization's well-being should focus on short- or long-term considerations. This emphasis on depth in cultural studies has been crucially important, in part because the methods most easily able to create in-depth understanding, such as ethnography and clinical interviews, had become unfashionable in the years when quantitative methods gained dominance in organizational studies.

Perhaps an example will help make this depth argument come alive. When Ouchi (1981) studied a particular electronics company, employees told a "second-chance" story about an employee who made a disastrous mistake. When the culprit was called to his boss's office, he feared he would be fired. Instead, his boss expressed faith that the employee would never make another such mistake and gave him a very tough assignment. This assignment was a testimony of the boss's faith that the employee could redeem himself because a second mistake would have done the company grievous harm. This story ended happily: The employee succeeded beyond his boss's fondest dreams and was thereafter one of the company's most loyal employees. A second and superficially unrelated manifestation of the culture at this firm was the company's promotion policy, sometimes labeled the spiral staircase. Before being promoted up a level, employees were moved laterally so they had a variety of functional experiences. In this way, all the high-level employees of the firm had extensive exposure to the problems of marketing, engineering, finance, human resources, and so on, giving them a broad perspective of the firm as a whole. Although these two manifestations (the story and the spiral staircase promotion policy) may seem unrelated, Schein might argue that they appear unrelated because this analysis so far has been relatively superficial, focusing on the level of artifacts. If the interpretation were to go deeper, as Schein argues it should, the researcher might conclude that both manifestations illustrate a tacit, basic assumption about the benefits—to individual employees and to the company as a whole—of taking a long-term perspective.

Not everyone (including myself) agrees that artifacts and values are necessarily superficial. A cultural artifact, such as a story or a ritual, is important because of how people interpret its meanings. Those meanings need not be superficial; they may reflect deep assumptions. In this way, I argue that artifacts, values, and assumptions do not necessarily reflect separable, varying levels of depth. A cultural researcher should seek deep meanings associated with each type of cultural manifestation. In a superficial cultural study, interpretations and meanings can reflect, for example, formulaic expressions of espoused values in a "corporate values" statement. Alternatively, interpretations may reflect deeply held personal values that take the form of basic assumptions, sometimes so taken for granted that they are difficult to articulate. Such basic assumptions may include "walking the talk"—values inferred from, and congruent with, behavior. Other kinds of interpretations of events and artifacts are less value laden and more like cognitive conclusions, or beliefs, about "how things are." Some of these beliefs may have the characteristics of basic assumptions. In each of these examples, what is important is not the cultural manifestation but how people interpret it. The depth of a researcher's analysis of these interpretations—that is, the patterns of meaning underlying a collection of cultural manifestations—can (and I argue should) approach the depth of understanding that Schein terms "basic assumptions." It is important to note, however, that even at the level of deep assumptions, collectivity-wide consensus may not emerge. In a single context, some assumptions might generate collectivity-wide consensus. Other assumptions might be common to some subcultures but not others. Finally, some assumptions might be so ambiguous that clear agreement or disagreement among substantial numbers of people would be unlikely.

Depth of understanding clearly has its advantages, but it is obtained at a cost: the time it takes to gain in-depth understanding. Although this is a pragmatic concern, rather than a theoretical issue, it merits consideration. An anthropologist, for example, may invest years in learning a language, traveling to a distant land, and enduring physical discomfort, emotional isolation, and other forms of hardship. He or she may spend 1 or 2 years doing participant-observation and then another 1 or 2 years deciphering and interpreting field notes. The final product of all this effort is (usually) a book-length ethnography because the complexity of this kind of data is difficult to carve up in journal-length articles. This is a large time investment, particularly in universities in which tenure decisions are usually made after the first 7 years of employment.

Organizational ethnographers share some, but not all, of these problems of time investment. As long as an ethnographer studies an organization within a familiar culture, the problems of physical and emotional hardship, travel, and language differences are minimized. The etic-emic dimension, however, is difficult to manage in a relatively familiar organizational culture, and many of the other difficulties of ethnographic research remain. Some obstacles to ethnographic research are intensified in organizational studies. In the academic departments in which many organizational researchers work, there is not much understanding of the assumptions underlying ethnographic methods and even less sympathy with putting "all one's eggs in a single basket"—a book—rather than publishing numerous refereed journal articles. An organizational ethnographer pays these costs and deals with worrisome publication decisions, in part, because of a conviction that depth of understanding is crucial. Imagine, then, an ethnographer's reaction to a study claiming to understand a culture on the basis of a questionnaire or a short-term qualitative study involving a few months of observation or interviewing or both. Appreciation seems unlikely.

Given all this emphasis on depth, who would advocate a "superficial" approach to studying culture? There are pragmatic reasons for doing so. Doing a good ethnography is difficult and very time-consuming. Also, when it is finished, it is still only a study with a sample size of one. Although several publications can result from a single ethnographic study, sooner or later a researcher may want to go back to the field to study a different context. Given the realities of modern academic and family life, however, most researchers do only one long-term ethnography—the dissertation. The time involved in each study means that an ethnographic researcher is unlikely to be able to use his or her own data to make comparisons among significant numbers of cultures or to build empirically based, theoretical generalizations about culture. Some culture researchers may not want to do so, but for those who do, less time-consuming methods for studying cultures are essential. Depth must be sacrificed, in these instances, if generalization is the goal.

This dichotomy, however, like the others discussed previously, is overdrawn; it is important not to regard the issue as a dichotomous choice between depth or superficiality. There are many ways to gain a multifaceted, moderately unsuperficial understanding of a culture, even using short-term qualitative methods or innovative survey measures. All methods can be designed and applied in slapdash or probing ways, making some degree of depth a possibility worth striving for, even in a study that seeks to generalize across many cultures.

Effects of Intellectual Disputes on Organizational Studies: The "Paradigm Proliferation" Disputes

Disputes about objectivity and subjectivity, etic and emic research, generalizability and context-specific knowledge, focus and breadth, and level of depth are of particular relevance to cultural research, but they also have surfaced, to varying degrees, in organizational studies as a whole. Scholars have engaged in a fierce debate about whether these disputes have had favorable or unfavorable effects on the development of organizational theory and research. The results of this debate have implications for the state and reputation of cultural theory and research.

Within organizational studies in the United States, disputes about these issues have been framed as the "paradigm proliferation problem." In the 1960s and 1970s, a single paradigm (focused on neopositivism and quantitative methods) held sway among most U.S. organizational scholars. In the early 1980s, the renaissance of interest in cultural studies and, more broadly, qualitative methods, activated many of the intellectual disputes described previously. As a result of these and other intellectual influences, there is currently a lack of consensus within organizational studies about what theories are worth studying, what methods are valid, what values and interests should be pursued, and what epistemological assumptions are merited (e.g., Burrell & Morgan, 1979; Clegg & Dunkerly, 1977; Donaldson, 1985; Nord & Connell, 1998; Silverman, 1970; Smircich, Calás, & Morgan, 1992). Thus, the intense disputes within cultural studies are mirrored, to a weaker extent, in the organizational field as a whole. Therefore, it is worth considering how the paradigm proliferation debate developed within organizational studies.

A paradigm offers a way of approaching scientific work, as Van de Ven (1997) explains:

> A paradigm is a worldview, a general perspective, a way of breaking down the complexity of the real world. As such, paradigms are deeply embedded in the socialization of adherents and practitioners, telling them what is important, what is legitimate, what is reasonable. Paradigms are normative; they tell us what to do without the necessity of long existential considerations. (p. 2)

I argue, in accord with Donaldson (1985), that the concept of a paradigm has been overused; the various intellectual disputes discussed previously do not fall easily together into well-defined, competing paradigms. Positions in these various disputes, however, do tend to cluster. For example, some organizational scholars favor being-realism, representational epistemologies, etic research, and the search for empirically based and generalizable theory, preferring a relatively narrow focus with relatively less concern about issues of depth. Other organizational scholars prefer becoming-realism, postrepresentational epistemologies, emic research, and breadth and depth of understanding. Of course, there are exceptions to these clusters—different ways to mix and match preferences regarding these issues. Whether these differences represent different paradigms or simply a cacophony of different opinions about fundamental issues is less important than the dialogues that have ensued.

One particularly vociferous debate occurred primarily in the United States. Recent recipients of a major award from the U.S. Academy of Management articulated opposing reactions to these developments. In his award acceptance speech, Pfeffer (1993) argued that the proliferation of research paradigms in the field of organizational studies had eroded the field's prestige in the rest of academia, making it difficult for us to garner resources and impeding the cumulative development of knowledge. Pfeffer argued that, for the advancement of the field and the enhancement of knowledge, a board of elite researchers should select a small number of research topics on which all organizational researchers would have to work.

The next year's award recipient, Van Maanen (1995a, 1995b), took umbrage at Pfeffer's call for the dominance of a few elite-approved research topics, which Van Maanen labeled "Pfefferdigms." Van Maanen (1995a, p. 133) argued that any elitist determination of what topics were worth studying was "insufferably smug; pious and orthodox; philosophically indefensible; extraordinarily naïve as to how science actually works; theoretically foolish, vain, and autocratic." Van Maanen viewed the proliferation of paradigms as a sign of the moral and intellectual health of the field and called for "letting a thousand flowers bloom" as an effective means of encouraging innovative research.

Subsequently, a third award recipient, Van de Ven (1997), spoke vehemently against the ways in which advocates of particular paradigms had demeaned and devalued research conducted from other paradigmatic orientations. Van de Ven used neopositivist language to argue that empirical evidence could resolve the competing claims of paradigms: "Valid empirical evidence is the ultimate external arbitrator for sifting and winnowing among our paradigms and for advancing those that provide empirically better explanations than others" (p. 9). Van de Ven is making assumptions about the objectivity of data and its determinant value in a theoretical dispute. The assumption that theoretical (and possible paradigmatic) differences of opinion can be empirically resolved is a basic tenet of neopositivism (e.g., Campbell & Stanley, 1966).

Many other scholars, working from different (not neopositivist) epistemological or methodological positions, would challenge Van de Ven's assumptions in this regard.[2] For example, Burrell and Morgan (1979) made a strong and influential argument for "paradigm incommensurability"—that is, evaluating contributions by the standards of an author's own paradigm, not the standards of others' paradigms. These authors carried paradigm incommensurability a step further, arguing that research within paradigms should be kept separate so that lesser known paradigms could develop without outside interference.

Hassard and Pym (1990) and Weaver and Gioia (1994) called for an end to this "smug protectionism." As calls for paradigm incommensurabilty became less accepted, uncertainty increased (Fleming & Stablein, 1997):

> Now paradigm differences must be taken seriously, not ignored or granted "separate but equal" status (Reed, 1996). Today, we are left with the uncertainties that characterize the 1990s regarding definitions, meaning, method, the nature of theory, and the role of the theorist (Clegg & Hardy, 1996).

The Culture Wars

The uncertainties that spread throughout the field of organizational studies at the turn of the century, giving rise to the paradigm proliferation debates, are even more intense within the domain of organizational culture studies. Because advocates of opposing views have been drawn to the study of culture, these disputes have surfaced and been argued particularly vociferously. In addition to their theoretical and methodological differences, cultural researchers are deeply divided on the question of whose interests and values merit representation and advocacy (e.g., Alvesson & Melin, 1987; Barley, Meyer, & Gash, 1988; Calás & Smircich, 1987; Stablein & Nord, 1985). When cultural studies come to contradictory conclusions, these fundamental disagreements make it difficult to adjudicate conflicting conclusions, perhaps with further empirical research, and arrive at some truth on which all parties would agree.

The intellectual disputes described in this chapter have made it nearly impossible to write a cumulative history of "what we have learned" so far about cultures in organizations. For example, when Peter Frost and I were asked to contribute a handbook chapter reviewing the accomplishments of culture research to date, we found it impossible to write the usual enlightenment tale of knowledge advancement. Instead, we (Martin & Frost, 1996) described cultural theory and research using a "culture wars" metaphor.[3] We described culture research as a series of ongoing battles between opposing viewpoints. We began with the "revolutionary vanguard" who spearheaded the renaissance of interest in cultural studies in the 1980s. Next, we described attacks and counterattacks by armies representing opposing theoretical viewpoints, a skirmish between quantitative and qualitative methodologists, a metatheoretical move to alter "the battle lines," and a postmodern[4] attempt to rout all armies from the field of battle.

Although we had fun using the culture wars metaphor to review the cultural literature, these intellectual disputes (a local version of the paradigm proliferation debate) have had serious consequences. Because it is difficult to present a cumulative picture of what has been learned from culture research, the perceived worth of this area of inquiry has been difficult to explain and understand, making it easier for critics to marginalize and devalue work in this area. When a theoretical domain, such as cultural research, challenges neopositivist assumptions about the empirical resolution of theoretical differences, it runs the risk of being dismissed by some as unverifiable and therefore empty rhetoric. For example, in Van de Ven's (1997) award acceptance speech, he notes,

> Then there are the endless rhetorical diatribes of neomodernists—culture theorists, critical theorists, postpositivists, feminists, Saussurean linguists. They are taking the discursive turn to deconstruct one another, and particularly the schools in Pfefferdigm. They lay bare the belly of the positivists. (p. 5)

Although critical, feminist, postmodern, and linguistic theoreticians offer cultural researchers fine intellectual company, this remark seems to me to be an attempt to marginalize and devalue cultural research. Even if Van de Ven did not intend this, he may have influenced others to do so.

If we are to counter attempts to marginalize and devalue cultural research, we need to make ourselves understood, build on each other's work, and begin to explain to the rest of the field why what we are doing is important. This is difficult, in part because cultural researchers do not have commonly accepted, unproblematic conceptual definitions. Therefore, it is essential that each cultural study clearly defines the concepts and operationalizations that it is using. To help in this task, in Chapter 3, I explore some different ways to define culture and examine what we study when we claim to be studying culture.

Notes

1. A geometer practices geometry.

2. For the purposes of summarizing this debate, I put aside for the moment differences of opinion about whether or not these are truly paradigmatic disputes (Donaldson, 1985).

3. *Culture wars*, in popular usage, refers to multicultural conflicts among representatives of different groups, defined usually by race, gender, ethnicity, class, or ideology.

4. Because postmodernism is so different from the intellectual traditions that preceded it, brief introductions in a text such as this do not do justice to it. For readers who want to read more about postmodernism, Alvesson and Deetz (1996) offer a clear introduction to postmodernism, contrasting it to critical theory. Martin and Frost's (1996) review of the cultural literature, described in this chapter, is written in a postmodern spirit; it describes unresolved conflicts among intellectual positions regarding cultural issues rather than telling a more modern tale of progress toward greater knowledge based on empirical findings. For a deeper discussion of postmodern approaches to culture, see Alvesson and Willmott (1996), Berg (1989), Calás and Smircich (1991), Czarniawska-Joerges (1988), Grafton-Small and Linstead (1987), Jeffcutt (1991), and Letiche (1991).

 *3*

Pieces of the Puzzle

WHAT IS CULTURE?
WHAT IS NOT CULTURE?

This chapter addresses the "granddaddy" of dilemmas in this domain: What is culture? What is not culture? This chapter begins by examining a variety of definitions of culture, exploring the theoretical implications of how culture is defined. Next, I turn to the related issue of how culture is operationalized (an *operationalization* is the way a given concept is measured in a particular study). Pieces of the cultural puzzle are defined, with vivid examples of cultural manifestations drawn from a variety of culture studies. In the course of defining and giving examples of these cultural manifestations, three intellectual traditions of relevance to cultural theory will be introduced: functionalism, critical theory, and postmodernism. Manifestations of culture include rituals, stories, humor, jargon, physical arrangements, and formal structures and policies, as well as informal norms and practices. Content themes (such as values or basic assumptions) are used to

capture and show the relationships among interpretations of the meanings of these manifestations. These are the building blocks needed for
you to understand the theoretical assumptions underlying a culture
study, summarize the content of any cultural portrait, and, if you wish,
develop your own answers to the questions: What is culture? What is
not culture?

Defining Culture

Table 3.1 lists a variety of definitions of culture. I use this table to
make it easier to read this section of the chapter, referring to each definition by the number of the definition in the table. These definitions were
selected because they reflect the range of definitions of culture currently in use among organizational culture researchers. Definition 1
(Sathe, 1985) and Definition 2 (Louis, 1985) in Table 3.1 illustrate two
theoretical features common to most such definitions: the use of the
word "shared" and a reference to culture as that which is distinctive or
unique to a particular context. Not all researchers agree that culture is
shared and unique, however, as will become evident in the following
discussion.

Ideational and Materialistic Approaches

The first two definitions have another characteristic in common:
Culture is conceptualized in terms of meanings or understandings.
These are cognitive aspects of culture, and therefore such definitions
are referred to as ideational. Ideational definitions of culture emphasize
subjective interpretations, whereas material aspects of culture can be
described in objectivist terms, or their meanings can be interpreted
subjectively. Definition 3 (Sergiovanni & Corbally, 1984) is similar to
Definitions 1 and 2 in that culture is defined as shared, but Definition 3
adds to this ideational emphasis a consideration of the material conditions in which these ideas develop. Materialist manifestations include the material conditions of work (e.g., the plush carpet of an executive suite and the noise and dirt on an assembly line) and the size of
employees' paychecks and other indicators of their material well-being.
Advocates of including material manifestations of culture argue that
an exclusive emphasis on ideational elements of culture would foster

Table 3.1   Definitions of Organizational Culture

1. "Culture is the set of important understandings (often unstated) that members of a community share in common" (Sathe, 1985, p. 6).
2. "[Culture is] a set of understandings or meanings shared by a group of people. The meanings are largely tacit among the members, are clearly relevant to a particular group, and are distinctive to the group" (Louis, 1985, p. 74).
3. "A standard definition of culture would include the system of values, symbols, and shared meanings of a group including the embodiment of these values, symbols, and meanings into material objects and ritualized practices. . . . The 'stuff' of culture includes customs and traditions, historical accounts be they mythical or actual, tacit understandings, habits, norms and expectations, common meanings associated with fixed objects and established rites, shared assumptions, and intersubjective meanings" (Sergiovanni & Corbally, 1984, p. viii).
4. "Cultural arrangements, of which organizations are an essential segment, are seen as manifestations of a process of ideational development located within a context of definite material conditions. It is a context of dominance (males over females/owners over workers) but also of conflict and contradiction in which class and gender, autonomous but overdetermined, are vital dynamics. Ideas and cultural arrangements confront actors as a series of rules of behavior; rules that, in their contradictions, may variously be enacted, followed, or resisted" (Mills, 1988, p. 366).
5. "An organization might then be studied by discovering and synthesizing its rules of social interaction and interpretation, as revealed in the behavior they shape. Social interaction and interpretation are communication activities, so it follows that the culture could be described by articulating communication rules" (Schall, 1983, p. 3).
6. "[Culture is] the pattern of shared beliefs and values that give members of an institution meaning, and provide them with the rules for behavior in their organization" (Davis, 1984, p. 1).
7. "To analyze *why* members behave the way they do, we often look for the *values* that govern behavior, which is the second level. . . . But as the values are hard to observe directly, it is often necessary to infer them by interviewing key members of the organization or to content analyze artifacts such as documents and charters. However, in identifying such values, we usually note that they represent accurately only the manifest or *espoused* values of a culture. That is, they focus on what people *say* is the reason for their behavior, what they ideally would like those reasons to be, and what are often their rationalizations for their behavior. Yet, the underlying reasons for their behavior remain concealed or unconscious. To really *understand* a culture and to ascertain more completely the group's values and overt behavior, it is imperative to delve into the *underlying assumptions,* which are typically unconscious but which actually determine how group members perceive, think, and feel" (Schein, 1985, p. 3).

(Continued)

Table 3.1   (Continued)

8. "In a particular situation the set of meanings that evolves gives a group its own
    ethos, or distinctive character, which is expressed in patterns of belief (ideol-
    ogy), activity (norms and rituals), language and other symbolic forms through
    which organization members both create and sustain their view of the world
    and image of themselves in the world. The development of a worldview with its
    shared understanding of group identity, purpose, and direction are products of
    the unique history, personal interactions, and environmental circumstances of
    the group" (Smircich, 1983a, p. 56).

9. "Culture does not necessarily imply a uniformity of values. Indeed quite differ-
    ent values may be displayed by people of the same culture. In such an instance,
    what is it that holds together the members of the organization? I suggest that we
    look to the existence of a common frame of reference or a shared recognition of
    relevant issues. There may not be agreement about whether these issues should
    be relevant or about whether they are positively or negatively valued. . . . They
    may array themselves differently with respect to that issue, but whether posi-
    tively or negatively, they are all oriented to it" (Feldman, 1991, p. 154).

10. "Culture is a loosely structured and incompletely shared system that emerges
    dynamically as cultural members experience each other, events, and the organi-
    zation's contextual features" (Anonymous reviewer, 1987).

11. "Members do not agree upon clear boundaries, cannot identify shared solu-
    tions, and do not reconcile contradictory beliefs and multiple identities. Yet,
    these members contend they belong to a culture. They share a common orienta-
    tion and overarching purpose, face similar problems, and have comparable expe-
    riences. However, these shared orientations and purposes accommodate
    different beliefs and incommensurable technologies, these problems imply dif-
    ferent solutions, and these experiences have multiple meanings. . . . Thus, for at
    least some cultures, to dismiss the ambiguities in favor of strictly what is clear
    and shared is to exclude some of the most central aspects of the members' cul-
    tural experience and to ignore the essence of their cultural community"
    (Meyerson, 1991a, pp. 131-132).

12. "When organizations are examined from a cultural viewpoint, attention is
    drawn to aspects of organizational life that historically have often been ignored
    or understudied, such as the stories people tell to newcomers to explain 'how
    things are done around here,' the ways in which offices are arranged and per-
    sonal items are or are not displayed, jokes people tell, the working atmosphere
    (hushed and luxurious or dirty and noisy), the relations among people (affec-
    tionate in some areas of an office and obviously angry and perhaps competitive
    in another place), and so on. Cultural observers also often attend to aspects of
    working life that other researchers study, such as the organization's official poli-
    cies, the amounts of money different employees earn, reporting relationships,
    and so on. A cultural observer is interested in the surfaces of these cultural man-
    ifestations because details can be informative, but he or she also seeks an in-
    depth understanding of the patterns of meanings that link these manifestations
    together, sometimes in harmony, sometimes in bitter conflicts between groups,
    and sometimes in webs of ambiguity, paradox, and contradiction" (Martin,
    Chapter 1, this volume, p. 3).

SOURCE: Adapted and expanded from materials presented in Martin (1992a).

misunderstanding by permitting a de-emphasis on the vastly different material conditions that characterize work at different levels of an organization's hierarchy. Czarniawaska-Joerges (1992) explains why it is important to include material manifestations:

> Organizational theorists have located new aspects of organizational life and its function to study during the second half of the decade. Among these we can find jokes, coffee breaks, how people are dressed, how they behave at the corporation's Christmas party, how they sit at meetings, how they get fired (the "rite" of getting fired), what stories about present and former figures of authority are told, and so on. . . . It could be argued that these are of marginal importance compared to, for example, the organization's hierarchy and the way in which work is organized, controlled, and carried out. (p. 108)

For example, materialist culture researchers would argue the low pay, dirt, and noise that assembly line workers often endure, or the relative quiet and luxury of the executive suite, must be considered if a cultural study is to offer a rich understanding of these disparate working experiences. In this way, material definitions of culture facilitate discussion of intergroup conflicts. Therefore, Definition 4 (Mills, 1988) is important because it stresses conflict in addition to what is shared, at least within subcultures; Definition 4 also includes both ideational and material aspects of culture.

   Two kinds of materialist approaches to the study of culture can be distinguished. Some materialist definitions include material manifestations as part of culture, as can be seen in Definition 3's inclusion of "material objects" and Definition 4's incorporation of "definite material conditions." Other materialist approaches assume that ideational considerations constitute culture (the cultural "superstructure"), whereas material aspects of working life are essential to consider but are not defined as part of culture (the structural "base"). According to this latter point of view, the materialist base consists of attributes such as job descriptions, reporting relationships, pay practices, and formally mandated policies and procedures, which are not part of the cultural superstructure. Culture, then, consists of the ideational elements, such as beliefs and values, that emerge to explain and reinforce a materialist base. Whether one defines material conditions as important to study but not part of culture or includes material conditions as manifestations of a culture, materialist approaches agree that it is essential to examine the material conditions that characterize a cultural context. In contrast, ideational definitions of culture exclude such material conditions.

Focus and Breadth

When many types of cultural manifestations are studied, including informal norms, rituals, stories, physical arrangements, and formal and informal practices, this produces a holistic view of a cultural context, referred to sometimes as a "generalist" study of culture. Materialist studies of culture, for example, are likely to include many types of cultural manifestations, as can be seen in Definitions 3 and 4. In contrast, other more narrow studies define culture in terms of just one or two manifestations, as can be seen in Definition 5 (Schall, 1983) and Definition 6 (Davis, 1984). Definition 5 defines culture as communication rules, whereas Definition 6 has an emphasis on beliefs and values. Studies that rely on narrow definitions of culture are referred to as "specialist" studies. Specialist studies assume that one or a few manifestations can stand in for, or represent, an entire culture because interpretations of more types of manifestations would be consistent. Consistency is a crucial and highly debatable theoretical assumption, as will be shown in Chapter 4.

Level of Depth of Interpretation

Depth is also an important component of some definitions of culture, as can be seen in Definition 7. As discussed in Chapter 2, Schein's (1985) approach to depth in Definition 7 (see also Schein, 1999) distinguishes three levels of depth: artifacts, values, and basic assumptions. As explained in Chapter 2, I argue that this approach to the question of depth confounds the content of a manifestation, such as a story, with the depth of the interpretation of that manifestation. I and others argue that any cultural manifestation can be interpreted superficially, or its interpretation can reflect deeply held, unconscious assumptions. Most cultural researchers do not address the issue of depth when they define culture, preferring to discuss that issue when they describe their choice of methods.

Recap

To review the dimensions of definitional disagreement presented so far, I consider one more definition of culture. Definition 8 (Smircich, 1983a) includes several ideational manifestations of culture (i.e., meanings, beliefs, and worldviews) and uses several words or phrases (such as "activities" and "environmental circumstances") that may allude to material conditions. Because many types of manifestations are mentioned (including language, history, norms, activities, and rituals), this definition stresses breadth of manifestations studied. The definition assumes that culture is both shared and unique. Questions of depth of understanding are not explicitly mentioned.

Areas of Theoretical Disagreement Implicit in Definitions of Culture

Is Culture Shared?

We can examine these definitions of culture and see how they imply fundamental theoretical disagreements. Most definitions of organizational culture include an explicit focus on what is shared (e.g., Definitions 1-3, 6, and 8). In contrast, some definitions stress conflict between opposing points of view rather than that which is shared (e.g., Definition 4). Even conflict definitions, however, tacitly presume that some views are shared by subcultures (e.g., owners and workers). Culture is less often defined as an incompletely shared system, allowing for a wide variation across interpretations. An example of this last "incompletely shared" view is given in Definitions 9 (Feldman, 1991), 10 (Anonymous reviewer, 1987), and 11 (Meyerson, 1991a). Although these three definitions allow for a "common frame of reference" concerning which issues are relevant, no clear unity and no clear conflicts characterize this view of culture as ambiguity; cultural members may agree that certain issues are an important part of their frames of reference but disagree regarding the particulars of each of those issues, creating ambiguity. Thus, even the word "shared" fails to elicit agreement among cultural researchers. My definition of culture, with which I began this book, is listed as Definition 12 in Table 3.1. Mine is a generalist rather than a specialist definition, including a broad range of ideational and material manifestations of culture, emphasizing depth of interpretation but allowing for shared meanings, conflict, and an ambiguity similar to that described in Definitions 9, 10, and 11. Thus, I believe that culture includes conflict and ambiguity as well as that which is shared. The debate about whether culture includes only that which is shared is one of the primary foci of Chapters 4.

Is a Culture Unique?

Many definitions and discussions of culture include a second common characteristic: the assertion that a culture is "unique" or "distinctive," claiming (usually without evidence) that its characteristics are seldom, if ever, to be found in other organizations (i.e., Definitions 2 and 8) (see also Clark, 1972; Gregory, 1983; Schein, 1985; Selznick, 1957; Van Maanen & Barley, 1984). This emphasis on uniqueness is important because if a culture is unique, then its study is likely to yield few theoretical generalizations. One reason why definitions of culture often include the assertion of uniqueness is that cultural members often believe, and take pride in, the idea that their organization's culture is unique (Martin, 1992a, pp. 109-110; Martin, Feldman, Hatch, & Sitkin, 1983). For example, Young (1991) found that women working on an assembly line in Britain had formed a close-knit culture that, they were sure, was unique:

Production director: Oh, I'll tell you, it's a unique little world of its own down there. They all have their own little events which they organize, and they've got their own lot of interests. (p. 93)

Machinist: All that stuff over on the [bulletin] board, that's all old biddies really. They all do that. It's their way of sayin' 'ow special they think they are; 'ow they've been 'ere longest an' all that. Just sort of tryin' to put all the others down. (p. 102)

There are many reasons why cultural members like to think of their culture as unique. An organization often defines the goods or services it produces as distinctive to carve out a well-defined niche in a market. In a similar fashion, members often view their cultures as distinctive (e.g., Clark, 1972; Gregory, 1983; Selznick, 1957). Particularly in individualistic societies, people generally want to be viewed as separate and special—a "unique" individual (e.g., Snyder & Fromkin, 1980).[1] All these factors combine to make cultural uniqueness desirable. Of course, because cultural members work within the boundaries of their culture, and probably have intimate knowledge of only a few other cultures, it is difficult for them to know whether their cultural uniqueness claims are justified.

Cultural researchers are presumably in a better position to assess the validity of uniqueness claims because they read case studies of many cultures and can determine that a cultural manifestation, claimed to be unique in one context, is observed in a variety of other contexts. Cultural researchers, however, often seem to take uniqueness claims at face value, including uniqueness or distinctiveness as one aspect of their definitions of culture and claiming that the perception of uniqueness increases organizational identification and commitment (e.g., Clark, 1972; Schein, 1985; Selznick, 1957, p. 8). So many cultural researchers include uniqueness claims as part of their definition of culture that Ott (1989, p. 52; see also Pedersen & Dobbin, 1997) concluded that one of the "very few areas of general consensus about organizational culture [is that] each organizational culture is relatively unique."

Contrary to Ott's (1989) claim, however, here too there is dissensus. For example, in Table 3.1, Definitions 1, 3 through 7, 9, and 10 do not include explicit claims of uniqueness. Many researchers challenge the assumption of uniqueness (e.g., Bockus, 1983; Martin et al., 1983; Riley, 1983; Trice & Beyer, 1984; Van Maanen & Barley, 1985, p. 32). Cultural members may believe their organization's culture is unique, but often what is believed to be unique to a particular context is found elsewhere as well (Martin, 1992a, p. 111), a contradiction labeled the "uniqueness paradox" (Martin et al., 1983). For example, when people tell stories that illustrate "what makes this place special," these anecdotes share the characteristics of the seven common story types found in most organizations. Similarly, when people describe rituals that they think of as unique, the basic dramatic structure, roles, and scripts of the ritual usually fit within one of several common ritual types (Trice & Beyer, 1984). Studies of the cultures of large corporations reveal that certain value themes (such as concern for quality of goods and services or customer satisfaction) are commonplace. In accord with the uniqueness paradox, members cite these common themes as evidence of the "uniqueness" of their culture (e.g., Bockus, 1983; Siehl & Martin, 1990). (These common types of stories, rituals, and content themes will be described later.) These examples suggest that claims of cultural uniqueness should be met with some skepticism, as some scholars have done:

Turner (1986, p. 111) stated, "We note, then, that organizational entities may not be possessed of a distinctive and uniquely unified culture,"
and Van Maanen and Barley (1985, p. 32) noted, "The phrase 'organizational culture' suggests that organizations bear unitary and unique cultures. Such a stance, however, is difficult to justify empirically." The
work of these authors suggests, for example, that claims of uniqueness
might not be found as frequently in nations in which collectivist, rather
than individualist, values predominate. A resolution to this disagreement about cultural uniqueness, labeled a "nexus approach" to the
study of culture (Martin, 1992a), is presented in Chapter 5.

What Culture Researchers Study
When They Claim to Be Studying Culture

The fundamental nature of theoretical issues raised by these varying
definitions of culture is underscored by a final source of conceptual
confusion. Conceptual definitions should correspond to the way those
concepts are operationalized in a particular study. Unfortunately, cultural studies often define culture one way and operationalize the concept differently, further contributing to the theoretical and empirical
confusion that characterizes this domain of research. Therefore, I will
ignore definitions for the moment and examine what researchers actually study when they claim to be studying culture.

Researchers have studied many types of cultural manifestations. Because some of the readers of this book may want to examine these cultural manifestations in their own research, this chapter includes many
definitions. Citations to specialist studies that focus on each type of
manifestation are included. The style of this discussion of cultural manifestations is unusual. Usually, a cultural study describes a manifestation in context, giving interpretations of its meanings in that context.
Because any given manifestation can be viewed and interpreted in a variety of ways, by different cultural members and by different researchers, this chapter could easily become too long. Here, manifestations are
taken out of their cultural context. Because manifestations are usually
studied to interpret them, however, some examples of interpretations
are needed; therefore, sample interpretations are given for stories and
rituals only. Four types of cultural manifestations will be described:
cultural forms (such as rituals, organizational stories, jargon, humor,

and physical arrangements), formal practices (such as pay schemes and hierarchical reporting structures), informal practices (such as norms), and content themes.

Cultural Forms: The Esoterica of Cultural Analysis

Cultural forms include rituals, organizational stories, jargon, humor, and physical arrangements including architecture, interior decor, and dress codes. Forms are the esoterica of cultural analysis. Until the 1980s, most organizational researchers and practitioners studied formal practices (such as written policies and formal organizational structures) and informal practices (behavioral norms—the unwritten rules). The espoused values of leaders, managers, and other employees have also been studied, often through attitude surveys. Until the 1980s, however, most organizational researchers did not study cultural forms, such as rituals and stories (as exceptions, see Clark, 1972; Pettigrew, 1979; Selznick, 1957). Since then, it has become clear that such an omission is a mistake. These cultural forms can provide important clues to what employees are thinking, believing, and doing.

Rituals: The Celebration and Sanctification of the Mundane

I begin with an example of a ritual. MFC, Inc. (a pseudonym) is a very small company that makes relatively large amounts of money by manufacturing metal foam. Even after years of refining the manufacturing process, MFC employees sometimes have trouble in the crucial last step, and if this happens the foam can fail to form properly—an expensive mistake. The "pour time" ritual at MFC transforms this last step of the manufacturing process into an elaborate rite. Every workday, as this crucial step in the process approaches, the beginning of a ritual is

> signaled by a call, "pour time." Workers in the machine shop promptly stop their work and head for the pouring area. The half-dozen participants include all of the production personnel: two shop machinists, two foam technicians, the shop supervisor, and Bryan Anderson [a pseudonym], vice president for production. The men don white smocks, safety glasses, and asbestos mitts. A roughly cylindrical vessel is removed from an oven and placed on a special altar. A crucible filled with molten metal is lifted from a

furnace in a carefully orchestrated motion requiring two men, one at each end of a special, 6-foot long caliper. The two men carefully pour the molten metal into the waiting vessel and then move quickly away. Seconds after the pouring is complete, flames shoot out from the bottom of the vessel. Two of the watching men use fire extinguishers to douse the flames, while two others rush in to encircle the bottom of the vessel with putty. A cap is then placed on top and insulation is wrapped around it. Various machines are turned on, in sequence, to assist formation of the foam, and the vessel is left to cool. (adapted from Rifkin, 1985, p. 6)

A ritual is like a drama (Rosen, 1985; Trice & Beyer, 1984). It consists of a carefully planned and executed set of activities, carried out in a social context (an audience), with well-demarcated beginnings and endings (like a play) and well-defined roles for organizational members (like a script). Sometimes, costumes and props are even used. Rifkin's (1985) description of the foam-making ritual exhibits all these dramatic characteristics. From the opening line, "pour time," the spectacle is carefully choreographed. Props and costumes have a religious aura. Attention is riveted on a sacred vessel, which the costumed high priests place on an "altar." The dangers of fire and molten metal (not to mention financial loss) raise the level of dramatic tension until the possibility of failure has been eliminated—temporarily—and the sealed vessel is put aside to cool.

Rituals have another distinguishing characteristic: They are repeated. For example, the foam-making ritual is enacted daily. Such repeated rituals have been referred to as rites to distinguish them from ceremonies, which are ritualized events that occur only once (Trice & Beyer, 1984). For example, one kind of ceremony has been called a "wake" (Harris & Sutton, 1986). This is a one-time party, held by former employees of an organization that is going out of business. Participants in an organizational wake exchange names and addresses, promise to keep in touch, and consume food and alcoholic beverages. They also express sadness and anger and offer each other emotional support for the future. The death of the organization ("I guess this means it is really over") is acknowledged explicitly, although friends make plans to stay in touch. This example of a wake ceremony illustrates another attribute of rituals: They often include other cultural forms, such as stories or jargon. For example, participants in a wake often give speeches that include jargon only cultural insiders could decipher. Organizational stories, featuring key events in the company's history, may be told. Humor is used to relieve the tension and sadness, often with jokes only insiders would understand. Sometimes, employees' personal office spaces are dismantled and, more rarely, company property may be defaced or destroyed. Photographs of friends may be taken to keep memories alive.

Rituals such as wakes usually mark transition points in employees' careers, the life cycle of products, or the history of the organization as a whole. For example, the "pour time" ritual marks a daily transition point in a manufacturing process, whereas a wake marks a transition in the life cycle of an organization. Other common types of transition rituals are defined in Table 3.2.

The annual sales convention held by the Mary Kay cosmetics company combines many of the common types of rituals described in Table 3.2. New and newly promoted employees are introduced (initiation). Mary Kay rewards high performers (enhancement) with prizes, such as diamonds and pink Cadillacs. This convention can also be seen as a renewal ritual, drawing attention to and renewing the enthusiasm of the sales force while drawing attention away from other more problematic issues (product development delays, missed shipping deadlines, or competition from other cosmetics companies). It is also an integration ritual because even those employees who are not singled out for recognition join in the fun and build relationships with each other and with the company as a whole.

Rituals offer an opportunity to show how the functionalist intellectual tradition has influenced cultural theory and research. The typology of rituals offered in Table 3.2 is an example of a functional cultural analysis (as functionalism was defined in Chapter 1, this volume). The typology is based on the outcomes anticipated from each type of ritual—enhancement, integration, and so on. A ritual fitting the descriptions in Table 3.2 would not, of course, be a unique cultural manifestation, although specific details of its implementation might be distinctive. Trice and Beyer (1984) expand this functional analysis, adding depth of interpretation, by arguing that rituals can have both technical and emotional, manifest and latent functions. The usefulness and the limitations of this kind of functional analysis can be demonstrated by analyzing the "pour time" ritual in these terms. The purpose of the "pour time" ritual may seem purely technical—to complete the last step of the foam manufacturing process. Also, undoubtedly, this manifest technical objective explains much about what is going on. However, it is

Table 3.2 Common Types of Rituals

Initiation rituals focus on the indoctrination of new or newly promoted employees, such as police recruits or a Japanese bank's newest crop of recent college graduates (e.g., Rohlene, 1974; Van Maanen, 1976).

Enhancement rituals bring recognition to good performance, such as when valued employees are flown to the Caribbean or young professors are given tenure (e.g., Trice & Beyer, 1984; Van Maanen & Kunda, 1989).

Degradation rituals celebrate the opposite—the defamation and removal of poor performers, particularly those in leadership positions (e.g., Gephart, 1978).

Renewal rituals, such as the "pour time" ritual, seek to strengthen group functioning by resolving one set of problems while drawing attention away from others.

Integration rituals provide an opportunity for employees to solidify their interpersonal relationships in a context in which family members are (usually) welcome and the formality of hierarchical relationships can safely and temporarily be suspended. For example, at a Christmas party, top executives chat informally with subordinates and their spouses, often talking of hobbies or children. At a party with music, male and female employees often dance and even flirt with each other, partially and temporarily suspending some of the sexual taboos associated with relationships at work. At a company softball game, the star of the day or the captain of a team may be a low-ranking employee, while the president of the company may be exposed as a poor batter. It is important that top executives participate in integration rituals, in part because hierarchical relations cannot be temporarily suspended or reversed in their absence. Too much insubordination, flirtation, or loss of control is usually not condoned. Not surprisingly, alcohol is often involved in these events.

(Continued)

not necessary to have several employees stand around while the metal is poured, however, when one or two would be sufficient to help with auxiliary tasks such as extinguishing the fire. On a more latent technical level, this carefully executed routine draws attention to the difficulty of the crucial last step of the manufacturing process and ensures that everyone is paying attention. The pouring ritual also has emotional connotations. On a manifest emotional level, the group enacts the importance of teamwork. On a more latent emotional level, any problems that might disrupt cooperation and feelings of closeness within the group must be temporarily put aside as attention is focused on a way in which the team works smoothly together. To the extent that such problems stem from strains in the relationship between the boss and his subordinates, the "pour time" ritual uses emotions to legitimate existing systems of power and authority.

Table 3.2 (Continued)

Conflict reduction rituals are a special kind of integration ritual designed to repair relationships strained by a conflict or by work-induced stress, such as a dead-
line, a controversial decision, or a bad outcome. They provide a context in which it
is safe to relax, rebuild good feelings among participants, and let off steam. As in
other integration rituals, if conflict is to be successfully reduced, hierarchical relationships need to be minimized or temporarily suspended; food and alcohol are often involved. For example, a work team may decide to go out for drinks or dinner
after a difficult meeting.

Ending rituals mark a transition from insider to outsider, for example, when a
transferred employee is given a good-bye party by coworkers, a newly retired employee is given a ceremony and a gift, or an organization about to dissolve gives its
employees a wake.

Compound rituals include two or more of the ritual types mentioned previously.
Many of the most involving rituals are compound. For example, the Mary Kay company holds a noisy, fun-filled annual convention for the sales force employees who
sell the firm's cosmetics door to door in their neighborhoods. Most of these salespeople are women, usually with no more than a high school degree. They work
hard, often combining their work for Mary Kay with the usual responsibilities of a
stay-at-home spouse. For these employees, the convention is a rare opportunity to
leave family responsibilities behind and be recognized for their other accomplishments. The convention is designed to heighten the sense that this is a special event,
in part by incorporating other cultural forms. For example, physical arrangements
are used to give the event glitz and glamor, like that associated with the Academy
Awards in Hollywood. Mary Kay wears a floor-length sequined gown. As the music
reaches a crescendo, she appears, slowly rising from below the stage, on a dais.
The audience also dresses up. In this setting, pink feather boas and bunny ears are
normal.

SOURCE: Adapted from Trice and Beyer (1984).

So far, this functional analysis of manifest and latent, technical and
emotional outcomes has tacitly assumed a managerial point of view.
For example, it is in management's interest to reinforce current systems
of power and authority. The functions of this ritual can also be analyzed
from a critical theory viewpoint, however. Critical theory offers a critique of efforts by managers to control the minds and behaviors of employees, particularly those who labor at the bottom of organizational
hierarchies. Critical theory has its roots in Marxism, the Frankfurt
school (Adorno, Horkheimer, Marcuse, and Habermas), and the theories of Foucault. (Alvesson and Willmott [1992] and Alvesson and
Deetz [1996] offer good introductions to critical theory.) When critical
perspectives are applied to cultural studies, the focus is on interpretations of meaning that differ according to one's status within an organi-

zation, with particular attention paid to the interests and opinions of lower-status employees (e.g., Rosen, 1985; Young, 1989).

The focus and power of critical analysis can be illustrated with the "pour time" ritual. A critical analyst might note that the boss, Bryan Anderson, is present in order to observe any mistakes made by the workers at a time when such errors would be particularly costly to the company. The description of the ritual reinforces the inequality between labor and management by referring to the boss, but not the workers, by a proper name. The boss's presence is a visible, although silent, threat that mistakes will be noticed and perhaps punished. In addition, a critical theorist might note that there is an egalitarian twist to the legitimation of power and authority in this ritual. Higher-ranking employees such as Bryan Anderson are temporarily standing aside, whereas lower-level employees take center stage. For the purpose of this ritual, they all wear the same uniform—white smocks and safety equipment. This can be interpreted as a temporary reduction of management-labor inequality and as a tacit acknowledgment of the importance and difficulty of lower-ranking jobs. In this way, the ritual may serve to increase workers' commitment to the firm without any adjustment in the magnitude of inequality between labor and management pay rates.

These managerial and critical interpretations of the "pour time" ritual implicitly assume that the meanings of these activities are unequivocally clear and stable. Even if workers and managers interpret the ritual differently, they do so in certain and unequivocal terms. It may be, however, that the meanings of a ritual are more ambiguous than clear, even to participants. For example, Kunda (1992), in a study of participants in an elaborate corporate ritual, described how employees enacted their roles, and delivered their scripts as prescribed, when "on stage." Their overtly conforming behavior, however, masked inner ambivalence. As they passed in and out of belief in the "appropriate" view of the ritual's meaning, the participants marked these transition points with softly murmured sarcastic comments and, off stage, gently self-mocking jokes. Similar signs of acceptance and resistance can be seen in Kondo's vivid description of an ethics retreat sponsored by her company at a corporate training school in Japan. One of the exercises required participants to stand in front of a group of employees, facing Mt. Fuji, and scream filial greetings ("Mother! Father! Good morning!") to the mountain at the top of their lungs. Kondo (1990), a participant-observer at this retreat, described her reactions as follows:

Not a few of us demonstrated considerable embarrassment during this event, but here the school capitalized on its keen knowledge of psychology. Every word was rewarded with a shout of encouragement and appreciation from the gallery. The group applauded after each person finished. Typically, shouters would have the traces of embarrassed smiles on their faces as they bowed to the others. The squad's encouragement made an embarrassing, difficult exercise infinitely more tolerable. . . . Above all, the point was to throw all our energy into the shouting. It matters not who is loudest or longest. The lesson is to try to the utmost of your ability. These lofty sentiments aside, shouting filial greetings at Mount Fuji elicited a good deal of satirical comment from my co-workers [when the group later returned to work] at the Sato factory. Suzuki and Yamamoto, the young artisans who were later known for their "uncooperative" attitudes when they themselves came to the [training school], would parody the exercise by crying out, in a strangled falsetto, "*Otosan, okasan*," as they feigned tears and dramatically staggered around the shop floor. (pp. 86-87)

Kunda's and Kondo's approaches to the study of rituals, capturing layers of ambiguity, resistance, and ambivalence, are all too rare, although similar analyses have been done by Meyerson (1994) and Rosen (1991).

This discussion of rituals has included a definition of rituals, distinguished repeated rites from "one-time" ceremonies, and offered a typology of rituals commonly used to mark organizational transitions. Interpretations of sample rituals illustrated the influence of functional, managerial, and critical theory traditions on cultural theory and research. Before proceeding to the next cultural form, organizational stories, it is important to note that not all analyses of rituals are functional and that most rituals can be interpreted from managerial, critical, and ambiguous points of view.

Organizational Stories and Scripts

Organizational stories consist of two elements: a narrative, describing a sequence of events, and a set of meanings or interpretations—the morals to the story. The details of a narrative and the interpretations of its meanings may vary, depending on who is telling the story, the audience, and the context. Some variations on a story theme will help illustrate these ideas. Some IBM employees tell the "green badge" story about a security supervisor who dared to challenge Thomas Watson, Jr.,

the intimidating chairman of the board of the company.[2] According to
one version of this story (Rodgers, 1969), the supervisor was

> a 22-year-old bride weighing 90 pounds, whose husband had been sent over-
> seas and who, in consequence, had been given a job until his return. . . . The
> young woman, Lucille Burger, was obliged to make certain that people en-
> tering security areas wore the correct clearance identification.
>   Surrounded by his usual entourage of white-shirted men, Watson ap-
> proached the doorway to an area where she was on guard, wearing an orange
> badge acceptable elsewhere in the plant, but not a green badge, which alone
> permitted entrance at her door.
>   "I was trembling in my uniform, which was far too big," she recalled. "It
> hid my shakes but not my voice. 'I'm sorry,' I said to him. I knew who he was
> all right. 'You cannot enter. Your admittance is not recognized.' That's what
> we were supposed to say."
>   The men accompanying Watson were stricken; the moment held unpre-
> dictable possibilities. "Don't you know who he is?" someone hissed. Watson
> raised his hand for silence, while one of the party strode off and returned
> with the appropriate badge. (pp. 153-154)

This story can be interpreted many different ways. IBM employees
might conclude, "Even Watson obeys the rules, so you certainly should"
or "Uphold the rules, no matter who is breaking them."

Organizational stories, such as the green badge narrative, are often
confused with organizational sagas, myths, and personal anecdotes,
which may not be known to large numbers of employees and/or which
do not claim to represent what actually happened to organizational
members or both.[3] To avoid this conceptual confusion and clarify what
is being discussed here, it is important to define an organizational story
as follows:

1. The central elements of an organizational story are known by a large number of
   people. For this reason, organizational stories are more informative about a cultural context than are personal anecdotes about a storyteller's experiences,
   which are not known to many other employees.

2. An organizational story focuses on a single event sequence. In contrast, an organizational saga (or the biography of a company founder or leader) summarizes
   years of events and is far more lengthy than a single organizational story.

3. An organizational story's central characters are members of the organization. An
   organizational story does not concern people or events outside the organization,

restricting attention to narratives that are more likely to be informative about a particular cultural context.

4. An organizational story is ostensibly true. Organizational stories implicitly claim to be an accurate representation of "the facts." Of course, others may disagree.

The green badge story is of particular interest because versions of this story are told in a wide variety of large and small, public and private organizations. For example, the "safety glasses" story, told by a plant supervisor at another company, sounds quite similar:

I started on a plant tour with him (the president), having planned the route we would take throughout the plant. He, however, took me wherever he wanted to go—in this case, the production line. He rolled up his sleeves and leaned over one of the assembly line workers and asked her how things were going. She interrupted him abruptly and said firmly, "I'm sorry, but you can't come in this area without your safety glasses." He apologized, red with embarrassment, went back to get his safety glasses, and then came back and complimented her on her guts. They chatted for quite some time. He was very impressed that she had challenged his behavior without being intimidated. (paraphrased from Wilkins, 1979)

Wherever I have found this story, there are two central roles in it: the high-status rule breaker and the lower-level employee who challenges the infraction. The attributes of the two protagonists amplify the status differences between them, although exact details may be unique to a particular culture. In all versions of the story I can find, the high-status figure is an older male. In the beginning of the story, he does something that makes his status clear. For example, Watson enters accompanied by an entourage. In the safety glasses story, the president ignores the plant manager's plans for his tour. Furthermore, the lower-status employee is usually a young female. Story details pinpoint her lower status. Lucille Burger is young, she weighs only 90 pounds, her marital status (new bride) is mentioned, and her uniform is too large. In the second version of the story, the assembly line worker sits while the president leans over her shoulder to comment on her work. (As more women enter high-status executive positions, it will be interesting to see if this kind of story persists and if status remains associated with gender in the same ways.)

In both these stories, the inequality between the two protagonists sets up a tension: Will the high-status person pull rank and be angry at the attempt to enforce the rules? In the versions of the rule-breaking story presented previously, rather than pulling rank, the authority figure complied with the rule. This outcome could be different, however, as shown in a third version of the rule-breaking story. Charles Revson, the head of the Revlon Corporation, was worried that employees were not coming to work on time, although he seldom arrived much before noon (Tobias, 1976):

> Everyone was required to sign in in the morning. Everyone. Even Charles signed in. One day, when Revlon was in the process of moving from 666 Fifth Avenue up to the General Motors Building, in 1969, Charles sauntered in and began to look over the sign-in sheet. The receptionist, who was new, says "I'm sorry, sir, you can't do that." Charles says, "Yes, I can." "No, sir," she says, "I have strict orders that no one is to remove the list; you'll have to put it back." This goes back and forth for a while with the receptionist being very courteous, as all Revlon receptionists are, and finally Charles says, "Do you know who I am?" and she says, "No, sir, I don't." "Well, when you pick up your final paycheck this afternoon, ask 'em to tell ya." (pp. 98-99)

The green badge and safety glasses versions of the rule-breaking story seem to portray the high-status employee, and by implication the focal organization, in a relatively favorable light. In contrast, the "sign-in sheet" version places Mr. Revson, and by implication the Revlon organization, in a more negative light. These similarities and differences among the various versions of the rule-breaking story can be captured using the concept of a script. A *script* is a cognitive framework that underlies an organizational story, the skeleton of a story that remains after the nonessential details have been stripped away (Schank & Abelson, 1977). A script has four defining characteristics:

1. A script specifies a well-defined set of characters or roles.
2. It contains a single, fixed sequence of events.
3. In addition, some events in a sequence may be optional.
4. When one of several alternatives may occur, these options are referred to as script branches.

These four elements can be seen in all the versions of the rule-breaking story presented previously. Two roles are well-defined: a high-status executive and a lower-status subordinate who has responsibility for ensuring rule compliance. Four events always occur in a fixed sequence. First, the high-status person did something that drew attention to his or her authority. Second, the high-status person broke a company rule. Third, the subordinate challenged the rule infraction. Fourth, the high-status person either did or did not comply. This either/or action alternative provides an example of a script branch, like a branch in a decision tree analysis. In an optional fifth step, evident in the safety glasses and sign-in sheet versions of the story, the high-status person reacted to the confrontation either by complimenting or by condemning the subordinate.

Script analysis has been used to develop a typology of stories frequently told in a wide range of organizations (Martin et al., 1983). These common story types include the rule-breaking story discussed previously and stories concerning the following: Is the big boss human? Can the little person rise to the top? Will the employee be fired? Will the organization help an employee to move? How will the boss react to mistakes? How will the organization react to obstacles? In accord with the uniqueness paradox, these common stories are often presented as evidence of a culture's uniqueness. This typology of common stories, like the typology of common rituals, is an example of a neopositivist approach to cultural research, relying on counts and categorical or dichotomous classifications. Such typologies are empirically derived, ostensibly objective truth claims, amenable to modification based on further empirical evidence.

Although script theory and classifications of common types of stories can help capture similarities, and some kinds of differences among stories, other kinds of differences, particularly in interpretation, are more effectively captured with other sets of conceptual and methodological tools. For example, a story might be told differently depending on who the storyteller is. Furthermore, a storyteller may vary the content of a story, and therefore its meanings, depending on the context in which the story is told. What you might say to the boss might be different than what you might say to a coworker. Imagine how a story's details might vary depending on whether it is told on a stage, in the men's room, or at the water cooler. Such differences in interpretation apply to other cultural manifestations as well.

Other meanings of stories emerge if an analysis considers what the story does not say. Such a focus on silences and on reading between the lines of a story text is characteristic of postmodern analysis. Because postmodern insights have contributed to cultural theory, it may be useful, for those who are unfamiliar with it, to introduce postmodernism very briefly here (see also introductions by Cooper and Burrell [1988] and Alvesson and Deetz [1996]). *Postmodernism* is an intellectual movement that has spread from Europe to North America and beyond, offering a serious challenge to any theory that makes a truth claim, forcing scholars from the humanities and many social sciences to rethink the basic assumptions of their disciplines. Postmodern scholars (such as Baudrillard, Lyotard, and, his protestations to the contrary, Derrida) have used textual deconstruction (a precise form of logical analysis of language use) to show how theoretical rhetoric hides its own weaknesses as it attempts to claim an inviolable place from which objective truth can be espoused. Postmodern contributions to cultural theory are plentiful. For example, Linstead (1991) examined how advertisements reflected cultural assumptions about consumers. Calás and Smircich (1991) and Willmott (1987), among others, dissected historical contexts in which well-known cultural theories or business practices had developed. Postmodern scholars (like neopositivist scholars working independently, such as Markus and Kitayama [1991]) also offered a new view of the self that is relevant to cultural work. Rather than a unified, autonomous self, these scholars drew a fragmented picture of the self, reflective of surrounding, often contradictory personal, textual, historical, and cultural influences.

Postmodern cultural scholarship challenges the assumptions of neopositivist and critical organizational theorists, taking apart any truth claim to show how it masks and skirts issues that undermine its validity. Mainstream organizational researchers were enraged at postmodernist attacks on the supposedly impregnable bastion of the scientific method. These critics denounced postmodernism as a form of nihilism and moral relativism: What was left, these critics asked, if anything could be deconstructed? Seeking a reply to these critics, postmodern organizational scholars attacked a difficult problem: How to reconcile the endless ambiguities of deconstruction with the clarity required for a commitment to action in organizations (e.g., Willmott, 1994).

Postmodern work has great relevance for cultural studies. Postmodernists could deconstruct any cultural theory using analysis of metaphors, dichotomies, silences, marginal asides, and footnotes in a scholarly text to show what complications and difficulties are being elided (merged together, without drawing attention to this melding) and masked by these abstractions. This or any other book could be deconstructed. For example, the typologies of common rituals and stories offered previously could easily be deconstructed, showing how these mutually exclusive categories mask overlap, oversimplify distinctions, and hide information not easily classified. Organizational stories are also easily deconstructed. For example, I (1990a) deconstructed a story told by a top executive describing how his company "helped" a pregnant employee who was about to give birth by cesarean section. The company put a video player in her hospital room so she could watch the launch of a product she managed. I deconstructed the story text progressively, showing how the company would have reacted differently had, for example, the employee been a man undergoing a heart bypass operation. Deconstruction also revealed some intriguing differences between the launch of the baby and the launch of the product, making it clear that the company was helping itself rather than its female employee and her child. Deconstruction is a powerful tool, as yet underused by cultural scholars. In addition, postmodernism has deep implications for how we write about the cultures we study—issues that are discussed in Chapter 9.

Jargon: The Special Language of Initiates

When outsiders enter a culture, one of the first manifestations of culture they will notice is jargon, the special language that only cultural insiders seem to comprehend (Clark, 1998). Despite this salience, relatively little cultural research has focused on jargon. Two types of jargon can be distinguished: technical and emotional. *Technical jargon* is task oriented and appears to be emotionally neutral. For example, lawyers and secretaries at the Neighborhood Legal Assistance Foundation spoke of "intake dispositions" and "litigation cost requests." At the Center for Community Self-Help, members became familiar with the "alphabet soup" of organizations involved in the worker-ownership movement: PACE, ICA, NCEO, AWOK, and WOSCO.[4]

In contrast, *emotionally laden jargon* is more overtly concerned with feelings (e.g., Ignatow & Jost, 2000). For example, "idea hamsters" on the "bleeding edge" are metaphors of life and death in Silicon Valley, the U.S. mecca for high-technology entrepreneurship. Nicknames are another type of emotional jargon. Many organizations use family names to refer to top management, a choice that can reflect familial closeness, conventional sex roles, the hierarchical distance and emotional ambivalence usually associated with patriarchal corporate relationships, or all these. For example, at B. F. Goodrich, business expenses charged to the company were "compliments of Uncle Benny," a reference to Benjamin Franklin Goodrich, the founder of the firm. Phillips Petroleum employees referred to "Uncle Frank" Phillips, whereas Honda had both an "uncle" and a "dad." Other emotional nicknames draw a line between cultural outsiders and insiders. For example, U.S. Navy personnel derogatively referred to members of the Marines, a rival service, as "jar heads." Land-loving civilian workers in a Navy yard were dismissed as "sand crabs." In contrast, Navy pilot insiders got praised as "jet jockeys," "zoomies," and "Airedales" (Evered, 1983, pp. 136-139). Emotion is generally an understudied aspect of cultures, and so the focus on emotionally laden jargon is a useful advance; more research on emotional aspects of cultures in organizations is needed, however.

Jargon also refers to place or position names. For example, at IBM, the "penalty box" was a temporary, unexciting position in which an employee paid for inadequate performance, whereas "Siberia" was a dead-end position—so useless that the offender usually resigned. At Revlon Corporation, the negative atmosphere, evident in the rule-breaking story discussed previously, also permeated the jargon. For example, the headquarters building at 666 Fifth Avenue was called "sick, sick, sick."

Jargon may seem trivial, or at best a necessary precursor to understanding a culture, but it can be used to develop unexpected insights. For example, at a large high-tech corporation named GEM Company (a pseudonym), some jargon appeared to be purely technical and emotionally neutral (e.g., "Master Order Form"). Other terms were more obviously emotional and value laden (e.g., "working the issue," which referred to the value placed on confronting disagreement and continuing discussion until consensus was reached). At GEM Company, Siehl and Martin (1988) tested new employees' familiarity with various cultural manifestations after 2 and 8 weeks on the job. The new hires were given multiple-choice vocabulary tests asking for the meanings of both technical and emotional jargon terms (with different versions of the test appropriately counterbalanced so respondents were not tested twice on the same words). Results indicated that new employees became familiar with cultural manifestations in a predictable order. Technical jargon was learned first, perhaps because it was essential for getting tasks done. Next, emotional jargon was learned. Other cultural manifestations were learned much later. For example, knowledge of the "correct" (most common) interpretation of organizational stories increased rapidly during the 6-week period of the study. A more difficult test attempted to assess general knowledge of the culture. Selected words in memos and letters from top management were blacked out. New employees had to fill in the blanks. After 2 weeks of employment, error rates were very high, and 4 weeks later they had improved significantly, although many errors were still being made. These results suggest that jargon may provide a linguistic foundation for other, more complex forms of cultural knowledge. This study, however, was conducted in an established, large, and stable corporation. It is important to learn if such results would be found (I doubt it) in a turbulent industry, such as high technology, or in a rapidly growing start-up company in which employees are constantly being hired and lines between old guard and newcomers are blurred.

There has been some research on jargon use in companies that are distinctive due to the intensity of the ideological commitment of their employees. In these companies, technical jargon and emotional jargon sometimes merge. For example, at Environmental Volunteers, Incorporated, organizational members are usually volunteers with a deep commitment to environmental issues who spend time teaching children about nature. These volunteers use technical jargon that has emotional overtones, particularly suitable for their school-age audiences. For example, "tree cookies" are thin, cross-sectional slices of trees that are used to explain how forests effectively adapt to crises such as fires and droughts. "Weird Willy" is a cardboard cutout bird used to explain why birds often need both beaks and claws to survive. Another example comes from the Trust for Public Land, a nonprofit organization that protects land from development by buying it and then giving it to state and federal park agencies. Most staff and volunteers at this philanthropic organization have a deep commitment to environmental issues; they do not think of themselves as engaging in a commercial enterprise, although the land involved is very expensive. Members of the Trust for Public Land never complete real estate "deals" or "sell" land—they "convey" it. A third example comes from Fashion Dynamics, which is a small, direct sales organization that places great emphasis on motivating its sales personnel. They refer to BD (burning desire to sell) and LUCK (labor under controlled knowledge, which refers to the need to take personal responsibility for whatever happens). In each of these examples, ostensibly technical jargon has emotional overtones.

Why are technical and emotional jargon easily distinguishable in some contexts and not in others? The Environmental Volunteers Incorporated and the Trust for Public Land are organizations that exist for ideological purposes. Members join because they believe fervently in these ideologies. Similar fervor and commitment can be found in some private sector companies, such as Fashion Dynamics. In such a context, technical tasks and personal values may be difficult to separate. In contrast, people may join other private sector firms and some public sector organizations for more pragmatic, economic reasons. In these contexts, employees may find it easier to separate their values and emotional concerns from their technical responsibilities. Thus, jargon may be an insightful and unobtrusive measure of why and whether people are committed to their work.

Some jargon relies on metaphors. For example, violent language permeates the jargon used to describe mergers and acquisitions (Hirsch & Andrews, 1983). "Sharks" are extremely predatory takeover experts, the worst of whom is called "Jaws." "Shark repellent" is a protective strategy used to keep sharks away. Other metaphors of violence use the language of cowboy movies. "Hired guns" are the lawyers and investment bankers that specialize in this business. An "ambush" is a clever, premeditated, and swift takeover attempt. A "shootout" determines the final outcome of the battle for control. Other metaphors for mergers and acquisitions are sexual. "Studs" are aggressive potential acquirers, and "sleeping beauties" are vulnerable target companies. "Cupid" is a role played by merger brokers. "Sex without marriage" is an extended negotiation for a friendly takeover that is never finalized. "Rape" is a hostile takeover, sometimes accompanied by looting of a firm's financial resources. Finally, "afterglow" is the postmerger euphoria of acquiring or acquired companies or both, which usually soon dissipates. These metaphors stress sex and violence, with strong overtones of competitiveness and aggression. In this way, metaphors tap the emotional aspects of life in particular kinds of organizations and industries, alluding to emotions that may not be socially acceptable to express more directly.

A wide range of researchable issues emerges even from this short examination. Jargon seems to vary in the depth of emotion expressed and the speed with which it is learned by new cultural members. Degree of familiarity with particular vocabularies might provide a sensitive index for drawing the boundaries of cultural membership, assessing employee morale, or measuring the extent to which new employees have "learned" a culture. The metaphoric emphasis on sex and violence, found in the mergers and acquisitions business, is striking and would easily lend itself to psychoanalytic or feminist analysis.

Humor: Drawing the Line With Laughter

Intriguingly, sex and violence surface in another cultural manifestation: humor. In contrast to studies of humor in organizations, examples of organizational stories, rituals, and even jargon are often intrinsically interesting. The same cannot be said for organizational humor, which is usually unfunny to an outsider. It is probably therefore fortunate that few organizational studies have focused on humor (as an exception, see Hatch and Ehrlich [1993]). You have been warned.

Much humor research has focused on blue-collar workers. For example, a 6-year ethnographic study in a machine shop found that most humorous incidents involved either physical slapstick or "dirty tricks" (Boland & Hoffman, 1983). One favorite joke involved the "goosing" of coworkers with broomsticks or steel tubes. Another popular trick was "bluing." The perpetrators would surreptitiously cover a machine handle with indelible blue steel marking ink and then laugh gleefully when the unsuspecting operator grabbed the "blued" handle and then touched his face or clothes. Recent research has begun to analyze the sexual associations of this kind of humor, focusing on the ways men enact their masculinity at work. Collinson (1992), for example, studied humor in a truck assembly plant, exploring the ways men used humor to express conformity, resistance, and control, particularly in situations in which their masculinity was undermined by low status and low pay.

Humor was also studied at a petroleum refinery in Texas (Siehl, 1984). Researchers interviewed a random, stratified sample of employees in groups of 10 to 12 people. Although none of the interview questions focused on humor, all instances when people laughed were recorded. Gender and race were the themes that most frequently provoked laughter. For example, one group was asked to define what the term "sponsor" meant. A man replied, "A big brother." A woman in the group pointed out that a sponsor could be a "big sister." Everyone laughed. Then one man added, "Or, a little sister." Another incident was triggered by a Caucasian man's reference to hiring "unqualified people on quotas." An African American woman in the group said, "You're just racist." The man laughed and responded, "I didn't mean you. You're a good engineer." She answered that he would not know how to recognize a good engineer. This, too, was greeted with laughter. Gender and racial humor were also observed outside the group interview setting at the petroleum refinery, such as when one researcher overheard Caucasian workers laughing at a joke about Reagan and "niggers." Physical slapstick had a similar tone. For example, one favorite anecdote concerned one of the few women who held a blue-collar position. She put on her hard hat after lunch only to find that a raw egg yolk had been placed inside. These "humorous" incidents had sexist and racist content, raising the question of whether different kinds of humor might have been expressed, had the researchers (a Caucasian man and woman) been a single-sex or mixed-race team.

This kind of humor is not limited to blue-collar workers. Newly hired sales executives at GEM Company also favored ethnic and sexual jokes (Siehl & Martin, 1988). During a 2-week training program for these executives, all instances of laughter were recorded. At first, most newcomers who attempted to be funny offered familiar ethnic jokes and sexual innuendoes with little explicitly organizational content. After just a few days, however, the trainees' humor changed. The jokes were still familiar, but now the ethnic and sexual targets were members of competitive organizations or people from other divisions of GEM Company. Both at the start of the training program and after a few days, jokes were being used to distinguish insiders from outsiders, and at both time periods women and minorities were the focus of these jokes. Racial, ethnic, and sexist jokes are a widespread characteristic of humor inside and outside organizations, at least in settings in which members of some demographic groups are numerically rare. What distinguishes organizational versions of these jokes is that outsider status is also being defined by membership in competing organizations or other parts of the employing organization; telling and laughing at these kinds of jokes may be a subtle measure of the extent to which employees are feeling identification with the organization for which they work.

Humor bridges uncomfortable moments, offers a way of releasing tension, and permits people to express that which they otherwise might be forbidden to say. Meyerson (1991a), for example, explored the ways social workers used humor to release the inevitable tensions of working in a profession in which success with clients was ill defined and in many cases unlikely. Meyerson, unlike the humor researchers cited previously, focused on groups of social workers, examining the helpful, tension-breaking role a single cynical joker played in group meetings. The social workers' jokes were full of irony and multiple meanings; the space created by these ambiguities permitted laughter. A similar emphasis on the role of ambiguity in humor can be found in Gherardi's (1995b) examination of gendered jokes told by professionals working together in Italy. These jokes often had flirtatious and sometimes directly sexual content. According to Gherardi, women and men welcomed such jokes as a way of breaking the discomfort caused by the entry of women into previously all-male high-status positions. Both of these studies point to the importance of ambiguity in humor and suggest that humor may have different tones and functions in different occupational and national cultures.

Humor in organizations is another domain in which systematic research is clearly needed. A classification of types of organizational humor, for example, might provide a useful starting point. Forms of humor based on gender, race, or ethnic identity, as well as the more organizationally specific jokes about competitors and coworkers from other groups, seem to draw attention to boundary lines between cultural insiders and outsiders. What other kinds of jokes are told and what functions might they serve? Cross-cultural comparisons of gendered jokes, for example, might be interesting. Would U.S. women be as likely as Italian women to enjoy flirtatious humor, or would they be worried about encouraging sexual byplay in a work environment? When a focus on women and minorities is combined with an emphasis on sexual violence or aggression, humor becomes a rich source of data for studies of prejudice. In-depth analysis of the tension-expressing functions of humor would also be informative. For example, symbolic or psychoanalytic analyses of the humor in the machine shop might explore the counterbalancing of affection and hostility among these men. Other, more sophisticated forms of humor undoubtedly are prevalent in organizational contexts and, if the simpler forms of humor are any indication, these too should provide rich data for study.

Physical Arrangements: Architecture, Decor, and Dress

Architecture, interior decor, and dress norms are particularly powerful cultural clues, in part because they are so easy to see. Some consul-

tants, for example, pride themselves on being able to "size up" an organization's culture during the brief time it takes to drive up to a building,
greet the receptionist, and walk to the office of the person they are meeting. Even a brief, "bare bones" description of an organization's physical
arrangements can be quite informative. For example, descriptions of
General Motor's (GM) architecture, interior decor, and dress codes suggest much about this firm's culture (Wright, 1979):

> The General Motors Building, where about 7,000 people work, is the most
> impressive structure in midtown Detroit whether viewed from air, the win-
> dows of skyscrapers in downtown Detroit 4 miles to the south, or the cement
> channels of the nearby Edsel Ford and John Lodge Freeways. The giant let-
> ters "GENERAL MOTORS" atop the building can be seen 20 miles away on a
> clear night. (p. 16)

In this headquarters building, as described by Martin and Siehl (1983),
the offices of GM's top management team were

> located in an I-shaped end of the fourteenth floor of this building. . . . Even
> on this floor, office decor was standardized. The carpeting was a nondescript
> blue-green and the oak paneling was faded beige. When (one executive
> requested something different) the man in charge of office decoration was
> apologetic, but firm, "We decorate the offices only every few years. And they
> are all done the same. It's the same way with the furniture. Maybe I can get
> you an extra table or lamp." (pp. 57-58).

Dress norms at GM were also strongly enforced (Martin & Siehl, 1983):

> GM's dress norms in the 1960s required a dark suit, a light shirt, and a muted
> tie. This was a slightly more liberal version of the famous IBM dress code
> that required a dark suit, a sparkling white shirt, and a narrow blue or black
> tie. (p. 57)

Even within GM, some diversity in decor and dress was allowed. One
GM executive, John DeLorean, used physical arrangements to facilitate
the development of a counterculture, different from the rest of the company (Martin & Siehl, 1983). For example, when he was promoted to
head the Chevrolet division, DeLorean used decor changes to symbol-
ize his declaration of independence. The division's lobby and executive
offices were refurbished with bright carpets, the paneling was sanded

and restained, and modern furniture was brought in. Executives were allowed "within reasonable limits" to decorate their offices to fit their individual tastes. Because physical arrangements are so visible, subtle variations can have a major impact. In his own dress, DeLorean role modeled an apparently carefully calibrated willingness to deviate from GM's dress norms (Martin & Siehl, 1983):

> DeLorean's dark suits had a continental cut. His shirts were off-white with wide collars. His ties were suitably muted, but wider than the GM norm. His deviations were fashionable, for the late 1960s, but they represented only a slight variation on the executive dress norms. (p. 61)

The previous examples illustrate the ways in which physical arrangements, such as dress norms and interior decor, can be a rich source of information about a culture. The DeLorean study also suggests that physical arrangements can be used by skilled managers to signal what kind of cultural changes they would like to see evolve in their own organizational domains. Despite evidence of the power of physical arrangements, research in this area is rare. Although some architects and social scientists have examined the psychological and sociological effects of physical arrangements, only a few organizational culture researchers have drawn on this literature (e.g., Davis, 1984; Gagliardi, 1990; Hatch, 1990; Pfeffer, 1992). Because there is no way textual descriptions can fully capture the physical manifestations of a culture, this is a research area that calls for innovative audio and visual methodology. Sound recordings (e.g., of noise levels), photographs of the insides and outsides of buildings, and videotapes of hallway traffic and conversations could be analyzed.

Even this brief discussion makes it easy to see the symbolic richness and interpretive potential of cultural forms. The study of physical arrangements, humor, jargon, stories, and rituals has already challenged claims that cultural research is "old wine in new skins." Many critical questions, however, have not been addressed. There are other cultural forms that have not been studied. For example, "artistic" products (such as brochures, logos, and advertisements) might be studied as manifestations of a culture, particularly from a semiotic or aesthetic point of view (Strati, 1992, 1999). Cultural members are embodied; photographs of their faces and bodies, tape recordings of their voices, and videos that capture nonverbal communication would enrich cultural studies. In addition, technological innovations (such as e-mail, video conferencing, and working from home) affect working environments in ways cultural researchers might be well equipped to explore. As these examples indicate, cultural forms are not really esoterica. They can provide important clues to what employees are thinking, believing, and doing. Because these aspects of culture are just beginning to be studied, however, they offer many opportunities for research. On a map of the cultural terrain, cultural forms would be labeled "terra incognita." I would add to the map "Dig here" for intellectual treasure hunters.

Formal and Informal Practices

Although cultural forms have traditionally been dismissed as esoteric and therefore not important, practices have long been the primary focus of attention in organizational research. In contrast to informal practices, formal practices are written and are therefore more easily controlled by management. Four types of formal practices have been of particular interest to culture researchers: structure, task and technology, rules and procedures, and financial controls. Because these are familiar concepts, they are described very briefly.

The mechanistic versus organic distinction captures some of the variance in organizational structure. A mechanistic structure can be captured with an organizational chart that contains job descriptions, reporting relationships, and so on. When a structure is more organic, job descriptions are usually more vague and flexible, often tailored to the skills of particular people or the demands of particular projects; hierarchical reporting relationships are complicated by cross-functional teams, dual reporting relationships, temporary project assignments, and so on. Other aspects of structure include the shape of a hierarchy (steep or flat), the criteria for differentiation (functional, product line, geographical, etc.), and the balance of integrating and differentiating devices.

Formal practices also include technology and task considerations—that is, what employees are required to do to produce whatever goods or services the organization offers. The technology associated with heavy manufacturing, for example, differs considerably from that associated with the delivery of services, such as executive training or accounting.

The tasks associated with interactive jobs, such as management, contrast with the tasks performed by a skilled technician working alone.

Formal practices are often expressed in the form of rules and procedures. Many of these focus on entry into and movement within the organization's hierarchy (e.g., hiring specifications, promotion criteria, and performance appraisal systems). Large organizations, particularly government agencies, often have elaborate handbooks of rules and procedures, whereas smaller, more entrepreneurial organizations try to minimize this kind of "red tape." Financial controls are a particularly important aspect of formal practices. These include accounting procedures, pay and benefit allocations, and budgeting processes. Although these may be recorded in the form of rules and procedures, access to some of this kind of information (such as pay levels) is sometimes highly restricted.

In contrast to formal practices, informal practices evolve through interaction and are not written down. Informal practices often take the form of social rules (e.g., Lundberg, in press). These rules are seldom written down because this would reveal an inconsistency between what is formally required and what actually happens. For example, when DeLorean was promoted at GM he tried to change the formal performance appraisal system to include only objective criteria, such as sales figures, rather than the subjective criteria, such as "gets along well with coworkers," that had been so important to the rest of GM. Although DeLorean's subordinates appeared to go along with this change in formal practice, informally they continued to let subjective factors influence their judgments. Obviously, they did not leave a written trace of this unapproved deviation from formal requirements (Martin & Siehl, 1983). Sometimes, informal practices create a limited or temporary space in which formal requirements can be relaxed. For example, British police are formally prohibited from drinking alcohol while on duty. They do so, however, both on and off the job and, while drinking, certain forms of behavior become temporarily acceptable. If a policeman is drunk or is drinking, he can make jokes about authority figures and express anger, fear, and affection in ways that would otherwise be unacceptable. These informal practices cannot be found in any handbook of police procedures, but they provide an important outlet for the pressures associated with this kind of work (Van Maanen, 1986). Similar drinking practices are found in Japan. As both these examples indicate, formal and informal practices are often inconsistent.

Some cultural studies are open to finding that interpretations are inconsistent across various manifestations, and, not surprisingly, these studies are more likely to include both formal and informal practices. Cultural studies that assume that interpretations of various cultural manifestations are consistent seldom examine both formal and informal practices; when they do, they tend to focus only on those formal and informal practices that are mutually consistent. This is indicative of a common problem in cultural studies: Researchers operationalize culture by focusing on types of manifestations that are more likely to produce results that confirm, rather than contradict, their theoretical presuppositions.

Content Themes: Espoused and Inferred

A content theme is a common thread of concern that underlies interpretations of several cultural manifestations. Content themes can be cognitive (beliefs or tacit assumptions), or they can be attitudinal (values). Sometimes, themes are espoused—for example, when top managers offer a list of their company's "core values." Other themes are inferred deductively by a researcher or an employee, such as when assumptions are inferred from behavior. Usually, espoused themes are relatively superficial because they are espoused to make an impression on an audience, whereas themes that are inferred deductively, by researchers or employees, reflect a deeper level of interpretation.

When content themes are espoused deliberately to external audiences, such as the general public or members of the immediately surrounding community, these themes may be sincerely espoused as an accurate reflection of an organization's activities, or they may be "corporate propaganda" that bears little relationship to what actually happens within the organization. In either case, espoused values represent an attempt to influence an individual or an organization's "aura" or "reputation" (Christensen & Kreiner, 1984). As Schein explains (1985) in one of his definitions of culture cited previously, espoused values

focus on what people *say* is the reason for their behavior, what they ideally would like those reasons to be, and what are often their rationalizations for their behavior. Yet, the underlying reasons for their behavior remain concealed or unconscious. (p. 14)

Because espoused values are an attempt to create an impression on an audience, usually portraying the organization in an attractive light, they tend to be highly abstract and somewhat platitudinous—the organizational equivalent of motherhood and apple pie. For example, Siehl and Martin (1990) quantitatively analyzed annual reports of 100 randomly selected *Fortune* 500 firms in the United States to determine what content themes were most frequently espoused in these public documents. Most firms offered bland espoused values, such as improved productivity, profitability, and humanist concern for employee well-being. Some of these firms also emphasized product quality, innovation, and customer service. A smaller number of firms added social responsibility to the communities surrounding the corporation. Firms with poor financial performance often discussed general economic conditions as an excuse for not producing better earnings. It may be useful to classify this study using the issues of dispute described in Chapter 2. This study assumed that content themes could be measured objectively and etically. We sought generalizations about content themes. This is a specialist study focusing on a single cultural manifestation—content themes espoused in public documents; therefore, we were not attempting to gain depth of understanding. This cluster of characteristics describes many quantitative studies of culture.

Content themes can be expressed at a variety of levels of abstraction. More abstract themes, of course, will be more likely to be common across organizational cultures. When themes are expressed less abstractly, they are more likely to be common to fewer cultures. Less abstract themes also may seem less banal. For example, in a study of 21 U.S. corporations of varying sizes (Goodhead, 1985), larger firms tended to discuss employee well-being in language that stressed hierarchy (valuing elite status), paternalistic values (such as a familial type of loyalty to the firm), or "Protestant ethic" (calling for hard work and sacrifice). Smaller firms and organizations composed primarily of professionals discussed employee well-being in terms that were meritocratic (rewards for contribution and professionalism) or cooperative (teamwork). A few smaller firms preferred an egalitarian form of employee well-being (ideas from anyone and freedom).

It is interesting to consider trade-offs among content themes. Some data suggest that executives may place greater stress on humanitarian values, such as warmth and friendliness, in contexts in which pay inequality between labor and management is particularly large (Martin &

Harder, 1994). In other words, to reverse the slogan adopted by a union of secretaries, employees may be given roses (gestures of friendliness) as a substitute for more bread (pay). This cynical interpretation of externally espoused values has caused many cultural researchers to worry about the ways in which externally espoused values can be manipulated. These researchers prefer to infer themes deductively from what is observed. For example, employees may take a short-term time perspective whenever decisions are made, or they may assume the best, or the worst, about their fellow employees. Espoused content themes and inferred content themes may be quite different. For example, in an organization in which top management is articulating "corporate value statements" that do not reflect employees' values and experiences, espoused and inferred values will be inconsistent.

In summary, content themes can be externally, self-consciously espoused, or they can be inferred deductively from what people do and how they interpret their surroundings. Cultural studies can focus on one or both of these types of content themes. Content themes can be very superficial, or if they are deduced from observed behavior or inferred from probing, honest conversations, they can reflect a deeper level of analysis. As can be seen from the examples of content themes cited previously, often these themes do not tap emotional concerns; if they did so, cultural analyses could be deepened.

Summary: The Question of Depth of Interpretation

I believe that cultural forms, such as stories, rituals, and physical arrangements (which are sometimes referred to as artifacts), are not necessarily more superficial or less important than deeply held assumptions. Thus, the various cultural manifestations described previously do not represent separable, varying levels of depth. A cultural researcher should seek deep interpretations associated with each type of cultural manifestation. A cultural study can be superficial, focusing on interpretations that reflect, for example, formulaic expressions of espoused values in a "corporate values" statement. Alternatively, a cultural study can focus on deep interpretations that take the form of basic assumptions, sometimes so taken for granted that they are difficult to articulate. Such basic assumptions may include "walking the talk"—when a person's expressed values and assumptions are consistent with how he or she behaves. Other kinds of interpretations of events and artifacts are less value laden and more like cognitive conclusions about "how things are." In each of these examples, what is important is not the cultural manifestation itself but how people interpret it. The depth of a researcher's analysis of interpretations of manifestations can (and I argue should) approach the depth of understanding that Schein terms "basic assumptions."

From Definitions and Operationalizations
to Theories of Culture

This chapter has covered a lot of ground. We have seen that many culture researchers define culture in approximately the same way—in terms of cultural manifestations that are shared by most cultural members. Often, they will also define culture as that which is unique about a context. We have seen that if we analyze how culture researchers operationalize culture—that is, examining what they actually study when they claim to be studying culture—we find a great variety of approaches. Some researchers study the meanings employees give to stories about leaders and colleagues or rituals they engage in at work; other researchers also examine more familiar attributes of organizations, such as hierarchical structures, the physical layout of the workplace, and pay systems, claiming that they too are studying manifestations of an organization's culture. To make matters more confusing, we have seen that cultural studies sometimes break a taboo, defining culture in ways that do not coincide with the ways they operationalize the concept and/or the results they find. For example, some interpretations of a cultural manifestation may not, in fact, be shared by most cultural members; some cultural manifestations studied may not be unique.

For these reasons, it is a good idea to disregard how culture researchers define culture and examine instead at how they operationalize it. When this analysis of operationalizations is done systematically, often glimpses of a cultural theory emerge. Cultural manifestations are consistent or not, cultural members appear to agree or not, and interpretations are singular and clear or multiple and ambiguous. Because culture researchers do not agree what we should study when we claim to be studying culture, and because our definitions of culture do not always agree with how we operationalize the concept, it is no wonder that we also disagree about what we have learned, so far, about culture. There is hope, however. Although it may first appear that cultural researchers disagree drastically about the theoretical conclusions they draw from their research, as shown in Chapter 4, there may be ways to understand why these differences have occurred and how advocates of different theoretical approaches might combine their insights and learn from each other.

Notes

1. Individuation has been conceptualized as an essential stage in the maturation process, whereby a child separates from parents (Maslach, 1974), and "deindividuation" has been studied as a potentially harmful loss of individual identity that can facilitate the expression of antisocial aggression (Zimbardo, 1969).

2. This material on stories and scripts is adapted from Martin (1982) and Martin et al. (1983).

3. An organizational story is a type of narrative—that is, a way of encapsulating knowledge organized around the intentionality of human action, expressed in a plot, which is the basic means by which specific events are put into one meaningful whole (Czarniawska, 1999). Narratives that are not organizational stories can be defined as follows: Organizational sagas are lengthy corporate histories containing many organizational stories (Clark, 1972). Myths are narratives presumed to be false; although myths are literally untrue, at their best they capture an underlying logic that expresses a kind of truth. Personal anecdotes are stories about the storyteller, not widely known by others.

4. Unless otherwise mentioned, examples of jargon are taken from material collected by students in my organizational culture class at Stanford University's Graduate School of Business.

 **4** Single-Perspective
Theories of Culture

This chapter focuses on a theory choice dilemma: What theoretical
perspective will you endorse, either as a reader or as a researcher?
Most organizational culture researchers have answered this question by
adopting one of three theoretical perspectives: the integration, differentiation, or fragmentation viewpoints.[1] In this chapter, I define and review the research supporting each of these perspectives. I show, using
dialogue, how and why advocates of these three perspectives disagree
with each other so vehemently. To set the stage, I review some of the
organizational culture literature, summarizing part of the large volume
of work that has been done in the past three decades. To do this, we need
some definitions.

Defining Three Theoretical Views
of Cultures in Organizations

The *integration perspective* focuses on those manifestations of a culture that have mutually consistent interpretations. An integration portrait of a culture sees consensus (although not necessarily unanimity) throughout an organization. From the integration perspective, culture is that which is clear; ambiguity is excluded. To summarize this in a metaphor, from the integration perspective, culture is like a solid monolith that is seen the same way by most people, no matter from which angle they view it.

The *differentiation perspective* focuses on cultural manifestations that have inconsistent interpretations, such as when top executives announce a policy and then behave in a policy-inconsistent manner. From the differentiation perspective, consensus exists within an organization—but only at lower levels of analysis, labeled "subcultures." Subcultures may exist in harmony, independently, or in conflict with each other. Within a subculture, all is clear; ambiguity is banished to the interstices between subcultures. To express the differentiation perspective in a metaphor, subcultures are like islands of clarity in a sea of ambiguity.

The *fragmentation perspective* conceptualizes the relationship among cultural manifestations as neither clearly consistent nor clearly inconsistent. Instead, interpretations of cultural manifestations are ambiguously related to each other, placing ambiguity, rather than clarity, at the core of culture. In the fragmentation view, consensus is transient and issue specific. To express the fragmentation perspective in a metaphor, imagine that individuals in a culture are each assigned a light bulb. When an issue becomes salient (perhaps because a new policy has been introduced or the environment of the collectivity has changed), some light bulbs will turn on, signaling who is actively involved (both approving and disapproving) in this issue. At the same time, other light bulbs will remain off, signaling that these individuals are indifferent to or unaware of this particular issue. Another issue would turn on a different set of light bulbs. From a distance, patterns of light would appear and disappear in a constant flux, with no pattern repeated twice.

These three theoretical perspectives are complementary in a specific way. Each perspective takes a different position on three dimensions, as summarized in Table 4.1: relation among cultural manifestations, orientation to consensus in a culture, and treatment of ambiguity.

Table 4.1 Complementarity of Three Theoretical Perspectives

	Perspective		
	Integration	Differentiation	Fragmentation
Orientation to consensus	Organization-wide consensus	Subcultural consensus	Lack of consensus
Relation among manifestations	Consistency	Inconsistency	Not clearly consistent or inconsistent
Orientation to ambiguity	Exclude it	Channel it outside subcultures	Acknowledge it

SOURCE: Adapted from Figure 3 in Meyerson and Martin (1987), Table 1 in Martin and Meyerson (1988), Table 1.1 in Frost, Moore, Louis, Lundberg, and Martin (1991), and Martin (1992a).

Single-Perspective Studies of Cultures in Organizations: A Review of the Literature

Because most empirical studies of cultures in organizations adopt one (or, rarely, two) of these three theoretical perspectives, I structure a review of this literature according to the primary perspective used. In this way, the three perspectives can be used to make sense of the morass of conflicting results that characterize cultural research. (More extensive reviews of this literature are available in Martin [1992a].) The studies referenced in this section of the chapter have been not been selected as exemplars of excellent research (for a critique of this approach, see Gagliardi, 1991), although you may decide that some may be. Instead, these studies have been selected as a small sampling of the many studies that have been done in the past three decades, with a focus on studies that may be of particular interest to organizational researchers.

Integration: An Oasis of Harmony and Homogeneity

In an integration study, each cultural manifestation mentioned is consistent with the next, creating a net of mutually reinforcing elements. For example, Ouchi (1981) described "theory Z" cultures as having a holistic concern for the well-being of employees, a long-term perspective regarding decisions about products and people, and a desire to control deviant behavior through "shared values" rather than rules and red tape. Note the ways these content themes consistently reinforce each

other. It would not make sense to care about the physical and psychological well-being of employees (e.g., giving financial support or time
off when necessary) if the company did not also take a long-term
perspective. Similarly, "shared values" would be unlikely if employee
turnover were high and short-term profit maximization goals were
foremost.

Collectivity-wide consensus is another hallmark of an integration
study, as can be seen in a description of the implications of concern for
employee well-being in theory Z cultures (Ouchi & Jaeger, 1978):

> The slowness of evaluation and the stability of membership promote a holis-
> tic concern for people, particularly from superior to subordinate. This
> holism includes the employee and his or her family in an active manner.
> Family members regularly interact with other organizational members and
> their families and feel an identification with the organization. (p. 688)

Although Ouchi's (1981) study of theory Z cultures relied on a random,
stratified sample of employees, most integration studies focus primarily on managers and professionals. For example, O'Reilly, Chatman, and
Caldwell (1991) studied accountants and not the clerical employees of
accounting firms, and Schein (1985, 1996, 1999) focuses on managers,
particularly those in top positions, and not the majority of lower-level
employees who might be more likely to deviate from top management's
espoused values.

Critics of the integration view argue that if a study claims to represent
the culture of an entire organization, then all kinds of organizational
employees should be studied, whether as informants in an ethnographic study or in a stratified, random sample, more likely in a quantitative study. Critics of the integration approach also observe that this
image of organization-wide harmony and homogeneity is difficult to
sustain, given the salience of inconsistencies, disruptions, conflicts, and
ambiguities in contemporary organizations. Some advocates of an integration view respond to this critique with a depth argument. They
acknowledge that deviations from integration do occur, such as inconsistencies, clashing interpretations, conflicts, and ambiguities, but they
do so at relatively superficial levels (e.g., stories, rituals, and values) that
do not represent the deeper essence of a culture: "The culture will manifest itself at the levels of observable artifacts and shared espoused values, norms, and rules of behavior . . . [but] to understand a group's

culture, one must attempt to get at its shared basic assumptions" (Schein, 1985, p. 27). For example, Barley (1983) looked beneath the diversity of funeral directors' activities to find a common underlying assumption: The best way to cope with death is to make it appear life-like, for example, in the preparation of the body.

Tacit, deeply held assumptions are detected when a researcher "pene-trates the front" of impression management strategies, searches for a pattern of interpretation underlying cultural forms such as stories and rituals, and gets down to the essence of what is really important. At this deep level, tacit assumptions are supposedly shared on an organization-wide basis. Thus, in integration studies, as Schein (1985, p. 18) argued, "Basic assumptions in the sense in which I want to define that concept, have become so taken for granted that one finds little variation within the cultural unit." Barley (1983) similarly assumes consensus in his study by referring to a prototypical cultural member, "the funeral direc-tor," thus tacitly excluding any mention of differences of opinion among funeral directors. McDonald (1991) offered a more explicit claim of organization-wide consensus in her description of the excite-ment felt by the (mostly volunteer) staff of the Los Angeles Olympic Organizing Committee. At a staff party, a vice president, recently re-turned from a road trip with the Olympic torch relay teams, remarked that he had witnessed

> the runner going over a winding road in the hills of West Virginia and en-countering a man standing alone on the top of a hill with a trumpet play-ing "America the Beautiful" as the torch passed. There was not a dry eye in the house. The speaker himself broke down, overcome by emotion, and could not continue for several minutes. The staff filed out to the strains of ceremonial music, clutching their commemorative mugs and pins reading "Team 84" that were handed to them at the exit. (p. 37)

"Not a dry eye in the house" is a statement not only of consensus but also of clarity; the meanings of this event were apparently clear to all, as in the other integration descriptions mentioned previously. Schein (1991b) summarized the integration approach as follows:

> What this "model" does say, however, is that only what is shared is, by def-inition, cultural. It does not make sense, therefore, to think about high or low consensus cultures, or cultures of ambiguity or conflict. If there is

no consensus or if there is conflict or if things are ambiguous, then, by definition, that group does not have a culture with regard to those things. (pp. 247-248)

Berger (1967, p. 23, as quoted in Wuthnow, Hunter, Bergesen, & Kurzweil, 1984, p. 26) also defined culture in integration terms as that which is clear and not ambiguous: "An area of meaning carved out of a vast mass of meaninglessness, a small clearing of lucidity in a formless, dark, always ominous jungle."

It is important not to exaggerate the integration perspective, making it a parody of itself or a straw man, easy to criticize. After all, consensus does not imply 100% agreement. Some argue that the opinions of people in leadership, management, and professional positions should perhaps "count more," in the sense that they have more power to control the trajectory of a collectivity. Also, if you go deep enough, people will be found to share some tacit assumptions about fundamental issues, such as time or human nature (although it is debatable whether these kinds of widely held assumptions are part of *organizational* culture). Furthermore, integration studies usually do not deny the existence of deviation from what is ostensibly a shared culture. They may describe cultural consensus in careful language that does not assume total unanimity—for example, "in at least one funeral home" (Barley, 1983, p. 409) and "people who were comfortable in this environment" (Schein, 1991a, p. 23; see also Schein, 1999).

When deviations from the ideal of consistency, consensus, and clarity are acknowledged in an integration study, however, they are seen as regrettable shortfalls. Such a normative orientation can be detected by analyzing whether the deviation from integration is seen as a problem that needs fixing. For example, in an integration study, ambiguity regarding some issue might be recognized, but it would be described in negative terms, for example, as a stressor, resulting in emotional strain and performance decrements (e.g., Katz & Kahn, 1978). For example, Barley (1983) described how funeral directors viewed emotional outbursts from bereaved family members:

From the funeral director's point of view, acutely expressive behavior can interrupt the pacing of funeral events, upset the "dignity" of the scene, and thereby hamper his work. Expressive behaviors are unresponsive to planning, scripting, or routinization, and their probability cannot be predicted with accuracy. Nevertheless, funeral directors do attempt to divert such disruptions by influencing participants' perceptions in ways that they think might render the emotional tone of funeral scenes more manageable. (p. 43)

In an integration study, deviations from consistency, organization-wide consensus, and clarity are seen as a problem, and sometimes remedies are proposed. For example, Sathe (1985, p. 140; see also O'Reilly et al., 1991) encouraged job applicants to seek cultures that mirror their own values: "If fundamental and irreconcilable misfits between the individual and the organization are apparent, it may be best for the individual to leave. Biting the bullet may be less costly than an eventual withdrawal, for both parties." In an integration study, a pocket of subcultural resistance might be acknowledged, but such a subculture would be seen as needing to be "brought on board," perhaps by a combination of training and performance appraisal; remedies for ambiguity might include defining it as due to "poor communication," requiring a clarification of an organization's strategy or vision, a motivational speech, or more careful supervision (Kotter & Heskett, 1992; Porras & Collins, 1994; Schein, 1999). When deviations from integration are seen as shortcomings, then we are in integration territory.

What makes a study congruent with the integration perspective is a prevalence of descriptive material consistent with the integration view (consistency, organization-wide consensus, and clarity), plus a normative position: Deviations from integration are portrayed as regrettable shortfalls from an integrated ideal. The integration perspective is described in more detail in Martin (1992a, pp. 28-43). The definitions of culture in Table 3.1 that are consistent with an integrated view, usually characterized by a focus on aspects of culture that are shared, are Definitions 1 (Sathe, 1985), 2 (Louis, 1985), 3 (Sergiovanni & Corbally, 1984), 6 (Davis, 1984), and 8 (Smircich, 1983a). When researchers write reviews of the cultural literature, they usually focus on work congruent with only one perspective, define cultures in a manner congruent with that perspective, and exclude most theory and research written from other perspectives. For example, Ebers (1995), working from a neo-positivist position, classifies an array of cultural studies "accurately" into a typology that reflects the content of the cultures studied (usually based on content themes in espoused values). It is noteworthy that

Table 4.2   Examples of Single-Perspective Cultural Studies

Theoretical Perspective	Studies
Integration	Altman and Baruch (1998)
	Barley (1983)
	Bryman, Gillingwater, and McGuinness (1996)
	Deal and Kennedy (1982)
	Dellheim (1987)
	Denison (1990)
	Kotter and Heskett (1992)
	Lincoln and Kallberg (1985)
	Martin (1982)
	Martin and Powers (1983)
	McDonald (1991)
	O'Reilly (1989)
	O'Reilly et al. (1991)
	Ouchi (1981)
	Pettigrew (1979)
	Porras and Collins (1994)
	Rohlene (1974)
	Sathe (1985)
	Schein (1985, 1999)
	Selznick (1957)
	Siehl and Martin (1984)
	Sims and Gioia (1986)
	Sproull (1981)
Differentiation	Alvesson (1993a)
	Barley (1986)
	Bartunek and Moch (1991)
	Bell (1990)
	Boland and Hoffman (1983)
	Brunsson (1995)
	Christensen and Kreiner (1984)
	Gregory (1983)

(Continued)

Ebers is tacitly claiming to review all organizational culture literature, but he cites integration studies almost exclusively. Other predominantly integration-oriented reviews of the organizational culture literature include those by Denison (1990), Kotter and Heskett (1992), Ouchi and Wilkins (1985), Schein (1999), and Schultz and Hatch (1996). Empirical examples of integration studies (single perspective) are listed in Table 4.2.

Table 4.2　(Continued)

Theoretical Perspective	Studies
Differentiation (continued)	Jermier, Slocum, Fry, and Gaines (1991)
	Louis (1985)
	Martin, Sitkin, and Boehm (1985)
	Meyer (1982)
	Meyer and Rowan (1977)
	Mumby (1987, 1988)
	Riley (1983)
	Rosen (1985)
	Rousseau (1990b)
	Sunesson (1985)
	Turner (1971)
	Young (1991)
Fragmentation	Alvesson (1993b)
	Brown and Duguid (1991)
	Brunsson (1985, 1989)
	Cohen, March, and Olsen (1972)
	Daft and Weick (1984)
	Feldman (1989, 1991)
	Gherardi (1995a)
	Golden (1992)
	Hatch (1999)
	Hedberg (1981)
	Knights and Wilmott (1987)
	Koot et al. (1996)
	March and Olsen (1976)
	Meyerson (1991a, 1991b, 1994)
	Perrow (1984)
	Risberg (1999)
	Sabelis (1996)
	Starbuck (1983)
	Weick (1991)
	Westra (1996)

Differentiation: Separation and the Possibility of Conflict

Differentiation studies focus on cultural manifestations that have inconsistent interpretations (e.g., Brunsson, 1986). For example, Riley (1983) studied two large consulting firms in which professionals unfailingly praised teamwork and cooperation (espoused values). In contrast, informal conversations were full of metaphors (jargon, perhaps reflecting informal practices) of aggression and fierce competition:

> The interviews were filled with images of cards and players, wars, teams, battles, armies, pugilistics, and wounds. Game (with a particular emphasis on sports) and military (with a vicarious interest in espionage) scenarios repeatedly emerged along with a discerning sense of their use. (p. 247)

Meyer and Rowan (1977) also focused on inconsistency, which they referred to as "loose coupling." In the schools they studied, when school administrators spoke to external audiences, such as the school board or government funding sources, they stressed the importance of "the numbers"—of books, students, desks, and classrooms. In contrast, when school administrators and teachers talked to each other, they refrained from talking about these quantitative variables, stressing instead the informal processes of teaching and learning.

Differentiation studies, unlike integration studies, generally view differences, including inconsistencies, as inescapable and desirable, both descriptively and normatively. Dissenting voices are not silenced or ignored and subcultural differences are a focus of attention. For example, Van Maanen (1991) described the various subcultures among the workers at Disneyland as follows:

> A loose approximation of the rank ordering among these groups can be constructed as follows: (1) the upper-class prestigious Disneyland Ambassadors and Tour Guides (bilingual young women in charge of ushering—some say rushing—little bands of tourists through the park; (2) ride operators performing (coveted) "skilled work" such as live narration or tricky transportation tasks like those who symbolically control customer access to the park and drive the costly entry vehicles such as the antique trains, horse-drawn carriages, and Monorail; (3) all other ride operators; (4) the proletarian Sweepers (keepers of the concrete grounds); and (5) the subprole or peasant status Food and Concession workers (whose park sobriquets reflect their lowly social worth—"pancake ladies," "peanut pushers," "coke blokes," "suds divers," and the seemly irreplaceable "soda jerks"). (pp. 61-62)

In Van Maanen's description, it is unclear whether these subcultures exist in conflict with each other or accept their hierarchical relation.

In other differentiation studies, conflicts among subcultures are explicitly examined. For example, Barley (1986) studied how the introduction of computerized tomography (CT) scanners into hospitals altered the relationship between two subcultures. Radiologists found their former high status undermined by the technicians' skill in operating the new machines:

> The technologists began to regard the inexperienced radiologists with disdain. To account for the new interaction patterns, the technologists formulated the view that the radiologists knew less than they rightfully should and that their ignorance created unnecessary work and kept the CT operation from running smoothly. (p. 93)

Some differentiation studies examine a broader range of subcultures within the boundaries of a collectivity, including managerial, professional, and a variety of blue-collar employees in their analyses. Some subcultures differentiate (as in Van Maanen's and Barley's studies) along occupational lines. Sometimes, subculture differentiation proceeds along horizontal (functional) or vertical (hierarchical) lines, whereas in other organizations context-specific subcultures may emerge based on networks of personal contact at work, friendship, or demographic identities (such as race, ethnicity, or gender). It is not enough to assume that particular sources of difference cause subcultural emergence because sometimes this does not happen.

In studies that examine multiple subcultures, relationships among subcultures may be mutually reinforcing, conflicting, or independent (Louis, 1985). For example, Bartunek and Moch (1991) studied a Quality of Working Life intervention at a food manufacturing plant. They found a variety of subcultural reactions to the intervention, ranging from strong support to vehement opposition to indifference. There are two traditions of research within the differentiation perspective that are important to distinguish. Some studies emphasize relatively harmonious relationships among subcultures (e.g., Trice & Beyer, 1993), whereas other studies, written from a more critical theory perspective (Alvesson, 1993a), stress inconsistencies (e.g., Brunsson, 1985) and conflicts between subcultures at different levels of an organizational hierarchy (e.g., Mumby, 1988; Rosen, 1985). Chapter 5 explains ideological reasons why these two kinds of differentiation studies have emerged as separate traditions.

To the extent that ambiguity is acknowledged in a differentiation study, it is described as occurring in the interstices among subcultural

"islands" of consistency, consensus, and clarity. Gregory (1983) summarized the differentiation point of view well:

> More researchers have emphasized the homogeneity of culture and its cohe-
> sive function than its divisive potential. This paper suggests, however, that
> many organizations are most accurately viewed as multicultural. Subgroups
> with different occupational, divisional, ethnic, or other cultures approach
> organizational interactions with their own meanings and senses of priori-
> ties. (p. 359)

The differentiation perspective is described in more detail in Martin
(1992a, pp. 83-117). One of the definitions of culture in Table 3.1, Definition 4 (Mills, 1988), is consistent with a differentiation view. Reviews
of research that include discussion of subcultures can take two forms.
Some authors focus on single subcultures, in essence taking an integration view at a lower (group rather than organizational) level of analysis
(e.g., Ott, 1989; Trice & Beyer, 1993). Other authors do reviews that encompass all aspects of the differentiation perspective, including relationships among subcultures involving unequal access to power and
resources (e.g., Alvesson & Berg, 1992; Turner, 1990; Van Maanen &
Barley, 1984). Empirical examples of differentiation studies (single perspective) are listed in Table 4.2.

Fragmentation: Multiplicity and Flux

The fragmentation perspective is the most difficult perspective to
articulate because it focuses on ambiguity, and ambiguity is difficult
to conceptualize clearly (for helpful conceptual frameworks, see
Brunsson, 1985; Daft & Weick, 1984; Feldman, 1989; March & Olsen,
1976; Weick, 1999). Fragmentation includes more than the ambiguity
that derives from ignorance or confusion. It also encompasses the complications that the clear oppositions of dichotomous thinking omit. It
includes irreconcilable tensions between opposites, sometimes described as ironies, paradoxes, or contradictions (e.g., Alvesson, 1993b;
DiMaggio, 1997; Gherardi, 1995a; Hatch, 1997; Koot, Sabelis, & Ybema,
1996; Meyerson, 1991a, 1991b, 1994; Risberg, 1999; Sabelis, 1996; van
Marrewijk, 1996; Westra, 1996).
    When examining the relationships among cultural manifestations, a
fragmentation study moves beyond the clear consistencies of an inte-

gration view and the clear inconsistencies of a differentiation view. Ambiguity can be seen as abnormal, a problematic void that ideally should be filled with meaning and clarity. Alternatively, fragmentation studies are more likely to view ambiguity as a normal, salient, and inescapable part of organizational functioning in the contemporary world. Many social workers, for example, are comfortable with ambiguity and accept it as a normal part of their working lives. Meyerson (1991a, p. 138) studied social workers who viewed their work in shades of gray rather than the clearly black or white oppositions seen in differentiation studies: "When [other social workers] come to me for a simple, clear solution, I tell them: 'Life is gray. If you want black and white, go to Macy's. Black and white are in this year.'" When culture is studied from a fragmentation perspective, ambiguities take center stage and are usually not viewed as abnormal, escapable, or problematic.

From a fragmentation viewpoint, relationships among manifestations are conceptualized in multivalent terms as partially congruent, partially incongruent, and partially related by tangential, perhaps random connections. For example, recall the clear oppositions in Meyer and Rowan's (1977) differentiation description of loose coupling in schools and contrast their view to Weick's (1979) fragmentation perspective on the loose coupling phenomenon:

> A loosely coupled system is a problem in causal inference. For actors and observers alike, the prediction and activation of cause-effect relations is made more difficult because relations are intermittent, lagged, dampened, slow, abrupt, and mediated. Actors in a loosely coupled system rely on trust and presumptions, are often isolated, find social comparison difficult, have no one to borrow from, seldom imitate, suffer pluralistic ignorance, maintain discretion, improvise, and have less hubris because they know the universe is not sufficiently connected to make widespread change possible. (p. 122)

Even the physical arrangements in an office can be interpreted as expressing a variety of kinds of ambiguity, as Tom (1986) found in her study of the Women's Bank in New York City:

> Of the trainers, only Elaine has an office of her own.... All the other trainers and trainees work in open areas. Some trainees are assigned desks of their own when their jobs require that they have a permanent workplace. Many

trainees do not actually belong in any one place at all but must sit where they
can find a place close to the task they are performing. All trainers have desks
of their own, usually somewhat larger than the trainees' desks. In general, the
assignment of space is confused and fluid. People often lose things that they
leave sitting in a space they had carved out for themselves when someone else
appropriates the space. People use others' desks when they are vacant, and it
is not uncommon for Elaine to be forced to vacate her office. (pp. 58, 62)

Fragmentation studies often explore irony and paradox—irreconcilable tensions that coexist in an uneasy balance (e.g., Schultz, 1992).
For example, Wels (1996) studies paradoxes encountered by expatriate
managers in Sino-Western joint ventures. Going beyond the usual generalizations about Asian cultures being collectivist rather than individualist, Wels (see also Koot et al., 1996; Sabelis, 1996) takes a view
sensitive to paradox:

Thus on the one hand the Chinese seem to adhere to group-orientation
whereby individual gain is tempered by group loyalties . . . on the other hand
and at the same time they strive for personal advantages. In many instances
these observations lead to the dilemma and question whether "the Chinese"
are group-oriented or individualistic. My argument would be not to make a
choice between the two, but to conclude that, as both perspectives have
sound arguments and are embedded in thorough empirical data, the Chinese simultaneously are collectivistic and individualistic. For such a life with
paradoxes Chinese "(c)hildren are taught to be selfless and to defer to collective norms, but they are also expected to gain recognition through achievement" (Pye, 1991:448). In these circumstances people must learn to pre-
tend and to a certain extent act as if they were selfless. They have to make a
show of denying that they act in their own interests. Behind this façade
and building of collectivism they must manoeuvre, use strategies, in order
to gain respect and individual benefits. Because everybody has to operate in
this way, everyone fears and is suspicious of "the other" trying to take advantage for his or her own benefit under the guise of an image of self-denial.
(pp. 136-137)

Risberg (1999) also uses the fragmentation perspective (although she
focuses on ambiguity rather than irony or paradox) to analyze the acquisition of a Swedish crane manufacturing company. She concludes,

The ambiguity approach has helped us see that a post-acquisition process cannot be understood in one clear way. There are ambiguities in interpretations of situations and statements. These ambiguities illustrate the multiple realities within the organization and during the post-acquisition process. The ambiguities can be held at different levels: interpersonal as well as intrapersonal; interorganisational as well as intraorganisational. (p. 177)

Fragmentation focuses on multiplicities of interpretation that do not coalesce into the collectivity-wide consensus characteristic of an integration view and that do not create the subcultural consensus that is the focus of the differentiation perspective. Instead, there are multiple views of most issues, and those views are constantly in flux (e.g., Golden, 1992), as can be seen in Meyerson's (1991a) account of the job descriptions of social workers:

Boundaries seem unclear because the occupation of social work includes a wide range of tasks and responsibilities, many of which are performed by members of other occupations. In a hospital, social work can include everything from concrete discharge planning—such as placing an individual in a nursing home—to less well-defined clinical work with patients and families. Yet nurses also plan discharges; psychologists counsel; and members of the clergy coordinate community resources. Thus, insiders as well as outsiders hold diffuse ideas about what social work is and about who is and is not a social worker. In addition, technologies seem ambiguous because what one does as a social worker (e.g., talk to clients) seems loosely related to what results (e.g., how clients behave). (p. 136)

The fragmentation perspective is described in more detail in Martin (1992a, pp. 130-167). The definitions of culture in Table 3.1 that are consistent with a fragmentation view are Definitions 9 (Feldman, 1991), 10 (Anonymous reviewer, 1987), and 11 (Meyerson, 1991a). Reviews focused primarily on the fragmentation view of culture include those by Feldman (1991), Jeffcutt (in press), Koot et al. (1996), Meyerson (1991b), and Risberg (1999). Empirical examples of fragmentation studies (single perspective) are cited in Table 4.2.

As these introductions to the single perspectives demonstrate, these are complex, internally coherent theoretical positions. Therefore, it is not advisable to cut short the treatment of a perspective by using only one element of its definition (e.g., "the differentiation perspective focuses on subcultures"). Such a simplification reduces the internally congruent complexity of a theoretical perspective to a level of analysis. These three perspectives, in a sense, are worldviews, and as a result sometimes adherents of one perspective react to cultural research done from another single perspective with disdain—sometimes even with a kind of intellectual anger. To make these conflicts come alive, in the following section I present them in the form of an (admittedly exaggerated) argument among three cultural researchers.

Three Characters Argue About Theory

Imagine you are at an academic convention. You walk outside and see, at a cool, shaded table, three culture researchers engaged in a loud "knock-'em-down" argument. Being interested in culture (which you must be if you are still reading this book), and enjoying a good argument, you approach and they invite you to join the conversation. Then, they proceed to ignore you while they continue arguing. Because the protagonists in this discussion are meant to represent composite views rather than specific individuals, they are referred to by the names of the theoretical perspectives they represent. Although the following argument uses individual researchers to represent the three perspectives, in practice it is particular empirical studies, not individual researchers, that can be described using these labels.[2] Researchers sometimes shift from one theoretical perspective to another as their interests change or as they study different kinds of contexts.

Integration: So, surely we all agree that culture is what people share—the social glue that holds people together—whether that glue be values, a shared sense of purpose, deep tacit assumptions, or simply habits of behavior.

Differentiation: No. Listen to yourself, Professor Integration: "Surely, we all agree . . .?" "What people share . . ." This is the kind of homogenizing language that makes your views seem to silence those who disagree. You cannot study managers and professionals and assume that their views are the same as the viewpoints of lower-level employees. The problem with your approach is that even if lower-level employees tell you they agree with top management's views, or with your views, they may be telling you what they think you want to hear. Lower-level employees know you discuss the results of your research mostly with management. You need to get lower-level employees to open up to you and trust you. If you observe their behavior on the job or get them comfortable enough to speak freely in front of you, you will find that more disagreement exists than is allowed for in your world of assumed harmony and unity. Organizations are full of conflicts of interest. For example, engineers may care about designing a technical tour de force of a product, with many features, whereas sales staff may ask whether those fancy features are really what customers want. Top executives may articulate core values, mission statements, or corporate strategies that everyone is supposed to endorse, but lower-level employees may well have another agenda. People with little choice may exhibit conforming behavior, but what values and beliefs do they really hold? If you just accept superficial rhetoric and don't get beneath the surface of the officially accepted view to see what else exists, then you will miss a lot. To claim to understand an organization without focusing on differences such as these—this is willful blindness. Similarly, to claim to describe a whole country's culture, without exploring differences in the experiences of rich and poor, urban and rural, different ethnicities and religions, and men and women—this is folly.

Integration: Well, you are right that we live in an increasingly differentiated world, full of conflicts. That's the problem. Organizations and countries today are riddled by balkanization, as people of different backgrounds disdain the melting pot model of assimilation and instead strive to preserve their differences. That is precisely why we need more of a sense of a community, more awareness of and respect for what we share. Even if you are right that much of what exists is differentiation, what we need is more unity.

Differentiation: You have dreams of unity that are based on a denial of difference. This is why so many people, especially those who come from less dominant countries, wince when talk of "globalization" makes it seem that the preferences and interests of a few powerful countries are shared by all. You are assuming a cultural homogeneity that may be just a façade or may not exist at all. When you look deep enough into claims of unity, you can see opposing points of view that are being silenced. The "melting pot" is infamous; it's just another name for the demand that immigrants conform to the values and behaviors mandated by the most powerful members of a society. When you deny the importance of those who disagree with whatever view is dominant, in effect, you are silencing their voices. Important differences get "swept under the rug" so the illusion of unity is preserved.

Integration: Illusion of unity? Nonsense. First of all, I pride myself on the depth of inquiry in my research. When you go deep enough, you find that many people share assumptions so taken for granted that they aren't even articulated, for example: Are people trustworthy and competent? Is a short- or long-term time frame appropriate? If you go deep enough, you find consensus. And don't make this consensus claim a straw man; I never would claim *all* people agree—just many. There are always conflicts and disagreements, but these are not desirable. When diverse people find the values, goals, and convictions they share, they can act together, in organizations, in nations, and even in international alliances. The more diverse we are, the more important consensus becomes, if we are to act together. This is, after all, what organization means.

Fragmentation: Let me get a word in. You guys are arguing about your differences and not looking at what you share. Both of you are assuming clarity—clarity about what people share or clarity about what disagreements they have. You are right, Professor Differentiation, clear consensus is rare in this constantly fluctuating, multicultural world. But you are also wrong, in that conflicts are seldom clear-cut dichotomies between opposing points of view. Ambiguity, not clarity, is the hallmark of contemporary life. And ambiguity is more than just individually idiosyncratic views concerning whatever is unknown, or whatever is unexplainable by other viewpoints. Ambiguity includes multiple, contradictory meanings that are simultaneously true and false, paradoxes, ironies, and irreconcilable tensions. Given the lives we lead, ambiguity is the essence of any adequate cultural description. You both have left out the most important thing.

Integration: Harrumph. Ambiguity is not culture; it is the absence of culture.

Differentiation: There are some clear rights and clear wrongs in this world, and by focusing on ambiguity, you endorse a kind of moral relativism.

Fragmentation: Let's be practical. If people experience their lives as riddled with ambiguity, a clear theory—or a theory of clear conflict—may be comforting to you, but it won't offer much insight because it endorses such an oversimplified view of how the world works. Maybe you could see my point of view if we shift levels of analysis for a minute. Consider how you as an individual experience everyday life. One moment you might think of yourself as a professor; the next moment another identity, for example, your age or the fact that you are a father, might become relevant. Different parts of your compound identity become salient, depending on what you are thinking and what is going on around you.

People fluctuate in this way because their self-concepts are fragmented. And sometimes, the parts do not fit together coherently, and things fall between the cracks. We are full of inescapable contradictions. Remember what Whitman wrote? "Do I contradict myself? Very well then, I contradict myself. I am large, I contain multitudes." And if individuals are this complex, then just imagine how much ambiguity there is in the cultures of an organization or a nation. Good cultural research should capture these complexities, rather than excluding them.

Although these three hypothetical professors are admittedly a bit extreme in their views, cultural researchers frequently have arguments such as this. We argue face to face, in restaurants, seminars, and convention symposia. We take a position in these arguments when we include and exclude points of view in literature reviews, accept or reject journal submissions, and decide whom to hire. The consequences of theoretical arguments such as these are very real, not just for academics, but also for the people we reach through our work as teachers, executive educators, consultants, and writers. Individuals and companies have spent large amounts of money hoping that organizational culture will provide some answers to some of their most intransigent problems. When culture research offers oversimplified answers, it runs the risk of being discarded—as yesterday's fad, old wine in new bottles, or simply a waste of money. Because organizational research sometimes has real consequences, outside the ivory tower, the theoretical argument introduced previously is not just of interest to hair-splitting academics. All cultural researchers have to take a position in this ongoing argument— a position that will affect others and themselves.

Distinguishing Culture, Climate, Organizational Identity, and Image

The distinctions among the three theoretical perspectives can be used to begin to explain how organizational culture is connected to related concepts, such as climate, organizational identity, and image. Some argue that organizational culture and climate have much in common (e.g., Denison, 1990; Schneider, 1990) and that the primary difference is methodological; climate researchers have relied almost exclusively on quantitative surveys, whereas culture researchers often prefer qualitative methods. Others disagree (Schneider, 1990; Schwartz & Davis, 1981). One way to resolve this dispute is to examine what climate researchers study when they claim to be studying climate. Denison (1990) makes the argument for the similarity between organizational culture and organizational climate in the following terms:

> First, both concepts focus on organizational level behavioral characteristics and implicitly argue that organizational units are a viable level for the analysis of behavior. This assumes some degree of consistency and behavioral integration within an organizational system, and also assumes that the foundations of that consistency (assumptions, meaning, beliefs, patterns of behavior) are a useful way to understand the actions taken by organizations and individuals within them. Second, both concepts cover a wide range of phenomena. Topics range from the deeply held assumptions that form the basis of a culture to the actual practices and patterns of behavior that are rooted in those assumptions. Although culture researchers have paid more attention to the former and climate researchers the latter, the overlap between the two has been considerable. (pp. 23-24)

Although Denison (1990) claims that both concepts cover a wide range of phenomena, in the terms defined previously, most climate studies measure either content themes (beliefs, values, or basic assumptions) or informal practices (behavioral norms), avoiding cultural forms such as stories, physical arrangements, jargon, and rituals. In the terms used previously, climate researchers tend to do relatively narrow specialist studies, focusing on just one or two types of manifestation. If such studies are to claim that a narrow subset of manifestations represents an entire organizational climate or culture, the researcher must assume (as Denison noted previously) that all the manifestations of climate or culture, if measured, would be consistent with each other—for example, that assumptions are consistent with practices, stories, physical arrangements, and so on. Culture researchers who accept this integrationist assumption about consistency would be more comfortable with viewing climate and culture as closely related; indeed, some integrationist researchers who claim to be studying culture do so with survey measures of content themes or informal behavioral norms that bear a striking resemblance to climate surveys (e.g., Denison, 1990; Kilmann, Saxton, Serpa, & Associates, 1985). In contrast, many differentiation and fragmentation culture researchers prefer to define and operationalize culture in terms that allow for inconsistency across the interpretations of a broader variety of manifestations, in effect claiming that culture and climate are conceptually quite different.

Organizational culture is also closely related to organizational identity and image, although Hatch and Schultz (1997, p. 5) have done a careful job of distinguishing among these three concepts. Organizational identity refers broadly to what members perceive, feel, and think about their organizations. It is assumed to be a collectively, commonly shared understanding of the organization's distinctive values and characteristics. Albert and Whetten (1985) offered an influential (and integrationist) definition of organizational identity as that which is (a) central, (b) enduring, and (c) distinctive about an organization's character. Image, however, is "not what the company believes it to be, but the feelings and beliefs about the company that exist in the minds of its audiences" (Bernstein, 1992, as cited in Abratt, 1989, p. 68). Hatch and Schultz expand this definition of image, noting that it should also include the ways organizational members believe others view their organization (see, for example, Dutton and Dukerich's [1991] study of the employees of the New York Port Authority, who were disturbed by the public image of their organization when it treated homeless people harshly). Hatch and Shultz (p. 6) define organizational culture as "the internal symbolic context for the development and maintenance of organizational identity" and present a model that shows the interdependence of culture, identity, and image in terms of overlapping processes:

> Organizational images are then projected outward and absorbed back into the cultural system of meaning by being taken as cultural artifacts and used symbolically to infer identity: Who we are is reflected in what we are doing and how others interpret who we are and what we are doing. (p. 11)

Organizational identity and image research shares some theoretical assumptions germane to some, but not all, culture research. For example, note that Albert and Whetten's (1985) definitions of image tacitly assume organization-wide consensus among employees ("collective" and "commonly shared") and distinctiveness, an echo of the "shared" and "unique" aspects of many integrationist definitions of culture. Hatch and Shultz's (1997) model shows overlap among identity, image, and culture, suggesting some degree of consistency, again in congruence with integration (but not differentiation and fragmentation) views of culture, although these authors are careful to allow for disjunctions as well. I believe that research on organizational identity and image, having to date relied heavily on integrationist assumptions, would be much enriched by a full consideration of the relevance of ideas drawn from differentiation and fragmentation cultural research. For example, consider the recent disputes about accidents and deaths due to Firestone tire failures on Ford vehicles. It is reasonable to presume that high-level employees may view these two corporations differently than most accident victims and their families, and that there may be considerable ambiguity concerning the images, identities, and even the possibility of long-term survival of both these companies. In doing such research, it would be important to sustain the delicate balance modeled by Hatch and Schultz, keeping these three concepts distinct but noting their overlaps.

This chapter began with a dilemma: What theoretical perspective will you endorse, either as a reader or as a researcher? So far, three possible, single-perspective answers to that question have been described: the integration, the differentiation, and the fragmentation views. Most cultural research to date (approximately 80%) tacitly uses one of these three theoretical perspectives, which is why I used these three terms when I reviewed the literature in this chapter and in other publications. There is another alternative—one that I endorse: All three of these perspectives could be combined in a single study (Martin, 1992a; Martin & Meyerson, 1988; Meyerson & Martin, 1987). This alternative is the focus of Chapter 5.

Notes

1. The three perspectives, separately and in combination, were first introduced in Meyerson and Martin (1987) and Martin and Meyerson (1988). Some of the material in this chapter and in Chapter 5 is drawn from these papers and from Martin (1992a), in which these ideas are explained in much more depth.

2. This conversation is based on material first published in Martin (1992a, pp. 8-10).

5   A Three-Perspective
Theory of Culture

In this chapter, I advocate using all three of the theoretical perspectives introduced in Chapter 4 in a single cultural study. I discuss examples of several three-perspective studies of organizations so you can see how the different viewpoints highlight very different aspects of a culture. Common misunderstandings of the three-perspective approach will be highlighted. Attributes, limitations, and blindspots in the three-perspective approach will be discussed, and other ways of thinking about culture will be introduced. If you are a cultural researcher, this chapter will leave you with some questions: Which theoretical perspective will you choose to use? One of the three perspectives? Will you vacillate across the perspectives, from study to study, depending on your objectives? Will you use some combination of these three perspectives in a single study? Will you prefer some other theoretical approach? To introduce these theoretical approaches to the study of culture, I begin with an example.

Before proceeding, one important issue merits discussion. Most organizational researchers use objectivist, representational language in reporting the results of their investigations. The objectivist and subjectivist approaches to the study of culture, introduced in Chapter 2, are discussed again at the end of this chapter in relation to the three-perspective approach. I sometimes use objectivist, representational language in this book—for example, "Schultz (1991) found evidence that people in organizations can easily shift their viewpoints and behavior to fit changing interactional contexts" and "A cultural portrait is more complex and inclusive if a culture is regarded, at any single point in time, from all three perspectives." Like many cultural researchers, however, I prefer a more subjectivist approach to the study of culture and a less representational style of writing. It is possible to avoid objectivist (representational or "realist") language when writing about cultural research, but this is difficult to do. Language use and representation are complex issues that merit a chapter of their own (Chapter 9, this volume). In the meantime, please be tolerant when I fall into using representational language.

The Organizational Learning Seminar

As a student or a faculty member, we have all attended seminars. At Stanford University, there was an unusual, very popular doctoral seminar taught by a professor in the School of Education. When I first heard about this seminar, I thought (in single-perspective terms) that it might provide a good example of the fragmentation perspective. At this seminar (described more fully in Martin, 1992a),

> ambiguity wasn't just acknowledged. It was relished. At the first meeting of the seminar the professor asked each student to write down, individually, what he or she wanted to learn and expected to contribute. No attempt was made to reach consensus on these issues. The professor then asked when and where the students wanted to meet and who wanted to lead the next class discussion. Confused, the students attempted to get him to define the topic of the course (listed in the catalogue as "organizational learning"). The students also asked for guidance: "What kind of student presentations should be given?" The professor consistently refused, with a smile, to provide this kind of structure. He was, however, agreeable to all the alternatives suggested. Finally, he was coerced into leading the second class session himself. . . . He led an open-ended discussion of two papers, one of which was titled

"Organizational Learning." In subsequent classes, none of the student presentations followed this example. A few of these sessions seemed, according to the students, to have "no" relevance to organizational learning. When asked, the students said they were not disturbed by this lack of focus on the course's ostensible topic ("We didn't know what to expect, anyway"). Most students defined a bad student presentation as a "formal talk." The "best" presentation was made by a student who put three brief diagrams on the board and started the group "playing around with ideas." At the last class session, the professor announced, "I think this is an appropriate time to distribute the class syllabus." In a spirit of "How can I know what I am thinking until I see what I say?" the syllabus listed the readings assigned by the student presenters for previous class sessions. Many of the students smiled in appreciation of this gesture. (pp. 175-176)

When I described this seminar to a class studying culture, I used it to illustrate the importance of ambiguity in the study of culture. The students in my culture class (some of whom had also attended the "organizational learning" seminar) were quick to correct me, saying my description did not capture important aspects of the seminar. For example, there were two subcultures of students in the class: research oriented and applied, in accord with a differentiation view of the seminar's culture. The research-oriented students reveled in the ambiguities of the class and were delighted to ponder complexities indefinitely. The applied students lost patience, accusing the research-oriented students of being "navel-gazing theoreticians," enveloped in the action paralysis that occurs, they thought, when ambiguity is pervasive. When the applied students took over the class and ran discussions, they presented case studies of specific applied problems. They were excited by the diversity of backgrounds and experiences represented by the students in the seminar, and they hoped a variety of inputs would generate useful solutions to applied problems they had been unable to solve. Each of the applied students remained a true believer in an unambiguous view of the world, although as a result of the class they found themselves more willing to experiment with novel (unambiguous) solutions to problems. These two subcultures had very different views concerning what the "organizational learning" seminar was about and why it could be a useful seminar for them to take.

Another student said I had also missed evidence of basic assumptions that most of the students shared, in accord with the integration perspective. For example, despite the professor's attempt to avoid a traditional leadership role, if you were to walk into the organizational learning seminar room you would see one person, much older than the rest, who was always listened to when he spoke. This was the person who would assign grades when the seminar concluded at the end of the quarter. In addition, there were institutional constraints: The seminar met at a particular time in a university-furnished room, and students received credits toward a degree. These formal and informal practices suggested that the professor and the students shared some basic assumptions about how to teach and how to learn in a university setting.

These students were correct: A broader view, encompassing these different perspectives, gave me a better understanding of the "organizational learning" seminar. This, then, raised a question that required me to reflect about my own limitations as a cultural researcher. Why had I, at first, seen only ambiguity when I heard about this seminar? I am research oriented, and so perhaps I had not fully understood the applied students' priorities. I may have drawn mental borders around the seminar's culture, assuming that the applied students were border crossers and not quite full members of the culture of the research-oriented doctoral program that sponsored the seminar. Also, because I am a professor, perhaps I was uncomfortable surfacing and thereby opening to question some assumptions about how to teach and who should grade in a university setting. For all these reasons, and perhaps others of which I am not conscious, in this context a theoretical viewpoint that emphasized ambiguity, rather than conflict between differing viewpoints or basic shared assumptions, was easiest for me to see. Although the ambiguity emphasis offered useful interpretations of the seminar's activities, the other less obvious (to me) perspectives offered equally intriguing insights. For example, the shared assumptions view made me aware that aspects of the situation that I had taken for granted (e.g., a teacher's giving grades) need not be taken for granted or viewed as unalterable.

I include this self-analysis here to model how such reflexivity can be helpful to a cultural researcher who finds one or more of the three perspectives described later "irrelevant" in a given cultural study. The importance of including such reflexivity in cultural studies is explained further in Chapter 9. Because a seminar is of interest primarily to academics, however, in this chapter I also summarize many studies showing how the three-perspective approach can be applied to the study of organizations.

Three-Perspective Definition of Culture

In this chapter, I take a clear advocacy position, arguing for using all three of these perspectives, not just one, when studying a culture. It is important to clarify my own position in the theoretical arguments outlined later because I cannot claim to offer an uncritical or even-handed review of the cultural literature in this chapter. To explain the reasons for my advocacy position, I return to the informal definition of culture with which I began this book and that is also listed as Definition 12 in Table 3.1:

> When organizations are examined from a cultural viewpoint, attention is drawn to aspects of organizational life that historically have often been ignored or understudied, such as the stories people tell to newcomers to explain "how things are done around here," the ways in which offices are arranged and personal items are or are not displayed, jokes people tell, the working atmosphere (hushed and luxurious or dirty and noisy), the relations among people (affectionate in some areas of an office and obviously angry and perhaps competitive in another place), and so on. Cultural observers also often attend to aspects of working life that other researchers study, such as the organization's official policies, the amounts of money different employees earn, reporting relationships, and so on. A cultural observer is interested in the surfaces of these cultural manifestations because details can be informative, but he or she also seeks an in-depth understanding of the patterns of meanings that link these manifestations together, sometimes in harmony, sometimes in bitter conflicts between groups, and sometimes in webs of ambiguity, paradox, and contradiction.

In the terms introduced in previous chapters, this informal definition takes a subjective perspective, focusing on ideational concerns and depth analysis (i.e., "in-depth understanding of patterns of meaning"). It also mentions material cultural manifestations (e.g., "the ways offices are arranged" and "dirty and noisy" or "hushed and luxurious" working environments) and has a broad rather than narrow, specialist selection of manifestations. Most important, in the last sentence it mentions varying kinds of patterns of meaning, underlying those manifestations, using code words that anticipate (incompletely) each of the three theoretical perspectives: harmony (integration), conflict between groups (differentiation), and webs of ambiguity, paradox, and contradiction (fragmentation).

I define culture more formally, then, as consisting of in-depth, subjective interpretations of a wide range of cultural manifestations (a generalist rather than a specialist view), both ideational and material. Culture, I argue, should be viewed from all three theoretical perspectives, not sequentially but simultaneously. In accord with the integration view, some aspects of the culture will be shared by most members, producing consistent, clear interpretations of manifestations. The hallmarks of the integration perspective are consistency across manifestations, collectivity-wide consensus, and clarity. In accord with the differentiation perspective, other aspects of the culture will be interpreted differently by different groups, creating subcultures that overlap and nest with each other in relationships of harmony, independence, and/or conflict. The defining characteristics of the differentiation perspective are inconsistencies across manifestations, with consensus and clarity only within subcultures. Subcultures can exist in harmony, conflict, or independently of each other. Finally, in accord with the fragmentation view, some aspects of the culture will be interpreted ambiguously, with irony, paradox, and irreconcilable tensions. The fragmentation view focuses on ambiguity, excluding the clarity implicit in both consistency and inconsistency. Rather than seeking consensus within cultural or subcultural borders, the fragmentation perspective finds only transient, issue-specific affinities.

Taken together, the three perspectives oppose each other on the three dimensions of comparison: the relationship among cultural manifestations, the orientation to consensus in a culture, and treatment of ambiguity (see Table 4.1). Because they take different positions on these three dimensions, the three perspectives complement each other in a precise way. If an empirical researcher uses all three of these perspectives in a single study—which is the point of view I advocate—the three perspectives offer a wider range of insights than is available from any single viewpoint. Each perspective has conceptual blind spots that the combination of the three does not. For example, the integration view is blind to ambiguities, and the fragmentation and differentiation views are blind to that which most cultural members share. In this sense, the three perspectives combine well with each other, offering a conceptual sweep that no one of these perspectives can encompass. These three dimensions, which I use to contrast the three perspectives, emerged inductively from a review of the culture literature, and so there is no a priori theoretical justification for these particular dimensions and perspectives. The three cultural perspectives, however, have proven useful in the analysis of other domains of organizational studies, such as institutional theory (e.g., Aldrich, 1992), suggesting that fundamental processes of wider applicability may be found if these three viewpoints are approached deductively as well.

Researchers and cultural members often find one of these three perspectives easier to understand and use, making it their personal "home" perspective. To speak reflexively, I have adopted an advocacy stance in this chapter because I have two home perspectives, differentiation and fragmentation. As you may have determined when I presented the single perspectives in Chapter 4, I find it very difficult to present the integration view in an even-handed way because it seems to me that an integration viewpoint silences all dissent and ignores crucially important ambiguities. Thus, taking an even-handed three-perspective view is difficult for me. It can, however, be done. When a researcher or a cultural member has a home perspective, the other perspectives should be studied; indeed, analyses conducted from "non-home" perspectives often produce the most unexpected and helpful insights. A home perspective is the most accessible in the mind of a researcher or cultural member; the other perspectives are usually suppressed or repressed beneath the surface of awareness. With some help from fellow scholars or cultural members, hidden or difficult to see perspectives can be surfaced, and when they are, they often offer keys to understanding that would otherwise be inaccessible. For example, aspects of a culture that once seemed incomprehensible or unrelated may suddenly make sense.

Sometimes most members of a culture share a home perspective; sometimes they do not. In time, home perspectives of both researchers and cultural members may change. These hidden or suppressed perspectives are crucially important because they may carry clues to understanding how cultural members may react in the future if currently suppressed viewpoints and opinions become dominant. Some cultural members and researchers do not seem to have home perspectives. Instead, these people easily switch from one theoretical perspective to another, eventually using all three. Such perspective switchers can be valuable collaborators and informants in a cultural study.

The three-perspective view of culture can be difficult to grasp. Reasons for these difficulties will be discussed later, after some relevant literature has been reviewed. One issue is best discussed before proceeding further, however. Researchers ask the following question: If three perspectives offer a broader view of a culture, deepening understanding, then why are not four or five perspectives better? The answer, obviously, is that more may indeed be better. There is a law of diminishing returns, however, as more and more perspectives are used to examine a single cultural context. These three perspectives make a particularly helpful combination because they complement each other in a precise way, as detailed in Table 4.1. It is difficult to imagine a fourth or fifth perspective that would focus on these dimensions of comparison (degree of consistency across manifestations, degree of consensus, and orientation toward ambiguity) and take a uniquely different position on each. Because these three perspectives complement each other in this way, their combination has an impressive scope. Furthermore, because most cultural research to date has focused on one of these three perspectives, the three-perspective approach to studying cultures offers a way to draw on and contribute to all this prior work. Because these three perspectives focus on the same unifying dimensions, however, theoretical approaches that examine culture from a quite different vantage point, such as the aesthetic approach (e.g., Strati, 1999), have much to contribute. Therefore, other cultural viewpoints, with references, are included in a later section of this chapter.

Three-Perspective Studies of Cultures in Organizations at a Single Point in Time

To illustrate this approach, several three-perspective studies of organizational cultures are described in the following sections. Each offers a broader range of insights than would be available had only one of these theoretical perspectives been used.

OZCO

OZCO is a pseudonym for a large, multinational corporation that has been the subject of numerous laudatory studies portraying it as one of the "excellently managed," "strong culture" companies (e.g., Ouchi,

1981; Pascale & Athos, 1981; Peters & Waterman, 1982; Porras & Collins, 1994). Like most of the firms in the technology industry, OZCO has been buffeted by a turbulent, highly competitive environment, but these studies uniformly describe the company as a haven of consensus, harmony, "family feeling," and commitment. Deb Meyerson and I studied this firm using a variety of methods, including interviewing employees off-site in settings in which they felt comfortable and free to speak frankly. Here, I cite excerpts from those interviews, selecting quotations that exemplify one of the three perspectives. To give a focus for the excerpts, I explore employees' reactions to the company's "family feeling." (For a more complete description of the methods and results of this case study, see Martin, 1992a, pp. 22-44, 83-129, and 197-199; Martin & Meyerson, 1988).

The first quotation comes from Denise (all names are pseudonyms), who worked on product marketing in the firm's headquarters building. Denise's desk was located in an open office space. Low partitions separated desks (as in the famous cubicles portrayed in Dilbert cartoons), and there were few solid walls or doors. According to Denise, "People get involved in each other's personal lives simply because they overhear each other on the phone. There is no privacy, so a family atmosphere is fostered." Stuart, like Denise, took an integration view, agreeing that the company's family rhetoric was indeed consistently enacted:

OZCO is like family. . . . Even in the nicest, friendliest family you are going to find some reward and punishment mechanisms. You expect that even if it is hidden, there are high-level discussions about this subtle control strategy. Even though I've had some high-level dealings, I haven't seen evidence of this. The parents don't seem to talk about them. This good homey feeling is pretty deep; I haven't seen that fade away. The battling is more like two brothers battling than competitive strangers. I keep thinking that there have to be things going on that I'm not seeing, but I don't think so.

What was Stuart missing in his vision of OZCO as a "good homey" family? One key is his use of the word "brothers" to describe coworkers. Ouchi studied companies, including OZCO, from an integration perspective. In one of his few criticisms of these firms, which he referred to as Type Z organizations, Ouchi (1981, p. 91) concluded, "Type Z companies have a tendency to be sexist and racist. . . . That is, the top management is wholesome, disciplined, hard-working, and honest, but unremittingly white, male, and middle class." When upper- and middle-class white men dominate the top levels of an organization, they tend to hire and promote demographically similar others who share their values, a process Kanter (1977) labeled "homosocial reproduction." Ferguson (1984) described the process as follows:

> The more similarity there is in outwardly identifiable characteristics, such as race, sex, dress, language, and style, the more likely is an aspirant to be seen as the "right kind of person" and given access to positions of discretion and power. Thus, the patterns of racial, sexual, and class stratification of the larger society are reproduced in the organization. (p. 106)

Martin and Casscells (1985) used data from the Equal Employment Opportunity Council to determine if, as Ouchi predicted, firms lauded in integration studies were in fact more likely to be dominated by white males. We compared randomly selected groups of organizations with firms in the same industry that had been described as having cultures characterized by consistency, organization-wide consensus, and clarity—labeled "strong culture" firms (such as IBM, Levi-Strauss, Procter and Gamble, Cummins Engine, and Hewlett-Packard). These strong culture companies (which included OZCO), compared to the randomly selected firms in the same industry, were indeed more likely to be occupationally segregated by race and gender, with women and minorities clustered at lower hierarchical levels in "pink velvet" and "black velvet" ghettos, whereas top managers were mostly white males.

Does this mean that the integration perspective offers a better way of looking at "strong culture" companies such as OZCO? Do these companies really have cultures that are "stronger" in the sense of generating more consistency, consensus, and clarity? I do not think so because all three perspectives provide useful insights into any culture. Ouchi's (1981) study, like any integration study, operationally defined culture in terms of consistency, organization-wide consensus, and clarity. Aspects of organizational life that did not fit within these conceptualizations (perhaps those most likely to be voiced by women and minorities) were excluded as "not part of the culture." Meyerson and I used a broader definition of culture, including differentiation and fragmentation views of culture. The differentiation view of the OZCO culture showed a very different interpretation, for example, of the company's claims of being like a family. Sally, a human resources consultant at

OZCO, said, "Along with this very nice, humanitarian theme goes the midwestern mommy and daddy: Daddy makes the decisions and Mommy does the supplementary stuff." Not all differentiation views of OZCO focused on gender issues. Other employees, such as Aida, who was a personnel clerk, pointed to an inconsistency between managerial family rhetoric and the reality of company practices:

> I guess I hired on with the company just by their reputation. . . . They (reputedly) treated their employees very well and it had a type of family atmosphere, and that once you were hired on at OZCO, you were treated almost like one of the family and you never got thrown out of the company. They treated you very well. They cared about you—that sort of thing. . . . I must admit, I don't hear that today. . . . You don't have that feeling of closeness.

Finally, some employees spoke of "family feeling" at OZCO in ambiguous terms congruent with the fragmentation viewpoint. For example, Ron, who worked on the operations staff, said

> I'm beginning to wonder if they really care. I don't know. Well, the thing is from my experiences and from other peoples' experiences that I know of, when you try and take [problems] high up, it seems to be—everybody seems to try and hush you up and pass it by you and say, "Yes, we'll look into it." And then you start hearing all the different stories that everybody is telling and it never gets told as it really is.

Examining this brief sampling of quotations from the larger OZCO study, we can see that there was no single, objectively correct view of the family feelings at OZCO. Instead, the term *family feeling* was abstract and ambiguous; different employees interpreted it differently. Similar variations were found in relation to other content themes at OZCO: egalitarianism, innovation, and a concern for employee well-being.

A broader conceptual and operational definition of culture, including all three perspectives, offered a wider range of insights—I would argue a deeper understanding—of OZCO. The integration perspective offered a picture of harmony and unity built around the content themes espoused by top management. This view may be of comfort to those top managers, but it is not useful if it does not reflect the views of a wider range of the company's employees. As seen in the differentiation and fragmentation views of the OZCO culture, there was considerable skepticism, doubt, and confusion regarding these espoused themes. This is useful information because it suggests that the rosy view of the employees quoted in the integration portrait presents only part of the cultural picture. The integration perspective includes a normative orientation, viewing deviations from consistency, organization-wide consensus, and clarity as a problem needing to be fixed. An integrationist might view the state of affairs portrayed in the differentiation and fragmentation views of OZCO as a problem and advocate changing the culture to make it more unified, perhaps through firing, hiring, or training employees so they would be more likely to agree with top management's viewpoint.

A differentiation study of OZCO, particularly if it was written from a critical theory perspective, might argue that lower-paid, lower-status employees are unlikely to buy into the harmony and unity views of top managers; at least the differentiation view of this culture presented dissent rather than silencing dissenting opinions through exclusion as "not part of the culture." A fragmentation scholar might add that the clarities of the integration view, as well as the clear dissent evident in the differentiation view, oversimplify those ambiguities that characterize everyday life in this organization; if cultural research is to be useful, it must encompass and represent these kinds of complexities. Such observations, however, do not address the kinds of cultural change that advocates of the differentiation and fragmentation views might suggest. These change recommendations will vary depending on the interests the researcher wants to serve, as detailed in Chapter 6.

In the next section, I make this argument in more precise theoretical terms using a matrix framework to summarize the integration, differentiation, and fragmentation views of the OZCO culture. This matrix framework can be used to summarize the results and decipher the theoretical underpinnings of most single- or multiple-perspective cultural studies.

A Matrix Approach to Understanding Culture

Because how culture is defined is often decoupled from how it is operationalized, it is helpful to ignore definitions of culture temporarily and summarize the results of a cultural study in the form of one or more matrices. When content themes are combined with cultural forms and formal and informal practices, we have the pieces of a cultural puzzle. We can explore how interpretations of these cultural manifestations relate to each other by summarizing the results of a cultural study—the pieces of a cultural puzzle—in one or more matrices. Columns in a matrix are types of cultural manifestations (such as rituals or stories) and rows, linking interpretations of these manifestations, are context-specific content themes (such as the need to take a long-term perspective or the company's concern for employee well-being). A matrix is useful because it shows precisely how culture has been operationalized: Is it a narrow specialist or a broad generalist study? Is it ideational or material in its focus? Such a matrix clearly exposes what a given researcher has actually studied when he or she claimed to be studying culture. A matrix analysis is useful for summarizing the results of other people's studies, or it can be used to summarize the results of your own cultural research. It is meant as a supplement—not a substitute—for a full description of research results, whether these results are written in prose (as in an ethnographic portrait) or represented in statistics.

Such matrices are also useful because too often a cultural study is just a richly detailed description; the underlying patterns of interpretation and theory of culture are difficult to decipher. When such a study is summarized in a series of matrices, theoretical assumptions become easier to see because the patterns of interpretations, across manifestations, are made evident. The cell entries in such matrices, and the underlying patterns of interpretation of those cultural manifestations, show how a researcher has answered the following questions: What is culture? What is not culture? Often, it is the empty cells and omissions that will be most important in making this diagnosis. Used in this way, a matrix is a prompt for deductive theorizing: You can see what has been studied, and how it has been interpreted, to determine what theory is in use. You can determine if a study has used only one of the theoretical perspectives described previously or if it has used more than one.

To build a matrix, start by listing the types of cultural manifestations across the top as column headings. It is helpful to begin with formal practices because these are the most familiar to most organizational researchers. Informal practices should be listed next, to the right of formal practices, and then cultural forms should be listed: rituals, stories, jargon, humor, and physical arrangements. (If other innovative types of cultural forms are studied, these can be inserted where they seem most appropriate.) This ordering of manifestations facilitates the

comparison of formal and informal practices to determine if they reinforce or undermine each other. Listing informal practices next to
rituals is also helpful because these two types of manifestations can be
difficult to distinguish. For example, daily gatherings around a coffee-
pot are usually an informal practice, but in some cultures these gatherings can have some of the elements of a ritual. Stories and jokes can also
be difficult to distinguish. Is a funny anecdote about fellow employees
an organizational story or simply an example of humor? The definitions in Chapter 3 can be helpful in distinguishing one type of manifestation from another. Listing similar manifestations in adjacent columns
can draw attention to ways in which these conceptual distinctions, like
all categories, are "fuzzy sets." The point is not to adhere to these definitions and orderings exactly but to be precise and explicit about whatever distinctions you find most useful.

Once you have listed formal practices, informal practices, and the
various cultural forms as column headings across the top of your matrix, you can move to the vertical axis, listing various content themes
down the left-hand column. It is helpful to separate externally espoused
content themes from those themes that are inferred by the researcher or
organizational member. Each row of the matrix, then, consists of a content theme and several cultural manifestations that are relevant to that
theme. An example should make the usefulness of a matrix more evident. An integration view of OZCO is summarized in Table 5.1 (all of
the OZCO matrices discussed here are adapted from Martin, 1992a).

The matrix in Table 5.1 is built around three content themes externally espoused by the company's top management: egalitarianism, innovation, and a concern for employee well-being. A variety of cultural
manifestations show these themes translated into action. The various
content themes and manifestation interpretations are consistent and
reinforce each other. (Two additional matrices, presented later, are built
around the same three espoused themes in order to maximize compara-
bility across the three matrices to be presented here. In most three-
perspective studies, however, when culture is viewed from different
theoretical perspectives, some new content themes emerge with each
perspective.) Each cell of this first matrix is consistent with all other
cells, creating an underlying pattern of integration. According to this
view of the OZCO culture, top management's espoused content themes
are said to be enacted, creating a culture that seems harmonious and
unified.

Table 5.1 An Integration Matrix View of OZCO

| Content Themes | | Practices | | | Artifacts | | |
External	Internal	Formal	Informal	Stories	Ritual	Jargon	Physical Arrangements
Egalitarian sharing		Participation in stock plan and profit sharing	"Management by walking around" as status equalizer	Strategic planning not the "OZCO way"	President's behavior at award ceremonies	"Retirement village"	Casual dress
		Answer own phone					One cafeteria
		Perk distribution based on need, not status		"Nine-day fortnight" story			Open offices
		Consensual decision making					
		Lateral promotions					No reserved parking
		No mass layoffs; voluntary time off					
Innovation		New products aimed at market-place	Products developed at rate of eight per week			"Play"	
		Centralized recruiting	Engineers design products for other engineers			"On the bench"	
		Teleconferencing					

(Continued)

Table 5.1 (Continued)

Content Themes		Practices		Artifacts			
External	*Internal*	*Formal*	*Informal*	*Stories*	*Ritual*	*Jargon*	*Physical Arrangements*
Holistic concern for employee well-being		Relocation voluntary; assistance for spouse	Facilitate self-help day care arrangements	"Second chance" story		"Family"	Open offices facilitate personal contact
		Scholarship funds	New employees sent flowers				
		Flex hours	Blame training rather than individual	"Cesarean" story		"Workforce rebalancing"	Offices decorated with personal mementos
		Self-improvement programs					
		No short-term contractors					Recreation facilities
		Voluntary time off for everyone					

SOURCE: Adapted from Table 3.1 in *Cultures in Organizations: Three Perspectives* by Joanne Martin, copyright © 1992 by Oxford University Press, Inc. Used by permission of Oxford University Press, Inc.

When the aspects of a three-perspective study consistent with the integration view (or the elements of a single-perspective integration study) are summarized this way, the entire study can be represented using a single matrix. All cell entries will be consistent with each other. In this way, integration studies are a bit like a hologram—any piece represents the whole because all pieces are consistent with each other. Because an integration study posits organization-wide consensus, only one matrix is needed. All cell entries should have a single, clear interpretation, with ambiguities being excluded from an integration study.

The second view of the OZCO culture is summarized in Table 5.2. In this matrix, the enacted themes contradict the espoused themes, and a variety of cultural manifestations and their interpretations suggest that the espoused themes misrepresent how business at OZCO is "really" carried out. The inconsistencies in this matrix, particularly between espoused and enacted content themes, create an underlying pattern of difference, congruent with a differentiation theory of culture.

Although this matrix focuses on the same three themes as the first matrix, in many organizational cultures a differentiated view would focus on different themes than would an integrated view of the culture. In addition, there are a variety of differentiation theories of culture. If distinctive subcultures exist, each subculture could be represented by a different matrix, with different content themes, if needed. At OZCO, for example, there were a variety of subcultures, some reflecting hierarchical differences (e.g., top management vs. assembly line workers) and some functional differences (the most noticeable being the clash between marketing and engineering). Although Meyerson and I did not do this, we could have developed a matrix for each of these subcultures.

In summary, the aspects of a three-perspective study consistent with the differentiation view (or the elements of a single-perspective differentiation study) can be represented in a single matrix with inconsistent cell entries (such as when informal practices are inconsistent with espoused content themes or formal policies). Alternatively, a differentiation study with multiple subcultures can be represented in a series of matrices—one for each subculture. If multiple matrices are used, it will also be useful to create a schematic map showing the relationships among the subcultures (mutually reinforcing, conflicting, or independent) at a higher level of analysis. According to the differentiation view, ambiguities should not be present within a subcultural matrix but, rather, should be reflected in the interstices (or points of contact)

Table 5.2 A Differentiation Matrix View of OZCO

| Content Themes | | Practices | | | | Artifacts | |
External	Internal	Formal	Informal	Stories	Ritual	Jargon	Physical Arrangements
	Egalitarianism challenged		Management by walking around as means of control			"Upstairs"	Seating in cafeteria by status and function
			Perk distribution based on managers' pull and surplus budget			"The labs"	Higher partitions for engineers than for marketing
			Authority and status may override consensual decision making				Open offices cause discomfort
			Ranking encourages specialization				Casual dress, and so on, cause intrusion into personal lives
			Opportunities for lateral promotion dependent on power of manager				
			Voluntary time off has differential impact				

Impediments to innovation	Autonomous division with independent systems of: product appraisal evaluation incentives accounting	Divisions each do recruiting on the side Division "coffee clatches" Divisions develop spinoff products independently	
	Group level integration in response to "lack of links"	Engineers develop products in "play" without marketing considerations	
Lack of holistic concern for employee well-being		Humanitarian policies in lieu of fair play "Family" implies patriarch and "Daddy" gets paid more No female general managers, few minorities, and women clustered in "pink velvet ghettos"	"Caesarean" story questions sensitivity to employee's family

SOURCE: Adapted from Table 5.1 in *Cultures in Organizations: Three Perspectives* by Joanne Martin, copyright © 1992 by Oxford University Press, Inc. Used by permission of Oxford University Press, Inc.

among subcultures. In this way, subcultures can be conceptualized as islands (or archipelagos) in a sea of ambiguity.

When a culture is viewed from the integration perspective, only one, clear interpretation of the meaning of each manifestation is given, presumably because all cultural members share that interpretation. When a culture is viewed from the fragmentation perspective, multiple interpretations of a manifestation are offered because the meaning of a manifestation is ambiguous rather than clear. Ambiguities can occur for many reasons, including confusion, ignorance, or inherent contradictions such as paradoxes or ironies. A fragmentation view is illustrated in the third OZCO matrix, presented in Table 5.3.

When the aspects of a three-perspective study consistent with the fragmentation view (or the elements of a single-perspective fragmentation study) are summarized using a matrix, cell entries offer multiple, ambiguous interpretations. Looking across cell entries, nothing is clearly consistent or clearly inconsistent. No organization-wide or subcultural consensus is evident. Ambiguity is prevalent everywhere.

In this way, matrices can be used to analyze the results of studies that take radically different positions regarding the dilemma, What is culture? What is not culture? For example, if a study's results are summarized in matrix format, it is easy to assess the breadth of the manifestations examined in a given study. Narrow studies focus on only one or two types of cultural manifestations, such as organizational stories or communication rules. Such studies produce matrices with only one or two columns filled with cell entries. At this point, I use the matrix framework to explain further why I prefer to define culture using all three perspectives, study a broad rather than a narrow selection of manifestations, and include both ideational and material aspects of culture.

Narrow studies, focusing on a single manifestation, may be informative about how that manifestation is interpreted in a particular context. It is not possible, however, to represent an entire culture by studying only one or two types of cultural manifestation, such as content themes (e.g., values) or informal practices (e.g., norms). For a study to claim to represent an entire culture, a broad range of manifestations (i.e., a more completely filled matrix) needs to be studied. All three OZCO matrices show that a broad variety of cultural manifestations were studied. To understand the limitations of narrow specialist studies of culture, consider a study that focuses only on organizational stories. A study of stories in a single organization can deepen our understanding of how

Table 5.3 A Fragmentation Matrix View of OZCO

Content Themes		Practices		Stories	Ritual	Artifacts	
External	Internal	Formal	Informal			Jargon	Physical Arrangements
	Ambiguity about egalitarianism	Performance evaluation process and criteria unclear	Norms of distributing "perks" unclear	Foreign transfer story			Goals and effects of open offices unclear
			Confusion about policy implementation and decision-making process across divisions	Ignorance about lateral promotion policy story			
			Confusion about how lateral promotion and foreign transfer works				
			Implementation of voluntary time off unclear				

(Continued)

Table 5.3 (Continued)

Content Themes		Practices		Stories	Ritual	Artifacts	
External	Internal	Formal	Informal			Jargon	Physical Arrangements
	Confusion about innovation	Unclear evaluation criteria	Unpredictable changes in structure "as needed"			"Dogs"	
		Ranking process compares "apples to oranges"	Confusion about divisions, responsibilities, and interrelationships				
		Confusion about product introduction process					
	Ambiguity about concern for employee well-being	Unclear relocation policy	Confusion about "family"				
			Personnel department is powerless and unpredictable				
			Commitment to female employees' and families' well-being unclear				
			Lack of cohesive subcultures				
			Poor communication causes confusion				

SOURCE: Adapted from Table 7.1 in *Cultures in Organizations: Three Perspectives* by Joanne Martin, copyright © 1992 by Oxford University Press, Inc. Used by permission of Oxford University Press, Inc.

stories function in that context. Also, when stories are gathered from many cultural contexts, a researcher can legitimately develop generalizations, for example, about what kinds of stories are commonly told in large corporations (Martin, 1982; Martin, Feldman, Hatch, & Sitkin, 1983; Martin & Powers, 1983; Martin, Sitkin, & Boehm, 1985). It is a mistake (one that I have made), however, to claim that an analysis of the stories told in an organization represents a portrait of that firm's culture. If a different type of manifestation, such as formal practices or rituals, had been studied, different interpretations might emerge (allowing for subcultural differences and ambiguous meanings) and quite different conclusions might be drawn. This is not a problem of story studies only; any narrow study focusing on one or two cultural manifestations faces the same limitations. The only way one could assert that a study of one or a few manifestations represented an entire culture would be to assume that the interpretation of all manifestations would be consistent, generating organization-wide consensus. This is an assumption acceptable only from an integration perspective.

Matrices can also be used to diagnose whether a given study is materialist or idealist or both. Materialist studies tend to include formal practices, especially pay rates, and physical arrangements (including the dirt and noise or quiet luxury of a work environment)—the material aspects of organizational life. In contrast, ideational studies (like symbolic analyses) focus on *interpretations* of some kinds of cultural manifestations and content themes—the cognitive and perhaps emotional aspects of culture. Whether or not a researcher defines materialist aspects of organizational life to be part of culture or uses a base-superstructure distinction (defining culture in ideational and not material terms), I believe that it is important that any cultural study examine the relationship between ideational aspects of culture and the material conditions of work; all three OZCO matrices do this. Often, the materialist aspects can illuminate the reasons for important differences in interpretation. Without such a grounding in the material aspects of working life, ideational studies can sometimes become so abstract, and in a sense idealistic, that pragmatically important aspects of organizational life can disappear from analysis, thereby limiting understanding. Critical theorists point out, aptly I believe, that if a cultural portrait is to include the views of those at the bottom of a hierarchy, it is essential to consider how the material aspects of their working lives differ from those of top managers (including the type of work done and the pay received as well as the working environment).

The matrix framework can also be useful to those who seek to develop theoretical generalizations about cultures in organizations. Some researchers, such as ethnographers, are interested primarily in developing a deep understanding of a single cultural context. Others, working from a neopositivist tradition, may want to develop theoretical generalizations, for example, about what kinds of cultures or subcultures emerge in particular kinds of organizations. If you are interested in developing generalizations across cultural contexts, matrices can also be used to compare the results or the theoretical orientations of a set of cultural studies of single contexts. How similar are the content themes in different cultures? Are there common types of rituals or stories that emerge in all organizations of a given size, age, or industry? Do these cultures have similar subcultural configurations? Do the same kinds of ambiguity emerge? Generalizations such as these can help us determine, for example, whether claims of cultural uniqueness are justified.

In these ways, a matrix analysis can delineate what a given study has included and excluded when it claimed to be examining culture. As you know by now, my answer to the questions "What is culture? What is not culture?" is that the better cultural studies include both materialist and idealist concerns, examine the broadest possible range of cultural manifestations, view any claim of cultural uniqueness as an empirical question, and use all three theoretical perspectives in a single study—not assuming that culture is only that which is shared. You, of course, may come to different conclusions. To further explore the insights that can be derived from cultural studies that use all three perspectives, several studies are discussed in the following sections.

Sumerbank

A state-owned conglomerate in Turkey, named Sumerbank, was studied by Baburoglu and Göcer (1994). This was an umbrella enterprise, encompassing 39 manufacturing plants, 47 bank offices, and 437 retail stores in industries ranging from steel to shoes and textiles. Baburoglu and Göcer described the culture as strongly integrated on four mutually consistent content themes: social responsibility, school, family, and colony. Stakeholders other than employees, such as family, were included as cultural members, all of whom referred to themselves as "Sumerbankians." The employees all lived in homes near the Sumerbank factory, and some employees even married each other. The

children of employees played with each other, went to school on Sumerbank scholarships, and some even became second-generation employees of the company.

This integration view, however, was only part of the culture at Sumerbank. The firm had long known that it was ultimately facing privatization, and despite this advanced warning they were unprepared. There
were no reliable profitability figures for separate business units, and
business strategy had long been production driven rather than market
driven. To achieve the competitiveness required for survival, Sumerbank needed to minimize redundancy and maximize sales volumes—
tough goals in an organization whose mission, as stated in its charter,
contained no mention of productivity or efficiency. These inconsistencies were worrisome: "In Sumerbank, the employees know what a
'Sumerbankian' means, but do not know what 'being productive'
means. It is time for them to learn this as well" (Baburoglu & Göcer,
1994, p. 50). Baburoglu and Göcer described this as a "Janus-faced" culture clash between the integration of the "Sumerbankian" way of life
and the conflicting demands of the move to privatization. The authors
saw a straightforward conflict between two clearly opposing ideologies,
as a differentiation perspective would suggest.

In addition, Baburoglu and Göcer (1994) reported that many employees were ambivalent. The Sumerbankians saw the desirability of being more competitive in the marketplace and believed that, in some
ways, they would personally benefit from the transition. At the same
time, many of these same people saw clear drawbacks and irreparable
damage to a valued way of life. In accord with the fragmentation view,
these contradictions were irreconcilable tensions causing confusion,
fear, anxiety, and especially ambiguity. Thus, data reflective of all three
perspectives—at the same time—presented a more complex view of the
culture(s) at Sumerbank than any single theoretical perspective could
offer. In this cultural portrait, the two less visible perspectives (differentiation and fragmentation) pointed to a complex future, when the integration commitment to school, family, colony, and social responsibility
would be a faint but fond memory.

A School

A grade school (kindergarten through 12th grade) was studied by
Stevenson and Bartunek (1996). Focusing on personal stories and a

network analysis of informal patterns of communication, Stevenson and Bartunek found all three perspectives to be useful in describing this culture. In accord with the integration perspective, most people told favorable personal stories about their work at the school, often about situations in which employees had helped each other through difficult times. Administrators told the most positive personal stories, such as the following:

> Ray Linder was the business manager here for 4 years. We were very close friends. One night, after we had dinner, Ray walked toward home. The next morning, when he did not appear for work, we sent someone to his house. They found him murdered. I immediately wanted to go over to his house to see what happened. Realizing that I could not be stopped, Dana (the principal) and Carlotta came with me. Throughout the week and the months that followed, the school community, led by Dana, supported me in my/our grief in many different ways. This is a very brief sketch, leaving out many details. However, the point is that you are never left to face anything alone. You are a member of a community here. (p. 92)

Like many integration accounts, this story merges I and we, stresses feelings of collectivity-wide community, and talks of understanding and support coming from a leader (in this case, Dana) and from peers.

The administrators were the dominant group in the school in terms of formal authority. In accord with the differentiation perspective, however, personal stories from teachers and some staff showed a pattern of conflict with the administration (Stevenson & Bartunek, 1996, p. 99). For example, one teacher spoke of conflicting feelings during a graduation ceremony:

> There was much talk about love, achievement, and integrity. Among the graduates was a . . . student [who] had missed most of my classes during her senior year. . . . This girl failed science and should not have graduated. . . . I was asked by the administration, however, to give her another exam which would allow her to pass and graduate. She did both, and the school did the girl a disservice. (p. 88)

This resentment-of-the-administration content theme was shared by people in structurally equivalent roles in the networks that characterized informal interaction in the school. This network analysis also produced quantitative evidence that was considered as congruent with a fragmentation viewpoint:

> The employees did not belong to clearly defined cliques and the large number of overlapping social circles precluded the development of shared cultural viewpoints within them. This result makes clear that "finding" a coherent clique or group, especially when the definition of group is expanded to include informal as well as formal functional groupings, is sometimes difficult. The differentiation perspective notion that there are frequently clearly defined subgroups may sometimes be too simple. (p. 101)

Stevenson and Bartunek concluded that the "effects predicted from the integration, differentiation, and fragmentation perspectives are likely to be jointly present in organizations" (p. 1).

Other Three-Perspective Studies

Other three-perspective studies have examined a variety of contexts. For example, Damon (1997) studied the birth of a culture in a new media company in Britain. In this longitudinal case study, Damon delineated commercial, professional, and creative tensions that evolved as employees created a culture characterized by integration, differentiation, and fragmentation. Enomoto (1993) used three perspectives to examine truancy in multiethnic urban high schools. Aurelio (1995) used Jungian analysis of archetypes to tap deeper, more unconscious aspects of cultural dynamics in a large, urban hospital. Jeffcutt (in press) used three perspectives to study a temporary organization for unemployed women in Britain. Takashi (1997) used theoretical modeling and quantitative analysis to study culture and innovation, using the three perspectives, in a sample of 403 managers in 361 large companies in Japan. On a more theoretical level, Koot, Sabelis, and Ybema (1996) discussed how the three perspectives are intertwined. These authors drew on postmodern approaches to demonstrate the importance of paradoxical, multilayered behavioral interpretations. Kilduff and Corley (2000) use network analyses to capture elements of all three perspectives. As these examples indicate, the three perspectives can be used to study cultures in a wide range of organizations and countries.

Three-Perspective Views of Cultural Change

The usefulness of a three-perspective approach to studying cultures may be easier to understand if we consider cultural change. In the following sections, I use three perspectives to describe the birth of an Internet venture and the transformation of the Peace Corps when President Nixon revamped President Kennedy's initial vision.

The Birth of a Start-Up Company

Startup.com (a pseudonym) was a fast-growing entrepreneurial venture in the turbulent Internet industry. This start-up company developed software for the Internet to help busy people schedule meetings at convenient times. To describe how the culture of this company changed, the following summary makes a simplifying assumption in the interests of brevity: The researcher and most of the cultural members viewed the culture in the same way. To make this account easier to follow, Figure 5.1 diagrams the three-perspective view of the cultural change process described here.

In its first months of its existence (Time 1), the new company struggled to invent itself, hire people, produce goods or services, market them, and meet its payroll. At this point, nothing was settled, and the predominance of ambiguity and uncertainty made the fragmentation aspects of this culture salient. Therefore, at Time 1, the home perspective seemed to be fragmentation, represented above the double line in Figure 5.1. At the same time, however, beneath the double line were elements of the hidden perspectives. In accord with the differentiation view at Time 1, inconsistencies abounded as managerial pronouncements, however well-intentioned, were not translated into action because so many tasks needed to be done. Rudimentary subcultures were starting to form. For example, employees who had substantial equity in the firm sometimes had different agendas and levels of commitment than employees with less of an equity stake. The "old guard" employees felt some distance from the new hires. At the same time, the integration perspective was also hidden beneath the double line in Figure 5.1. In accord with an integration view, most employees shared the stress and exhilaration of being part of a start-up, participating in the frantic rush to get products shipped so payroll commitments could be met. All three perspectives were relevant, but the hidden perspectives, below the

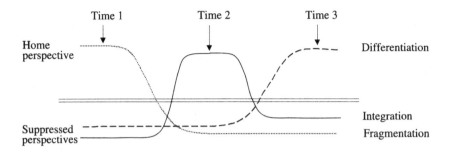

Figure 5.1. A Three-Perspective View of Cultural Change at a Start-Up Company
SOURCE: Adapted From Figure 9.1 in *Cultures in Organizations: Three Perspectives* by Joanne Martin, Copyright © 1992 by Oxford University Press, Inc. Used by Permission of Oxford University Press, Inc.

double line in Figure 5.1, contained the seeds of what would be most important in the future.

At Time 2, several months after venture funding was first received, organization-wide concerns took precedence as the company faced the threat that venture capitalists would be unwilling to provide a second round of financing. Integration seemed to become the home perspective as most employees joined the all-night and all-weekend efforts to get the product released in time to impress the venture capitalists and start bringing in revenues. Also at Time 2, below the double line in Figure 5.1 there were hidden perspectives: the ambiguities and uncertainties of the fragmentation view and the inconsistencies and subcultural separations characteristic of the differentiation view. Because so much had changed so rapidly, and because so many new employees had been hired but not fully socialized or trained, ambiguities and uncertainties lurked just beneath the consciousness of most employees. Everything seemed to be changing all the time—the constant flux characteristic of the fragmentation view. Also, subcultures had definitely emerged. Most noticeably, the marketing staff had banded together, worried that the complex user interface built by the engineers would be too difficult to understand, making consumers flee the company's Web site before they fully understood the advantages of the complex tools they were being offered. The engineers were also unified—in opposition to the marketing staff's endless attempts to add "help instructions," "buttons," and other graphics on the Web screens designed to make the user interface easier to use for the consumers. These "bells and whistles," the engineers said, ruined their elegant software and made it more likely to break down. These were tense times, but the home perspective was integration, as everyone pulled together to meet deadlines and help the company survive.

By Time 3, some time later, the start-up company had reached adolescence, if not maturity. Payroll worries and the venture capital crisis were dim memories. The second round of financing was apparently about to come through, and a large corporation was expressing interest in buying the entire enterprise. With rapid growth, the company now had dozens of employees, and they had begun to separate into clearly delineated subcultures that were easy to see, making differentiation the home perspective. Marketing and engineering were still separate subcultures, although they were coexisting in relatively happy symbiosis now that their management had changed. The top executive team was now quite separate from the rest of the employees—a subculture unto itself. Lower-level employees, especially the technicians and clerical workers, felt distant from the professionals and especially from the top management team. In addition, the women managers and professionals had formed their own subculture, going out to dinner and the movies regularly to get away from "the boys." At the same time, below the double line in Figure 5.1, two hidden perspectives were integration (focused on pride in the company's unique product and its new, tenuous hope of profitability) and fragmentation (based on the confusing residues of the company's rapid growth in a constantly changing industry and worries about continuing financing prior to a buyout or a public stock offering). These hidden perspectives contain clues to how the culture might change in the future.

Peace Corps/Africa Under
Presidents Kennedy and Nixon

One of the most detailed three-perspective studies of cultural change described the creation and transformation of the Peace Corps in Africa (Meyerson & Martin, 1987) under two presidential administrations. As you may know, the Peace Corps was founded, with great excitement, during the administration of President Kennedy. Young, idealistic, middle-class volunteers were recruited, mostly from colleges, to help people in developing countries. In the words of one of the Peace Corps' leaders (Shriver, 1986, p. 18), "An idea, to conquer, must fuse with the will of men and women who are prepared to dedicate their lives to its realization." This heady rhetoric was to mobilize Peace Corps volunteers and staff; working and living together with people from host countries, they were going to change the world. In the Peace Corps at this time, especially in the African division, integration seemed to be the home perspective.

At the same time, inconsistencies could be detected, especially as the appointed Peace Corps staff (a Peace Corps/Africa director, directors for each host country, and training and administrative personnel) began to distance themselves from the volunteers, becoming a separate subculture. For the most part, the volunteers had relatively little contact with each other. They lived in isolated villages or in some urban areas. Despite this lack of contact, in some host countries the volunteers began to coalesce into rudimentary subcultures. Rare cross-country meetings gave volunteers a chance to share information about common concerns. The volunteers involved especially in educational projects found it useful to trade teaching materials and techniques, leading to the development of some close relationships and the beginning of a cross-country project-oriented subculture. Differentiation, then, was one of the hidden perspectives at Time 1.

The fragmentation perspective was also relevant although less visible at this time. There was constant flux as volunteers arrived, served a short term (usually 2 years), and then were replaced. In addition, turnover among country directors was high. Volunteers' contact with staff members was rare and, in the opinions of many, not particularly productive. Even veteran volunteers were uncertain about how to cope with unfamiliar problems. An ability to live with ambiguity was an essential job requirement. Transient issue-specific concerns developed, although there was much disagreement about what the problems were, where they had surfaced, or how they should be resolved. For example, debate focused on such issues as whether it was appropriate to be teaching English; what, if anything, should be done about love affairs and pregnancies among volunteers; and how to cope with unfamiliar illnesses and dangers. Some individuals became involved in one or more of these issues, at least for a time, whereas because of isolation or distance or

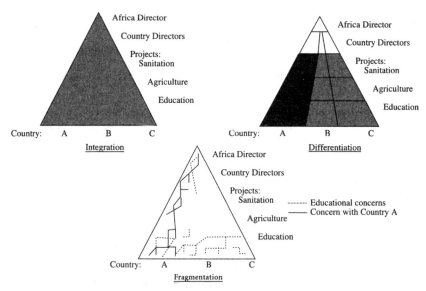

Figure 5.2. A Three-Perspective View of Cultural Change at the Peace Corps/
Africa: Time 1
SOURCE: Adapted from Meyerson & Martin, 1987; reprinted in *Cultures in Organizations: Three Perspectives*
by Joanne Martin, copyright © 1992 by Oxford University Press, Inc. Used by permission of Oxford University
Press, Inc.

both, others remained ignorant or uninvolved. This three-perspective
view of cultural change in the Peace Corps at Time 1 is summarized in
Figure 5.2.

Life in Peace Corps/Africa did not change much under President
Johnson's administration. When Nixon was elected, however, there
were dramatic changes. President Nixon, unlike Presidents Kennedy
and Johnson, believed that the Peace Corps had become a haven for
those with suspect political views, a sinecure for middle-class liberal
arts graduates with no marketable skills. An integration view of the
"new" Peace Corps, instigated by Nixon and his appointees, focused on
changes in the kinds of volunteers that were recruited. Senior citi-
zens and blue-collar workers with practical skills in irrigation, plumbing, and farming were encouraged to join the Corps. Teaching of
English was deemphasized because this kind of project had been especially attractive to those volunteers who had suspect (liberal) political
views. This integration view of the new Peace Corps was based on a
mandate for a different kind of volunteer and a different mission for the
organization.

The upheaval caused by the change in policies from Washington, D.C., was exacerbated by an environmental change in Africa. A major drought spread across the continent, causing a realignment of project assignments. Thirsty crops needed to be replaced by drought-resistant grains, and water-based sanitation and irrigation projects had to be abandoned. As governments changed in response to the crisis, and sometimes in response to violence, the Peace Corps shifted its host countries. The subcultural configuration of the Peace Corps under President Nixon was quite different than it had been under President Kennedy.

These changes in direction caused confusion. The fragmentation perspective captures some of these reactions. Turnover was high as many idealists left and more diverse and pragmatic staff and volunteers took over. Rumors abounded. Some said Nixon was planning to defund the Peace Corps within a year or two. Morale slumped, and most volunteers were looking for other jobs. Although many shared these worries, there was little consensus about what to do. Some issues galvanized widespread concern but not consensus. For example, volunteers engaged in a wide range of projects (e.g., planting, irrigation, sanitation, and building bridges) were searching for effective ways to teach. Consensus was difficult to obtain, however, because it was very difficult to persuade village elders to build a new well or cook untraditional grains. Therefore, educational concerns produced widespread but loose and transient connections among staff and volunteers during the Nixon years. A similarly transient wave of concern spread when one country faced the threat of political violence, although it was unclear to many whether that threat was a sign of progress or deterioration. This three-perspective view of cultural change in the Peace Corps at Time 2 is summarized in Figure 5.3.

Not a Stage Theory of Change

Even in this brief account of the cultural change process at Peace Corps/Africa, limitations of each perspective's approach to change can be seen. The integration viewpoint focused on leader-induced policy changes, mostly from Washington, D.C. A leader-focused view underestimates the impact of environmentally induced changes, such as the drought or upheavals in the governance structures of nation-states in Africa. The differentiation view focused on issues that were of great

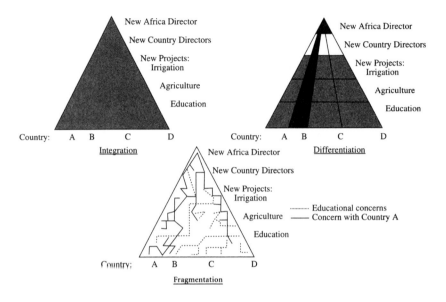

Figure 5.3. A Three-Perspective View of Cultural Change at the Peace Corps/
Africa: Time 2

SOURCE: Adapted from Myerson & Martin, 1987; reprinted in *Cultures in Organizations: Three Perspectives*
by Joanne Martin, copyright © 1992 by Oxford University Press, Inc. Used by permission of Oxford University
Press, Inc.

importance to volunteers, such as project-related difficulties and country-
specific concerns that affected subcultures differently. Finally, the ambiguities and uncertainty captured by the fragmentation perspective
were central to the experiences of volunteers and staff members who
were working in rapidly changing, relatively isolated settings. All these
aspects of change are important to understand. It is clear from these accounts that a three-perspective approach to the study of cultural change
offers insights inaccessible to any single perspective. The implications
of each perspective for the change process are summarized in Table 5.4.

The three-perspective view of cultural change is based on the premise
that at any point in time, all three perspectives are relevant. This approach, then, is not the same as views of cultural change that assume
that a culture passes from one perspective to another, one at a time.
Jonsson and Lundin (1977) provide an example of a single-perspective
stage theory of cultural change. These authors argued that cultures

Table 5.4   Implications of the Three Perspectives Regarding Cultural Change

	Perspective		
	Integration	*Differentiation*	*Fragmentation*
Role of leader	Leader centered	Teams of leaders can have secondary influence	Power diffused among individuals and environment (hegemonic discourses)
Role of environment	Can have some influence but is separate from culture	Environmental influences salient; can be external (jolt) or enacted (nexus approach)	Boundary between environment and organization permeable and in constant flux (nexus approach)
Action implications	Top-down control by leaders, or seek culture-strategy fit, or question normative ability to control culture	Little direct advice to managers or subordinate groups	Individual seen as powerless or as able to contribute intellectually to undermining hegemonic discourses

SOURCE: Adapted from Table 9.1 in *Cultures in Organizations: Three Perspectives* by Joanne Martin, copyright © 1992 by Oxford University Press, Inc. Used by permission of Oxford University Press, Inc.

move through three stages. Organization-wide enthusiasm for key ideas, which they label "myths," makes action possible (integration). Then, crises bring discouragement, the acknowledgment of ambiguity and anxiety, and sometimes action paralysis (fragmentation). To decide how to act, cultural members seek a return to clarity, as a new myth is substituted for the old one (a new integration). Other theories of change that focus on one perspective at a time include Bartunek (1984)[1] and Frederick (1985).[2]

Other scholars, such as Sales and Mirvis (1984)[3] and Greenwood and Hinings (1988),[4] go beyond a stage approach to argue that a large variety of tracks, or sequences of perspectives, can occur. These authors are in agreement with the three-perspective model that the sequence of events in a cultural change process cannot be predicted. For example, not all start-up organizations will have their home perspective shift from fragmentation to integration and then to differentiation. Any sequence is possible. To these views, I add that all three perspectives are relevant and should be studied at any and all points in a change process.

Common Misunderstandings
of the Three-Perspective Approach

The implications of the three-perspective approach can be clarified by exploring some common misperceptions.

Categories are not boxes, and perspectives cannot usually be used to describe individual researchers. Researchers sometimes object to their cultural research as a whole (e.g., "He is an integrationist researcher"), or one of their cultural studies (e.g., "That is a differentiation study"), being "put in a box" as an exemplar of one or more theoretical perspectives: "My study is more complicated than that." This is understandable because no one likes their work or themselves to be put in a box. When researchers object to a study or a review being "boxed" as an exemplar of a single perspective, it is usually because the study also includes some material congruent with other theoretical perspectives. When reviews and empirical research emphasize one perspective, with a secondary and cursory mention of other perspectives, however, these should be understood as predominantly single-perspective studies. A perspective is a category that can be used to classify a study that predominantly uses a single perspective. A perspective should not usually be used to classify the entire research output of an individual because many researchers use different perspectives across different studies as their views change or as they experiment with different ways of thinking about cultures. For example, I have done single-perspective and three-perspective studies, as have many other researchers. Thus, studies, not researchers, usually exemplify the perspectives. There are exceptions, however. A single-perspective label can be used appropriately for those culture researchers who choose to specialize exclusively in a single perspective, such as the protagonists in the argument in Chapter 4.

Perspectives are not merely levels of analysis. Sometimes a differentiation study offers a miniversion of the integration perspective, at a lower level of analysis, so that a subculture becomes an integrated culture—writ small. Studies of single homogeneous subcultures, such as "occupational subcultures" (e.g., Barley, 1983; Trice & Beyer, 1993), should be classified as integration studies if they are characterized by consistency, consensus, and clarity. If a study explicitly or tacitly deals with more than one subculture, however, then the culture is composed of subcultures that have relationships to each other. These relationships can be mutually reinforcing, independent, or conflicting (Louis, 1983, 1985). For example, at OZCO, top management and human resources subcultures usually reinforced each other, marketing and engineering subcultures were often in conflict, and assembly line workers remained uninvolved in many of the issues that absorbed their professional and managerial colleagues. The possibility of subcultural conflict is conceptually crucial because it permits a fuller exploration of the workings of power (e.g., Alvesson, 1996; Hardy & Clegg, 1996; Lucas, 1987; Mumby, 1987, 1988), as will be discussed in Chapter 6. For these reasons, the integration and differentiation perspectives are profoundly different: Differentiation studies of multiple subcultures are not a "microversion" of the integration view at a lower level of analysis.

In a variation of this kind of misunderstanding, the three perspectives are sometimes simplified as if they were "merely" three levels of analysis, with the integration view being the organizational level (sometimes measured quantitatively as a mean or a main effect, with low within-group variance); the differentiation view being the group level, allowing for intergroup conflict (sometimes measured quantitatively as significant between-group difference); and the fragmentation view being the individual level (measured perhaps as error variance). These are conceptual misunderstandings and oversimplifications (and statistical misrepresentations) because, as outlined in Table 5.5, the three perspectives differ from each other on all three levels of analysis. (Although Table 5.5 is framed at the organizational, group, and individual levels of analysis, the same arguments could be made at different levels. For example, the highest level could be a larger collectivity, such as an interorganizational alliance or a nation.)

The three perspectives each conceive of a culture in radically different terms: as a homogeneous unity; as a collection of subcultures; or as a gathering of transient, issue-specific concerns, constantly in flux. If subcultures are acknowledged, relationships among them can be diagnosed as mutually reinforcing, conflicting with each other, independent, or so ambiguously related that clear congruence or conflict is impossible to diagnose. The conception of the self that underlies each

Table 5.5   Levels of Analysis and the Three Perspectives

	Perspective		
Level of Analysis	Integration	Differentiation	Fragmentation
Organizational	Consensus throughout the organization; goal is assimilation and conformity	No organization-wide consensus; organization is cluster of subcultures	Issue-specific attention with no consensus; patterns of issue activation in flux
Subcultural	No important subcultural differences; subculture can represent whole	Relation of subcultures can be Enhancing Conflicting Independent	Subcultural boundaries uncertain, fluctuating, blurred, nested, overlapping
Individual	Self unified, constant, a member of the culture	Self composed of multiple subcultural identities	Self fragmented, in flux; no central unity

SOURCE: Adapted from Martin & Meyerson (1988), Table 1; Meyerson & Martin (1987), Figure 3; Frost, Moore, Louis, Lundberg, & Martin (1991), Table 1.1; and Martin (1992), Table 1.1.

perspective is also dramatically different, including a unified self (integration); a self divided into separable components (differentiation), such as when a person is a member of different overlapping, nested subcultures; and a postmodern, fragmented identity with porous boundaries, reflecting and refracting a variety of cultural influences (fragmentation). These differences in the conceptions of the self, underlying each of the three perspectives, are discussed in more detail in Martin (1992a, pp. 57-60, 94-96, 100-101, and 155-157). With such profound conceptual differences, at all levels of analysis, each perspective is deeply different from the others. The three perspectives are not just three levels of analysis.

Hidden perspectives are not less important, especially for those interested in predicting or influencing change. Although a home perspective may be easier to see, if a researcher looks hard enough, cultural manifestations and interpretations consistent with other perspectives will always become visible. Hidden perspectives that are not dominant or easy to see at one point in time may later become home perspectives. Therefore, hidden perspectives often provide a useful clue about what the future will hold. For example, if top management announces a restructuring of a firm, deep knowledge of various subcultures may help organizational members predict which subcultures will resist, which will cooperate enthusiastically, and which will try to remain aloof from the proposed changes. As another example, suppose a content theme such as the importance of innovation is seen as ambiguous. Some employees may label as innovative slight variations in current products and services the firm offers, whereas others may define innovation as requiring a radical departure from current operating procedures. Under some conditions, this ambiguity may be unimportant; adherents of both interpretations may be seen, and see themselves, as enhancing the firm's commitment to innovation. Should innovation be tied to annual individual bonuses, however, these differences in interpretation could become very important: Should only those whose contributions fit the more radical definition of innovation garner greater rewards? For reasons such as this, insight provided by the hidden perspectives can be important to cultural members as well as cultural researchers.

One of the three perspectives will not provide a more "accurate" description of a culture at a particular point in time. This is the most common misperception of the three-perspective framework. All three perspectives are relevant at any point in time; one is not temporarily more accurate than the others. To make the reasons for this position clearer, discussion about the objective and subjective distinctions, introduced in Chapter 2, may be relevant here. Perhaps you, as a cultural researcher, prefer an objectivist approach that judges theories by how accurately they represent a phenomenon under investigation (e.g., Ebers, 1995). If so, you might object to the three-perspective approach by asking the following: "Don't some cultures have more consensus than others, making the integration perspective a better fit?" "Aren't there other cultures that are obviously characterized by intergroup conflict, characteristic of a differentiation perspective?" "Aren't there a few cultures in which ambiguity is visible everywhere, making the fragmentation view the most accurate and useful theory?" "Can't one perspective be more accurate than another in its representation of a particular culture?" and "Isn't the presence or absence of subcultures or ambiguity an 'empirical question'?" If this is your point of view, you can use the ideas in this book to seek the contextually most appropriate theoretical perspective to represent a particular culture.

Alternatively (and this is what I recommend), you could suspend judgment, for now, and try a three-perspective approach: See what can be learned from labeling the view that seems dominant, to you or to cultural members—the home perspective—and continue to search for cultural manifestations and interpretations consistent with the other two perspectives. This may be difficult if you are used to assuming that theories can and should be evaluated to determine which offers the single most accurate representation of what you are studying. The three-perspective view is perhaps easier for those, like myself, who take a subjectivist approach to the study of culture, arguing in accord with Mumby (1994, p. 158) that "theories do not neutrally reflect the world, but rather that they construct it in a particular fashion." From this viewpoint, theories can be evaluated by their power to provide insights that might otherwise be overlooked rather than by how accurately they represent some objective reality. The three-perspective approach helps us view the world in a particular, socially constructed way, stemming from the viewpoint of the researcher and the characteristics of the context and the people being studied. As Fleming and Stablein (1999) suggest, "Just as an infrared nightscope allows the user to see in the dark, adopting a different theoretical perspective attunes the researcher to different aspects (wavelengths) of the scene." Therefore, I argue that a multi-perspective approach offers a wider range of insights than is available from any single-perspective vantage point. This is why any cultural portrait is more complex and inclusive if it is regarded, at any single point in time, from all three perspectives (Martin, 1992a, p. 174; Martin & Meyerson, 1988; Meyerson & Martin, 1987). No one perspective is empirically more accurate than the others—a home perspective is simply easier to see.

I realize that a subjectivist approach is anathema to many organizational researchers who believe that the purpose of research is to seek the most accurate view of a phenomenon, test (prove and disprove) hypotheses, and build generalizable theories. There is a small but important difference between advocating the greater inclusiveness of a three-perspective view and positing that a three-perspective view of culture is more accurate than other theoretical approaches. Like other subjectivists, I do not believe we can accurately, or even completely, represent what we see, and I believe that what we see bears a complex relationship to what others may see. Therefore, I try to refrain from making inappropriate and grandiose truth claims in this book. It is my hope that for those who remain uncomfortable with subjectivist assumptions, they will still be willing to try using three perspectives at a single point in time to find out what more they can see.

No matter how you "slice it," culture still cannot be defined only as that which is shared. The idea that culture is that which is shared is a Lazarus of a theory: It just will not die. For example, an advocate of this integrationist approach, struggling to deal with the three-perspective view, might argue the following:[5]

> Just because a culture doesn't have a shared set of views about issue X doesn't mean they don't agree about issue Y. Organizations aren't sustainable as social institutions unless they have some basic shared understandings about core ends and means, and legitimated patterns of behavior, such as routines or scripts. For example, take a local bank, in which employees do not agree about who has the most power, whether the board is doing a good job, whether their human resources policies are really family friendly, and so on. Still, they must agree that the organization's operations will comply with prevailing banking regulations, that the overall portfolio of loans should generate a profit, that request for loans above a certain amount require the approval of a committee, that the committee should consider the credit worthiness of applicants, and so on. I don't see how it is possible to argue that members don't share at least some common interpretations.

I would respond to this argument by saying that I agree that any organization will require, simply to survive, some common interpretations. The three-perspective approach to understanding cultures in organizations includes the integration view and thus could include all these shared interpretations, if they indeed were shared. The three-perspective approach would not, however, stop there. It would also give equal attention to signs of differentiation and fragmentation. In the terms used in the previous argument, culture includes issue X as well as issue Y. What people disagree about and what they find ambiguous are just as much a part of culture as what they share.

A more complicated objection to the three-perspective view, however, might return to the centrality of what is shared:

> Suppose we define culture as "a set of minimally shared meanings or understandings." This definition is agnostic regarding the extent to which those meanings are in conflict, ambiguous, and so on. For example, in some

organizations, members might agree that they share a wide range of assumptions and practices. In other organizations, members might generally agree that subcultures have different, sometimes conflicting orientations. And in still other organizations, the understanding shared by members might be that they don't agree on much at all (i.e., "You can't take anything for granted when you propose an idea"). This approach would, unlike the integration perspective, take no normative position regarding which of these cultures would be more desirable. Indeed, some people might find the integration culture boring, preferring the open free-for-all of the fragmented setting.

In accord with the three-perspective view, and contrary to the integration view, this argument does not assume that one perspective describes aspects of a culture that are normatively more desirable. There are several ways in which this argument departs from the three-perspective approach, however. The argument assumes that all or most members of a culture agree about how they would characterize that culture, leaving open whether that culture is integrated, differentiated, or fragmented. In other words, this argument assumes that most members of a culture share the same home perspective. The problem is that the members of a culture may disagree about which view of their culture is the home perspective. Furthermore, this argument is assuming that one perspective is more accurate than the others at a single point in time. In contrast, for reasons described previously, I have argued that all three perspectives should be used together simultaneously, at a single point in time, to search for "the patterns of meanings that link these manifestations together, sometimes in harmony, sometimes in bitter conflicts between groups, and sometimes in webs of ambiguity, paradox, and contradiction."

In summary, a particular culture is not more, or less, accurately represented by one of these perspectives. There is no such thing as an "integrated culture" or a "fragmented culture." There can, however, be a culture viewed from the integration perspective, and such a view is incomplete until that culture is examined from the differentiation and fragmentation perspectives (not to mention other theoretical viewpoints not yet discussed). To restate this argument in longitudinal terms, a particular culture does not pass from one perspective to another over time, for example, moving from early leader-centered integration to fragmentation to whatever. If one perspective seems easier to see than the others, then this will be the researcher's or the cultural members' home perspective; the other hidden perspectives will be visible too, if the researcher or the cultural member looks hard and in-depth. All three perspectives are relevant at any point in time.

Switching Perspectives

So far, this discussion has illustrated the three-perspective approach by showing how researchers can use all three perspectives in a cultural study. In addition, cultural members, like cultural researchers, use all three perspectives when they describe the cultures in which they work. To illustrate this, reanalysis of the OZCO interviews revealed numerous employees making remarks, in quick sequence, which fit more than one perspective. Stuart, for example, vacillated between perspectives as he described the distribution of special benefits ("perks"). Speaking from an integration view emphasizing the company's egalitarian approach to distributing resources, Stuart said, "If you have a reason, you get something better. Design people get better terminals. Salespeople have cars, but they need them. I have a schlocky desk, but that's ok. I can still do my work." Later, Stuart took a differentiation view, arguing that the distribution of perks was inegalitarian, reflecting a boss's access to resources: "If my manager has extra money, after everything is taken care of, then we get some perks."

Schultz (1991) also found evidence that people in organizations can easily shift their viewpoints and behavior to fit changing interactional contexts. She labels these contexts "symbolic domains" to distinguish them from physical locations and from functionally or hierarchically defined subcultural identities. In the Danish ministry studied by Schultz, the symbolic domains that evoked different patterns of behavior included daily routinized tasks; stories about the minister handed down from employees; individual and formal group meetings with the minister; and unplanned, ad hoc talk with the minister under crisis conditions. In each of these domains, reactions differed in predictable ways. Although this study does not separate integration, differentiation, and fragmentation viewpoints explicitly, data are congruent with all three perspectives.

It is easy to understand how people could shift perspectives easily. For example, while you are positioning yourself to view things from one perspective, it may be that at that point you are also more able to grasp other points of view. While studying many subcultures, you can see what they share. While studying shared themes, you may see how those themes have different meanings for some individuals, whereas other individuals remain ignorant or uninvolved. The ease with which people can shift perspectives suggests that adopting a three-perspective view should not be difficult for most cultural researchers once they put aside single-perspective theoretical blinders.

Simultaneity and Perspective Interplay

The core of the three-perspective approach is a proposition concerning simultaneity. If any cultural context is studied in sufficient depth (as in the studies of the academic seminar, OZCO, Sumerbank, the school, the Internet start-up company, and Peace Corps/Africa), some things will be seem to be consistent, clear, and indicative of collectivity-wide consensus. Simultaneously, other aspects of the culture will seem to coalesce into subcultures, enabling these subcultures to reinforce, be independent, or conflict with each other.[6] At the same time, still other elements of the culture will seem fragmented, in a state of constant flux, and infused with confusion, doubt, and paradox (Martin, 1992a, p. 4; see also Martin & Meyerson, 1988; Meyerson & Martin, 1987).

Although the three perspectives occur simultaneously, they can be presented separately, as I did in the descriptions of OZCO, the academic seminar, and the Peace Corps/Africa. I chose this writing strategy because I was concerned with protecting the three perspectives from pressures toward assimilation. Having examined a variety of three-perspective studies, presented in all kinds of ways, I see that it is not essential that the perspectives be presented separately. A clear account can repeatedly switch back and forth across perspectives (e.g., Hassard, 1988; Willmott, 1990), acknowledging the ways the boundaries between these conceptual categories can be blurred (e.g., Ybema, 1996, 1997). This approach follows Schultz and Hatch's (1996) recommendation for paradigm interplay:

> Interplay complements well-known contrasts between paradigms with connections proposed by postmodern critiques of modernist social science. Considered simultaneously, these contrasts and connections position the researcher to move back and forth between paradigms and invite researchers to see and use the diversity of organizational theory in new ways. (p. 529)

Although the three cultural perspectives fall short of being full-blown paradigms (Martin, 1992a, pp. 15-16), this interplay of connections among the perspectives is facilitated by their common grounding in three dimensions of inquiry: relation among manifestations, orientation to consensus, and treatment of ambiguity. By encouraging perspective interplay, perhaps we can preserve and enhance the playfulness, spirit of innovation, and awareness of irony and reflexivity that has enlivened the renaissance of interest in cultural phenomena while avoiding some of the turgid, self-limiting, and self-aggrandizing effects of any theoretical framework (see Gagliardi, 1991).

Dangers of Perspective Interplay

It is important to give each perspective full consideration, respecting and retaining differences among the viewpoints. Paradigm interplay requires the simultaneous recognition of both contrasts and connections among paradigms. To do this in an even-handed fashion, the researcher first shifts between and then withdraws an equal distance from the paradigms being represented (Schultz & Hatch, 1996, p. 543). With this approach, interplay should permit, and ideally facilitate, the exploration of the complex conceptual differences among the three theoretical perspectives. This is easier said than done, however. Often, one perspective is given precedence, the other two are included only as minor themes, and the resulting empirical study or review is tacitly or explicitly described as representing all three kinds of cultural research. In three-perspective research, it is essential that representations of the field of culture literature, and empirical studies of a particular culture, give all three perspectives comprehensive and even-handed coverage. This can be achieved by discussing each perspective in turn, or it can be done by perspective interplay, as Schultz and Hatch recommend.

Characteristics of
Most Organizational Culture Research

The three-perspective approach evolved from my review of the organizational culture literature. If approximately 80% of the cultural studies work tacitly from one of these three perspectives, and approximately another 10% use two or three of these perspectives to study a single cultural context, then we are now in a position to talk about the characteristics of this large subset of the organizational culture litera-ture. Generally, this research usually does not separate functionalist and symbolic aspects of culture. Often, these studies avoid the corporeal, emotional, and aesthetic aspects of organizational life. Most, but not all, of these studies tend to underestimate the importance of environmen-tal influences on the content of organizational cultures. Usually, organi-zational culture research treats cultural boundaries as stable, imperme-able, and clearly defined. These characteristics are discussed in the following sections.

The Blurring of Functionalist and Symbolic Approaches

Both functionalist and symbolic studies have been conducted using one or more of the three perspectives. The three-perspective approach deliberately blurs boundaries between these two very different kinds of cultural research by offering a theoretical framework that can be used in both symbolic and functional research. It is important to acknowledge, however, that functionalist approaches to the study of culture are hotly debated. Many cultural researchers tacitly or explicitly support the functionalist view, arguing that culture is important primarily (and sometimes only) if it can predict productivity or firm performance or help firms survive. Examples of functionalist studies include those by Kotter and Heskett (1992), Porras and Collins (1994), and Schein (1999). (For a meta-analysis of the increase in numbers of functionalist, managerial studies, see Barley, Meyer, & Gash, 1988.) Other cultural re-searchers consider functionalist approaches anathema, in part because functionalist studies tend to take a managerial point of view, arguably ignoring or even working against the interests of nonmanagerial em-ployees. Antifunctionalist cultural researchers often prefer an approach to the study of culture that emphasizes symbolic meanings, uses culture as a metaphor rather than a variable, and refrains from any functionalist interpretations (e.g., Gagliardi, 1990; Grafton-Small & Linstead, 1987; Jones, Moore, & Snyder, 1988; Schultz, 1995; Smircich, 1983a; Smircich & Calás, 1987; Strati, 1992; Turner, 1986; Young, 1989). Because of this hotly contested dispute, any theory that blurs the boundaries between functionalism and symbolism is therefore deservedly suspect. Because of the importance of this issue, particularly the question of whose interests are served by different kinds of cultural research, Chapter 6 focuses on interests and claims of neutrality.

Avoidance of Corporeal, Emotional, and Aesthetic Aspects of Organizational Life

Strati (1999) articulates the need for a broader, more aesthetic view of organizations with his usual wit:

> Most of the research and analysis published in the area of organizational theories and management studies described the following somewhat bizarre phenomenon: As soon as a human person crosses the virtual or physical threshold of an organization, s/he is purged of corporeality so that only his or her mind remains.... The prevalent image conveyed by the organizational literature until the mid-1970s, in fact, was that organizations are made up of ideas which meet and merge on the rational level; ideas, therefore, devoid of eroticism, beautiful or ugly sensations, perfumes and offensive odours, attraction and repulsion. Organization theory and management studies depicted organizations in idealized form by depriving them of their earthly features of physicality and corporeality. (pp. 3-4)

Organizational research in the 1980s began to examine physical aspects of organizational life, most notably in cultural studies of such manifestations as interior design, architecture, dress norms, and the noise or luxury of working environments, as discussed in Chapter 3. Strati (1999, p. 6) observes that recently researchers (e.g., Degot, 1987; Ramirez, 1987; Rusted, 1987) have studied organizational aesthetics without referring to the physical structures of organizations, for example, by using analogies with art, examining aesthetic sentiments and judgments about the beauty of an organization, and studying how aesthetic judgments are negotiated in aesthetic practices. Thus, an aesthetic approach to the study of organizational cultures offers an aesthetic, corporeal, and (to a lesser extent) emotional understanding of organizational life, in contrast to the rational models that dominated previous theory and research (for introductions to aesthetic research of direct relevance to cultural theory, see Gagliardi [1990, 1996], Hatch & Jones [1996], Strati [1999], and the 1987 special issue of *Dragon*, edited by Benghozi). Given the increasing emphasis on emotional issues within the rest of organizational theory, these approaches in particular

seem to offer opportunities for future cultural research, left largely un-
touched by single- and three-perspective studies of culture.

Cultural Boundaries as Stable,
Impermeable, and Clearly Defined

The cultural research reviewed so far in this book has assumed that
the boundaries of a collectivity, such as an organization, coincide with
the boundaries of a culture, making it unproblematic to speak inter-
changeably of employees and cultural members. In fact, we live in a
world in which such boundaries are constantly being broached, moved,
and made problematic by "downsizing," rapid expansion, and extensive
use of temporary workers. Virtual employees work from home offices.
Executives fly from one national office to another. Competing organizations partner with each other in complex networks of alliances. I
could go on, but my point is clear. Boundaries of cultures and organi
zations cannot be assumed to coincide. Employees may or may not be
cultural members to differing extents that wax and wane over time.
Boundaries should not be conceptualized as stable, impermeable, or
clearly defined. For all these reasons, the ways in which cultural theories
(including the three-perspective approach) have conceptualized boundaries need rethinking. As will be shown in Chapter 10, once the topic of
boundaries is opened, many of the basic assumptions of cultural theory
come into question in interesting ways.

A Nexus Approach to the Study of Culture

One more limitation of many, but not all, single- and three-perspective
studies merits more extensive discussion. Often, these studies focus attention within the boundaries of an organization, thus not adequately
dealing with the impact of environmental influences on the contents of
cultures. One way to address this issue is to return to the discussion of
uniqueness presented in Chapter 3. If culture is defined as that which is
unique, and if little is in fact unique, then the phrase "organizational
culture" is a misnomer; if the cultures or subcultures being studied
cross organizational borders, they would be better described as occupational subcultures. This is the conclusion drawn in Gregory's (1983)
study of the occupational subculture of computer programmers in the

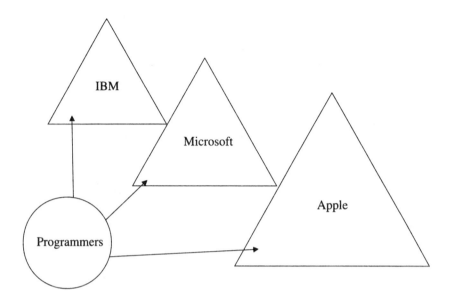

Figure 5.4. Adaptation of Gregory's (1983) Model of Occupational Cultures

Silicon Valley in California. Gregory found that programmers had the same occupational culture no matter which organization they worked for, as illustrated in Figure 5.4. A cynic might observe that Gregory chose to study a geographical location and occupation in which "company hopping" was the norm. Her theoretical challenge, however, merits serious consideration.

Studies that challenge uniqueness claims, such as Gregory's (1983), have many theoretical implications. Cultural members' opinions about what is unique may be misguided in the sense that often what is believed to be unique to a particular context is found elsewhere as well. This is the uniqueness paradox (Martin et al., 1983). If we restrict attention to only those cultural manifestations that are unique, in that they are not found elsewhere, we would be able to study only a small portion of what goes on. Therefore, we need to acknowledge that an organization is unlikely to be an isolated, unique "island of history," unaffected by the society that surrounds it (e.g., Sahlins, 1985). Instead, an organization is likely to be penetrated by a variety of influences from the surrounding environment (see also Schneider & Barsoux, 1997).

An example can illustrate the implications of this reframing. The Trust for Public Land is a small nonprofit organization that uses charitable donations of money and land to transfer ownership of undeveloped tracts to local, state, and federal park systems (Martin, 1992a, pp. 111-112). When this organization was studied, the professional staff consisted primarily of lawyers, most of whom shared a deep commitment to environmental conservation. Other professionals were accountants. Although many of the accountants also shared a commitment to conservation, for most of them their primary professional identification was not to the organization but to the profession of accounting. For these accountants, regular national conferences with accountants from other organizations were very important. At the Trust for Public Land, the remaining employees were clerical staff, few of whom shared the environmental ideology that provided the organization's rationale for existing. Most of the clerical staff worked at the trust because the pay was reasonable and the location was convenient. Unlike the lawyers and accountants, most of whom were white men, the clerical workers were, with few exceptions, women of Hispanic backgrounds. Many of these Hispanic women shared commitments to the primacy of family and the value of open disclosure of personal and work-related emotions to coworkers. Louis (1985, p. 79) labels these extraorganizational cultural influences "feeder cultures" (Figure 5.5).

Studies such as this suggest a resolution to the uniqueness paradox. An organization can be conceptualized as a nexus (Martin, 1992a, pp. 112-114) in which a variety of internal and external influences come together. The research cited previously suggests that only a few cultural manifestations will be truly unique. Therefore, we need to distinguish three types of cultural manifestations: those that are truly unique (a small proportion), that is, those that are found in only one cultural context; some that are falsely believed to be unique; and those that are acknowledged to be not unique.

Nonunique manifestations reflect influences external to the focal organization. What is unique and organizational, then, will be the particular content and mix of these influences as they come together within the permeable, fluctuating boundary of a collectivity, such as an organization. This is the nexus approach to the study of culture, as diagrammed in Figure 5.6. The nexus approach implies that although it is an awkward circumlocution, strictly speaking we should say "cultures in organizations" and not "organizational culture." The phrase "cul-

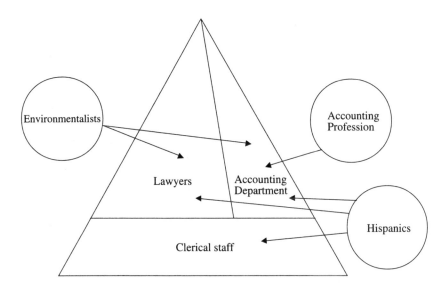

Figure 5.5. "Feeder" Cultures at the Trust for Public Land
SOURCE: Adapted from Figure 6.2 in *Cultures in Organizations: Three Perspectives* by Joanne Martin, copyright © 1992 by Oxford University Press, Inc. Used by permission of Oxford University Press, Inc.

tures in organizations" does not assume that the influences that come together within an organization are consistent with each other, and it does not restrict attention to that which is unique to a particular context. (Admittedly, I use the more common phrase, organizational culture, in this book because it is easier.)

The nexus approach is also relevant to prior discussions of depth. It suggests the following hypothesis: When a basic assumption generates collectivity-wide consensus, it is likely that this assumption is a reflection of cultural influences from outside the collectivity. For example, in the Peace Corps/Africa study, such external influences included the change of presidential administrations in Washington, D.C., and the impact of a drought and the threat of a violent uprising in Africa. Another example focuses on the kinds of deep, basic assumptions that are the subject of Schein's (1985, 1996) cultural research; these too may have sources external to an organization. Assumptions about the trustworthiness of people, for example, may stem from children's relations with parents and community members rather than from interactions among adults within a particular organization. Similarly, a short-term

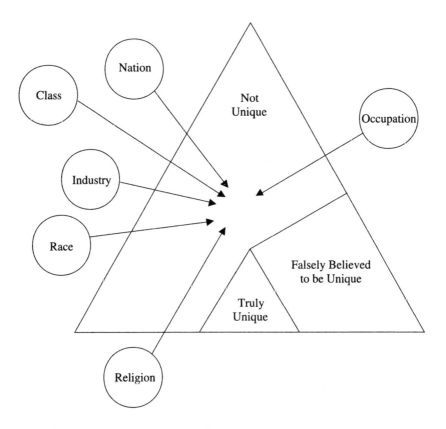

Figure 5.6. The Nexus Approach to Cultures in Organizations

SOURCE: Adapted from Figure 6.2 in *Cultures in Organizations: Three Perspectives* by Joanne Martin, copyright © 1992 by Oxford University Press, Inc. Used by permission of Oxford University Press, Inc.

time perspective may not be unique to a particular firm, but it may be appropriate because of external conditions shared by most firms in a particular industry. For example, firms in the Internet industry must cope with a rapidly changing, turbulent market in which very rapid product innovation is the norm. Under such conditions, a short-term perspective may be necessary for survival. In contrast, in the milk container industry, product innovations are rare, and the market is stable, making a long-term perspective more viable. As both of these examples suggest, it seems reasonable to view a collectivity as a nexus in which a variety of external cultural influences affect which basic assumptions are shared and which are not.

This chapter was very long, but it takes some length to deal with complex theoretical issues. There is one more type of concern, however, that merits examination before you can address the theory choice dilemma: the question of whose interests are being served by the various theoretical perspectives discussed so far. This is the focus of Chapter 6.

Notes

1. In Bartunek's (1984) study of cultural change in a religious order, an environmentally triggered crisis caused confusion, making ambiguity salient. She concludes, "The crisis challenges the validity of the organization's interpretive schemes, suggesting that they are no longer adequate. During such crisis periods all organizations experience a loss of former certainty" (p. 364) (a fragmentation view). Subcultures in the religious order suggested alternative resolutions of the problems (differentiation). Eventually, according to Bartunek, a new synthesis was achieved, one that reflected power differences among the subcultures (a new integration). Bartunek, like Jonsson and Lundin (1977), focuses on one perspective at a time (the home perspective, not the hidden perspectives) and offers a linear, rationally explainable, unidirectional movement across stages in the cultural change process. This kind of linear sequence of stages, focusing on one perspective at a time, is found in other studies of cultural change (e.g., Brunsson, 1985; Miller & Friesen, 1983; Morgan & Ramirez, 1984; Torbert, 1976; Tushman & Romanelli, 1985). Similar unidirectional stage sequences can be found in theories of change that do not focus on culture (e.g., Greiner, 1972; Kimberly, 1979; Kimberly & Miles, 1980; Kimberly & Quinn, 1984).

2. Other scholars focus on one perspective at a time but challenge the assumptions of unidirectional linear progress across stages. For example, Frederick (1985) describes a pattern of oscillation between integration and differentiation. He argues that organizations seek requisite variety because they need to adapt, by changing their culture, to the demands of the marketplace. Requisite variety is obtained at a cost because it undermines the consistency and consensus of a culture. Too much differentiation creates instability, intensifying pressures to increase integration. Too much integration reduces a culture's ability to adapt and find requisite variety. Frederick believes that alternation between these integrating and differentiating forces forms the basis for cultural change. Frederick's oscillation approach is a stage theory of change that focuses on one perspective at a time.

3. Sales and Mirvis (1984) examined cultural collisions in the acquisition process, delineating the interplay of integration, assimilation, and rejection—change processes that include echoes of all three perspectives.

4. Greenwood and Hinings (1988, p. 303) explore a variety of change trajectories and conclude that "not all organizations pass through transitions or the same set of stages, nor do they depart from similar positions or have common destinations." Greenwood and Hinings's approach is unlike the three-perspective approach in that it views only one perspective as relevant at a given time.

5. I am grateful to Dave Whetten, the colleague and friend who served as my editor on this project, representing Sage Publications and the editorial committee of organizational scholars who supervise the **Foundations for Organizational Science** series, to which this book belongs. His comments were particularly useful in this section of the chapter.

6. To my regret, I undermined the simultaneity aspect of the three-perspective approach in earlier writings when I argued that although observation can yield insights congruent with all

three perspectives simultaneously, it can be helpful to write up those results separately for each perspective, one perspective at a time: "Pressures toward assimilation would undermine a perspective's inherently oppositional stance toward the other viewpoints, threatening its conceptual and political integrity. A multiperspective view of culture must vacillate among the three viewpoints, presenting each in turn. When it is used this way, a three-perspective approach is both possible and desirable" (Martin, 1992a, p. 187); "What is to be learned from culture research is, in part, the usefulness of preserving the differences between these social-scientific perspectives and deepening rather than eradicating the conflicts between them" (p. 5). This separate-presentation recommendation has caused some understandable confusion. Some researchers seem to have concluded that I abandoned the conviction that all three perspectives offer insights at a single point in time. I never have done so. The three-perspective framework is based on and is congruent with studies that have found observations fitting more than one perspective at a single point in time (e.g., Kunda, 1992; Riley, 1983; Sackmann, 1997; Turner, 1971; Van Maanen & Barley, 1985; Ybema, 1997; Young, 1989). The confusion, however, suggests that this recommendation should be revisited. There were several reasons why I had argued that although the three perspectives occur simultaneously, they should be presented separately. I was concerned with protecting the three perspectives from pressures toward assimilation. To write succinctly and present clearly understandable ideas, however, there is an understandable but unfortunate tendency to reduce the complexity of the perspectives. To avoid confusion, I now emphasize only the simultaneous relevance of all three perspectives, without recommending they be written up separately.

6 Interests and
Claims of Neutrality

People sort patterns of experience, preferring some patterns more than others. Interests are patterns that focus on the well-being of specific individuals or, more likely, groups of people (Nord & Connell, 1996). Having interests is the opposite of being disinterested or impartial. Culture studies have differing interest orientations. These interest orientations are difficult to decipher because they are usually tacit rather than explicit. Most organizational culture studies are written in the managerial interest, aiming to help managers improve the productivity and performance of their organizations. In contrast, other organizational culture studies are quite critical of managerial actions and priorities. Finally, many organizational culture studies (especially neopositivist empirical studies) are ostensibly value neutral, striving to reach conclusions unaffected by a researcher's personal value or interest preferences.

Whether one believes in the possibility of value neutrality or not, it is important to ascertain the interest orientation of cultural studies, especially those studies that appear at first to be value neutral. We need to ask, "Whose interests are being served by this research?" Managerial, critical, and ostensibly value-neutral interest (descriptive) positions merit discussion because they influence what theories are seen as relevant, which informants are seen as important to study, and what conclusions are drawn (Alvesson, 1993a, makes this point cogently). For example, studies that claim neutrality are characteristically silent about conflicts of interest between more and less powerful employees. Ostensibly value-neutral cultural portraits often describe the status quo without recording any objections to these practices or any alternative views of how organizational functioning could and should change. Tacit, unexamined, and unchallenged interest orientations can interfere with the interpretation and understanding of cultural research.

Interests, then, are the focus of this chapter. Interests present dilemmas for a researcher, raising questions such as the following: "How might I reinterpret the findings of a given study to take into account its interest orientation?" "What is my personal orientation regarding interests?" "Do I believe that value-neutral research can offer a mirror image of some objective reality, not serving any interest group more than another?" "If I believe value-neutral theory is not possible, whose interests do I want to serve in my cultural research?" "How might my interest preferences affect my research in nonobvious ways?" and "What blind spots should I anticipate?" If each of us is to develop individually tailored answers to these questions, a more structured treatment of interests is needed.

The Critical Challenge

Because so much organizational (and cultural) literature assumes value neutrality, or does not explore interests explicitly, a brief history of how interests have been reflected in organizational research may be helpful. Interest in interests intensified when critical theorists challenged the managerial assumptions implicit in much organizational research. The critical theorist most frequently cited, with regard to interests, is Habermas. He (1971) distinguishes three kinds of research: technical, practical, and emancipatory. In the specific sense in which Habermas defines these terms, *technical research*[1] implicitly uses theory to try to manipulate the environment and produce predicted effects. The implicit goal of research in the technical interest is control—of employees by management and owners of an organization. Technical research is usually conducted in the managerial interest. In contrast, according to Habermas, *practical research*[2] is not conducted with the goal of controlling the environment or producing predicted effects. ("Practical" may seem to be an odd terminology because many organizational researchers would define practical research as applied work, conducted in the managerial interest.) The goal of "practical" research, according to Habermas, is to develop a deep understanding of context-specific knowledge to develop action-oriented understanding within a community, fostering moral sensibility, consensual decision making, and so on. "Practical" research is ostensibly value neutral—that is, in the terms I use here, it is written in the descriptive interest.

In contrast to both technical and "practical" research, the goal of *emancipatory research*[3] is to promote what Habermas (1971) calls an "ideal speech situation" whereby two or more people can interact without one dominating the other in any way. Emancipatory research questions assumptions about the current situation. Thus, it escapes the inherent conservatism of most empirical research, which afterall must by definition study the status quo (Martin, 1992b). Emancipatory research, by definition, has an explicit critical edge, usually focusing on conflicts between labor and management, the oppression of workers with low-paid jobs, or the silencing of the concerns and needs of women, racial or ethnic minorities, and so on. Within the cultural domain, these are the traditional concerns of much, but not all, differentiation research (Alvesson, 1993a).

Stablein and Nord reviewed a broad spectrum of cultural research in 1985 using Habermas's (1971) categories of technical, practical, and emancipatory research. They concluded that almost all the cultural research at that time was written in the technical interest, often with an explicitly functionalist and managerial orientation. Stablein and Nord then described several studies that were more emancipatory, and they encouraged cultural researchers to do more of this kind of research. Smircich and Calás reviewed the culture literature in 1987 and concluded (pp. 18, 39) that it had become "dominant, but dead," meaning that this initially innovative domain of research had come to be, like most of the rest of organizational studies, dominated by managerial interests. In 1988, Barley, Meyer, and Gash reviewed both academic and practitioner-oriented cultural research, mostly published in the United States, and came to similar conclusions about the predominance of managerial research. The 1990s brought a proliferation of critical culture studies that challenged managerial assumptions. More recent reviews of the cultural literature (e.g., Martin, 1990a; Martin & Frost, 1996) have found a proliferation of research that fits the second and third of Habermas's categories. Although technical research still predominates, particularly in the United States, many hermeneutic "practical" studies (mostly purely descriptive) have been conducted. In addition, a substantial number of emancipatory studies have begun to emerge.

Managerial, Critical, and Descriptive Interests

In this chapter, I focus on three kinds of interests of particular relevance to cultural studies: managerial, critical, and descriptive. These three categories bear some relationship to Habermas's interests, but my focus here is more limited in that, unlike Habermas, I do not include in these labels any presumptions about epistemology or method preferences and I focus exclusively on interests as they pertain to cultural research. Managerial interests focus on the manipulation and control of employees to improve the efficiency of an organization, for example, by managing culture to increase commitment, loyalty, productivity, and even sometimes profitability. Managerial interests are familiar to organizational researchers and so do not need further explanation here.

Cultural studies written in the critical interest recognize conflicting preferences and interpretations in organizations, showing how some preferences are privileged and institutionalized, whereas others are ignored and suppressed (e.g., Alvesson, 1996). Critical cultural research often has an antimanagerial tone. It challenges the legitimacy of authority, asks whether "shared" values are in fact shared, and asks why some people adopt values that seem not to serve their interests, in effect showing what some label "false consciousness" (e.g., Kunda & Van Maanen, 1999). Other critical cultural research asks, in the emancipatory tradition, not what is but, rather, what could be. This kind of critical research asks "What is necessary for the transformation of structures?" (Riley, 1983, p. 436) and seeks to "free people from frozen social relations" (e.g., Alvesson & Willmott, 1992, p. 453) so they can exercise greater control, individually and/or collectively. Critical research in the emancipatory tradition seeks to approach an ideal, in which there are no domination-subordination relationships among participants in a collectivity and in which people are free to explore their beliefs with autonomy and responsibility (as in what Habermas [1971] termed an "ideal speech situation") (e.g., Alvesson & Willmott, 1995).

Critical cultural studies are not immune from criticism. Interestingly, despite its agenda of societal transformation, critical cultural research often abstains from spelling out what action should be taken in a given context, except perhaps by increasing disadvantaged people's cognitive awareness of their own disadvantaged position. One justification for critical cultural research's shortage of action recommendations is the emancipatory goal of freeing people to make their own decisions and take responsibility for the consequences (Stablein & Nord, 1985, p. 18). Making action recommendations, according to this view, would not be the responsibility of a critical researcher. Critical cultural researchers often lack reflexivity in the sense that they usually do not reflect, in print, about the interest-related limitations of their own views. For example, critical researchers may ask managerial researchers to use reflexivity to undermine managerial claims to knowledge and privilege, but critical researchers seldom undermine their own work or challenge the ways in which they privilege their own opinions. It is important to note that critical cultural studies, like cultural studies written in the managerial interest, can be judged positively or negatively depending on who is doing the evaluation (the researcher, lower-level employees, managers, shareholders, or others).

Finally, there is descriptive research written in the descriptive interest, claiming (usually implicitly) to be value neutral. Many researchers believe that value-neutral work is possible, and arguably more desirable (in the sense that it is "better science"), than work that makes its interest orientation explicit (e.g., Campbell & Stanley, 1966; Runkel & McGrath, 1972). These scholars are assuming that a study can mirror a culture without distortion—in a sense presenting an "objective" view that is not tainted or distorted by the researcher's values or interests. In contrast, if a study is viewed as constructing, rather than just mirroring, a culture, then what the researcher constructs and how he or she constructs it necessarily reflect the researcher's values and interests. In this sense, claiming value neutrality is a value position, and it is difficult, if not impossible, to do value-neutral research. According to this view, with which I agree, scholars should be self-reflective about how their interests may have affected their empirical and theoretical work (e.g., Calás & Smircich, 1996; Clegg & Hardy, 1996; Reed, 1985; Stablein & Nord, 1985).

This debate about value neutrality is not an argument I can resolve here, and I want this book to be useful to those who may not share my views. Therefore, I have included a third category of interests, labeled "descriptive," in the analyses discussed later. This is a residual category to be reserved for those cultural studies that have sought to avoid an obvious commitment to either managerial or critical interests. For example, a descriptive study might provide an articulation of a variety of interests in an even-handed fashion, or it might try to avoid any obvious interest orientation. If a study is cited in the "descriptive interests" category, this label should not be misinterpreted as a judgment that the cited study is, in fact, value neutral. Instead, descriptive studies have an interest in appearing value neutral.

Three Characters Argue About Interests

Many culture researchers prefer to be silent, or at least subtle, about their interests, in accord with my grandmother's advice to refrain from talking about politics (or religion) in public. Such silence and indirection does a disservice, of course, to those who want to understand more fully how interests affect the development of theory and research. Fortunately, those three professors whom we left arguing a few pages back are unusually outspoken about their interest orientations. Also, because this is an informal conversation, they express their views more frankly, and perhaps more extremely, than they would in a scholarly publication. As you will hear as we eavesdrop, these professors combine theoretical orientations and interests in the ways we observe most often in the cultural literature. The integration scholar prefers work done in the managerial interest, the differentiation researcher prefers studies written in the critical interest, and the fragmentation scholar, in the descriptive tradition, does not take an explicit interest position:

Integration: The exciting thing about culture is that it is so useful to managers. When leaders offer clearly defined corporate vision statements, backed by well-articulated objectives and corporate values, they can generate enormous amounts of commitment and goodwill among employees, increasing productivity and ultimately profitability. And for a leader, there is the promise that your personal values can be reflected in corporate values, giving you a kind of (temporary) organizational immortality through the organization's culture.

Differentiation: There you go again, telling managers what they want to hear. Value homogeneity is an illusion that top executives love to believe in. Lower-level employees, if you would listen to them, would tell you a different story. Lower-level employees sometimes interpret executive rhetoric about customer satisfaction, quality, or increased productivity simply as another excuse to get them to put aside their personal values (perhaps an emphasis on the quality of relationships with coworkers or the priority of family) and work harder. Conflicts of interest between labor and management should not be ignored. There are also differences of habit and opinion, not to mention conflicts of interest, between creative people and "bean counters," between technological wizards and technophobes, etc. And women and minorities may sometimes be uncomfortable with policies and informal practices based on the values and priorities of their white male "superiors." You need to listen to difference.

Fragmentation: You both oversimplify. What one manager sees as desirable, another may abhor. And sometimes managers understand the interests of lower-level employees and take them to heart, trying to create organizations that work in their interest. And you, Professor Differentiation, see conflicts in such black-and-white terms. Sometimes interests do not congeal along such clearly defined group lines. And within each of these groups, there is much variance. There are women and minority males who think just like their white male colleagues; skin color and reproductive plumbing do not predict opinions in any straightforward way.

Integration: If you don't have people pulling together, in a common direction, how can you get people to work together as a team? A strong corporate culture provides the glue that holds people together in tough times and motivates them to pull together when a change plan needs to be implemented. Besides, everyone benefits. The key to success is strong cultural control. If management is unified, and if they are willing to repeat their messages in talk and in action, time and time again, they can create strong cultures that generate excitement, commitment, and productivity. Aren't you interested in helping managers learn how to create and control corporate cultures, so employees' working lives will be more satisfying and productive? What would you recommend that managers do? After all, if the company goes out of business, employees will lose their jobs. Mergers and acquisitions are expensive, in time and money, and they often fail because of a lack of a unified culture. Your theory of culture has got to allow for and facilitate managerial control, for the benefit of all employees. Otherwise, no practitioners and few organizational researchers will be interested.

Differentiation: Well, my students and colleagues are more interested in a theory that explains and perhaps even helps alleviate inequality than they are in a theory that perpetuates inequalities unthinkingly. What is important to any scholar is to develop a theory of culture that captures what people's everyday working lives are like, not what top management wishes they were. Scholarship is not management consulting and it is not wishful thinking. You sound like a "value engineer." I doubt value consensus can be induced and manipulated as easily as you seem to imply. In any case, culture is more than values; it includes habits, policies, material conditions of work, pay scales, and a myriad of other things that are not just fancy words. And when you speak of change, you primarily talk of planned change—planned by top management. Cultural change is more likely to be a nonplanned response to an environmental jolt or the product of long-term struggle among groups with varying degrees of power to impose and resist change. You need to pay less attention to the powerful and more attention to subordinated groups, if you really want to understand the process of cultural change. You think primarily from a top manager's point of view.

Fragmentation: Cultural change is even more complex, and less discretely punctuated, than either of you acknowledge. Yes, there are planned change programs and discrete environmental "jolts," not to mention "bottom-up" changes, but most cultural change in organizations is a process of constant flux. And the interpretations of those changes are multiple; people don't agree what change is intended, why, or even what exactly has changed. One person's change is another's stagnation. Change is a part of culture; it is culturally constructed and so its meaning lies in the eye of the beholder. Professor Integration, there is a false clarity inherent in words like "shared values" and "strong cultures"; these concepts represent an attempt to impose order on flux and deny ambiguities. Better to admit the complexity and try to understand it. Culture is not clear and top management teams don't control its trajectory. And Professor Differentiation, the world is also not clearly divided into oppressors and the oppressed; these divisions are oversimplifications that exaggerate conflict and define it in terms of clear oppositions. The world is far more ambiguous than either of you are willing to admit.

Differentiation: You, Fragmentation, sound like a belly-gazing academic, paralyzed by complexity. If we focus on ambiguity and what you call "flux," how can we ever use culture to improve the working lives of lower-level employees? Or, indeed, all employees? Get out of your ivory tower and produce some ideas we can use on the shop floor and with the clerical staff!

Integration: You talk a good game, Professor Differentiation, but what are the practical action implications of your work? In your research, you seem to do a lot of criticizing of management and a lot of detailing how various subordinated groups "suffer oppression" on the shop floor or the construction site. Every once in while, you even describe how some group resists its subordination, by little gestures that don't, in the long run, really change anything. I'm the only one here who really works to improve the lives of working men and women, and when I do it by focusing on managers rather than lower-level employees—well, that's appropriate. Managers have the power to make a difference.

This disagreement seldom takes place the way it is portrayed here—as a frank, face-to-face argument. Interests are seldom expressed so overtly. Often, scholars leave these interest preferences unstated, or indirectly alluded to in code, such as when professors decide who to promote to tenure, what dissertation topics are worthwhile, or whose work should be included in a prestigious handbook. All researchers are involved in such considerations as gatekeepers and/or someone who might be included or excluded. Therefore, we all need to be able to determine what interests are implicit in ostensibly value-neutral research.

Exploring the Intersections of Theory and Interests

Although these particular interest orientations—managerial, critical, and descriptive—correlate with particular theoretical viewpoints, none of the theoretical perspectives forces a researcher to adopt a particular stance regarding interests. These theories and interests are conceptually orthogonal dimensions of analysis, although some combinations will occur more frequently than others. To examine the interests implicit or explicit in a wide variety of cultural studies, I use two dimensions of analysis—the three theoretical perspectives and the three kinds of interests. Table 6.1 summarizes this review in a three-by-three design, with cells containing references to studies that represent intersections of each of these theoretical perspectives with each of these kinds of interests.

Table 6.1   Examples of Single-Perspective Cultural Studies Reflecting Managerial, Critical, and Descriptive Interests

Integration Studies	Differentiation Studies	Fragmentation Studies
Integration studies with managerial interests	Differentiation studies with managerial interests	Fragmentation studies with managerial interests
Deal and Kennedy (1982)	Abolafia and Kilduff	Cohen and March (1974)
Denison (1990)	(1988)	Eisenberg (1984)
Kilmann (1985)	Brunsson (1986)	Kreiner and Schultz (1995)
Kilmann, Saxton, Serpa,	Cox (1993)	McCaskey (1988)
and Associates (1985)	Martin and Siehl (1983)	Perrow (1984)
Kotter and Heskett (1992)		Risberg (1999)
O'Reilly and Tushman		Weick (1983, 1991)
(1997)		
Ott (1989)		
Ouchi and Jaeger (1978)		
Peters and Waterman		
(1982)		
Porras (1987)		
Porras and Collins (1994)		
Schein (1985)		
Trice and Beyer (1985)		
U.S. General Accounting		
Office (1992)		

(Continued)

In Table 6.1, I focus on single-perspective studies written in the managerial, critical, or descriptive interest. Studies were assigned to cells in Table 6.1 based on their predominant theoretical perspective and interest, although others may be mentioned as secondary themes. For each cell, in the following sections I try to describe at least one study in-depth so that the reader can see how interests were deciphered, sometimes from ostensibly value-neutral texts. Unfortunately, I read only English (and a little French), so I relied on studies published in or translated into English, usually in North American or European journals and books. Table 6.1 is meant as a first step toward explicating the role of interests in cultural research. The next step would be to explore interplay among the three theoretical perspectives I focus on and make the borders among these theoretical categories permeable, deconstructing the "boxes" in Table 6.1. Finally, although it is beyond the scope of this book, it would be interesting to add consideration of the interests implicit in other theories, such as aesthetic approaches, that are

Table 6.1   (Continued)

Integration Studies	Differentiation Studies	Fragmentation Studies

Integration studies with critical interests
  Foucault (1977)
  Martin and Meyerson
    (1997, 1998)
  O'Reilly (1989)
  Sewell and Wilkinson
    (1992, 1998)
  Van Maanen and Kunda
    (1989)
	Differentiation studies with critical interests
	  Alvesson and Billing
	    (1997)
	  Bartunek (1984)
	  Bartunek and Moch
	    (1991)
	  Bell, Denton, and
	    Nkomo (1993)
	  Collinson, Knights, and
	    Collinson (1990)
	  Cox and Nkomo (1990)
	  Jamison (1985)
	  Lucas (1987)
	  Marshall (1984)
	  Martin (1994)
	  Mills (1988)
	  Mills and Hatfield (1997)
	  Riley (1983)
	  Rofel (1989)
	  Rosen (1991)
	  Smircich and Morgan
	    (1982)
	  Turner (1986)
	  Van Maanen (1991)
		Fragmentation studies with critical interests
		  Alvesson (1993b)
		  Feldman (1989, 1991)
		  Grafton-Small and Linstead
		    (1995)
		  Letiche (1991)
		  Sabrosky, Thompson, and
		    McPherson (1982)
		  van Marrewijk (1996)
		  van Reine (1996)

Integration studies claiming descriptive interests
  Barley (1983)
  Martin, Feldman, Hatch,
    and Sitkin (1983)
	Differentiation studies claiming descriptive interests
	  Barley (1986)
	  Van Maanen and Kunda
	    (1989)
		Fragmentation studies claiming descriptive interests
		  Levitt and Nass (1989)
		  Meyerson (1991a)

orthogonal to the three perspectives discussed here and thereby open doors to new forms of understanding how interests affect cultural theory and research.

Integration Studies With Managerial Interests

Studies written in the managerial interest seek ways to use culture to improve the efficiency of an organization by increasing loyalty and commitment, giving employees a reason to work harder and increase productivity. In these functionalist studies, culture is viewed as helping organizations in their tasks of internal coordination and external adaptation (Schein, 1985). For example, the General Accounting Office (GAO) of the U.S. government audited the Defense Department and concluded it needed a change in its "inventory management culture." At the request of Senator John Glenn, the GAO (1992) obtained recommendations from academic experts in "changing or perpetuating" an organizational culture. The GAO chose to consult with experts who had worked primarily within the integration perspective (e.g., Terrence Deal, J. Steven Ott, Vijay Sathe, Edgar Schein, and Alan Wilkins). These experts recommended (GAO, 1992, p. 3) that the Defense Department

> display top management commitment and support for values and beliefs;
> train employees to convey and develop skills related to values and beliefs;
> develop a statement of values and beliefs;
> communicate values and beliefs to employees; and
> use a management style compatible with values and beliefs, and so on.

The values and beliefs referred to previously are not spontaneously exhibited by lower-level employees or observed in the normal course of work. Instead, these are values and beliefs of managers, relevant to the desired change in business strategy. The strategies quoted previously from the GAO report to Senator Glenn are designed to repeatedly reinforce a set of managerial values and beliefs using consistency to generate collectivity-wide consensus to new policies and practices. This is what is meant by "value engineering," a colloquial term used to describe integration studies that advocate managerial control of cultural change (e.g., Kilmann, Saxton, Serpa, & Associates, 1985; Trice & Beyer, 1985).

O'Reilly and Tushman (1997, cited in Buell, 1997) take the efficiency argument a step further. Using the hallmark characteristics of the integration perspective, such as consistency and consensus, these authors advocate managing the culture by altering formal practices and other kinds of cultural manifestations. They advise managers to foster "ambidextrous" cultures that celebrate stability, building on the capacity to adapt by making small, incremental changes while simultaneously fostering the capacity to lead revolutionary change when necessary. An ambidextrous corporate culture, they argue (as quoted in Buell, 1997), can impact a firm's profitability, either positively or negatively:

> An important part of the solution for ambidextrous firms is massive decentralization of decision making, with consistency achieved through information sharing, strong financial controls, and individual accountability. But couldn't such a scheme easily lead to fragmented strategies and operations? The answer . . . is strong social control, exercised through the corporate culture. Culture is the key both to short-term success and, if not managed correctly, long-term failure when it creates obstacles to innovation and change. (p. 7)

Many culture researchers and popular management gurus have similarly argued, in accord with the integration view, that homogeneous, tightly unified cultures can provide a key to profitability. As in the previously mentioned GAO recommendations, companies are advised to create a "strong," internally consistent culture. Such a culture is said to generate collectivity-wide consensus through strong forms of social control or more subtle means of fostering "voluntary" conformity through shared values (e.g., Deal & Kennedy, 1982; Kilmann et al., 1985; Kotter & Heskett, 1992; Ott, 1989; Ouchi & Jaeger, 1978; Ouchi & Wilkins, 1985; Porras, 1987; Porras & Collins, 1994).

Critics observe that claims of a culture-profits link are usually based on short-term studies of small numbers of companies, without adequate comparison groups. For example, *Business Week* ("Who's Excellent now?", 1984) followed up Peters and Waterman's (1982) "strong" culture companies and found that, contrary to the culture-profits hypothesis, these companies had had unexceptional profit records. Systematic studies of the culture-profits relationship are rare (e.g., Denison, 1990; Kilmann, 1985; Ouchi & Jaeger, 1978)—for good reasons. Because profitability is caused by many variables (the industry, the state of the economy, market conditions, etc.), a large sample of organizations must be studied, making in-depth examinations of so many cultures difficult if not impossible. As a result, culture is often measured relatively superficially, for example, with questionnaires that ask employees to agree or disagree with statements regarding values and practices they may have observed at work. Siehl and Martin's (1990) review of this literature concluded that the culture-profit hypothesis remains unproven because of the vast number of variables impacting

firm profitability (many unmeasured in these studies) and the shortcomings of the ways in which culture was measured. Subsequent studies
of the culture-profits hypothesis (e.g., Kotter & Heskett, 1992; Porras &
Collins, 1994) share these shortcomings.

Siehl and Martin (1990) were not sanguine about the chances that the
culture-profits hypothesis would find conclusive support. To examine
this hypothesis more thoroughly, a team of culture researchers would
have to pool time and resources in a longitudinal, multivariate study
(with many control variables) of the cultures and profitability records
of a large, systematic sample of organizations in a single industry. Siehl
and Martin referred to this approach as the "Methuselah project" in
honor of the biblical figure who lived an exceptionally long life; it would
probably not be a practical dissertation topic. Even if a strong correlation between culture and financial outcomes remained, after a research
project included all the necessary comparison groups and control variables (most notably, the noncultural variables that influence profitability, such as market conditions, business strategy, and economic conditions, etc.), this hard-earned correlation could never prove a causal
argument about profitability. The culture-profits hypothesis remains
popular for obvious reasons, but it also remains unproven, despite
heroic efforts to overcome these methodological difficulties.

Integration Studies With Critical Interests

The integration perspective easily lends itself to managerial applications. It is more difficult to imagine an integration study written from a
critical point of view. Of course, there are many studies that describe the
culture of lower-level employees with an antimanagement tone, but
either explicitly or implicitly, these studies build a contrast between two
subcultures (one managerial and the other lower rank), making them
exemplars of the differentiation perspective. To be both critical and
integrated, a study must provide an internally consistent, consensus-
generating portrait of a culture in which all is clear, deviants are punished, no subcultures coalesce, and—to make it critical—the net result
would be harmful to participants in the culture.

One possibility is Foucault's (1977) study of an ideal prison. He described an arrangement of cells and prison guard observation posts
in a "panopticon" in which every action of every prisoner (and most
guards) is constantly observable. Foucault also studied educational in-

stitutions. He (1980) described the physical arrangements of desks in classrooms and the plethora of petty rules regulating all aspects of behavior in schools (no wiggling, line up by height or first initial of last name, no gum chewing, etc.). Foucault showed how power operated through these apparently inconsequential microprocesses, creating near total conformity and an unquestioning acceptance of how things were to be done. In other words, educational institutions teach conformity through the creation of organizational cultures characterized by repetition of the same themes (consistency), creating unquestioning acceptance of demands for conformity (consensus) inside and beyond the schoolyard. In Schein's terminology, Foucault is describing the creation of basic, shared assumptions, and he is doing so in terms that are highly critical of the institutions he studies. In the panopticon study, he does not focus on differences between prisoners as a subculture and guards as a subculture, and with few exceptions he does not explore opportunities for prisoners to resist their enculturation. A similar orientation can be seen in studies that draw critical comparisons between cultures, portrayed from an integration viewpoint, and religious cults, revival meetings, and attempts to brainwash employees (e.g., O'Reilly, 1989; Van Maanen & Kunda, 1989).

Martin and Meyerson (1997, 1998) used Foucault's ideas in a study of seven of the eight highest-ranking women executives at Link.Com, a pseudonym for a large, multinational technology firm. These women coped with common problems (difficulty getting promoted; lack of adequate mentoring; their inability and unwillingness to "fit in" with their male colleagues' apparent enjoyment of bragging contests, shouting, fierce arguments, and endless competitions; feelings of isolation; salary levels lower than those of comparable men; etc.). The women tended to take individual responsibility for these difficulties, blaming themselves rather than asking what it was about the environment that caused these problems. Most of these women, most of the time, did not see that these problems could be traced to the fact that they were all working in an aggressively masculine culture. Men had created the norms, policies, and practices of this culture, and, not surprisingly, male executives were more comfortable and found it easier to succeed in this environment. Both the men and the women executives were often blind to the dynamics of gender, viewing the culture as gender neutral. Male and female employees at this company shared tacit assumptions about the culture's gender neutrality, meritocracy (the prevalence of practices that distributed promotions to the deserving), and individual responsibility (for whatever outcomes were received). The one woman who most actively worked to improve the status of women in the company was usually a lone voice; her individual efforts helped a few individuals but did not achieve lasting system change. These seven women never coalesced into a subculture, although a few developed friendships in pairs; therefore, this cannot be characterized as a differentiation study. This study illustrates how a study, conducted from the integration perspective, points to themes that were shared, even though the participants were not clearly conscious of these issues and were not explicit about them in their individual cultural descriptions. Nevertheless, the study has a critical tone. It draws on feminist theory to delineate the ways that gender works in an apparently gender-neutral culture (see also Mills, 1988) to the disadvantage of women and the advantage of men.

Ironically, despite their affinity with the goals of those who are disadvantaged in organizational hierarchies, critical integration studies seldom offer guidance to those who would change cultures in an emancipatory way (Smith, 1993). In critical integration studies, in part because of an apparent lack of subcultural bonding, resistance to the powerfully dominant culture is minimal, individual rather than collective, and sporadic—a far cry from the "can-do" orientation of the managerially oriented value engineers. Critical integration studies, however, do offer an explicit and powerful critique of the ways in which management appropriates and tries to manipulate culture for instrumental purposes to the detriment of lower-level employees (e.g., Sewell & Wilkinson, 1992, 1998).

Integration Studies Claiming Descriptive Interests

Smith (1993, p. 420) urged organizational researchers to "move away from their prescriptive underpinnings and their emphasis on changing cultures and organizations for particular ends." She also suggested moving closer to the cultural perspectives of anthropologists and sociologists, who view culture as lived experience, an integral part of organizational life, rather than a variable that might be manipulated for instrumental (or presumably exploitative?) purposes. Integrative research with descriptive interests tends to take the position that Smith advocated, often with an explicit refusal to view cultures as malleable. For example, Uttal, 1983, observed that cultures are too elusive and hidden to be accurately diagnosed, managed, or changed. Barley et al. (1988, p. 44) noted, "Culture operates as a form of normative control beyond the volition of the individual. . . . While cultures might control people, it was almost unthinkable that people could control culture."

To examine the implications of this reluctance to consider controlling cultural change in the interests of one interest group or another, it will be helpful to examine one study in depth. Barley's (1983) study of funeral directors emphasized consistency, consensus, and clarity, in accord with the integration perspective. Barley drew his data from and generalized to funeral directors only and did not attempt to discuss the viewpoints of other people who work in funeral homes, such as embalmers, hearse drivers, or those who set up chairs and move caskets. Therefore, this is an integration study of a single occupational subculture rather than a study of a larger collectivity. Although a funeral director may be the manager of staff at a funeral home, the organizational level of analysis was not the focus of this inquiry. Barley's study refrained from an overt managerial or critical tone in its descriptions of what funeral directors do and why they do it, and in this sense it can be considered as being written in a descriptive interest. In other words, this study was trying to refrain from explicit advocacy of particular interests, in part by being silent about individuals and groups who might have other points of view about funerals.

Here, the distinction between functional and interpretative research can be helpful (Schultz, 1995). Functional research treats culture as a variable, searching for causal links to outcome variables, such as employee commitment, control, and profitability, whereas interpretative work regards culture as a root metaphor—a lens for studying organizational life (Smircich, 1983b). Therefore, interpretative work will be more likely to be written in the descriptive interest. Does such work escape functionalism and attain value neutrality? If we are intent on finding a hidden instrumental focus, we could argue that Barley (1983), for example, emphasized how the funeral director sought to create an illusion of life in the midst of death to have a "successful" funeral without excessive outbursts of emotion. These are functional objectives. Barley precluded the critical examination of these objectives by refusing to explore the viewpoints of those who might object to the funeral director's emphasis on the illusion of life, such as the bereaved, other employees at the funeral home, or perhaps those who contemplate their own death. Insofar as a funeral director is a manager, of funeral participants if not of funeral home employees, this can be described as a study conducted in the managerial interest. We cannot resolve the value neutrality dispute here, but it does seem fair to say that most studies written in the descriptive interest can, if analyzed deeply enough, be seen to contain the seeds of other, particular interests.

Differentiation Studies With Managerial Interests

Differentiation studies, written in the managerial interest, delineate the subcultural lines of cleavage in an organization and refrain from criticizing management. Such studies do not urge the erasure of subcultural differences but, rather, seek to preserve difference and encourage different ways to achieve managerial objectives, such as commitment, productivity, performance, or organizational survival. For example, Martin and Siehl (1983) describe how the dominant culture of General Motors (GM) emphasized deference to authority, fitting in, and demonstrating loyalty. Martin and Siehl then analyze how Vice President John DeLorean created a counterculture in his division of GM that directly challenged the values of the dominant culture. For example, DeLorean discouraged deference to authority, even his own, and role modeled how divisional employees could deviate, within carefully calibrated limits, from the dominant culture's norms—for example, regarding dress codes:

> GM's dress norms . . . required a dark suit, a light shirt, and a muted tie. This was a slightly more liberal version of the famous IBM dress code that required a dark suit, a sparkling white shirt, and a narrow blue or black tie. . . . [In contrast] DeLorean's dark suits had a continental cut. His shirts were off-white with wide collars. His ties were suitably muted, but wider than the GM norm. His deviations were fashionable [for the time], but they represented only a slight variation on the executive norms of the dominant culture. (pp. 57, 61)

DeLorean also used formal practices to reinforce these alternative values. For example, he gave pay bonuses to those who resisted demands for unquestioning loyalty, especially when their resistance resulted in better divisional sales. In this way, DeLorean led a balancing act, deviating in some ways while continuing to give priority to the dominant culture's emphasis on selling more cars, maximizing profits, and controlling employees. Martin and Siehl have written a managerial account; the deviance in DeLorean's division substitutes one form of managerial control (that of the dominant culture) for another (that of the manager of the counterculture) without ever challenging managerial dominance over subordinates or the primacy of the corporation's financial goals.

In a more complex example of a managerially oriented differentiation approach, Brunsson (1986, p. 166) demonstrated how various "feeder cultures," constituencies external to the organizational cultures being studied, created pressures to do many things at once: "For example, companies are required, by powerful counterparts, not only to make high profits but also to provide many jobs, good employment conditions, and little pollution." According to Brunsson (p. 171), organizations respond to these demands by developing internal differentiation (internal subcultures that share the values of particular external constituencies) and encouraging inconsistencies across cultural manifestations: "Organizations may reflect inconsistent norms by systematically creating inconsistencies between talk, decisions, and products. They can talk in consistence with one group of norms, decide according to another, and produce according to a third." These inconsistencies mask the ways in which the organization's culture deviates from management's rhetorical promises to their external constituencies. This is a form of "organizational hypocrisy" that facilitates public perception that managers are meeting the conflicting external demands on the culture. This example of a differentiation managerial study is more complex than the DeLorean study because in Brunsson's studies (1986, 1988, 1989) the variety of responses to these conflicting pressures cannot always and easily be seen as in the managerial interest. It is perhaps not surprising that differentiation studies that emphasize inconsistent cultural interpretations would be inconsistent in other ways as well. In general, the inconsistencies Brunsson describes seem to make members of these cultures less able to act, and therefore, paradoxically, their organizations are more apt to survive (Brunsson, 1986). Another differentiation account, written from a managerial interest, is provided by Abolafia and Kilduff (1988). In some senses, especially when he argues for the positive effects of diversity in organizations, Cox (1993) offers a managerial approach to cultural differentiation that is nonetheless sensitive to differing views of minority and majority members.

Differentiation Studies With Critical Interests

Most critical differentiation accounts focus on conflicts of interest between classes, as enacted within an organization—for example, be-

tween labor and management. Jaggar (1983) explained cogently why
managers might prefer the legitimation implications of an integration
view and why lower-ranking employees might seek a more critical differentiation perspective:

> Because their class position insulates them from the suffering of the
> oppressed, many members of the ruling class are likely to be convinced by
> their own ideology; either they fail to perceive the suffering of the oppressed
> or they believe it is freely chosen, deserved, or inevitable. They experience
> the current organization of society as basically satisfactory and so they ac-
> cept the interpretation of reality that justifies that system of organization.
> They encounter little in their daily lives that conflicts with that interpreta-
> tion. Oppressed groups, by contrast, suffer directly from the system that
> oppresses them. . . . The pervasiveness, intensity, and relentlessness of their
> suffering constantly push oppressed groups toward a realization that some-
> thing is wrong with the prevailing social order. Their pain provides them
> with a motivation for finding out what is wrong, for criticizing accepted
> interpretations of reality, and for developing new and less distorted ways of
> understanding the world. These new systems of conceptualization will re-
> flect the interests and values of the oppressed groups and so constitute a repre-
> sentation of reality from an alternative to the dominant standpoint. (p. 370)

Most critical studies of cultures in organizations refrain from using
neo-Marxist phrases such as the interests of the "ruling class," but they
do point without equivocation to whose interests are being served, and
not served, in attempts to engineer values and manage cultural change,
as Turner (1986) explained:

> The dedication and quasi-religious commitment which the new manager
> seeks to instill into his employees sometimes sits a little oddly with the
> nature of the company goal: It may be inspiring to hear of sales staff risking
> their lives in a snowstorm to ensure that the company goal of regular delivery
> of supplies is maintained, but when the reader learns that the product is a
> high-salt, high-calorie junk food, doubts about whether some of this shin-
> ing dedication is perhaps misplaced begin to arise. (p. 108)

Empirical studies also fit within this tradition of cultural research.
For example, Smircich and Morgan (1982) described how the president
and the staff of a large insurance company had conflicting interpretations of a new management initiative:

For the president, [the initiative] sought to define the situation in a way that created a high priority, future-oriented program. . . . [He stressed] the relative success of [the initiative] in getting rid of the backlog of work. For the staff, [the initiative was] . . . the act of a manager who was afraid to confront the real issues, who insisted on seeing the organization as a team, whereas the reality was that of a poorly managed group characterized by narrow self-interest, and noncooperation at anything but a surface level. (p. 267)

Whereas Smircich and Morgan focused on a top executive, Van Maanen (1991) described tensions between first-line supervisors and ride operators at Disneyland as follows:

Supervisors in Tomorrowland are, for example, famous for their penchant of hiding in the bushes above the submarine caves, timing the arrivals and departures of the supposedly fully loaded boats making their 8½-minute cruise under the polar icecaps. That they might also catch a submarine captain furtively enjoying a cigarette (or worse) while inside the conning tower (his upper body out of view of the crowd on the vessel) might just make a supervisor's day—and unmake the employee's. In short, supervisors, if not foremen, are regarded by ride operators as sneaks and tricksters, out to get them and representative of the dark side of park life. (p. 61)

Differentiation studies written from a critical perspective often follow gender and race to find fault lines in the apparent unity of a dominant culture (e.g., Alvesson & Billing, 1997; Bell, Denton, & Nkomo, 1993; Collinson, Knights, & Collinson, 1990; Cox & Nkomo, 1990; Marshall, 1984; Martin, 1994; Mills, 1988; Mills & Hatfield, 1997). Siehl (1984), for example, found that the humor of male oil refinery workers was often targeted at minorities who had, under recent affirmative action policies, infiltrated their ranks. Women, for example, were likely to find raw eggs broken into their hard hats. Similarly, in Bartunek and Moch's (1991) study of the Quality of Working Life intervention, male machinists used humor to express their reactions to women who worked in the packing department:

One story, told on several occasions in our presence, compared machinists' tool boxes with women's purses. One machinist would tell another that he owned his own work tools. He then would ask how much the other machinist thought these tools were worth. After several low estimates, the first machinist would proclaim that his work tools were worth several thousand dollars. The machinists would then change roles, the second asking the first how much his tools were worth. After the second machinist proclaimed the true value of his tools, the first machinist would ask the second, "And what do the silly bitches carry in their purses?" Together the two participants would call out "Kotex!" Those listening, usually under the windows of the cafeteria, would smile and nod approval. (p. 112)

As the previous examples illustrate, critical differentiation studies examine interactions among representatives of subcultures, with an eye for inequalities. Whether they simply describe conflicts of interest or move into the language of domination and oppression, these scholars go beyond a neutral description of the status quo. For the most part, these are empirical studies or reviews of empirical studies; these authors usually do not take it on themselves to examine alternatives to current arrangements that might come to exist, in accord with the emancipatory goals of many critical studies. These critical differentiation studies, however, do communicate clearly their normative position that current arrangements work to the advantage of the advantaged while ignoring or perpetuating the subordination of those lower in the hierarchy. Other studies with critical differentiation elements include Bartunek (1984), Jamison (1985), Lucas (1987), Mills (1988), Riley (1983), Rofel (1989), and Rosen (1991).

Differentiation Studies Claiming Descriptive Interests

These studies describe inconsistencies, subcultural differences, and the channeling of ambiguity without adopting an explicit managerial or critical vantage point. For example, Barley (1986) contrasted the subcultures of technologists and radiologists, representing their different points of view in some detail, while refraining from explicitly considering the ways in which these differences might further or impede the goals of hospital administrators. Of course, any conflict consumes employees' time and energy, and any conflict could have implications for the efficient functioning of a task-oriented group, but these concerns were not Barley's primary focus. Similarly, Van Maanen and Kunda (1989) described, without exploring managerial or critical implications, the viewpoints of two kinds of engineers:

Of most interest is the contrast between hardware and software engineers. The former are described by the latter as narrow, concrete, speak "technologese" rather than English, undereducated, hard drinking, interested only in the blood and guts of the machine. The latter are seen by the former as undisciplined, loose, airy-fairy types, dreamers, talkers not doers. (pp. 73-74)

Fragmentation Studies With Managerial Interests

Fragmentation studies view ambiguity as the essence of a culture, and they allow for multiple interpretations of the meaning of that ambiguity. Some fragmentation studies written in the managerial interest take a normative position: that ambiguity has negative effects, for example, on organizational efficiency. An extreme example is provided by Weick's (1991) description of a crash at the airport in Tenerife. The fog was thick, one flight crew was in a rush because of flight time regulations, and it was difficult to turn large airplanes (such as the two KLM and Pan American 747 jets waiting for instructions) on the narrow runways. Normal levels of ambiguity at the airport were intensified, according to Weick, for many reasons:

> Controllers at Tenerife were also under pressure because they were short-handed, they did not often handle 747s, they had no ground radar, the centerline lights on the runway were not operating, they were working in English which was a less familiar second language, and their normal routines for routing planes on a takeoff and landing were disrupted because they had planes parked in areas they would normally use to execute these routines. (p. 122)

Contrary to claims that fragmentation studies are of interest only to belly-gazing academics, Weick described the important practical consequences of this ambiguity in terms that would deeply concern airport managers (not to mention airline travelers):

> After the KLM plane made the 180 degree turn at the end of the takeoff runway, rather than hold as instructed, they started moving and reported, "We are now at takeoff." Neither the air traffic controllers nor the Pan Am crew were certain what this ambiguous phrase meant, but Pan Am restated to controllers that they would report when they were clear of the takeoff runway, a communique heard inside the KLM cockpit. When the pilot of the

KLM flight was asked by the engineer, "Is he not clear then, that Pan Am?," the pilot replied "Yes" and there was no further conversation. (pp. 118-120)

Thirteen seconds later, the KLM jet tried to take off. It hit the Pan Am aircraft in its path, and 583 people were killed.

Other fragmentation studies written in the managerial interest take a normative position that ambiguity has positive effects, for example, on organizational performance. In his study of the nuclear accident at Three Mile Island, Perrow (1984) explored the dire consequences of not having enough ambiguity. Perrow concluded that such accidents were "normal," in the sense of being unavoidable in such a centralized, tightly coupled system in which automatic warnings and employee training could not predict or counteract the kinds of complex faults that were most likely to occur. Asked by management to recommend a better approach, Perrow suggested reliance on ambiguous systems: decentralized, loosely coupled, simple to fix, and simple to understand, with none of the complex negative synergies that can cause complex failures in more integrated plans. It seems reasonable to presume that such acceptance of ambiguity would have similar positive effects, from a managerial viewpoint, in the cultures of companies in the Internet industry, in which constant change is a given, the company has virtual employees who work from home or elsewhere, conventional job descriptions are often obsolete within weeks, and valuation of the company's worth (or stock) is highly volatile.

Fragmentation studies with a managerial interest, which allow for multiple interpretations of the meanings of ambiguities, include Cohen and March's (1974) study of college presidents, McCaskey's (1988) examination of the managerial uses of ambiguity, Risberg's (1999) study of mergers and acquisitions, and Kreiner and Schultz's (1995) study of cross-national technology development projects. Fragmentation studies with a more pronounced managerial interest, but with less exploration of multiple interpretations of ambiguity, include Weick's (1983) description of universities and Eisenberg's (1984) study of the political usefulness of ambiguity.

Fragmentation Studies With Critical Interests

Feldman (1989, 1991) studied policy analysts at the U.S. Department of Energy. These analysts were supposed to focus on well-defined problems and produce reports outlining solutions that could be used by politicians. Instead, Feldman (1991, pp. 154-155) concluded, "Analyses do not lead to positions that are promoted through politics. Analyses do not even support positions chosen by politicians. Analyses are being produced, but it is not clear for what or for whom." A similarly critical view is evident in Sabrosky, Thompson, and McPherson's (1982) description of the U.S. military as an "organized anarchy" in which decisions were (contrary to the rhetoric of military commanders) not made in a disciplined, rational fashion:

> Information still becomes lost in the system, directed to the wrong people, or both. Similarly, during a crisis, the wrong people may try to solve a problem because of their prowess at bureaucratic gamesmanship, or the right people (because of mismanagement or oversight) may be overlooked or sent elsewhere. (p. 142)

Perhaps with a cynical smile, Sabrosky et al. quoted Rourke's (1972) conclusion that such apparent fragmentation may, in certain circumstances, have some positive effects:

> The existence of bureaucratic inertia, fragmentation of authority, and relative lack of efficiency may be a collective blessing in disguise in certain circumstances. Elected and appointed officials are not always paragons of intelligence and wisdom, and the inability of the military bureaucracy to execute rapidly some radical (or reactionary) executive proposals could have some inadvertent utility. (p. 52)

"Inadvertent utility" is a far cry from value engineering; the critical orientation of each of these accounts is easy to see. Letiche (1991) focused on a consulting intervention in the product design division of a multinational corporation. Working from the fragmentation perspective, and using postmodern approaches, Letiche critiqued the traditional, modernist conceptions of management and organizational behavior that underlay the design of the consulting intervention. Letiche offered an iconoclastic way of reinterpreting the intervention that focused on multiple interpretations of ambiguities. Employees found this approach to be quite practical because it seemed closer to the ways in which they experienced organizational life and because it offered new ways of viewing employee control and performance improvement. Other critical fragmentation studies include Alvesson (1993b), Grafton-Small and Linstead (1995), van Marrewijk (1996), and van Reine (1996).

Fragmentation Studies Claiming Descriptive Interests

Studies fitting this description are perhaps the most common type of fragmentation research. Some fragmentation studies written in the descriptive interest explicitly strive to attain a balance between critical and managerial interests. For example, Meyerson (1991a) described social work in the following ambivalent terms:

> One social worker mentioned that being "the elbow in the system's side" was her professional responsibility. Others viewed themselves as the patient's advocate. However, because social workers work in organizations where they have little formal power, they must comply with and even become exemplars of the system to gain legitimacy. . . . Thus, although some social workers believed that their role was to change or resist the status quo, they also believed that to be effective they must work within and thereby perpetuate the status quo. Social workers must simultaneously advance reforms and preclude them, critique the medical model (of social work, which defines the client as a patient with problems to be "cured") and enforce it. (p. 140)

This avoidance of either a managerial or a critical bias (focusing instead on ambivalence regarding both alternatives) is echoed in Levitt and Nass's (1989) study of textbook publishing. The editors were unclear about fundamental issues such as how to judge the quality of a book or predict whether it (or they personally) would succeed or fail:

> The editors consistently described their work in gambling terms, such as "a lottery with bad odds," "an attempt to hedge one's bets," or "a crapshoot." . . . The sense of confusion experienced by participants inhabiting this haphazard and unpredictable universe is captured in the following comment from a sociology editor: "Editors can become schizophrenic. You think a manuscript is good and it doesn't make money. Then you get a manuscript that you think is bad, and it makes money—but not always." (pp. 191-192)

In these descriptive fragmentation studies, action implications of work were unclear, making any attempt to manage these cultures a preordained exercise in futility.

Affinities Between Particular
Theories and Particular Interests

To conclude this odyssey through the nine cells of Table 6.1, I consider how Lee Iacocca (1984) described his early days as CEO of Chrysler Corporation. Not surprisingly, Iacocca wrote in the managerial interest. To the extent that he saw ambiguity and differentiation, he was not pleased:

> I watched in amazement as executives with coffee cups in their hands kept opening the door and walking right through the president's office. Right away I knew the place was in a state of anarchy. Chrysler needed a dose of order and discipline—right away. . . . Chrysler didn't really function like a company at all. Chrysler in 1978 was like Italy in the 1860s—the company consisted of a cluster of little duchies, each run by a prima donna. It was a bunch of mini-empires, with nobody giving a damn about what anyone else was doing. What I found at Chrysler were 35 vice presidents, each with his own turf. There was no real committee set up, no cement in the organizational chart, no system of meetings to get people talking to each other. I couldn't believe, for example, that the guy running the engineering department wasn't in constant touch with his counterpart in manufacturing. But that's how it was. Everybody worked independently. I took one look at that system and I almost threw up. That's when I knew I was in really deep trouble. (p. 152)

Iacocca reacted to this "anarchy" with normatively explicit disdain (a fragmentation view written in the managerial interest). He went on to offer an action plan that exemplified an integration view, again written in the managerial interest. He advocated firing people, rather than value engineering, to achieve the homogeneity and unity he desired:

> There was so much to do and so little time! I had to eliminate the 35 little duchies. I had to bring some cohesion and unity into the company. I had to get rid of the many people who didn't know what they were doing. I had to replace them by finding guys with experience who could move fast. And I had to install a system of financial controls as quickly as possible. (p. 165)

In contrast to Iacocca's distaste for ambiguity, scholars working from a fragmentation viewpoint usually see ambiguity as the inescapable, and sometimes even desirable, essence of the cultures they study. For example, Becker (1982) critiques the simplicities and order of the integration perspective and the way it defines culture as excluding ambiguity. Instead, Becker argues that the fragmentation view is most appropriate for describing the complexities of contemporary life in industrialized societies:

> Many anthropologists have a kind of temperamental preference for the simplicity, order, and predictability of less complicated societies, in which everyone knows what everyone else is supposed to do, and in which there is a "design for living." If you share that preference, then you can turn culture into an honorific term by denying it to those social arrangements which do not "deserve" it, thereby making a disguised moral judgment about those ways of life. But that leaves a good part of modern life . . . out of the cultural sphere altogether. (p. 518)

This discussion of the nine cells of Table 6.1 does not capture the fact that some combinations of these theoretical perspectives and interests are more common than others. The integration view has an affinity for managerial interests, particularly because many integration studies endorse the idea that managers can control and change cultures. Differentiation studies tend to take a critical perspective, in part because the existence of subcultures and the possibility of subcultural conflict open the door to consideration of power, inequality, and the dynamics of domination. Fragmentation studies tend to be descriptive because the clarities of both the managerial and the critical vantage points tend to be incongruent with the complexities of a study that focuses on multiple interpretations of almost everything. Because of these affinities between theoretical perspectives and interests, some cells in Table 6.1 remain empty or nearly empty, indicating a kind of research that is rare. For example, differentiation studies conducted from a managerial perspective and integration studies that take a critical perspective are difficult to find. There are relatively few fragmentation studies of any kind, although this kind of research is rapidly becoming more common, particularly in international studies of culture in which a conceptual framework for thinking about contradictions and complexities is essential (e.g., Koot, Sabelis, & Ybema, 1996; Sackmann, 1997). A culture researcher searching for underresearched topics could consider Table 6.1 a map to unexplored territory and, possibly, the research equivalent of buried treasure. A more cautious or cynical researcher might ask,

"Are there good reasons why researchers have avoided an exploration of this particular intersection of theory and interests? If so, how will I deal with these anticipated difficulties?" With this question, I return to the dilemmas that began this chapter.

Resolving Theory and Interest Dilemmas

Each cultural researcher has to find an individually appropriate resolution to the theory and interest dilemmas that are the focus of Chapters 5 and 6:

What theoretical perspective will I endorse? One of the three viewpoints described in these pages? Some combination of these three perspectives? One of the other theoretical approaches? Some theoretical view not mentioned in this book? Or will I vary in the theories I use, depending on the objectives of a particular study?

How might I reinterpret the findings of a given study to take into account its interest orientation? What is my personal orientation regarding interests? Do I believe that value-neutral research can offer a mirror image of some objective reality, not serving any interest group more than another? If I believe value-neutral theory is not possible, whose interests do I want to serve in my cultural research? How might my interest preferences affect my research in nonobvious ways? What blind spots should I anticipate?

When making these interest decisions, first and foremost, you and I have our own values to consider. We each need to consider who we are, and who we are becoming, as we search for our research voices and identities. These issues are important and difficult, even for seasoned researchers. Most researchers want to do research that reflects their own beliefs and priorities; otherwise, why be a researcher in a world in which other occupations may offer greater rewards on many dimensions?

Shortcomings of My Own Resolutions to the Dilemmas

At this point, it may be appropriate to engage in some reflexivity, outline how I have resolved these theory and interest dilemmas, and share how I view the advantages and disadvantages of my choices (which might, in some ways, be similar to your choices). As you know by now, I advocate use of all three theoretical perspectives in a single study. With regard to interests, my choice has changed. Early in my career, I wrote in the managerial interest (e.g., Martin, Feldman, Hatch, & Sitkin, 1983; Martin & Siehl, 1983; Siehl & Martin, 1984). During these years, I lost awareness of the extent to which my writing was reflecting the managerial orientations of most of my colleagues at the business school at which I work, perhaps because I was untenured (for a bit of an autobiography on this issue, see Martin [in press]). Occasionally, I have also written in an ostensibly value-neutral, descriptive style (e.g., Martin, 1982; Martin & Meyerson, 1988), reflecting my neopositivist training. Recently, I have made a conscious effort to make my cultural work more congruent with my personal political values; it now has an explicit critical tone (e.g., Martin, 1990a, 1994; Martin & Frost, 1996; Martin, Knopoff, & Beckman, 1998; Martin & Meyerson, 1998).

Because I do not believe that value neutrality is possible, I believe that cultural researchers should reflect openly, in print, about their own interests and how these have affected the research being described. Just as I believe it is not possible to do value-neutral research, however, I also believe that, even with the best intentions of evenhandedness, balance is a goal that is very difficult if not impossible to achieve. Therefore, in this book I have tried for balance, most of the time, but also explicitly revealed my own preferences. There is a different approach. Cultural researchers can attempt to represent both managerial and critical viewpoints even-handedly, within the bounds of a single study. Such evenhanded interest portrayals have an advantage: They tend to disarm some critics who would advocate the use of a particular, single-interest orientation.

Of course, there are drawbacks to trying to represent both managerial and critical interests even-handedly. The argument will be complex, the text long, and advocates of particular theoretical perspectives or interest orientations may regard your work as a "sellout" trying to please everyone. It also may be more difficult to build a distinctive reputation if you include multiple theoretical perspectives and multiple interest orientations, for reasons Strober (1990) described well:

> Scholars often make their mark in academia by becoming associated with a particular position and entering into frequent doctrinal debates while stubbornly defending their particular orthodoxy. After all, to the extent that academics measure their own and others' success by the number of entries in

the citation index, it pays not necessarily to be right, but to be clearly identi-fied with a particular position and then to be attacked and to counterattack frequently. Academics often gain little from seeking commonalities among denominations or building bridges across sets. (p. 238)

No matter how many theoretical perspectives or interests you include, there will always be someone who criticizes your work for excluding others. Studies that encompass multiple theories (such as the three-perspective approach) may be criticized by journal editors and review-ers who believe that, in any given context, one theory can be pitted against another to determine which provides "the most accurate" description. Such traditional empiricists may say, "How can all three perspectives be valid? Isn't one going to offer a more accurate descrip-tion than the others? Isn't a 'hidden' perspective just another name for a perspective that has received less empirical support in a given context?" Regarding this and other issues, I hope that Chapters 5 and 6 have pre-pared you to respond. No matter which perspective(s) and which in-terest(s) you choose, Chapters 5 and 6 should help you anticipate what objections are likely to be raised, giving you time to consider how you will respond. In other words, at the next argument among the three pro-fessors, what will your contribution to the conversation be?

Pragmatic Considerations

Deciding what you think about these theory and interest dilemmas is not just a question of personal preferences. Despite our desires to have our scholarship remain steadfastly in touch with our personal values, it is important to acknowledge that institutional constraints create pressures that push us toward particular theoretical viewpoints and in-terests. Researchers who share similar interests and theoretical perspec-tives tend to cluster in particular departments and types of institutions. Critical cultural scholars may find it more congenial to work in a labor relations institute or in some sociology departments, particularly if they prefer to work in the differentiation tradition. Managerially ori-ented cultural researchers may prefer a business school, in which their students may particularly appreciate the integration perspective. Cul-tural researchers who work with a descriptive interest and/or who pre-fer the fragmentation viewpoint may find their homes in relatively tol-erant, interdisciplinary settings.

There are good reasons for these clustering dynamics in university settings. After all, similarity is a key to attraction and liking. In addition, people with power tend to select others who are similar to them in demographic characteristics as well as attitudes, training, and interests—a process Kanter (1977) referred to as "homosocial reproduction." People seek out others who share their beliefs so that on "safe territory" interest issues can be discussed more openly and more deeply. Such "safe" discussion forums can be harshly characterized as preaching to the converted or, more sympathetically, seen as a much-needed place to discuss difficult problems with those who are already "on board" regarding basic issues. If you work in an institutional context in which your colleagues do not share your interest preferences, you may have to go outside that institution to find collaborators and critics who will help your work. This was my solution when I was untenured and first became interested in culture. A virtual "dream department" of generous culture scholars throughout the country critiqued my drafts and helped me determine what kind of cultural research I wanted to do.

I hope this detailed description of differences—indeed, fierce arguments—among cultural researchers will not discourage people new to this area. Organizational culture research is a remarkably open field of inquiry, in part because of these differences. This is why so many innovative approaches to organizational studies, such as qualitative methods, postmodern scholarship, discourse analysis, and critical theories, have found a home of sorts within the cultural domain. This is, in part, what makes cultural research today so exciting. It is noteworthy that many of the studies cited in this book, and in this chapter in particular, were done by researchers new to the study of culture—in many cases by researchers just completing their PhDs. There are risks in doing cultural research; certainly, what the next important study will be and the "right" way to do cultural research are not clear. This uncertainty, however, means that creative work and new ways of thinking will be particularly welcome in this domain of research.

A Preview of Coming Attractions

Part I of this book has focused primarily on cultural research that has already been done. In Part II, this focus will shift to skills needed to do cultural research. Chapter 7 discusses the qualitative and quantitative methods debates as they have surfaced in cultural research, and it offers several hybrid methods that bridge these debates in useful and sometimes novel ways. Chapter 7 has been written to be useful (in combination with Chapter 2, which outlines the basic disagreements that underlie the culture wars) to all kinds of organizational scholars, not just those who do cultural research. Chapter 8 brings theory, interest, and methods choices together—where the rubber hits the road—in a series of hypothetical reviews of real culture studies. These reviews should help you anticipate and deal with criticisms of cultural research, no matter which theory and interest choices are made. Chapter 9 offers a variety of innovative ways to write about cultural data—innovative approaches that are more fully responsive to some of the epistemological, methodological, theoretical, and political complications that have been discussed. And so it goes . . .

Notes

1. The goal of technical research is to develop generalized knowledge that can be stated in terms of an abstract rule. This is sometimes referred to as nomothetic research, and it often takes the form of stating a theory, formulating a hypothesis, testing that hypothesis, and then revising the theory if necessary. So far, this sounds quite familiar because it describes well most of the quantitative research in organizational studies, particularly that done within a positivist or neopositivist tradition.

2. Research conducted in the practical interest is the kind of hermeneutic work done by historians, literary critics, and some anthropologists. The goal of this kind of research is to study meaning in a specific context as it evolves in interaction. The focus is on socially constructed meaning as it evolves within a specific material base. Therefore, the focus is not on an objectified construct. Instead, the objective is to develop ideographic knowledge that is not generalizable to other contexts and not stated in abstract terms. When a study shares these objectives but is written with more critical goals (e.g., Kondo, 1990), it is, according to Habermas (1971), written in the emancipatory rather than the "practical" interest.

3. Whereas technical research seeks generalizable theory regarding the invariant rules of social action, emancipatory research focuses on ideologically frozen relations of dependence that can in principle be transformed.

II

Doing Cultural Research

7   To Count or Not to Count?

It's not worth it to go round the world to count the cats in Zanzibar.
—Quotation attributed to Thoreau by Geertz
(1973, p. 16)

Is Geertz (or Thoreau) objecting to counting? Why? Is he being serious, or is he objecting to trivial research? Does he mean that all quantitative research is trivial, or is it that culture cannot be understood with quantitative methods? Is it that orientation toward cats is only one aspect of culture in Zanzibar so that cultural researchers should not focus only on cats if they want to understand the entire culture in Zanzibar? Is it that the numbers of cats represent a relatively superficial, material aspect of culture that says little about the subjective meanings of cats to the people of Zanzibar? Is it that counting is a research activity that can be done by anybody, even a cultural outsider, whereas a deeper understanding would require trying to understand how a cultural insider thinks? Perhaps cat counts, an admittedly limited measure, could be done in a variety of cultures and used as one of several indicators of a culture's orientation toward its natural environment; cultures could then be compared, at least on this one dimension. Is such comparison or generalization across cultures a worthwhile, even necessary, activity for cultural scholars, or is deep cultural knowledge necessarily context specific?

205

In these ways, this one quotation about cats in Zanzibar alludes to all
the fundamental disputes discussed in Chapter 2:

Is culture an objective or subjective phenomenon?

Can culture be understood from an outsider or etic point of view, or does an insider
    or emic viewpoint generate more insight?

Is generalization (or at least comparisons across cultures) desirable and possible, or
    is cultural understanding necessarily context specific?

Is breadth of cultural manifestations studied unimportant or essential?

Is depth of interpretation the single most important indicator of the quality of a cul-
    tural study, or are other quality criteria (such as appropriate comparisons)
    more essential?

As in the quotation about counting cats, when cultural researchers discuss methods choices, these discussions often deteriorate into dogmatic
debates about the worth (or worthlessness) of qualitative or quantitative approaches. Such debates are ultimately inconclusive because any
method has its strengths and inescapable limitations. It is more important to understand the advantages and disadvantages of any methods
choice, and to do this the disputes that underlie methods debates, re-
phrased previously as questions, need to be exposed and discussed in an
open-minded way (Martin, 1990b).

In the 1960s, quantitative and qualitative methods were increasingly
conceptualized as a dichotomy, even in methods courses. Such dichot-
omization obscures the variation within and between these two categories. Qualitative methods include long-term ethnographies based on
participant observation, short-term qualitative studies, textual and discourse analysis, and analyses of visual artifacts such as photographs.
Quantitative research includes experiments, surveys, archival studies of
large data sets, and content analysis (counts of categories of qualitative
data). When the qualitative-quantitative distinction is phrased as a
dichotomy, it often excludes or marginalizes useful intermediate approaches—hybrid methods that span the quantitative-qualitative divide, such as content analysis. (See Table 7.1 for examples of all these
methods choices.) This chapter uses the questions listed previously to
discuss the strengths and limitations of a wide range of quantitative,
qualitative, and hybrid methods for studying cultures.

Table 7.1   Examples of Quantitative, Qualitative, and Hybrid Studies of Culture

Quantitative	*Qualitative*
Barley, Meyer, and Gash (1988)	Barley (1983)
Cooke and Rousseau (1988)	Bartunek (1984)
Denison (1990)	Boland and Hoffman (1983)
Friedman (1983)	Botti (1995)
Hong, Morris, Chiu, and Benet-Martinez	Brunsson (1985)
(2000)	Collinson (1992)
Kilmann, Saxton, Serpa, and Associates	Gregory (1983)
(1985)	Kanter (1977)
Martin (1982)	Kondo (1990)
Rousseau (1990b)	Kunda (1992)
	Martin, Feldman, Hatch, and Sitkin
Hybrid	(1983)
Barley (1986)	Martin, Knopoff, and Beckman (1998)
Deacon, Bryman, and Fenton (1998)	Martin and Meyerson (1998)
Gundry and Rousseau (1994)	Meyerson (1994)
Martin, Sitkin, and Boehm (1985)	Mills (1995)
Martin, Su, and Beckman (1997)	Mills and Hatfield (1997)
Ouchi (1981)	Pettigrew (1979, 1985b)
Roberts, Rousseau, and LaPorte (1994)	Rosen (1985, 1991)
Rousseau (1990b)	Weick (1991)
Siehl and Martin (1984)	Wilmott and Knights (1995)
Stevenson and Bartunek (1996)	Young (1989)

Methodological Dilemmas in Cultural Research: An Overview

Cultural researchers face methods dilemmas, whether they acknowledge them or not, each time they design or evaluate a study. What kind of study design will give answers to the questions of interest? What are the theoretical implications of that method choice? How might this method choice be criticized? Which of these criticisms are valid, and which should be disputed? These methodological dilemmas are the focus of this chapter and Chapter 8. This chapter begins by examining the strengths and limitations inherent in a wide range of methods choices, focusing on such issues as objectivity and subjectivity, etic and emic views, generalization and context-specific knowledge, focus and breadth, and depth of understanding. These issues explain, in part, how and why criteria for evaluating the adequacy of qualitative research differ from those used to assess quantitative work. A brief history of methods preferences in the field of organizational studies helps show why the methods debates among cultural researchers have been particularly fierce. This chapter explains how particular methods choices tend to cluster, in particular patterns, with the theoretical perspectives and interests discussed in Chapters 4 through 6. Exceptions to these patterns—that is, studies that offer novel combinations of manifestations, theories, interests, and methods choices—are explored, with citations to and summaries of illustrative studies. The qualitative-quantitative dichotomy is challenged and deconstructed, introducing various innovative, hybrid ways of combining methods.

In writing this chapter, I tried to be responsive to the fact that readers have varied kinds of methodological expertise. Some readers will want to skip over familiar material, whereas others may want to supplement this chapter's brief overviews with the cited references. I hope that you will devote most attention to those methods that are least familiar. Even if you have no intention of ever using a particular method, you may well be called on to evaluate (cultural or noncultural) research that does so. The citations in this chapter include introductory and more advanced material, so labeled. The advanced readings should be sufficient to prepare a researcher who wants to try an unfamiliar method, although a collaborator or adviser with expertise in this method will of course be helpful. One key limitation of this chapter merits note. Postmodernism questions the worth of all the methods choices discussed in this chapter and is careful to avoid any language that implies that an objective reality can be accurately portrayed using any kind of empirical data. Discussion of the postmodern challenge, and the ways in which it can be used to question and broaden cultural theory and research, will be provided in Chapter 9. Finally, in offering guidance to resolving methods dilemmas, I provide a range of issues to consider—from epistemological to pragmatic. I think it is important to discuss all these considerations, but they should not be confused with each other.

One Study Idea, Three Methods

Answers to the questions raised at the start of this chapter (and discussed in more detail in Chapter 2, this volume) tend to cluster. Cultural research that tries to assess culture as objectively as possible tends also to take an etic viewpoint, seek generalization, be willing to sacrifice breadth of understanding for careful and replicable measures of fewer cultural manifestations, and place relatively less emphasis on depth of understanding. More often than not, these studies tend to be quantitative, although interesting exceptions occur. For example, a few qualitative researchers seek generalizations based on systematic comparisons within and across qualitative case studies (in accord with the advice of Blau, 1965). A contrasting cluster of cultural studies defines culture subjectively and is more likely to seek an emic viewpoint, eschew generalization, and value breadth as well as depth of understanding. These studies are mostly qualitative and often take the form of short- or long-term ethnographies. In between these extremes, as will be shown, are a variety of hybrid methods that combine quantitative and qualitative approaches in useful and innovative ways.

For example, suppose you wanted to do a study regarding the following question: As a multinational corporation expands into different national cultures, how much should it standardize, trying to reproduce the headquarter's culture in each locale, and how much should it try to adapt to local cultural norms? Note that this question is phrased in a way that it could be addressed from any of the three theoretical perspectives, all of them, or none of them. Here, I focus on how this question might be addressed using quantitative, ethnographic, and hybrid methods.

A quantitative study might sample 100 multinational corporations using a standardized questionnaire measure of culture (e.g., Cooke & Rousseau, 1988; Denison, 1990; Kilmann, Saxton, Serpa, & Associates, 1985; Xenikou & Furnham, 1996) to ask random samples of managers to report on the behavioral norms that characterize working relationships in their locale. A similar questionnaire could be filled out by a random sample of managers working at the headquarters of each company. Statistical analyses could be used to assess the similarity of each locale's culture to the headquarters' culture, as measured by responses to the questionnaire. Corporations could be classified as "standardizers" (that tend to replicate the headquarters' culture in most locales) and "local adapters" (whose local company cultures tend to reflect the norms of the surrounding nation or geographical region). Perhaps even the profitability of standardizers and local adapters could be compared, controlling for relevant factors such as industry, recent economic conditions, and the competitiveness of the market. Perhaps standardization is more possible in some countries than others, depending on the similarity of the national cultures of the headquarters and local offices. Note the managerial and functionalist focus of this study. Its sampling procedures include only managers or professionals, although implicitly the claim is made to represent the culture of all the employees in the locale or at the headquarters. It also reflects the managerial interest in seeking links to profitability. Not all quantitative studies of culture will have these attributes (objectivity, etic, seeking theoretical generalization, narrow focus, and not much depth) and this managerial focus, but many do.

In contrast, an ethnographer might enter a single organization and stay 1 or 2 years as a participant-observer, working closely with people at all levels of the organization. With the help of a few well-chosen, articulate, and insightful informants, multiple interpretations of a wide range of cultural manifestations could be gathered. These interpretations would be relatively deep, given the length of time the researcher had been involved and his or her increasing acceptance as "one of us" by coworkers. For example, the ethnographer might find that local managers conform to headquarters' policies only when they have to do so—when headquarters staff can observe their behavior. In other instances, local staff might play on the ambiguities inherent in headquarters' policies, adapting them with subtlety to fit local customs. In this way, the study could show how appearances of standardization can mask local adaptive strategies. Such an ethnographic study would focus more on subjective, emic, context-specific knowledge, based on a breadth of cultural manifestations and a depth of understanding. Such a study could reflect a managerial, critical, or descriptive interest, although managerially oriented ethnographies are rare. Again, this cluster of positions on the disputed questions discussed in Chapter 2 is not necessary, but it does commonly occur.

A hybrid approach could measure the degree of standardization versus local adaptation by observing and collecting transcripts of employee group meetings and then content analyzing the discourse. This would have the advantage of letting employees' work-related talk, rather than the wording of researchers' questionnaire items, determine the cultural content viewed as relevant to a particular setting. Such a content analysis, however, would not be strictly emic because researchers would determine the content analysis categories based on how they interpreted what employees said. A content analysis of meeting transcripts would be quantitative: a count of the types of concerns employees raised at meetings in the headquarters and the local offices. The degree of overlap between headquarters and various local offices would be a measure of the degree of cultural standardization in a multinational corporation. Perhaps some local cultures would be more standardized (more similar to those of headquarters) than others, and qualitative data from hours of observing meetings could offer explanations for these disparities.

Because of the time-consuming nature of observation and the customized content analysis of the meeting transcripts, this hybrid study would probably have to focus on a small sample of multinational corporations and only a few locales in each. Ideally, the corporations and locales would be chosen to control for such factors as industry and national location, making a mix of context-specific and theoretical generalizations possible. Generalizations about degrees of standardization across corporations would nevertheless be problematic because the cultural content in each corporation, and potentially each locale, would differ. Such a hybrid study is not easily classified as objective or subjective, emic or etic, narrowly focused or broad, or superficial or in-depth. It could be managerial, focusing on opinions of only managerial and professional staff and seeking correlations between the degree of standardization and measures of profitability, or it could sample employee meetings at all levels, refrain from seeking correlations to measures of firm performance, and reflect either a critical or ostensibly descriptive interest.

Some historical background about the field of organizational studies, and the place of cultural studies within that field, will clarify the need for a broad approach to methods—one that encompasses qualitative, quantitative, and hybrid approaches.

A Brief History of Methods Preferences

Methods preferences are often defended in a heated fashion, in part because it is difficult to "teach old dogs new tricks" and in part because differing epistemological assumptions sometimes (e.g., Burrell & Morgan, 1979)—but not always—underlie methods choices. When a researcher advocates one method, researchers preferring other methods may believe that the worth of their training and life's work has been challenged. These methods disputes are less overt in some disciplines because members share a particular methodological preference. In the interdisciplinary domain of organizational studies, in contrast, methods debates are more common and more overt. Many organizational researchers are trained primarily in a single method, usually experimental, survey, or archival data analysis. Other organizational researchers may have the opportunity to learn a wider range of methods (e.g., in some sociology or political science departments and some organizational behavior groups in business schools and industrial relations departments). Even in these places, however, specialization in a particular type of method is usually an option. A few organizational researchers have the opportunity to learn both quantitative and ethnographic methods (e.g., in the industrial engineering department at Stanford's School of Engineering and in some business schools, such as Michigan and the Sloan School at Massachusetts Institute of Technology). Organizational researchers who are initially trained in such a wide range of methods are rare, although cultural researchers often learn both at some point in their careers.

Although organizational researchers collectively use a very wide range of methods, some methods are more widely accepted than others. In the mid-1960s, qualitative case studies of organizations were heavily criticized, whereas quantitative studies of large numbers of organizations proliferated (Blau, 1965). Since then, organizational studies have come to be dominated by quantitative methods, primarily surveys, archival data analyses, and experiments (e.g., Podsakoff & Dalton, 1987; Stablein, 1996). For example, there was a steady increase in the proportion of quantitative papers accepted by *Administrative Science Quarterly* between 1959 and 1979 (Daft, 1980, p. 629). During these years, qualitative researchers often had a difficult time getting their work published and accepted, particularly in the United States. In other countries, particularly in parts of Europe and Japan, qualitative research had a stronger foothold. Outside the United States, a widespread critique of the shortcomings of positivism, coupled with a fascination with the insights of critical theory and postmodernism, created a groundswell of dissatisfaction with tendencies to assume that quantitative methods are superior (more rigorous and "scientific") than qualitative approaches or to use neopositivist language ("these data prove that . . . "). This dissatisfaction stemmed, in part, from differing answers to the questions with which this chapter began.

In the 1980s, an international renaissance of interest in cultural studies of organizations occurred. Organizational culture research attracted many researchers who found quantitative methods to be narrow, dry, and restrictive of the kinds of ideas that could be explored. They hoped cultural research would offer a place where the strengths of qualitative methods would be appreciated and legitimated. Indeed, this is what has happened. In part because of the contributions of cultural researchers, qualitative methods became more broadly accepted in the 1980s and 1990s. Several new organizational journals are open to qualitative contributions (e.g., *Organizational Science, Organization, Journal of Management Inquiry,* and *Studies in Cultures, Organizations, and Societies*). In addition, there has been a noticeable increase in the number of qualitative studies accepted by older, more established journals. In the United States, however, quantitative methods still predominate outside the domain of cultural research.

This renaissance of interest in cultures in organizations in the 1980s produced hundreds of studies (e.g., Barley, Meyer, & Gash, 1988). Many of these cultural studies were empirical and of these, most used qualitative methods. Culture provided a theoretical excuse for relegitimating a wide range of qualitative approaches, including long-term participant-observation, short-term qualitative studies (sometimes referred to fondly as "smash and grab" ethnographies [Sutton, 1994]), conversational analysis, studies of visual symbolism, and narratives. At this time, quantitative culture studies were few and far between, although their numbers began to increase in the late 1980s and early 1990s. Some welcomed this quantitative development (e.g., "At long last, we are getting high-quality, scientific studies of culture" or "Now finally we can use cultural variables to predict performance, commitment, and turnover"). Others dismissed quantitative culture studies as a sign of the deterioration of the richness and innovation of early cultural research (e.g., "Such studies reify culture and reduce its rich complexity to a set of adjectives or a self-report questionnaire"). Many cultural researchers believed that quantitative studies of culture signified assimilation to the

mainstream methodological norms of the organizational field, destroying the distinctiveness and the creativity of the cultural domain and
making it "dominant, but dead" (Calás & Smircich, 1987).

Rationale for a Multimethod Approach

The negative repercussions of the methods debates continue to affect
cultural studies today. Because most organizational researchers were
trained in either quantitative or qualitative methods, what seems obvious and fundamental to one person may seem highly debatable, if not
dubious, to someone with different training and preferences. Therefore, no matter what method is chosen, a cultural researcher submitting
a study to a journal is quite likely to get reviews from advocates of differing methodological assumptions, sometimes making acceptance rates
low and the process of revision very difficult for editors as well as researchers. This is particularly a problem for qualitative researchers
submitting papers to journals for which the norms support a format
(literature review followed by hypotheses, methods description with
sampling procedures, data, discussion, and empirically derived theoretical conclusions) that is derived from and geared to the presentation of
quantitative data (as is the case in many mainstream U.S. journals).
These publication difficulties pose a major obstacle for cultural researchers, discouraging some from entering or remaining in the field
and making it difficult for those who do remain to find and judge the
value of prior research. Such norms also inhibit the development of cultural knowledge; if a person only appreciates, reads, and uses insights
from cultural studies using familiar methods, much of what has been
done will go unused, at least by many cultural scholars.

In this chapter, I attempt to address these problems by presenting all
sides of the methods disputes. This chapter encourages all of us to learn
enough about the methods we do not use so that (at a minimum) we can
judge, knowledgeably, whether a given study is executed well, even if the
methods used are not the ones we personally prefer. If we could learn
enough, and put aside our methods preferences long enough, to absorb
what can be gleaned from well-executed studies that use a wide variety
of methods, cultural theory and research would be enhanced (for a related multimethods argument, see Rousseau, 1990a). Methods preferences and choice of theoretical perspectives are often correlated in ways
discussed later. Therefore, if we read cultural research conducted with

methods and theoretical approaches other than our own, we might stop ignoring empirical findings based in different theoretical traditions. Theory development might cross the theoretical boundaries discussed in earlier chapters. Each of us would have more to draw on when generating new ideas and deciding what we think we know so far. Theory development would be more complex, and we would have a broader range of empirical findings to draw on. For example, studies conducted from one theoretical perspective would be encouraged to acknowledge that when cultural researchers are willing to look for cultural characteristics congruent with other perspectives, such characteristics are easy to find.

In addition, if we were open to various methods and theoretical views of culture, we would be more open-minded and well-informed when reviewing or assessing reviews of research done by methods with which we are relatively unfamiliar. Finally, a few researchers might be tempted to learn unfamiliar methods to match their research projects and methods choices in a more informed and variable fashion. Others might choose not to use multiple methods in their own research, but they could read and learn enough to draw on (and cite) studies conducted with differing approaches. Of course, some diehards will continue to read, work, and value only research conducted in accord with their own methods preferences, but their choices and opinions might continue to generate debate that is fruitful for other researchers.

Methodological Criteria for Assessing the Quality of an Empirical Culture Study

A cultural researcher, or even a reader of the cultural literature, needs to know how to assess the quality of studies that use a wide range of methods. The hybrid study discussed previously indicates that a quantitative versus qualitative dichotomy is too oversimplified (e.g., Cook & Reichardt, 1979) to be of use in describing the range of methods used in organizational studies of culture. Criteria for assessing the quality of studies, however, often retain this dichotomy and reflect the standards of either highly quantitative or purely qualitative methodology. Therefore, it is important to approach criteria for assessing quality with knowledgeable skepticism. Even familiar criteria may be based on assumptions that, for a given study, may not be appropriate.

Criteria used to judge the quality of cultural studies include attributes familiar to quantitative researchers, such as large sample size, random or systematic sample-selection procedures, reliability, and validity. Other criteria, more familiar to qualitative researchers, include
breadth and richness of a thick description, the depth of emic understanding, and the reflexivity (self-insight) with which the researcher
discusses the inevitable complications of his or her own attempts to understand the culture as an insider would. For all these criteria, the following discussion dissects the relevant underlying assumptions to provide a basis for deciding whether these criteria are appropriate when
judging the quality of a given study.

Before proceeding, it may be helpful to state why all this emphasis on
assessing quality is being condoned. First, at all stages of the research
process, like it or not, the quality of research is constantly being assessed—in thesis orals, in journal reviews, and simply when we read and
decide whether to consider a study's conclusions credible. Assessment
judgments are inevitable, and if cultural researchers are going to become willing to read the work done by researchers using unfamiliar
methods, it is essential to learn how to assess the quality of unfamiliar
methodological approaches. Undiscerning researchers have often dismissed whole classes of studies using such statements as "Qualitative
research is just a journalistic description of an 'n' of one" or "Quantitative studies of culture are so superficial they are worthless" (Martin,
1990b). We all need to know how to make more careful, knowledgeable
quality judgments, appropriate for the given methods of a study, even if
we choose to specialize in a single method in our own research.

Sample Adequacy and Its Effects

If a study is seeking to build empirically based generalizations, quantitative methodologists would argue that it is crucially important that a
sample be representative of the population that is being generalized
about. Also, if statistics are to be used, it is essential that the sample size
be sufficient to assess probabilities within reasonable confidence intervals. In a cultural study, these issues surface at two levels of analysis: the
collectivity and the individual.

At the collectivity level, the researcher has to decide how to select one
or more cultural contexts to study, such as work teams, organizations,
industries, or nations. If generalization is the goal, then the collectivity

or collectivities selected should be representative of a category, and generalizations outside that category should be eschewed. Therefore, for example, a study of computer companies should not be generalized to other industries, or a study of U.S. companies should not be generalized to companies in other countries—sins of overreaching that are commonly committed. Ideally, a large, randomly selected sample of collectivities should be studied if statistically based generalizations are to be made. If it is too difficult or time-consuming to study a large number of collectivities, then systematic sampling of a few carefully chosen comparison sites can be done. In small sample comparison studies, cultures can be studied with somewhat more breadth (multiple manifestations) and depth, but the sample size (of collectivities, not individuals), of course, is much smaller. The smaller the sample, the more easily it can be criticized as being nonrepresentative of any larger category, making it difficult to build empirically based theoretical generalizations. Because it is very difficult to study large numbers of culture with depth and breadth, however, large samples of collectivities ($N > 50$) are rare in the cultural literature; when they occur, these studies are usually criticized for having narrow and superficial measures of culture.

If a study does not seek generalization, then a collectivity can be chosen for a variety of reasons, including selecting a site because it is unusual. For example, organizations are sometimes selected because they exhibit innovative and admirable "best practices" (e.g., Peters & Waterman, 1982). Other organizational sites are studied because they claim to have found an unusual way of doing business (e.g., Martin, Knopoff, & Beckman's [1998] study of The Body Shop International, a large corporation known for its commitments to social change and environmental protection). Study of unusual sites can be justified by claims that such studies illustrate the limits of what is possible. In such cases, study of a statistical outlier is appropriate, provided that evidence is given supporting the choice (e.g., that the site is unusual in regard to a particular dimension). Sometimes, however, studies of distinctive collectivities claim to make links to organizational success or productivity, as did the Peters and Waterman study. To support such claims, appropriate comparison data are essential; for example, with regard to Peters and Waterman's study, we need to know if the same "best practices" were used in companies that failed, and if comparable success was also attained in companies that refrained from using these "best practices." More often than not, including my study of The Body Shop, some kinds of generalizations are made, albeit with some circumspection. Such generalizations need to be examined critically. It is not valid, however, to criticize a study because the study site is somehow unrepresentative of a larger class if no generalizations to that larger class are made.

Sampling procedures regarding individuals within collectivities can be similarly assessed. If a study were seeking generalization about the culture of an entire collectivity, then quantitative researchers would argue that it is essential that all members of that collectivity (the "population") or a random, stratified sample of those individuals be studied. If statistical procedures are used, a sufficiently large sample of individuals is needed. A few studies of cultures in organizations use large, random, stratified samples of individuals across all levels of a hierarchy (e.g., Martin, Sitkin, & Boehm, 1985; Ouchi, 1981; Rousseau, 1990a). Also, some qualitative studies of relatively small collectivities apparently (details are sometimes not given) study all, or almost all, members (e.g., McDonald, 1991; Meyerson, 1991a; Young, 1989).

Unfortunately, many culture studies examine a subset of members (usually drawn from particular strata of a collectivity) and then generalize, without sufficient empirical evidence, to the collectivity as a whole. For example, in his early studies, Hofstede (1980) and colleagues sampled male managers who worked for a single multinational company in a variety of nations and generalized—across class, gender, and organizational boundaries—to draw conclusions about national cultures. It is possible, even likely, that nonsampled women, manual laborers, rural residents, and employees of smaller, less prestigious firms in each country might have had quite different views of their respective national cultures. (Subsequent studies by Hofstede, Neuijen, Ohayv, & Sanders [1990] modified this sampling procedure, but many of the sample limitations were not removed and their effects were not fully explored.) These studies exemplify the most common error regarding sampling procedure: the part-whole fallacy—drawing conclusions about an entire collectivity on the basis of studies of only one strata of the population.

In organizational cultural studies, the part studied is usually a sample of managers and professionals, whose views are then said to be generally shared by other members of the whole organization (this was the case in the first of the three studies of the degree of cultural standardization in multinational corporations; see also the large number of managerially oriented culture studies cited in Barley, Meyer, & Gash [1988]). Because this error is very common, it is one of the most important methodological flaws in studies of cultures in organizations. Justifications for this sampling procedure include the assertion that such high-status people have the power to make a difference for others in the company. Sometimes, researchers will also assert that generalizing from a managerial sample is justified if these people "are knowledgeable about" and "really care" about the well-being of their subordinates. Would those same researchers be willing to generalize to an entire company based on the opinions of lower-status employees who were "knowledgeable about" and "really cared" about the well-being of their managers? Such generalizations ignore the possibility of conflicts of interest and fail to test their assumptions of homogeneity across nonsampled groups. Such a sampling procedure assumes, in accord with the integration perspective, that a culture is homogeneous across levels of a hierarchy. Many differentiation and fragmentation studies suggest that such assumptions about homogeneity are justified rarely and only in relation to a subset of the relevant content themes. In addition, even within a hierarchical level, such as top managers, distinctive subcultures may exist (e.g., managers with marketing vs. engineering backgrounds and male vs. female managers), making part-whole sampling procedures likely to be a source of bias and therefore erroneous generalizations.

In developing quantitative measures of culture, it will be essential not to reduce the conceptual complexity of the three theoretical perspectives to simple statistical measures. For example, Early (1995) equated the three perspectives with statistical terms. For example, the integration view could be represented as a mean response with low variance, the differentiation perspective as a significant between-group difference or an interaction term, and fragmentation as within-cell error variance. These analogies trivialize the complexity of these theoretical viewpoints. Cultures have many manifestations, with multiple, often conflicting meanings associated with them; these meanings and manifestations cannot simply be measured the same way and somehow averaged. For example, a survey question may be understood differently by members of different subcultures. The relationships among subcultures (enhancing, conflicting, and orthogonal) and the possibilities of a divided self with multiple, overlapping subcultural identities are keys to understanding the differentiation view of culture. These conceptual components of the differentiation view are not captured in the statistics described previously. A survey question may have multiple interpretations because its meaning is ambiguous. Fragmentation is certainly more than error variance because it requires deep analysis of contradictions, irreconcilable paradoxes, ironies, ambivalence, and the multiplicity of interpretations inherent in all these kinds of ambiguity (e.g., Feldman, 1989; Kondo, 1990; Kunda, 1992; Meyerson, 1991b). Thus, answers to a single survey question may, in effect, be drawn from several populations of different questions, depending on how the question is understood; therefore, concepts such as mean, variance, and error term do not have their customary, statistical meanings. Quantitative measures of culture need to take such complications into account.

Qualitative studies raise a different set of quality concerns when sample adequacy is considered. Because people who are similar in some way to the researcher, such as being of the same sex or a similar age, may be willing to talk more openly, these reasons for choosing informants can lead to biased sampling (a variant of what Kanter [1977] called "homosocial reproduction"). Those cultural members willing to confide in a researcher may also be somewhat marginalized members of a culture, with their marginal status giving them distance that enhances their insight and their willingness to speak openly with a researcher. It is important to acknowledge that most informants are not representative of a "modal" member of the culture, and that therefore the views of some types of cultural members may be misunderstood or underexplored, another version of the part-whole fallacy. Should a researcher rely on marginalized informants to suggest other informants, this larger "snowball" sample might be far from representative. Feminist anthropologists, for example, have argued that most early anthropologists were men, working primarily with male informants, and so they may have created incomplete and possibly misleading portraits of the cultures they studied (e.g., Rosaldo & Lamphere, 1974).

This biased sampling criticism, however, may be inappropriately applying a quantitative evaluation criterion to qualitative work. Most ethnographers are not seeking generalization or even representativeness; their priority is to gain a deep, emic understanding of a culture. Whereas quantitative study participants are sampled so that they will be statistically representative of some larger population, qualitative study participants, called informants, are chosen because of their experience, lucidity, and willingness to talk openly with the researcher. Although most ethnographers do not choose informants because of their representativeness, ethnographers do seek generalization in the limited sense that a sample of informants is said to provide insight into an entire culture. This implies that biased sampling of informants is suspect. If depth of emic insight is paramount, however, then a researcher has to be able to develop a personally close, confiding relationship with informants, and this simply may not be possible with any randomly selected individual. Some researchers argue that it is impossible to eliminate the sampling bias in qualitative research by adhering to more systematic sampling procedures because it is essential to have rapport with informants to elicit information from them. Other researchers argue that it is advisable to diversify a sample in a qualitative study or work with demographically different collaborators so that informants are drawn from all segments of the collectivity being studied. In the sampling domain, at the individual level, it seems to me that qualitative researchers might well pay more attention to the issues of individual representativeness so stressed by quantitative methodologists. Generalization to all members of a culture, when one has primarily studied members of one subgroup, seems suspect to me; maybe this conclusion, however, is simply evidence of bias due to my own quantitative training.

Bias Avoidance in Quantitative Cultural Studies

Quantitative methods texts emphasize the importance of a variety of measures of reliability and validity (for careful and clear explanations, see Runkel & McGrath [1972] and Cook & Campbell [1979]). These are various ways of seeking objectivity, in the sense of a two-way correspondence between a measure and what is being measured. For example, inter-item and test-retest reliabilities assess the extent to which a measure would produce the same results if some items were eliminated or if the measure were administered at different points in time. Internal and external validity measures assess the extent to which a measure actually measures the concept of interest. Reliability and validity measures are designed to eliminate, as far as is humanly possible, any effect of the individual beliefs or assumptions of the researcher so that any other researcher using the same methods would produce the same results.

These criteria for assessing quality are appropriate for evaluating quantitative cultural research. For example, experimental laboratory methods have been modified to create a kind of culture in a laboratory setting. Zucker (1977) created an "office" culture in an experimental setting, showing how norms persist even when individual group members exit and others enter. Other experimental researchers have refrained from creating new cultures in laboratory settings, preferring instead to activate preexisting cultural identities. For example, Hong, Morris, Chiu, and Benet-Martinez (2000) challenge the integrationist ideas that culture functions as a highly integrated, internally consistent, consensual, and static knowledge structure that, steadily and unwaveringly, is available to provide cultural interpretations of whatever is experienced. In contrast, Hong et al. offer a dynamic, social constructivist approach that argues that individual-level perceptions and judgments are influenced more by domain-specific knowledge structures that, through "frame switching," move in and out of activation. Hong and colleagues tested these ideas by studying bicultural individuals (e.g., Hong Kong students exposed to Western teaching or students studying in the United States having had extensive living experience in both the United States and China). It was hypothesized that these individuals would be capable of "flip-flopping" across their two cultural identities, depending on the context in which they found themselves.

The methods used in Hong et al.'s (2000) hybrid study are worth examining in-depth because they are innovative and because it is easy to anticipate how advocates of the qualitative and quantitative approaches might view the strengths and weaknesses of this study in different terms. To test their ideas, Hong et al. primed these bicultural study participants by exposing them to either U.S. or Chinese cultural icons, such as Marilyn Monroe or a Chinese opera singer. The participants were then asked, in ostensibly unrelated tasks, to interpret the behaviors of social animals (e.g., fish swimming in a group, with one fish behind or ahead of the rest). (Because such interpretations usually have anthropomorphic overtones, this task elicits participants' preconceptions about social relations.) When a cultural theory was potentially available (because both frameworks were in these bicultural participants), highly accessible (due to the priming of one of the two cultural frameworks), and highly applicable to the task, participants offered interpretations congruent with the primed cultural framework. For example, when explaining the behavior of the fish swimming ahead of the group, bicultural participants in the American (individualistic) cultural priming condition made more internal ("the deviant fish is the leader") and fewer external attributions than did similar participants in the (collectivist) Chinese culture priming condition. This series of studies supports the contention that culture consists of a series of discrete, concrete knowledge structures that are activated when primed and otherwise uninvolved in the interpretation of experience.[1]

A quantitative researcher might observe that this study design retains an ability to build theory based on solid quantitative data and experimental control. It also resolves a key problem in some prior experimental cultural research—the difficulty of operationalizing cultural identity. One cannot randomly assign individuals to national cultures. Usually, study participants from one country of origin—for example, Chinese undergraduates or managers—are contrasted with a closely matched sample of participants from a second country, creating two quasi-experimental conditions that are conceptualized as representing two entire national cultures (e.g., Markus & Kitayama, 1991; Triandis, 1989). By using priming of bicultural subjects, Hong and colleagues (2000) locate two cultural identities within an individual, allowing either to be activated and thus allowing true random assignment of subjects to experimental conditions, avoiding some of these methods problems.

By standard quantitative criteria, such as reliability, validity, and bias avoidance, the quality of Hong et al.'s (2000) study is high. Despite these strengths, this study might well be criticized by an ethnographer. Quantitative culture studies, such as that of Hong et al., often focus on abstract cultural dimensions that are etically derived by the researcher, such as individualism versus collectivism. An ethnographer might believe that such abstract dimensions bear little direct relationship to the deeper, more contextually specific modes of understanding—about both individualism and collectivism—that cultural members actually rely on in their everyday lives. A qualitative critic of this study might regret that Hong and colleagues do not attempt to study participants emically.

In addition, a qualitative critic might be worried about the narrowness with which culture is being operationalized here, with icons and an experimental task that asks participants to make causal attributions about why one fish swims ahead or behind other fish. Although Hong et al. (2000) offer a credible argument that such tasks elicit socially relevant anthropomorphic interpretations, it is a big leap from fish to everyday human behavior. (It is important to note that one study in this series does focus on human rather than fish behavior, and that other studies by these authors use different operationalizations of culture.) Nevertheless, studies of an abstract dimension, such as individualism-collectivism, do not (and do not attempt to) give us a detailed, context-specific understanding of the deep assumptions or emotions that underlie such abstract explanations. A qualitative critic of this kind of experimental research might call for a broader range of cultural manifestations with a more pragmatic or more emotional focus (everyday tasks, how people think about money, health, their physical surroundings, and stories, myths, rituals, etc.) to give a more richly textured, detailed understanding of the cultural underpinnings of everyday life. Hong et al. designed an innovative study, testing a provocative idea, but as the previous remarks suggest, its strengths may be more evident to quantitative researchers and its limitations more visible to qualitative researchers. In the cultural arena, with its multimethod audience, it is difficult to please most of the people most of the time.

Reflexivity in Qualitative Cultural Studies

When the quality of qualitative cultural studies is being assessed, quantitative evaluation criteria, such as reliability, validity, and bias avoidance, seem less easily relevant. It is not clear what such criteria mean once one has chosen a subjective, emic, depth approach to research. Therefore, quantitative researchers often do not know how to judge the quality of qualitative research. Fortunately, there has been considerable work on this subject (for a fine introduction, see Agar, 1986). Alternative criteria, such as reflexivity, are crucially important when evaluating qualitative research.

The rationale for reflexivity has been developed by ethnographers as well as feminist and postmodern theorists. These scholars have persuasively delineated a variety of ways that, even in ostensibly objective, quantitative research, the biases of a researcher can and unavoidably do influence the "results" found and the conclusions drawn. For example, feminist theorists show how the genders of researchers and cultural members affect what is experienced and how that experience is interpreted, making it clear that generalizing from one sex to another is a tricky business (e.g., Ferguson, 1993; Flax, 1990). Postmodernists delineate the ways in which two-way correspondence between a measure and what is being measured can never be attained, in part because all perceptions are shaped by prior experiences of ourselves and others (e.g., Cooper & Burrell, 1988; Moi, 1985; Weedon, 1987). From these vantage points, objectivity is an elusive target.

The response to this critique of objectivity need not be a relativist claim that "all options are equally valuable." Instead, many ethnographers, feminist theorists, and postmodernists stress the importance of researcher reflexivity—that is, the need to write in the first person ("I")—to analyze how the eye of the beholder affected what was seen. Speaking personally (as reflexivity requires), it is very difficult for me to write in this self-revealing manner because I have been trained to erase all traces of myself in my writing. To erase oneself in this manner, advocates of reflexivity would say, is to use a rhetorical means of enhancing my authority as a researcher. When the author is erased or made invisible, the text appears to represent reality directly and objectively, without bias. In contrast, much ethnography includes a detailed and open discussion about the researcher and his or her relationship (including emotions) with the people being studied. One of the best examples is Kondo's (1990) ethnography of a family-owned small business in Japan. Her openness about herself as a Japanese American female of a certain age and class background enriches the reader's understanding of the cultures she is describing.

> At first, then, as a Japanese-American I made sense to those around me as a none-too-felicitous combination of racial categories. As fieldwork progressed, however, and my linguistic and cultural skills improved, my informants seemed best able to understand me by placing me in meaningful cultural roles: daughter, guest, young woman, student, prodigal Japanese who had finally seen the light and come home. Most people preferred to treat me as a Japanese—sometimes an incomplete and unconventional Japanese, but a Japanese nonetheless. . . . That I, too, came to participate enthusiastically in this recasting of the self is a testimonial to their success in acting upon me. (pp. 13-14)

In time, however, Kondo's enthusiastic embrace of a Japanese self began to fade:

> As I glanced into the shiny metal surface of the butcher's display case, I noticed someone who looked terribly familiar: a typical young housewife, clad in slip-on sandals and the loose, cotton shift called "home wear" (homu wea), a woman walking with a characteristically Japanese bend to the knees and a sliding of the feet. Suddenly I clutched the handle of the stroller to steady myself as a wave of dizziness washed over me, for I realized I had caught a glimpse of nothing less than my own reflection. Fear that perhaps I

would never emerge from this world into which I was immersed, inserted
itself into my mind and stubbornly refused to leave, until I resolved to move
into a new apartment, to distance myself from my Japanese home and my
Japanese existence. For ultimately, this collapse of identity was a distancing
moment. It led me to emphasize the *differences* between cultures and among
various aspects of identity: researcher, student, daughter, wife, Japanese,
American, Japanese-American. (pp. 16-17)

Kondo's research focuses on the relationship between cultural identities
and the self. In the previous quotations, Kondo describes her transition
of understanding from a unified self reflective of a culture and conforming to it (characteristic of integration research) to a divided self,
reflecting various conflicting aspects of identity (more characteristic of
differentiation and fragmentation views). Her reflexivity illuminates
this theoretical transition.

Many contemporary researchers would judge the quality of a study,
particularly an ethnography, in part by its reflexivity—that is, the depth
of insight offered by the researcher into his or her own effect on and relation to the data being collected. Rather than minimizing this effect,
the researcher seeks to understand it fully—a dramatic contrast to the
objectives underlying the bias-reducing concerns of reliability and validity. Academics are prone to posturing, however. Perhaps a modest,
reflexive introduction can, in its own way, sometimes enhance the credibility of an author and thereby support his or her authority, although
ostensibly doing the opposite.

Judging Quality Differently

In addition to reflexivity, a variety of other criteria are used to evaluate qualitative research. For example, Golden-Biddle and Locke (1993)
analyze qualitative texts and conclude that the authors' preferred criteria include authenticity, plausibility, and criticality. Denzin and Lincoln
(1994) provide a helpful overview of varying opinions about how to
assess the quality of qualitative research. In addition, among the many
authors who argue that the qualitative-quantitative distinction has
been overdrawn, Nord and Connell (1998) try to develop criteria for
judging quality of research in both these traditions. They argue for nine
criteria for evaluating qualitative *and* quantitative research: precision,
plausibility, "acceptable" thought processes, inclusiveness, generality,

elegance, expansion, utility, and success in communicating. This is an interesting list. It includes some criteria similar to those of other authors (e.g., precision and plausibility), some criteria that seem to pertain more to writing than to the process of data collection (e.g., success in communicating), and others that might be debatable. Perhaps all studies need not seek inclusiveness and generality? Is there consensus about what is considered acceptable? Must all studies have practical utility? Although there are differences of opinion about how to assess the quality of research, it is clear that standards exist for both quantitative and qualitative studies. It is less clear that the same standards can be applied to research in both traditions.

Many argue that qualitative and quantitative studies cannot be evaluated using the same criteria. One reason for these different standards is that trade-offs among evaluation criteria are inevitable (McGrath, 1982) so that researchers can deliberately maximize some criteria only by accepting compromises on other quality dimensions (McGrath, Martin, & Kulka, 1982). For example, a method that is quite precise, such as an experiment, pays for that strength with weaknesses, for example, in scope (narrow) and "realism" (low external validity in some experiments). A cultural study that attains depth of understanding and breadth of cultural content probably has a small sample size of both individuals and collectivities. Given that some trade-offs among criteria are unavoidable, I argue that reviewers should understand the need for trade-offs and use different criteria for judging the quality of a study, depending on what method is being used. Unfortunately, as illustrated in the hypothetical journal reviews in Chapter 8, many reviewers do not hesitate to use criteria developed for quantitative research to assess qualitative studies and vice versa.

Hybrid Methods: Deconstructing the Qualitative Versus Quantitative Dichotomy

To further complicate the assessment of quality, many studies have deliberately attempted to bridge the qualitative versus quantitative dichotomy through the use of hybrid methods. Such methods involve the deliberate, and often innovative, combination of qualitative and quantitative techniques within a single study design, seeking a design that shares some of the strengths of both. For example, ethnographers might collect both qualitative and quantitative data simply to have more context-specific data. Unobtrusive measures and systematic sampling procedures have been integrated into the traditionally qualitative case study approach (e.g., Campbell & Stanley, 1966; Van Maanen, Dabbs, & Faulkner, 1982; Webb, Campbell, Schwartz, & Sechrest, 1966/1972). Barley's (1986) study of two occupational subcultures explored radiologists' and technicians' differing reactions to the introduction of a technical innovation using clever quantitative measures to supplement qualitative data. Other hybrid studies of culture include Gundry and Rousseau's (1994) use of critical incidents to communicate culture to newcomers and Roberts, Rousseau, and LaPorte's (1994) study of high-reliability cultures on nuclear aircraft carriers.

Although some hybrid studies seek to generate generalizable rather than context-specific research results, other hybrid studies are tailored to fit a particular context, aiming to develop rich context-specific insights rather than generalizations. Many of these studies use content analysis to transform qualitative data into quantitative data (e.g., Martin et al., 1983; Martin et al., 1985; Siehl & Martin, 1984; Stevenson & Bartunek, 1996). Some of these studies use a two-stage design, with a short period of qualitative data collection used to develop quantitative culture measures that are context specific. For example, Siehl and Martin studied the enculturation process using a "building-block" model to represent the order in which new employees would learn cultural knowledge. At Time 1, shortly after being hired, new employees were familiar with top management's espoused values (measured on Likert scales) and could correctly define much of the company's technical jargon and some of its more value-laden jargon (a vocabulary test format was used). At Time 1, these new employees were aware of a subset of four of the company's most commonly known organizational stories but did not interpret the meanings of those stories in the same way as employees who had worked at the company for a longer period of time. The new employees at Time 1 showed virtually no evidence of tacit knowledge (measured by being able to fill in words randomly blacked out in a memo from the company's president). When asked a series of questions about the company's values-in-use (derived from analysis of the company's actual practices), these new employees showed no pro-company biases in errors made. At Time 2, after a few months on the job, they had fully mastered almost all these elements of cultural knowledge, including making pro-company errors when assessing actual company practices. Only the last to be acquired, tacit knowledge measures showed room for improvement. These context-specific ways of measuring cultural knowledge could easily be adapted for the study of cultural learning in other sites to determine if the same building-block model of socialization processes is relevant. Perhaps certain kinds of formal socialization and training programs would change the rate of some types of learning.

Hybrid methods are controversial. Some have argued that such methodological hybrids inevitably highlight the weaknesses of their contributing components (e.g., Runkel & McGrath, 1972). Others have disagreed, arguing that hybrid combinations can generate insights otherwise unavailable (Martin, 1990b). Here, two context-specific hybrid studies are described and assessed to illustrate the range of insights and the types of criticisms that hybrid studies can generate.

Martin, Su, and Beckman (1997) surveyed virtually all members of a small publishing company. They asked subjects to complete a questionnaire, called the "Value Audit," that contained both quantitative and open-ended questions. The items focused on a series of "corporate values" developed by a top management team and revised by all members of the firm. The questionnaire repeated the "official" definition of each value and then asked subjects to translate the value into their own words. These personal interpretations of each value were then coded quantitatively to determine whether they were similar for most of the organizational members (in accord with the integration perspective), shared only by distinctive subcultures (in accord with the differentiation perspective), or viewed as having a variety of ambiguous meanings (in accord with the fragmentation viewpoint). In addition, employees' attitudes toward the values were also quantitatively assessed with 9-point Likert scales (e.g., "To what extent do you personally approve of the value?" and "Is the company committed to the value?"). Most important, study participants were also asked to write down stories about occasions during which particular values were or were not translated into action. These stories were quantitatively content analyzed to determine whether the corporate rhetoric was indeed translated into action and whether the employees approved or disapproved of the results.

This mix of qualitative and quantitative measures produced results congruent with a three-perspective view of the culture. According to the Likert scale averages, the vast majority of the employees viewed the company and themselves personally as strongly committed to translating these values into action. A more detailed analysis of the quantitative data, however, revealed a more complex picture. This apparent organization-wide value consensus was supplemented by higher and lower commitment, specific to particular values, in some subcultures. There was considerable ambiguity about the meanings, desirability, and enactment of a few values, such as valuing diversity, being innovative, and finding a good work-family balance. The stories employees chose to tell, and the variety of ways in which they translated the values into their own words, reflected the ambiguities involved in interpreting these highly abstract values. In addition, many employees were ambivalent about the company's ability to translate this value rhetoric into action. Because of the ways that the more open-ended measures tapped ambiguities and ambivalence, formal and informal feedback suggested that the results of this study seemed, in employees' eyes, to represent the company's culture well.

This study demonstrates that all three of the theoretical perspectives discussed in Chapters 4 and 5 can be studied using a hybrid approach. It is noteworthy, and also characteristic of other studies, that the most etic and quantitative measures, the Likert scales, produced the strongest evidence of organization-wide consensus about commitment to the values. Going beyond an oversimplified equation of the three theoretical perspectives with statistical measures of means, variance, and error terms, this study also used more qualitative measures, some of which were then transformed into quantitative data through content analysis. Importantly, the qualitative and hybrid content analysis measures revealed more evidence of subcultural formation, dissent, conflict, and ambiguity, congruent with the differentiation and fragmentation perspectives—not otherwise detectable. As is often the case with hybrid methods, this study met some of the criteria usually used for assessing the quality of quantitative studies, such as its sampling procedure (all-inclusive) and sample size (a very high response rate) as well as its inter-item reliability and inter-judge coding reliability scores. Like many qualitative studies, however, this research produced a portrait of this context rather than generalizable insights about culture in organizations. This hybrid "value audit" is easy to administer and score and could easily be adapted, using a different set of values, for use in other contexts (I am happy to share copies of this instrument). A "value audit" could focus on the values spontaneously expressed by a cross section of employees rather than on the espoused corporate values generated by a management team.

Hybrid methods entail inevitable trade-offs. This hybrid study was less successful in meeting criteria for assessing qualitative research. Most notably, the level of depth of understanding of the culture was relatively superficial. No long-term participant observation was used, and the values being studied were created by top management rather than elicited from employees or observed by researchers. This kind of questionnaire may have been a relatively ineffective way to tap the articulate and often emotional reactions of some employees, particularly those who felt constrained by their lack of ability to "write well" in response to the open-ended questions about value meanings and stories. In addition, despite guarantees of anonymity, some may have been reluctant to be frank in their reactions. Therefore, this was an etic study that focused on only two manifestations ("corporate" values and stories), attaining only a little breadth and modest depth of insight. The study's ability to meet quantitative criteria for assessing quality was purchased at a price that most ethnographers would say was too steep.

Another example of a hybrid approach, using only the integration perspective, examined the culture of a highly successful electronics company. Ouchi (1981) and colleagues used a random, stratified sample of employees, combining traditional quantitative survey methods, observations, and interviews to build a multimethod portrait of the company's culture. Interviews and surveys were structured combining closed and open-ended questions, both quantitative and qualitative. This study examined a wide range of cultural manifestations (including stories and rituals as well as formal and informal policies, dress, decor, and physical arrangements). This study comes closer than most to meeting quantitative criteria for quality while addressing the need for breadth and richly detailed description.

Trade-offs are inevitable in any method choice. Some criticisms of this study could be made on the basis of criteria usually used for assessing quantitative studies. For example, although this study produced context-specific information, some generalizations were also made, notably that companies with similar "theory Z" cultures would have high levels of commitment, productivity, and profitability. Such generalizations could be challenged on the basis of the nonrepresentative sampling of the small number of organizations studied in depth.

Although appropriate comparison groups of organizations were studied, these data were far less comprehensive and many control variables
necessary for a full examination of cultural effects on firm performance
were not measured.

Applying criteria usually used for assessing qualitative research, this
study could be criticized as being relatively superficial. The observation
periods for each work team were relatively short, as were interviews.
The research team maintained an etic stance, and its formal dress (suits,
like the dress of managers) and status (mostly white, male Stanford
University faculty and students) may have created distance, making it
particularly difficult for young managers and lower-status employees to
give frank responses. As in the Martin et al. (1997) study described previously, it is difficult to know if these methodological shortcomings
contributed to the findings of high organization-wide commitment.
Furthermore, both studies have little reflexivity on the part of the authors. Both Martin (as a member of the publishing company's board of
directors) and Ouchi (having served as a consultant to the company he
studied) may well have identified more with the company's top management than with its lower-level employees. As these examples indicate, hybrid studies run the risk of being criticized using both qualitative and quantitative criteria, setting a standard that, given the
inevitability of trade-offs, cannot be met. Hybrid studies, however, offer
a type of insight and a range of measures that can appeal to both kinds
of researchers.

Clusters of Methods Choices,
Theoretical Perspectives, and Interests

Although it is important to allow for exceptions, there are characteristic clusters of the types of manifestations studied as described in
Chapter 3, the theoretical perspectives discussed in Chapters 4 and 5,
the conflicting interests examined in Chapter 6, and the methods discussed in this chapter. For example, quantitative studies of culture usually focus on a single or a few types of cultural manifestation (usually
questionnaire studies of self-reports of behavioral norms, much like
those used in climate studies). Often in such studies, only those items
that generate organization-wide consensus are included as measures

of the culture, in accord with the integration perspective. Other items are usually simply not used. Similar conceptual limitations affect studies that rely on factor analysis to exclude items or data that do not generate organization-wide consensus. In effect, such studies define culture in integration terms and exclude (or do not seek) evidence of differentiation and fragmentation—finding what they set out to seek. Such results suggest (controversially) that the integration perspective may, in part, be a methodological artifact.

Of course, exceptions exist; a few studies use these quantitative data collection and analysis techniques to reflect differentiation and fragmentation views. For example, Rousseau (1990a) and Friedman (1983) use quantitative measures of self-reported behavioral norms to tap subcultural and collectivity-wide consensus. Even these studies, however, excluded any items that generated variance that did not generate organization-wide or subcultural consensus. In effect, this approach excludes items that might be best suited to tapping emically defined subcultures (not anticipated by researchers) and ambiguities. Purely quantitative studies have seldom attempted to assess evidence of the fragmentation view of culture, although they could do so. For example, a researcher could expand the Martin et al. (1997) approach, measuring variations in interpretations of content themes, stories, rituals, and even meanings associated with physical arrangements, such as dress norms and decor. The frequency (although not the content) of ironies, paradoxes, or contradictions could be recorded, tapping other aspects of the fragmentation perspective. There is no reason that the fragmentation perspective, which is so useful for understanding cultures in contexts such as government bureaucracies and rapidly changing Internet companies, should be left only to qualitative researchers.

As discussed previously, quantitative studies have a tendency to assume that data from samples of managers (and perhaps professional employees) can be safely generalized to an entire organization—a version of the part-whole error. This willingness to ignore potential differences in viewpoints and conflicts of interest among employees is contrary to the differentiation and fragmentation theories of culture. It fits well within a managerial interest orientation, in effect silencing dissent. In deciphering the interest orientation of quantitative studies, it is important to examine methods procedures, such as sample and variable selection, for clues. Many studies tacitly or explicitly claim value neutrality, even when a managerial orientation is evident. For example, some studies seek to measure culture as a variable, which can then be correlated with measures of outcome variables such as productivity, lower turnover, and profitability. Such outcome studies are almost always managerial in their interest orientation. Although it can be argued that such outcomes benefit all employees, these benefits are seldom distributed equally. A critical researcher might argue that lower-level workers may resent pressures to increase their productivity and may believe that increases in profitability benefit others, such as managers and shareholders, more than themselves. Turnover may decrease simply because workers have fewer alternative employment opportunities. Very few cultural studies that examine outcome measures of organizational effectiveness consider these alternative, critical views of the outcome variables they study.

Qualitative cultural studies have a different profile. For reasons explained previously, qualitative studies tend to focus on a broad range of cultural manifestations. Ideally, in emic research in-depth understandings penetrate the impression management and politeness facades that cultural members offer to outsiders, exposing differences of opinion, contradictions, conflicts, and ambiguities. It is rare that an in-depth ethnographic study takes a purely integration point of view (although exceptions do exist (e.g., Schein, 1985). More often, qualitative studies adopt a differentiation (e.g., Rosen, 1985; Van Maanen, 1991) or fragmentation (e.g., Feldman, 1991; Meyerson, 1991a) viewpoint. Although some qualitative studies adopt the point of view of the powerful, in the managerial interest (e.g., McDonald, 1991; Schein, 1985), often qualitative studies adopt an explicitly nonmanagerial, critical position (e.g., Jermier, 1985; Rosen, 1985; Van Maanen, 1991; Young, 1991). Although many qualitative studies, particularly recent studies, attempt some reflexivity (e.g., Kondo, 1990), the norm is still to tell a "realist tale" (Van Maanen, 1988), ostensibly written in the descriptive interest.

In summary, although exceptions are possible and do exist, methods choices, theoretical perspectives, and interest orientations cluster. Quantitative studies usually assume the integration perspective and adopt a managerial orientation. In contrast, qualitative studies are more likely to assume differentiation or fragmentation perspectives and to adopt a more critical orientation. Some of the specific studies examined in this book fit these generalizations, whereas others represent exceptions to these general rules.

Advantages of a Multimethod Approach
to the Study of Culture

To the extent that particular theoretical questions have not been examined with certain types of methods or from certain interest orientations, these "empty spaces" represent uncharted territory—possible
arenas for future research. If a problem has been addressed from one
cluster of methods, theories, and interests, then attacking the problem
from a different set of methods, theories, and interests might well yield
new insights (McGrath, Martin, & Kulka, 1982). Therefore, if we want
to deepen and extend the entire domain of cultural research, a multimethod approach, across studies, may be more useful than a collective preference for a particular kind of method. This does not mean that
we each have to be able to use a variety of disparate methods (although
that might be desirable and possible, perhaps by collaborating with
people with different methods expertise). It does mean that the collectivity of culture researchers will benefit from having a diversity of methods represented in our empirical work, which means that we must develop the ability to assess the quality of a wide range of methodological
approaches.

It is important to be clear about the purpose of a multimethod approach to this field. Conventionally, it has been argued that knowledge
in a field accumulates when different methods are used to address the
same problem (e.g., Campbell & Fiske, 1959; Jick, 1979; McGrath et al.,
1982). If these different methods yield similar results, this congruence
(labeled triangulation) is said to reinforce certainty about the validity
of the conclusions. In contrast, some critics of positivism argue that we
cannot be sure that triangulated results represent some objectively veri-
fiable truth. Even so, multimethod research is often worth doing. It is
expected, even desirable, that the use of multiple methods to address
the same idea would produce divergent results. Different methods draw
attention to different aspects of a phenomenon or demonstrate different ways of interpreting the same event or artifact (Martin, 1990b). An
excellent example of a multimethod study that produced apparently
contradictory quantitative and qualitative findings is that by Deacon,
Bryman, and Fenton (1998). These authors skillfully explored these discrepancies and used them to develop new insights not accessible with
any single methodological approach. It is likely that the quantitative,
qualitative, and hybrid methods used to address the question of cultural

standardization in multinational corporations would produce divergent findings. Each of these study designs taps aspects of the theoretical problem less easily examined with the other methods. One of the strengths of the cultural literature is that, collectively, cultural researchers have used a wide range of methods. For the advantages of that strength to be recognized, however, each cultural researcher needs to be able and willing to read, assess, appreciate, and draw appropriately on studies that use unfamiliar methods.

Resolving Methodological Dilemmas

This chapter began with a series of methods dilemmas that culture researchers must resolve for themselves. The kinds of methods generally used to address particular kinds of research questions have been described. The strengths and shortcomings inherent in a wide range of methods choices have been analyzed, focusing on such issues as objectivity and subjectivity, etic and emic views, generalization and context-specific knowledge, focus and breadth, and depth of understanding. Clusters of methods choices, theoretical perspectives, and interests have been described and illustrated. Exceptions to these rules of thumb have been explored, with citations to and summaries of illustrative studies. Hybrid methods, which in effect deconstruct many of these dichotomous ways of describing methods choices, have been described and illustrated to encourage exploration of this option.

Unfortunately or fortunately, it is not enough to make these methods choices thoughtfully. When or if studies are evaluated and researchers' scholarly reputations are produced, we enter into a dialogue with colleagues. That dialogue presents us with the evaluation and revision dilemmas that surface, for example, during the reviewing process. Because methods choices often cluster with theoretical preconceptions and interests, judgments about the quality of a study often do not exhibit an open-minded willingness to assess the inescapable trade-offs inherent in choices in any of these domains—precisely because of fundamental disagreements about how to answer the questions with which this chapter began. Evaluating a study as low quality in effect is refusing to learn from it. It is a crucial problem if evaluations do not use appropriate criteria for evaluating the quality of a particular study.

In Chapter 8, I write hypothetical reviews that offer a preview of the praise and the criticisms that you will need to anticipate and, in some cases, be ready to counter, whatever methodological choices you make. My multimethod views are not unusual anymore; the field is changing, and openness to various theories, interests, and methods is growing. No matter how you resolve theory, interest, and methods dilemmas for yourself, Chapter 8 should help you design and defend your own choices more skillfully and add to your ability to understand and evaluate fairly a full range of cultural studies.

Notes

1. Although my focus in this chapter is methodological, the series of studies by Hong et al. (2000) makes an important substantive contribution to the psychological literature on culture. These authors (and also Morris & Peng, 1994) reframe culture in terms of dynamic, domain-specific knowledge structures rather than the static, holistic approach of earlier culture-as-world-view research. This more focused and dynamic approach allows for the entire apparatus of cognitive theory and research to be brought to bear on cultural phenomena, opening a broad and exciting range of studies exploring cultural variation (including relevance and irrelevance) of such concepts as schemas and categorization. This approach is complementary to the work of other psychological theorists (e.g., Kitayama & Markus, 1994; Shweder, 1991) who are more involved in understanding the modes of thought and action that are unique to particular cultures. Together, these two streams of cultural research are revolutionizing our understanding of psychology, revealing that that which seemed (to North Americans at least) to be universal may indeed be culturally specific.

8

Putting It All Together

REVIEWS OF SAMPLE STUDIES

To produce an interpretation of the way a people lives which is
neither imprisoned within their own mental horizons, an
ethnography of witchcraft written by a witch, nor systematically
deaf to the distinctive tonalities of their existence, an ethnography
of witchcraft written by a geometer.

—Geertz (1973, p. 57)

Geertz, as an anthropologist, might find it quite normal to study witches, headhunters, or cockfighters. Those of us who study organizations focus our attention on people in somewhat more mundane occupations. Nevertheless, we, like anthropologists, face the difficulty to which Geertz (1973) alludes: It is difficult to find a balance between emic and etic methods. An emic account can become so immersed in the "native's" viewpoint (an ethnography of witchcraft written by a witch) that it loses any sense of how, in a larger context, being this kind of "native" is distinctive. Conversely, an etic account runs the risk of being so enamored of counting and measuring (an ethnographer of witchcraft written by a geometry expert) that the texture of life in a culture becomes lost. Also, just as a cultural study can become too emic or etic, so too a hybrid method risks becoming neither fish nor fowl, losing both the rich detail of an ethnographic account and the statistical precision of a careful quantitative study. Furthermore, the emic and etic issue is just one of many difficult choices, discussed in previous chapters, that a cultural researcher must make.

This chapter brings together many of the issues discussed so far, showing how they intersect in particular cultural studies (objective and subjective, etic and emic, generalization and context-specific knowledge, focus and breadth in cultural manifestations, and level of depth), theoretical perspectives (integration, differentiation, fragmentation, a three-perspective view, or some other approach), interests (managerial, critical, and descriptive), and methods (quantitative, qualitative, and hybrid). I have chosen to bring these issues together where "the rubber hits the road"; that is, to examine how they intersect during the peer review process. When we choose one end of a continuum, such as emic and etic or managerial and critical interests, we open ourselves to criticisms from advocates of the other end of the continuum who may well be the people reviewing our work. For example, it would be difficult and perhaps undesirable for a reviewer to ask that a qualitative study meet criteria appropriate for evaluating quantitative research, such as systematic random sampling, large numbers of cultural contexts studied, and evidence of intercoder reliability. Also, it would be difficult and perhaps inappropriate for a quantitative study to be required to meet the criteria appropriate for a qualitative study, such as depth of interpretation, long-term participant observation, and so forth. Although we know that choosing one answer to a dilemma makes it difficult to achieve the strengths of unchosen approaches, we nevertheless sometimes criticize studies precisely on these grounds.

These criticisms are expressed indirectly and tentatively when we author papers that include criticism in the text or when we talk face-to-face with the researcher whose work is being criticized. When external letter writers evaluate a tenure candidate's work, when journal reviewers and editors assess a manuscript for publication, and when people talk privately about a colleague's work, criticism is more open and direct, and often more extreme, in part because it is anonymous (as in a "blind" unsigned journal review) or confidential (as in selection and promotion decisions or a private conversation). The imaginary arguments scattered throughout the preceding chapters foreshadow some of these kinds of open and direct criticisms. Imagine, for example, that you decide to use a managerial, integrationist approach in your latest paper and your blind reviewer is the outspoken Professor Differentiation. Given his vehement advocacy of critical interests, can you imagine what he might say about your managerial integrationist study, no matter how well you designed it? Conversely, imagine that you are a devoted critical theorist who has used the differentiation perspective to delineate the mistreatment of union workers during a recent automotive strike. The reviewer of your paper is Professor Fragmentation, who also happens to be a strong advocate of the descriptive interest (i.e., she prefers refraining from obvious interest advocacy). She would like you to explore the ambiguities of both the union and the management positions in the conflict, presenting both points of view and emphasizing their internal contradictions and paradoxes. Reviews such as these are not uncommon, and when they are extreme they are particularly difficult to deal with. Reviews have a definite impact on scholarship, altering its content and determining whether it will be published. Such commentary cannot be dismissed or ignored without repercussions. The dilemma, therefore, is how to anticipate and deal with such criticisms.

Overview and Rationale
for Focusing on the Review Process

In this chapter, I review four studies. I summarize each study's logic and design and then write three short evaluations of it. The first review highlights the study's strengths, the second criticizes its weaknesses (sometimes unfairly using inappropriate criteria), and the third offers my own assessment. In my assessment, I summarize how each study exemplifies some of the key concepts presented in this book and then offer one or more ways to respond to the positive and negative reviews. The studies to be evaluated in this way are (a) an innovative quantitative study of culture (O'Reilly, Chatman, & Caldwell, 1991), (b) a combination of surveys and qualitative (historical) case studies examining the "strong" culture-effectiveness hypothesis in a large sample of organizations (Denison, 1990), (c) a hybrid (content analysis of stories) study of an entrepreneurial culture founded by a charismatic leader (Martin et al., 1985), and (d) a richly detailed (journal-length) ethnographic study of a Japanese-owned manufacturing company's collaboration with Italian employees (Botti, 1995). I chose my own study because I know its faults well, and I chose the others because they are well-designed and executed examples of a type of cultural research.

I have several objectives in this chapter. First, I hope that this material will help cultural researchers anticipate the range of reactions that a particular kind of cultural research may generate so that they can evaluate the appropriateness of those suggestions in a knowledgeable manner and decide what or if improvements are necessary. A critical reading of these reviews should help researchers avoid common pitfalls, anticipate arguments, and enter the fray of the review process well prepared to justify their theory, interest, and method choices. For consumers (readers) of cultural research, I hope this chapter will bring moments of recognition as they react to reviews with agreement, disagreement, and, I hope, a growing sense of how their criteria for assessing the quality of a study might be adjusted to encompass a wider range of theories, interests, and methods. Finally, we are all involved in the evaluation process as reviewers, journal editors, or writers of letters for job or promotion candidates. I hope these positive and negative reviews will heighten awareness of how an evaluator's preferences affect the content of evaluations, opening our minds to types of research that are less familiar or less consistent with our own preferences.

Hypothetical reviews have been written to honor the promise of anonymity made to journal reviewers. To present ideas concisely and clearly, the reviews are short and offer either strong praise or strong criticism. It is realistic to include reviews that contradict each other. Gottfredson (1978) found that reviewers agree fairly well when they are asked to list the desirable qualities of a generic manuscript, but they agree only very weakly when they are asked to evaluate whether a specific manuscript has those qualities. Starbuck (2000), early in his tenure as editor of *Administrative Science Quarterly,* coded 500 pairs of reviews (accept = +1, reject = −1, and revise = 0). The correlation between pairs of reviews was .12, accounting for only 1.4% of the variance. Mahoney (1977) similarly found that journal reviewers had poor inter-rater agreement. He also found that reviewers tended to be biased against manuscripts that reported results contrary to their theoretical views (as suggested by the reviewers' own publications). Reviewers who disliked the findings of a particular paper tended to find fault with its methods, whereas reviewers who approved of the findings tended to perceive the paper as methodologically strong. In summary, it is realistic to focus on reviews that disagree in their evaluation of a particular cultural study.

Furthermore, it is likely that the opinions of those researchers reflect their own theoretical, interest, and methods preferences.

In the cultural domain, compared to the rest of organizational studies, reviews are particularly likely to be both contradictory and extreme because of the wide range of preferences cultural researchers bring to the topic. The hypothetical reviews in this chapter, however, are more extreme than most actual evaluations. These reviews are overly harsh or too easily satisfied. Even in the cultural arena, most actual reviews tend to mix positive and negative commentary, focus more on substance than on methods issues, and temper extreme opinions with some tolerance for opposing points of view. I have written the hypothetical reviews in this chapter using exaggerated positive and negative reactions to make disputed issues clear and easy to see, not because all or even most reviews of cultural research are this extreme, unhelpful, or intemperate. Luckily, and increasingly, reviews of cultural research have become far more constructive and evenhanded than these hypothetical reviews suggest.

After these pairs of contradictory hypothetical reviews, I offer my own view of each study. I point out how each study and its reviews reflect the ideas introduced so far in this book, and I discuss alternative ways a manuscript author might respond to these commentaries. I do not mean to imply by this that I should have the last word (irresistible though this may be) or that most reviewers share my opinions about the concepts introduced in this book. I do try to be relatively evenhanded in presenting my assessments of each study. Here, however, some reflexivity is called for. Although I do appreciate qualitative, quantitative, and hybrid methods, I am less tolerant (as you may have gathered by now) of single-perspective theoretical approaches, especially when that single perspective is integration, written in the managerial interest, and when other cultural research traditions are not cited or used. Also I prefer breadth in a cultural study; I believe that a focus on one or a few cultural manifestations is misleading because (as predicted by the differentiation and fragmentation views) different manifestations are likely to give rise to different interpretations. Thus, although I try to be evenhanded, my own preferences come through when I express my own views in this chapter.

It is risky to write a chapter about the reviewing process; this is dangerous terrain ("Dragons lurk here."). Advancing a scholarly point of view by criticizing an individual scholar's work (even my own work) runs the risk of fostering polarization. I worry that this chapter might dampen some people's motivation to learn and try new practices and perspectives because they fear criticism from advocates of other viewpoints. This would be precisely contrary to the goals I outlined previously. Extreme views such as those illustrated in the hypothetical reviews, however, are in fact part of the review process, especially in the cultural domain and especially when reviews are blind or confidential. I believe that it is better to bring such extreme criticisms out into the open, away from the protections of anonymity and confidentiality, so that cultural researchers receiving such criticism are well prepared, know their options, and can respond with confidence, knowing they are not alone. Also, to the extent that readers of this chapter are participants in the review process, perhaps the increased awareness that comes from discussion of such extreme reviews will encourage all of us to become better informed about the varying criteria that are appropriate for evaluating various kinds of culture research.

Enough said. The four studies to be discussed are ordered beginning with the most purely quantitative, progressing through two hybrid studies, and ending with an ethnography.

Study 1: O'Reilly et al. (1991)

Overview

O'Reilly et al. (1991) scoured the academic and popular cultural literature of the early 1980s (e.g., Davis, 1984; Deal & Kennedy, 1982; Kilmann, 1985; Ouchi, 1981; Peters & Waterman, 1982; Schein, 1985), seeking value statements that were said to characterize "strong" cultures. They systematically reduced these items to a set of 54 value statements combined in an instrument called the Organizational Culture Profile (OCP). They used this instrument to assess the fit between an individual's values and an organization's culture. Study participants included large and small samples of undergraduates and informed professionals familiar with accounting firms (e.g., new and senior accountants, certified public accountants, middle-level managers, and MBA students).

Study participants were asked to sort the 54 items twice using a sorting method based on Stephenson's (1953) Q-sort approach. The logic of this approach is to have study participants, not researchers, decide which concepts (in this instance, which value statements) are and are not relevant. In the first sorting, study participants were asked to profile the culture of an organization for which they worked: "[Rate] the most characteristic aspects of the culture of your firm [in the form of] . . . norms or shared expectations about what's important, how to behave, or what attitudes are appropriate" (O'Reilly et al., 1991, p. 495). In a second sorting, study participants were asked to profile their own values by responding to the question, "How important is it for this characteristic to be part of the organization you work for?" In both the organizational and the individual profiles, items viewed as more characteristic or more important were given more weight, reflecting the study participant's opinions. A template-matching process was used to assess the fit between the (idiographic) value profile of an individual and the ratings of the organization's culture. Internal and test-retest reliability was good, as were measures of discriminant and other forms of validity. In accord with their hypotheses, O'Reilly and colleagues found that when the fit (congruence) between the organization's culture and the individual's values was greater, normative commitment was higher, job satisfaction was higher, individual intent to leave the company was lower, as was actual turnover.

Reviewer A

This is a fine paper, with careful methods described in great detail. The OCP measure is a strong contribution to the long-standing controversies regarding person-situation fit. Cultural researchers have long needed an easy-to-administer, quantitative measure of culture, such as the OCP. It was ingenious to base this measure on the Q-sort method, as cultural survey measures have been criticized for imposing researchers' conceptual categories on participants who may see other dimensions as more relevant. The Q-sort approach weights only those items that participants consider important, putting this kind of criticism to rest. Clear evidence of various types of reliability and validity are offered, a welcome improvement over the "looseness" of much of the prior cultural research, which has relied, all too often, on anecdotal case studies of single settings. The large numbers of working professional as well as student subject samples add considerable heft to the results, permitting generalization with more confidence than is normally the case in organizational studies that use only student samples. Although many cultural researchers have claimed to find a link between some kinds of cultures and commitment or organizational performance, this is one of the first studies to demonstrate such a link with solid, reasonably well-controlled data.

Another important strength of this study is its evident practical implications (detailed in O'Reilly, 1989; O'Reilly et al., 1991). Although I would have been interested to learn more in this paper about the observed differences among the major accounting firms (see Chatman, 1991, for some of these details), this evidence of the importance of person-culture fit in predicting commitment, job satisfaction, and turnover should help many new hires make better judgments about where to work. In addition, these results (and perhaps even use of the OCP) should help many firms save money on hiring, training, and socializing new recruits who ultimately perform poorly and leave the firm. Systematically screening job applicants, to see if they fit a culture, should benefit all. Because this instrument is objective and quantitative, claims of subjective bias or discrimination will be avoided. On a larger scale, systematic use of this instrument gives us a means for assessing how the values of cultures in different industries compare, and how, within an industry, firms differ from each other, perhaps giving one firm a competitive edge over another.

Reviewer B

The authors begin their discussion of culture by noting that cultures have usually been defined in terms of what is shared by all or most members of a culture. Such definitions of culture are indeed common, but they ignore those aspects of culture that generate disagreement, confusion, ambiguity, irony, contradiction, and so on. This theoretical narrowness is reinforced by the cultural measures these authors choose. O'Reilly, Chatman, and Caldwell (1991) acknowledge that cultural manifestations include assumptions, values, behavioral norms and expectations, and actual behavior, but proceed to justify a focus on a single manifestation, values, as "the defining elements around which norms, symbols, rituals, and other cultural activities revolve" (pp. 491-492). Rituals, stories, or myths, then, are "phenotypic outcroppings that reflect underlying beliefs and values" (p. 492). Such an assumption ignores the vast body of evidence, cultural and otherwise, suggesting that espoused values often are inconsistent with self-reported group norms, as well as interpretations of other cultural manifestations such as rituals and stories.

A focus on values is an especially narrow and problematic aspect of culture to study. Study participants are asked to rate values chosen by researchers, assessing whether those values are characteristic of their organization as a whole. Participants are not given an opportunity to offer other values more relevant to their workplace. These "value" measures are in essence self-reports of desired or actual behavioral norms. It is difficult to know what these measures are tapping. Participants' responses may be affected by their desire to have, or to show they have, a positive image or self-esteem, to manage the impression made on a researcher, or (if there is strong affect toward the collectivity being studied) to portray that collectivity as a generally positive or generally negative place to work.

Although this study has a desirable sample size and variety of study participants, it is noteworthy that these participants (undergraduate and MBA students, professionals, and managers at accounting firms) are all drawn from the professionally oriented middle class—as if secretaries, clerical workers, blue-collar employees, and custodians were not part of organizational cultures and as if their views of the cultures did not count. Subcultural differences, for example, between consultants and auditors, or across different levels of these strongly hierarchical firms, were not explored. Is it fair, then, to conclude that these "organizational cultures" are accurately characterized by organization-wide consensus about shared values, and that those values are deeper than but consistent with other (unmeasured) manifestations of the culture? In the few instances in which evidence that could contradict these preconceptions was collected, the authors do indeed find, for example, that person-culture value fit is related to value-based commitment but not to instrumental, compliance-based commitment, a measure closer to actual behavior.

These conceptual and methodological difficulties have important practical implications. For example, the authors may seem to have found an objective measure of cultural fit, untainted by subjectivity or bias. Subjectivity may well creep in, however, as study participants describe their personal value profiles in ways that enhance their self-esteem or project a positive, socially desirable image. Also, long-term employees may well be either alienated or highly satisfied with their employing firm, creating a positive or negative "halo effect" as they describe that firm's values. Also, accountants who differ from the average employee of an accounting firm, perhaps because they are female and/or African-American, or from a working class background, may find themselves exhibiting conforming behavior and keeping their atypical value profile to themselves. Do we really want a systematic way to screen out these "misfits"?

My Opinion

I begin by using the concepts introduced in this book to characterize this study. O'Reilly et al. (1991) summarize study participants' subjective views (their self-reports of values they consider as characteristic of a culture) in a profile of an organization's "culture." The language used to describe that profile (e.g., various measures of reliability and validity) treats the profile as if it were an objectively valid portrait of the culture. Subjective factors (as detailed by Reviewer B), however, may well have influenced study participants' responses to the OCP instrument, leaving this instrument poised between objective and subjective ends of a continuum. Similarly, it is difficult to agree with Reviewer A that this instrument is an emic measure because of the etic considerations raised by Reviewer B, again leaving the study poised between etic and emic extremes. The study explicitly tests a theoretically derived hypothesis and seeks to build empirically based generalizations. This is clearly a narrow, specialist study focused on a single type of cultural manifestation (self-reports of values). In-depth interpretations are not this study's primary objective.

Regarding theoretical and interest issues, this study defines culture as shared (implying organization-wide consensus), measures only a single cultural manifestation (implying consistency of interpretations across other unmeasured cultural manifestations), and excludes ambiguity; these are the hallmarks of the integration perspective. In the study's review of the cultural literature on page 491 and in the citations to cultural researchers used as sources of values, only integration studies are cited, as if cultural research from the differentiation and fragmentation traditions did not exist. The study is functionalist in its focus on links between culture and measures of firm performance; in its discussion of the practical implications of the results, the study is explicitly written in the managerial interest. For example, as Reviewer B points out in accord with critical theory, lower-level organizational employees are excluded when generalizations about "organizational" culture are made. Job candidates whose personal values do not fit most organizational culture profiles, perhaps because they come from a different kind of background than most other employees, would be excluded by analysis of average scores on the OCP, although these "marginalized" job candidates might not want this outcome or view it as justified.

In summary, the study authors define culture in integration terms, review primarily integration theory and research as support for their ideas, measure only those aspects of culture that fit the integration viewpoint, and then find results congruent with these assumptions. This could be seen as a narrow focus, which should be properly acknowledged, or it could be seen as a serious weakness that ignores essential elements of what cultures comprise. By now, it is clear that I tend to the latter view, but as a reviewer, a more evenhanded response would be to ask the authors to acknowledge their integrationist focus explicitly and perhaps justify it. At the end of the paper, ideas for future research might take a broader theoretical view of the cultural field, addressing some of the issues raised by Reviewer B or by cultural researchers from outside the integration perspective. Such an approach might broaden the appeal of the paper and leave it less open to criticism by those who do not share the preconceptions of the integration view of culture, which has been so heavily criticized.

As Reviewer A elaborates, however, this is a well-designed quantitative study. Within the constraints of the integration perspective, the authors measure effectively and in an innovative way what they set out to measure. The OCP does indeed provide an easy-to-administer measure of value consensus, defined from the integration point of view. The OCP's ease of administration, the care with which its psychometric properties have been investigated, its quantitative approach, and even its focus exclusively on an integration view are all characteristics that coincide with the preferences of managers, who would also be attracted by this study's findings of a link to firm performance. This study can be criticized for not fully acknowledging its theoretical, interest, and methods limitations, but within its choice domain this study is carefully and creatively designed and executed. Furthermore, in contrast to most other quantitative approaches to measuring culture, this study moves closer to the subjective and emic concerns that are so important to qualitative researchers. The next study moves closer still, spanning the qualitative-quantitative divide with a hybrid approach.

Study 2: Denison (1990)

Overview

Denison (1990) defines organizational culture as

the underlying values, beliefs, and principles that serve as a foundation for an organization's management system as well as the set of management practices and behaviors that both exemplify and reinforce those basic principles. These principles and practices endure because they have meaning for members of an organization. (p. 2)

Culture is measured, in this book, by a series of questionnaire items assessed with 5-point Likert scales indicating the extent to which a described behavior is viewed as characteristic of the organization; for example, "Is your performance adequately recognized and rewarded?" and "Does the organization have a real interest in the welfare and over-all satisfaction of those who work here?"

Variants of these items were used in a series of survey studies conducted by the University of Michigan Survey Research Center between 1966 and 1981. Samples of organizational employees varied in size and in the degree to which random, stratified sampling procedures were used. Denison (1990) rated the adequacy of these samples in terms of size and the extent to which all employees were sampled. In many samples, managers and professionals only or primarily were surveyed. Denison used many appropriate measures of firm performance (e.g., return on sales and return on investment), with a few control variables (e.g., industry). Thirty-four organizations were included. Data were checked for representativeness. Performance data were standardized by industry using 20 years of data from 556 firms in the Survey Research Center archives. Only one of the firms studied lost large amounts of money during the study period, and that outlier was investigated in-depth to determine if the results would change if it were included or excluded. Results did not change. Denison found, across industries, a positive correlation between these self-report behavioral measures of "culture" and organizational effectiveness.

These quantitative procedures were supplemented by several case studies. Qualitative methods varied across these cases. Denison (1990) generally read available corporate histories and interviewed approximately 25 employees of each firm (usually high-ranking managers or professionals or outside consultants known to be well informed about the company). The results of these case histories were used to inform and supplement the quantitative analyses. Therefore, this was a kind of hybrid study, although there was no attempt to combine qualitative and quantitative methods.

Reviewer A

The most important question, concerning organizational culture, is whether having a "strong" culture (consistent, shared) relates to firm profitability. Denison's careful quantitative study settles this question once and for all: "Strong" cultures do indeed correlate with important measures of firm performance, such as return on sales and return on investment. The care with which this study is conducted is commendable. The adequacy of employee sampling procedures is assessed in exceptional detail, and Denison tests whether the study results differ, depending on sample adequacy. The organizational sample size (34 firms) is reasonably large for a cultural study, and the statistics used are appropriate and reported in detail. Several statistically oriented appendices are helpful in this regard. Industry norms, for 20 years, are used to be sure that financial performance data are appropriately controlled, using an even larger sample of 556 firms. The questionnaire items (used to measure organizational culture) focus on issues that are familiar and important to managers, such as job design, leadership, and organizational climate. A few qualitative case studies, based on historical documents and interviews with key personnel flesh out these numbers, giving the details that make the statistics come alive. Denison concludes with a series of practical implications outlining how managers can become culture creators, adjusting a culture to maximize its consistency and ability to generate commitment. This is a superb study.

Reviewer B

This study exemplifies exactly what is wrong with the "corporate culture" literature. The author defines culture in terms of what is consistent with managerial goals. Any data that do not fit these definitions are excluded. Culture is measured, superficially, with questionnaire items about people's self-reports of certain behaviors that supposedly reinforce management's goals and values. There is no evidence that these self-reports reflect actual behavior and no evidence that these aspects of behavior are of great importance to employees, especially those who are not managers. Is this really a measure of culture, in all its complexity, as it is reflected in employees' everyday working lives? Denison is concerned (as shown by how he defines and measures culture) only in management's viewpoint. He is more comfortable than he should be with sampling procedures that focus on managers and professionals, not the rank-and-file employees who are the majority of employees in most firms. Finally, this book summarizes the results of studies of 34 firms conducted for other purposes, decades ago. Are the results therefore really focused on culture and are they out of date?

The substantive and methodological concerns outlined previously mean that no matter how many numbers are presented, and no matter how sophisticated the analyses of those numbers are, it is not clear that this study really measures culture, as culture relates to the working lives of the full range of employees in the firms surveyed. This study's overweening emphasis on managerial concerns, the definitional and measurement focus on only that which is consistent and shared, and the conceptually narrow measurement of culture (self-reports of behaviors relevant to managerial principles) means that this study's shortcomings undermine its claim to have found a clear relationship between culture and firm performance.

But what about the qualitative case studies? Don't these speak to some of the issues I raise in regard to the quantitative data? Absolutely not. The focus on corporate histories and archival documents means that Denison is getting the "official" story of the company's past, often written by managers or by writers approved by management. Such corporate histories generally emphasize, in glowing terms, the contributions and leadership of top managers and the enthusiastic participation of most employees. In such accounts, dissent, ambiguities, and difficulties are usually omitted or toned down. Echoes of the bias found in such corporate histories can be found in Denison's case descriptions, which tend to lionize top management, assume consensus, and take claims of responsibility for firm success at face value. For example:

> Founder and Chairman Don Burr was the central figure in the creation of this culture. He was teacher, preacher, strategist, and role model: a "street wise" pied piper leading an organization that was, in his own words, designed "to unleash the power of the individual." . . . The mission was infectious. The belief that a humanistic organization could revolutionize the industry, that commitment and involvement as equal team players could fulfill individual career ambitions, and the vision that an organization of owner-workers could prosper together all combined to produce phenomenal levels of activity and commitment. Everyone ate, breathed, and slept People Express in the early days. . . . People Express was a powerful example of a mission-based organization. . . . The root of this mission—that nothing was impossible for an organization that could unleash the power of the individual—may also have helped create the assumption that the organization could not fail. (pp. 113, 128)

It is true that, in preparation for writing these case studies, Denison and colleagues interviewed contemporary employees (about 25, a small sample). However, these interview subjects were not part of a random, stratified sample, but included primarily managers and professionals, top executives, consultants, and academic researchers who had worked primarily with the managerial ranks at the firm, and perhaps a few loyalists or rising stars. Such a sample is more likely to give a managerially approved version of history (one that emphasizes harmony and unity). This bias is exacerbated if the qualitative method used is a one-time interview rather than longer term observation, in contexts in which the employees "forget" the presence of researchers.

The demand characteristics of these qualitative methods (corporate histories, archived documents, and short-term interviews), the bias of these sampling procedures (of both documents and interviewees), and the evident managerial interests of the researcher all likely combined to limit, in predictable ways, the contents and conclusions of these case studies. It is useful to recall that People Express did fail. For all these reasons, the qualitative portraits of these corporate cultures are severely limited and obviously biased, making the conclusions of this study (to have found a link between culture and effectiveness) even more suspect.

My Opinion

This study takes an objectivist approach to culture using primarily etic sources, such as Likert-scaled questionnaire items and corporate histories. The author seeks to generalize about a relationship between "strong" cultures and measures of firm performance. The study is narrow in focus (e.g., self-reports of behavior in the quantitative data) and does not, even in the case studies, seek or attain much depth. Such characteristics are to be expected in most quantitative studies.

I agree with Reviewer A regarding the statistical care with which Denison analyzes his quantitative data. My major quibble, and it is an important one, is that these results are correlational and should not be interpreted to mean that culture *causes* firm effectiveness. In addition, in contrast to the careful and thorough quantitative analysis, the qualitative part of this study does not seek or attain the subjective, emic, contextually detailed, broad, or deep understandings found in longer term qualitative studies such as ethnographies. This is another way of saying that I agree with Reviewer B that the quantitative part of the study, which engages most of the author's efforts, is better executed than the qualitative part.

In my view, one of the study's most important limitations is its narrow quantitative operationalization of culture (self-reports of behavior). This operational narrowness is not reflected in the study's definition of the more holistic concept of culture. Furthermore, the studies on which this reanalysis is based were originally conducted to measure

such concepts as job design, job satisfaction, leadership style, and organizational climate. Although Denison attempts to distinguish culture
from these other concepts (as have others, such as Schneider, 1990), in
fact, many of the measures used here are exactly the same as those used
to measure climate, job design, and so on. In this study, there is no
attempt to tap the full range of symbolically rich cultural manifestations studied by other researchers, such as stories, rituals, and physical
arrangements.

The study clearly defines culture in integration terms. Interpretations
of cultural manifestations are consistent with each other ("management practices and behaviors that both exemplify and reinforce [man-
agement's] principles"). These manifestations are seen as generating
organization-wide consensus ("These principles and practices endure
because they have meaning for members of an organization"). Culture
is operationalized in accord with this definition, excluding from the
cultural realm (as Reviewer A notes) anything that does not fit this definition, such as subcultural differences and ambiguities. This is a single-
perspective study, and it does not meaningfully acknowledge or use
data to explore results of studies conducted from other theoretical perspectives. It seeks what it sets out to find tautologically. As you might
expect, I find this theoretical orientation severely limited in its scope. If
I were reviewing this study, I would at least ask that this exclusion of
other kinds of cultural theory and research be acknowledged and perhaps justified.

When a study uses only the integration perspective, it often is written
in the managerial interest. This can clearly be seen in the way this study
defines culture (in terms of management's principles and behavior
consistent with those principles) and the way it deals with sampling
procedures that are limited to the views of managers, professionals, top
executives, and their confidants (researchers and consultants). This
managerial interest is particularly evident in the data on which the
qualitative case studies are based and the study's conclusions (complete
with advice for managing culture to promote unity and managerial
control of employees' values and behaviors). This attribute can be seen
as either a strength (making applied implications clear) or a limitation.
It presents a problem when the author claims to be describing a firm's
entire culture (not just the management-consistent aspects of that culture) as it is viewed by all or most employees (not just the managers

and professionals). Unfortunately, this kind of totalizing language, characteristic of integration studies written in the managerial interest, is used throughout this study. Again, as you might expect from my acknowledgments of my own bias, I would have preferred a more balanced design, analysis, and discussion—one that included the views of dissenting individuals and groups, particularly those who viewed things in ambiguous terms or who viewed things differently than managers and top executives.

My views reflect my preference for studies that are broad and deep rather than narrow, that incorporate all three perspectives, and that include critical as well as managerial interests. These preferences are not unbiased, obviously, and neither are Reviewers A and B. As in my assessment of Denison's (1990) study, both Reviewers A and B overstate their cases and omit evidence contrary to their views, exhibiting the biases in the reviewing process found by Mahoney (1977). Reviewer A, for example, praises the study only for the ways in which it meets standard quantitative evaluation criteria and does not explore many of the study's limitations. Reviewer B focuses primarily on the shortcomings of the study's qualitative component and does not acknowledge its quantitative strengths. Reviewer B (like myself) overstates Denison's managerial emphasis, not fully acknowledging the extent to which Denison uses statistics to determine if omission of lower-level employees from some of his quantitative samples would change his conclusions. Reviewer B also takes a cheap shot regarding the failure of People Express, a fact that Denison acknowledges and explores. Like many actual reviews, none of these assessments, including my own, evaluate Denison's study in an evenhanded way.

It is tough for a study's author to be assessed in this format, and so it is only fair that I put myself, or at least one of my studies, under this scrutiny. I have chosen another hybrid study—one that challenges some of the assumptions of the integration view. Denison's (1990) hybrid study kept qualitative and quantitative approaches separate, each contributing a different kind of insight. Although ideally this kind of hybrid approach would keep the strengths of both methods intact, satisfying critics of both schools of thought, as we have seen in the contrasting views of Reviewers A and B, this cup can be seen as quite full or quite empty. In the next hybrid study to be critiqued, qualitative and quantitative approaches were combined using content analysis to transform narratives into statistics. This hybrid strategy can also be seen positively or negatively.

Study 3: Martin et al. (1985)

Overview

Martin et al. (1985) explicitly used the integration and differentiation perspectives. They observed that integration studies make organizational leaders—especially founders—a seductive promise: They can create a unified, internally consistent, consensually endorsed organizational culture, cast in their own image, reflective of their own personal values—a promise of a kind of organizational immortality. In contrast, differentiation studies of culture portray organizations in terms of heterogeneity and dissensus. Subcultures proliferate, differentiating themselves from each other, sometimes existing in harmony or indifference and other times erupting in conflict. According to the differentiation perspective, a leader or founder is only one of many sources for these shared understandings and misunderstandings. The integration and differentiation perspectives were positioned by these authors as opposing theoretical viewpoints. A two-stage study was designed to "test" which of these two views was the most accurate way to portray the culture of a small company recently started by a charismatic entrepreneur who was well respected by his employees.

In the first stage of this study, Martin et al. (1985) conducted 6 months of qualitative research—mostly observation, some participant observation, and some unstructured interviews (conversations). The aspect of the qualitative data collection activities, most relevant to this paper, focused on how employees defined the subcultures that were relevant to them at work. Employees talked of themselves as belonging to subcultures based on length of tenure with the company, level of hierarchy, and function, such as engineering or marketing. In the second stage of the study, the authors interviewed a random, stratified sample of 64 of the firm's 700 employees. In the structured interview format, these employees were asked to tell an event-specific version of the company's history. The following was the most important item: "Please tell us about the events which were important in shaping what the company is like today or what it will be like in the future." Follow-up probes asked for details of each event, what meanings the event held for them, and the importance of the event. The maximum number of events was 10. Employees were asked to recount only those events that "have happened to someone other than yourself" so that widely known events would be recounted.

Systematic content analysis was used to determine the extent of overlap between the founder's and the employees' views of these stories. For example, a critical incident in the company's history focused on a quality control problem. According to the founder, his actions created the solution (Martin et al., 1985):

> We were getting reports that 30% of all units were arriving at the dealers dead on arrival, that 80% of all units being shipped were requiring service work under warranty. An examination of why this happened showed that . . . the method used was to scream at an engineer until he agreed to have it fixed by the morning, whether he could or couldn't, whether he knew what was happening or not. . . . Information I received [was] filtered through levels of management, suitably laundered at each step on the way, so that by the time it got to me, I was hearing only what they wanted me to hear. . . . I decided to totally short circuit that by appointing five quality circles, five people in each circle, five people drawn utterly at random from the ranks of the non-supervisory personnel so that nobody, under any circumstances, could manipulate who would be on which quality circle. The moment that happened, I started to get all kinds of information. It had a tremendous effect, internally, externally, and caused a number of interesting incidents to occur. (pp. 109-110)

Although this founder was exceptionally well respected, very few of the employees' accounts of this crisis mentioned the founder's actions, the laundering of information, or the quality circles. Instead, the employees told this story by going into great detail about the design, production, and vending of the product, with particular emphasis on relations with distributors and suppliers. In addition, the employees generally attributed the quality turnaround to something the founder never mentioned: their own willingness to work hard, beyond the call of duty. For example, "A lot of bad [component of the product] was going out. I had to test [this component.] Everybody put [in] lots of hours, late hours, and they had shifts all night. Everybody really pulled together and made it work and fixed the whole thing" (p. 111).

Whereas many event histories were differently interpreted by the founder and the employees, other event histories tapped subcultural differences. Hierarchical and functional classifications of employees, especially, tended to interpret events differently, suggesting that these employee classifications had developed into distinctive subcultures. For example, engineers and marketers told event histories about a product upgrade crisis. Members of both subcultures agreed on the presenting problem (a product upgrade gone wrong), but each group attributed the problem's resolution to the heroic efforts of their own functional area, with little or no mention of the contribution of members of the other subculture.

Although hierarchy and functional subcultures were spontaneously mentioned in Stage 1 of the study, and evidence of these same subcultures was also found in Stage 2, this was not true for tenure subcultures. In Stage 1, "wild-eyed cowboys" were the old guard, present from the company's first days, whereas "suits" or "new hires" were hired recently. In Stage 2 of the study, however, no trace of these tenure-related subcultures was found in the event histories. Probing (qualitatively) for the reasons for these results, the research team discovered that between Stages 1 and 2, many of the wild-eyed cowboys left the company, dismayed with its increasing bureaucratization.

The founder was aware of the difference between his personal values (more like those of the wild-eyed ones) and those of the later hires. The founder moved the company toward more bureaucratization and encouraged the turnover that led those who shared his personal "cowboy" values to leave. The founder then hired people ("suits") with "big company experience" to take the places of the wild-eyed cowboys like himself. Rather than creating a culture cast in his own image, this founder announced his plans to resign; it was consistent with his own values, he said, to permit the company to evolve in the direction the employees believed was necessary. In the words of the founder, "Creating a culture is like surfing. You cannot make a wave. All you can do is wait and watch for the right wave, then ride it for all it's worth." Martin et al. (1985) noted that results of this study are consistent with organizational life cycle research that suggests most companies do not escape bureaucratization and increasing hierarchical and functional differentiation; like this company, most start-up companies eventually replace entrepreneurial "cowboys" with "suits" as they grow. In addition, this study challenges and undermines the seductive promise that some integration studies make to organizational leaders: that they can create a unified, internally consistent, consensually endorsed organizational culture cast in their own image and reflective of their own personal values—a promise of a kind of organizational immortality. Instead, in accord with the differentiation view of culture, this study suggests that groups of employees and a founder have dramatically different interpretations of critical incidents in the company's history.

Reviewer A

This study offers an unusual hybrid mix of methods. Like many quantitative studies, this study uses a random, stratified sample of employees and systematically content analyzes event histories. The content analysis is careful and detailed, with intercoder reliability and between-group tests of statistical significance used to determine which employee classification differences were important in shaping perceptions of the company's history. In accord with the assumptions underlying qualitative methods, however, the content of those event histories is determined by study participants, not researchers, and interpretations of the meanings of these events are subjective and multiple. The authors attend to interpretations that are shared by most employees and those that are shared by one subculture but not another.

The results indicate that even though this founder was much admired by his employees, his view of the company's history was quite different from theirs—compelling evidence of the difficulties of shaping a culture cast in a founder's own image. In part, he encouraged this disparity in views by encouraging "wild-eyed cowboys" such as himself to leave the company, replacing them with bureaucratic "suits." This study's systematic approach to studying company history lends a depth of understanding of the process that leads so many entrepreneurial companies to adopt bureaucratic practices willingly. Because so much organizational life cycle research indicates that this company's move toward bureaucratization is the norm, I am not worried about this being a case study of a single organization. The founder, however, could have behaved differently, perhaps staying on to resist the bureaucratization. For this reason, generalizations about the founder's behavior should be made with considerable modesty. Furthermore, although the results of this study show evidence of subcultural differentiation, it is not clear that this aspect of the company's culture, like the founder's behavior, can be generalized to other settings. The primary limitation of this study, then, is the fact that it is based on a sample size of one (organization).

Reviewer B

Sutton (1994) defined a "smash and grab" ethnography with reference to those who rob stores rapidly by smashing the windows, grabbing whatever is in sight, and running. A smash and grab qualitative study bears little if any relationship to the patient, deep participant observation of a true ethnographer, who spends a year, sometimes more, learning the language and culture of the people he or she is studying. Whereas a few ethnographers have long bucked the trend toward quantitative methods in organizational studies (e.g., Kondo, 1990; Kunda, 1992; Pettigrew, 1979, 1985b; Rofel, 1989; Van Maanen, 1991), inferior smash and grab ethnographies have invaded the "cultural" studies of organizational researchers. These short-term qualitative studies invoke the power and depth of insight of qualitative research but then fail to use the methods required to obtain high-quality ethnographic data.

This study is a classic example of a smash and grab study. Stage 1 of the research may have consisted of 6 months of ethnography, as claimed, but 2 to 20 hours of interviews and observations, per week, falls short of true participant observation and 6 months is a short time. Furthermore, the only result of that qualitative work, presented in this manuscript and of relevance to the rest of the paper, is the employees' ways of talking about their subcultural identities. One of those identities, length of tenure, turned out to be "statistically insignificant." I would say all these statistics are insignificant. The authors would have been better served by refraining from counting phrases in a content analysis. Instead, they should have stayed longer at the company, working alongside the employees, and coming to be accepted by them, penetrating the impression management "front" we all use with strangers. Two to 20 hours a week is insufficient for this process. Importantly, there is no reflexive discussion of the researchers and how their relationships with the employees might have affected what they saw, heard, perceived, or concluded. This is an inferior and superficial application of qualitative methods, which should be rejected. No revisions could fix what is wrong with this manuscript.

My Opinion

Like the previous study by O'Reilly and colleagues (1991), this study begins by collecting and aggregating subjective interpretations and then proceeds to reify those aggregations, as if they were objectively accurate characterizations of this organization's culture and subcultures. The study also hovers, like the study by O'Reilly et al., between the emic

views of study participants and the etically generated content analysis
categories of the researchers, perhaps moving a bit closer to an emic
view. The authors do not hesitate to move from this study of a single
organization to generalizing about the life cycles of entrepreneurial
organizations and the validity of the integration and differentiation
viewpoints. Also, like O'Reilly et al., this study is a narrow specialist
study focused on a single cultural manifestation (organizational stories, referred to as critical event histories). There is little evidence of the
authors seeking an in-depth understanding of the culture, although
that may underestimate the depth of insight that came from the 6
months of qualitative work that is not reported in any detail in this
manuscript. Overall, the language of this paper seems to be derived
from the hypothesis-generating, theory-testing rhetoric developed for
quantitative studies.

How does this 1985 study reflect my current preference for studies
that are broad and deep rather than narrow, that incorporate all three
perspectives, and that include critical as well as managerial interests?
The study's relevance to the integration and differentiation perspectives is explicit. The fragmentation view, with its focus on paradoxes,
contradictions, and ambiguities in accounts such as stories, could well
have been investigated usefully, but it was not. This study has a strength,
according to quantitative criteria for evaluation, in that its sampling
procedure and data reporting included employees from all levels of the
hierarchy and tried to determine if hierarchical differences affect interpretations. These elements are congruent with a critical interest, although this is not as explicit as I would now prefer. The study is clearly
not written in the managerial interest; its lack of an explicit critical
focus, and its use of objectifying language characteristic of quantitative
manuscripts, suggests that its primary focus is the descriptive interest.

The study has some strengths. It does show, within this context, that
the founder's view of the company's history and his personal values
were seldom reflected in the views of the employees, who disagreed not
only with him but also often with each other. Although the statistics
used (the percentage of employees who told a given critical incident
highlighting this or that interpretation and whether between-group
differences in particular interpretations were statistically significant)
were not sophisticated; they were appropriate. Because these measures
were derived from content analysis of employee-generated critical incidents, they did retain the actual content of what people said; specific

accounts of particular incidents were quoted. I think the study should have been written differently, however. A critical and a managerial interpretation of the results could be outlined, stressing the contrast and abandoning any language implying interest neutrality. In addition, I would refrain from writing in a style that is more suitable for quantitative than qualitative or hybrid studies.

Reflecting on this study, I would encourage my old self and my collaborators to draw more deeply on the qualitative data we collected and refrain from generalizing with such abandoned ease. Many of the suggestions of Reviewer B, who seems to be an advocate of long-term ethnography, would have improved the depth of insight in the study. An ethnography would, in many ways, have produced better qualitative insights. Regarding quantitative evaluation criteria, I believe that this study's major weakness is that its generalizations are based on a study of one founder of one company. Could another founder have been more successful in imprinting his or her values and version of history on his or her employees? Even if prior studies by other researchers produced results that supported the results of this study, it is always problematic to build generalizations based on a sample size of one. Therefore, this study's primary contribution lies not in its "theory testing" generalizations but in its demonstration of a hybrid method.

When a hybrid study is evaluated, reactions are often strongly positive or strongly negative. Reviewer A has the more appreciative reaction, stating that the hybrid method offers a systematic and creative way to portray the complexities of a company's history in the eyes of its employees. Reviewer B sees this hybrid approach as less worthwhile. As in most hybrid studies, my coauthors and I compromised some strengths of each of the methods we combined (e.g., McGrath, Martin, et al., 1982). It is easy to imagine a sophisticated quantitative archival or survey study of the culture creation process in many companies. In such a study, the variables studied and the depth of understanding of various views of the process would not be as deep (recall Denison's [1990] quantitative measures of culture), but other relevant questions about generalizability would have been addressed more authoritatively. Also, Reviewer B is correct in saying that this study falls short of the standards usually used to assess the quality of a full-scale, long-term ethnography. No revisions can address these problems, which are inherent in hybrid methods. The fate of this manuscript, therefore, must rest in the hands of those who read and evaluate it because in any hybrid study, the cup really is half full and half empty. In the final study to be discussed, I return to a purist approach, in this case, an ethnography—one that is unusual in its cross-national organizational focus and its journal-length format.

Study 4: Botti (1995)

Overview

Botti (1995) studied a Japanese manufacturing company, Nipponware, that initially tried to enact, in Italy, traditionally Japanese commitments (for "theory Z" corporate cultures, see Ouchi, 1981) to job security, promotion based on seniority, consensual decision making, out-of-school hiring, and so on. In 1987, the firm faced a market crisis and felt forced to move to an emphasis on lean production, increased flexibility, innovation, and job rotation, with a quality-oriented, small batch production system. This transformation would be wrenching in any case, but the culturally based misunderstandings between the Japanese owners and managers and the Italian managers and workforce made this change process even more complicated than is usually the case. Botti analysed this process longitudinally (length of research time is unclear) from a cross-cultural perspective. She used primarily interviews but also documentary study and some observation to develop understandings of what kinds of misunderstandings occurred and why. Interviewees (sampling details not included) seemed to include extensive contact with two Italian managers and considerable contact and/or observation of other managers, both Japanese and Italian, as well as some (perhaps more limited) observation and interviews with shop floor workers. This U.S.-born researcher reflexively analyzed her own limits (p. 58): "While 30 years spent in Italy helped me to make sense of what the Italians told me, language problems, cultural distance, and mutual efforts at politeness complicated my interviews with the Japanese." Botti resolved this difficult dilemma by relying primarily on the Italian's descriptions of their own behavior as well as that of the Japanese. She then proceeded to interpret the Japanese reactions in more depth by drawing on the extensive, and clearly relevant, Japanese literature on their managerial practices and cultural beliefs (e.g., Befu, 1963; Doi, 1973; Ishida, 1984; Nakane, 1970).

Botti (1995) presented a detailed portrait of the dilemmas experienced by the Japanese managers, left bereft of familiar or familial support in a strange country. Not surprisingly, they responded positively to friendly overtures from Italian supervisors of the shop floor, not realizing that the overtures carried expectations of future favors rather than deep personal friendship. As one Italian employee described it,

> From a purely personal point of view, some of the [Japanese] executives were really needy, and they reached out to the Italians. The Italians responded, but by welcoming the Japanese into their homes they were really after something else. . . . For instance, these [Italian] guys would go right to the [Japanese] managers and ask them for help and advice—about practical matters they understood perfectly well. The Japanese reacted in a very fatherly way to this kind of thing, and they never realized that they were being manipulated. So there was this kind of duping and misunderstanding in the very beginning, because the Japanese were innocent and naive in some ways. (p. 62)

When the Japanese did not respond with favors to these acts of "friendship," the Italians threatened work slowdowns and other forms of productivity sabotage to the consternation and surprise of the Japanese, who thought they were dealing with a different kind of relationship—with a different level of mutual trust and obligation. For example, the Japanese promoted three of their Italian "friends," who were members of the union, to positions as foremen. The Japanese did not worry about divided loyalties because in Japan it was customary to overlap these two roles:

> When the foremen manipulated their personal networks in order to limit some of the strikes, the Japanese considered their behaviour to be laudable and natural—used as they were to enterprise unions and to foremen who strove to achieve harmony within the company. What they didn't understand was that the foremen were making a personalistic, collusive use of their mandate and doing their bosses "a favour." The Japanese didn't understand that favours in Mediterranean patronage systems are always accompanied by an element of threat: that they *cost*. The Japanese didn't even appear to get the message when one of the foremen took to creating serious problems which—after useless recourse to outside experts—he then "resolved," thus reminding top management that he was indispensable for the regularity of the workflow. (pp. 63-64)

The result of incidents such as these was a crisis of misunderstanding that brought the plant, and its productivity, to a standstill. Eventually, a small group of Italian and Japanese managers managed to diagnose the problem and work out a cross-culturally complex resolution, rife with ambiguities that permitted some differences to persist without causing high levels of disruption. Botti's account included richly detailed, contextually specific descriptions of both Japanese and Italian cultures in a context in which one is transplanted within the other and both have to respond to environmental, market-driven demands for organizational change.

Reviewer A

This study offers a classic "thick description" of not one, but two national cultures, as they come together in a Japanese-owned manufacturing plant, located in Italy. Botti's cultural portrait is grounded in sensitivity to job and status differences within each of these national cultures. She works, with care and nuance, to understand the varying subjective experiences of the people she studies. She presents her analysis with extensive quotes and contextual details so the readers can feel "they were there" and have enough information to gauge the accuracy of the wide range of data reported. The writing is subtle, eloquent, carefully structured, and beautifully crafted. The account shows none of the hallmarks of the national stereotyping and oversimplification that mars much cross-cultural research, in part because of Botti's extensive knowledge of Italy (as a long-time resident) and her familiarity with a wide range of Japanese cultural research. This intellectual cross-cultural openness is welcome in a field in which even cross-cultural researchers seldom read scholarly literature from other countries.

That said, and despite its longitudinal focus, this study has weaknesses. It is not clear how long the researcher spent on site, what activities she observed or participated in, or how study participants did or did not react to her presence. There is little reflexivity, except for the remark about her 30 years in Italy, as opposed to her distant and polite relations with the Japanese. How did her sex or U.S. birth affect her interactions and perceptions? More detail about particular interactions would have strengthened the presentation of results: Who said what? What were the material conditions of the work site where this interaction took place? What were the class backgrounds and current financial status of the people studied? It seems (details about method are dismayingly few) that much evidence was collected in interviews rather than long-term participant observation, suggesting that this study may have been a short-term case study rather than a full-scale, longitudinal ethnography. Perhaps, however, this is simply due to the length limitations inherent in a journal publication. More methods details would help readers assess the quality of the data-gathering process and the depth of involvement that underpin this study's conclusions. More reflexivity would also be helpful for the reader. Despite these shortcomings, this study remains one of the most eloquent and insightful journal-length ethnographies published in recent years.

Reviewer B

This is a circuitously written, poorly organized description of a classic organizational change project (moving from a seniority and consensus-based Japanese system based on lifetime employment to a more lean and mean, flexible, small batch production system). This common transition takes place in an uncommon setting: a Japanese-owned plant in Italy. The study includes virtually no details about participant sampling procedures, sample size, interview content, sites observed, and so on. As is usually the case in such narrative accounts of single case studies, there is no attempt to address issues of reliability or validity, even without statistical measures. It is certainly not clear why we should believe that this U.S.-born researcher accurately perceives and recounts the opinions of either the Japanese or the Italian employees. The results of the study primarily consist of detailed descriptions of the various misunderstandings that arose between the Japanese managers and the Italians working at the plant. Botti explains how, over time, those misunderstandings were partially resolved, so lean production policies could be enacted and the firm could survive.

Botti gives us a detailed understanding of one unique context, with few if any applications to other situations. Perhaps because of this inability to generate generalizations or applications, Botti refrains from drawing many theoretically based conclusions. It is unclear what this research, or even this kind of research, can contribute to our theoretical or practical understanding of organizational change or cross-cultural communication.

My Opinion

Like most ethnographies, this study is written from a subjective and emic vantage point. It eschews most generalization, explores a wide variety of cultural manifestations, and seeks an in-depth understanding that penetrates the "front" of impression management strategies.

Although it makes no references to the three theoretical perspectives, it includes material consistent with all three. Differentiation appears to be its home perspective, but data indicative of integration and fragmentation views are also examined. The study alternates between Italian and Japanese and between high-ranking and low-ranking employees; it seems to have material congruent with both managerial and critical interests.

I admire this study and believe its richly contextualized descriptions of cross-national misunderstandings deepens understanding of both national cultures (see also Sackmann's [1997] fine edited collection of case studies). Although there is considerable rhetoric about "globalization" and the spread of multinational corporations, it is still rare to find deeply insightful descriptions of the kinds of difficulties that bring so many of these ventures to an expensive, rue-filled end. Despite these strengths, Reviewers A and B both find fault with this study for very different reasons. Some of these criticisms, I believe, are well founded (and could easily be responded to), whereas others are less appropriate.

Reviewer B makes a set of methodological and perhaps epistemological assumptions about the value of generalization, large samples, systematic sampling procedures, reliability, and validity. These assumptions about what makes research of high quality are more appropriate for quantitative than qualitative studies. Reviewer B mentions few of the usual qualitative criteria for judging methodological adequacy (long-term participant observation, insightful reflexivity about the effect of the researcher on the data collected, richness of contextual detail, etc.). I now provide a pragmatic discussion of how one might respond to a review, such as this one, that uses inappropriate evaluation criteria given the method used. If a journal editor were to request a full discussion of Reviewer B's suggestions, the author could explain why a larger sample of case studies of other contexts, or better indicators of reliability or validity, would not be appropriate given the goals of this study. Such an explanation might be a useful introduction to these issues for readers more used to quantitative approaches—a fine idea if one's goal is to increase the breadth of work cited and understood by cultural researchers. Reviewer B would be unlikely to be appeased by such an explanation, however. If the editor implies that Reviewer B must be appeased in a revision (unlikely in a journal such as *Organization* that understands and values qualitative work), this might well prove to be an exercise in futility for the author. In such a case, it might be advisable to submit the article to a journal that is more open to qualitative work. Reviewer A, however, makes many important suggestions, congruent with usual definitions of high-quality qualitative research, that merit careful inclusion, such as providing a better discussion of reflexivity and more methodological detail. Responding to Reviewer A's concerns would make the paper stronger.

Resolving Dilemmas

These contradictory, opinionated reviews, and some of the more broad-minded resolutions suggested for each study, offer ways to deal with the debates about issues, theoretical perspectives, interests, and methods that have been the focus of this book so far. Pragmatically, given the range of researcher preferences represented in the cultural literature, it is impossible to please all of the people all of the time. There is considerable evidence, however, that the intellectual climate for organizational culture research is becoming more receptive. Organizational researchers working in the cultural domain are increasingly aware of the problems of inappropriate evaluation criteria. More cultural scholars are learning how to evaluate unfamiliar methods and research designs. The organizational field as a whole is also changing, becoming (in some areas) more accepting of qualitative approaches. Some research domains, such as organizational identity, must face the same dilemmas that cultural researchers have been dealing with (whether identity should be assessed from an emic or etic viewpoint, whether interpretations of an organization's identity are multiple or single, and therefore supposedly consensual, etc.). There are more journal outlets of high quality that are open to qualitative research. In other words, this is a great time for organizational researchers to explore cultural questions. Intellectual developments in methods and epistemology have electrified the humanities and some social sciences, first in Europe and then slowly spreading throughout North America and throughout the rest of the world. Many of these developments (and disputes) have surfaced earlier in cultural studies than in other organizational domains, creating opportunities for innovation in theory, methods, and—as described in Chapter 9—ways of writing about cultures in organizations.

 **9**

Writing About Cultures

A CRISIS OF REPRESENTATION?

*Whether quantitative or qualitative methods are used,
representational approaches to knowledge production rest on a
privileging of the consciousness of the researcher who is deemed
capable of discovering the "truth" about the world of management
and organization through a series of representations.*
—Knights (1992, p. 515)

Many cultural researchers write in the traditional language of the social scientist, scientific journalese, and present results in traditional scientific style (theory, hypotheses, methods, results, and conclusion). When studies are written in this apparently objective, ostensibly factual style, it appears as if the author is saying, "Here is what is true." Ethnographic researchers are more likely to abstain from explicit claims of objectivity and "scientific" writing styles, but they too use writing strategies to enhance the authority of the author and the credibility of a text, making implied truth claims in a more indirect way. In such accounts, the I/eye of the author disappears, and what is left appears to be a picture of reality that you as reader would supposedly see and interpret in the same way as the omniscient, invisible author.

Recently, qualitative researchers, critical and postmodern theorists, and others have raised important challenges to the truth claims made in these kinds of scholarly writing. This is the "Crisis of Representation?" in this chapter's title. This chapter builds on these challenges, linking them directly to problems of representing knowledge when writing about culture in organizations. There are alternative ways to write that avoid many of these difficulties. Some of these alternatives eschew generalization, focusing instead on "thick" (i.e., richly detailed and multi-layered) descriptions of specific cultures. Other alternative writing styles lend themselves, in a carefully delimited way, to the development of cultural theory. I believe these are useful and legitimate ways to write, well suited to describe cultures in organizations. This chapter describes these various approaches to textual representation and illustrates them with a few, quite innovative texts that describe organizational cultures, written in ways you may have never imagined.

Writing Dilemmas

These challenges to traditional social science, coupled with the examples of new ways of writing about culture, will highlight a series of writing dilemmas all cultural researchers must either face or avoid: "Should I write in the traditional social scientific style, implying 'This is the truth about this culture,' or should I offer different, possibly conflicting perceptions and interpretations of the events and experiences of the people I studied?" "Should I state my observations, and those of others, in clear terms, or should I explore, in writing, the ambiguities of what people perceive, think, and feel?" "How can a researcher write a coherent account of a culture that is rife with uncertainties?" "Are accounts that acknowledge uncertainty somehow an attempt to present a more 'realistic' picture of how people in organizations actually view the complexities of their everyday lives?" "If so, isn't this just another truth claim dressed up in new clothing?" "In whose interest do I want to write—in the managerial interest, or do I want to focus on a change-oriented emancipatory political agenda that would improve the lives of workers who earn relatively little?" "How can I write an emancipatory account, given that empirical work, in effect, must study the status quo and not some idealized, future world?" "Should I acknowledge ambiguities and uncertainties if I am worried about sliding into moral relativism and abandoning commitment to the political and action-oriented

objectives of my research, which require a modicum of ideological certainty and a focused change agenda?"

Obviously, each of us has to find our own answers to these questions.
Whether you are a cultural researcher or just reading work in this domain, this chapter on writing and representation will help you understand why some of the best contemporary cultural research is written in
unusual styles. This chapter may also make the limitations of the traditional scientific writing style more salient to you. If you are a cultural
researcher, by the end of this chapter it is my hope that some new questions and new ways of writing about culture may suggest themselves
to you.

The Logic of More and Less Traditional
Social Scientific Writing Styles

The style and format of a traditional social scientific journal article
includes tightly reasoned, theoretically derived deductions; precisely
formulated hypotheses; crisp and succinct but thorough descriptions
of sampling procedures; operationalizations of concepts; exact measures; evidence of reliability and validity; and statistical tests with conventional ways of representing uncertainty (probabilities, with confidence intervals, and error terms). These components of the traditional
style are familiar, making omissions easy to detect. This structure rig-
idly constrains the theoretical conclusions that can be drawn from a
study, forcing hypotheses, data, tests, and conclusions to be tightly coupled. Such constraints strengthen the presentation of quantitative research (and even some hybrid and qualitative studies), improving the
quality of empirically based theoretical generalizations. This style also
lends social science, the poor cousin of "hard" science fields, a scientific
aura that gives credibility to these disciplines. Truth claims appear to be
empirically well-founded, objectively measured, and therefore to be
trusted. With this representational writing style, generalizable theory
based on empirical research can be developed in a straightforward
manner that is relatively easy to use in teaching PhD's what is known
and MBA's how to use what is known.

When this kind of traditional, representational writing style is used
for ethnographic research, some of its limitations become evident (e.g.,
Hatch, 1996). For example, many ethnographic studies begin with an

emic focus on what is in the minds of the people being studied rather than an etic focus that begins with hypotheses derived from theories in a researcher's mind. Therefore, for emic research, often grounded theory is preferred—hypotheses that emerge from data rather than hypotheses that are deduced from theory (Glaser & Strauss, 1967). Obviously, it would not be appropriate to write up the results of such a study beginning with a literature review and deriving hypotheses from that review. A different style of writing would be required. For reasons discussed in Chapter 7, characteristics of good quantitative research (such as large, random samples) are not suitable for some kinds of qualitative research. For example, ethnographers prefer to select informants not randomly but based on such personal attributes as insightfulness and willingness to confide in the researcher. Therefore, for these kinds of qualitative studies, discussions of sampling procedures and interrater reliability are unlikely to be appropriate or even relevant. For all these reasons, the traditional representational, social scientific writing style may not work well for some kinds of cultural studies.

Postmodern and critical theorists have deeper reasons for critiquing representational writing styles, claiming that such writing styles make truth claims in ways that mask uncertainties and indeterminacies as well as the managerial interests of some researchers. The quotation from David Knights (1992), with which this chapter began, illustrates this kind of critique of the truth claims implicit in traditional social scientific (representational) writing styles. As introduced in Chapter 2, a being realism epistemology underpins much objectivist social scientific writing, treating concepts such as culture as if they were unproblematic objects of analysis—"out there" in a form that anyone could recognize. In contrast, advocates of "becoming-realism" critique representational writing strategies as a rhetoric that hides conceptual uncertainties, making truth claims that, under close examination, cannot be substantiated. Theoretical generalizations (such as the three-perspective model in this book) have been critiqued as imperialistic, "totalizing" moves to subsume other people's ideas into a grand metatheory that lays claim to representing the truth (the whole truth, nothing but the truth) (e.g., Gagliardi, 1991). Critical organizational theorists challenge representational writing strategies of traditional social scientific writing on different grounds. As described in Chapter 6, critical theorists find that most organizational research, including most organizational culture studies (even those written in the ostensibly neutral descriptive interest), represents the interests of managers rather than the interests of those who have less power.

If a social scientist were to write honestly about what is known, and how it is or is not known, the ensuing writing style would have to be quite different than the rigid formalisms of the traditional, representational style that is the norm in many organizational journals. The strengths and advantages of the traditional, representational writing style are likely to be familiar to most readers of this book; the look, logic, and strengths of alternative styles of writing may be less familiar. Thus, in this chapter I focus on the advantages of alternative styles. Van Maanen (1988) offers one typology in a book that serves as a useful introduction to these ideas for organizational culture researchers.

Realist, Confessional, and Impressionist Tales

Van Maanen (1996) distinguishes realist, confessional, and impressionist "tales." These are narrative structures used for describing the results (or part of the results) of qualitative studies. (For more insight into writing strategies for cultural studies, see Clifford, 1988, 1997; Clifford & Marcus, 1986; Czarniawska, 1997, 1998; Geertz, 1988; Marcus & Fischer, 1986/1999). The realist tale is most common. The authority of the author is unchallenged in a realist tale. He or she has interpretive omnipotence—the all-knowing, all-seeing narrator whose view is truth. In such accounts, the author usually avoids the first person and uses impersonal or third-person circumlocutions ("the researcher" or "members of the culture think") or the passive tense ("informants were selected") in the main body of the text. (Interestingly, introductions, conclusions, footnotes, and appendixes sometimes break with the "realist" writing strategy of the rest of a text, pointing to places where authorial omniscience breaks down.) These impersonal textual strategies enhance the author's authority by making his or her embodied individuality (a source of potential human limitations, if not bias) disappear from the text. The tone is studied neutrality and objectivity; no doubts are revealed. Only one interpretation—that of the author—is possible. Because this writing style is so familiar, bland, and standardized, and so widely adopted in journals and other scholarly publications, it is a style that can appear "styleless," one that is devoid of writing skill and rhetorical strategies. This is misleading because this realist style is indeed a well-developed rhetorical strategy that enhances the apparent objectivity of the author by deleting almost all references to the more subjective and personal aspects of the research and writing process (Van Maanen, 1996):

> By treating writing as largely an individual product and language as secondary to facts, theories, and methods, we nourish and reward those whose performed identity approximates a highly stereotyped cold-eyed, dispassionate man or woman of science whose talk and publications merely code and record the facts uncovered by research. The office, corridor, and tavern talk, the lessons of socialization, the editorial work that helps shape and craft the written word are blithely ignored. (p. 379)

In addition, in a realist tale the author seems untroubled about generalizing from singularities (a particular behavior, exhibited by a particular person or persons, in a particular situation, at a specific time). Therefore, for example, Geertz's (1973) famous description of a Balinese cockfight is drawn from an amalgamation of cockfights he observed, creating a prototypical, representative cockfight. In addition, implicitly or explicitly, the author claims to represent the "typical" cultural member's view of this prototypical cockfight, without distortion ("The Balinese feel . . ."). When a realist tale acknowledges variation among cultural members, the author usually makes a generalization about a vaguely specified proportion of cultural members ("some" or "a few"), followed by quotations from individuals who, it is implicitly claimed, represent the median position in these majority or minority groups. Behavior is described so that it appears ordinary, natural, and normal. Theoretical concepts are illustrated with specific details, chosen by the author, which fit the definitions of these abstractions. This editorial role of the author—choosing some details and not others and quoting some informants and not others—is not mentioned in a realist tale. Thus, the author casts himself or herself as a valid observer of native views, capable of seeing "natural" behavior, describing it, and theorizing about it, without distortion, in "realistically truthful" terms. In Chapter 2, the discussion of epistemology indicated that a realist tale usually assumes being-realism and representationalism. Both quantitative and qualitative research can be described using variants of this kind of realist style.

Van Maanen's (1996) second writing strategy is a confessional tale. In such tales, the author's authority is personalized. The author tries to establish rapport with the reader, using the first person "I" (or eye) to imply that the author is somehow trustworthy, usually because he or she is like the reader in some way. Perhaps the most famous instance of this is Firth's (1936/1967) description of his arrival at an island, quoted and analyzed in Geertz (1988) and further contextualized by Pratt (1986). Firth tries to give the reader the sense of being there with him as his ship arrives at the island, where a chief waits on the beach:

> In the cool of the morning, just before sunrise, the bow of the *Southern Cross* headed towards the eastern horizon, on which a tiny blue outline was faintly visible. Slowly it grew into a rugged mountain mass, standing up sheer from the ocean.... The ship anchored on a short cable in the open bay off the coral reef. Almost before the chain was down the natives began to scramble aboard, coming over the side by any means that offered, shouting fiercely to each other and to us in a tongue of which not a word was understood by the Mota-speaking folk of the mission vessel. I wondered how such turbulent human material could ever be induced to submit to scientific study. Vahihaloa, my "boy," looked over the side from the upper deck, "My word, me fright too much," he said with a quavering laugh; "Me tink this fella he savvy kaikai me." *Kaikai* is the pidgin-English term for "eat."... Feeling none too sure myself of the reception that awaited us—though I knew it would stop short of cannibalism—I reassured him, and we began to get out the stores. Later we went ashore in one of the canoes.... At last the long wade ended, we climbed up the steeply shelving beach, crossed the soft, dry sand strewn with the brown needles of the Casuarina trees—a home-like touch; it was like a pine avenue—and were led to an old chief, clad with great dignity in a white coat and a loin-cloth, who awaited us on his stool under a large shady tree. (pp. 11-13)

As Geertz explains, this description encourages readers to believe they would react the same way as the author during this entry scene. The first sightings of the island and what happened as the boat drew closer to the beach are incidents written to maximize the reader's impression that he or she is beside the author on the boat, seeing what he has seen as the boat approaches the beach. This rapport is enhanced by the author's description of Casuarina trees as being "like a pine avenue." The author labels this a "home-touch," giving the reader a way to view Casuarina trees in familiar terms and at the same time making the reader feel a commonality with the author. Such a rapport between an author and a reader increases the author's credibility in the rest of the account, which in Firth's case is written primarily in the realist style.

Constructing a presumed similarity with the reader, however, is a tricky business. Although Firth wrote his account in 1936, some readers probably were discomforted then (and certainly would be now) by a description of the young male on the boat as "my 'boy.'" The young male speaks in pidgin-English, whereas the author's probably strained attempts to speak the native tongues are not recorded. Referring to the "natives" as "turbulent human material" might well be construed as demeaning and perhaps racist. Van Maanen (1996) acknowledges the gap between a reader and the writer. He advises authors to establish rapport in a confessional tale by portraying themselves as wily and suspicious of deceit, a distancing stance might prove more successful with contemporary readers of cultural research.

Confessional tales often tell of a progression from etic (outsider or stranger) to emic (insider or initiate) status. In such tales, the author often begins by telling about preconceptions held that will later be shown to be erroneous. The initial contact with the culture is usually described in some depth (as in Firth's arrival on the beach), followed by some incidents in which misunderstandings occurred or hardships had to be endured. Next, the author is tested in some way and then is rewarded, perhaps by being invited to participate in a formal initiation ceremony. Finally, some evidence of acceptance as a member is forthcoming. Only after such a progression is it credible that the author claim to be "just like everyone else" or to "blend into the background." This too is a form of truth claim that the author, after a long and possibly difficult or embarrassing period of cultural socialization, becomes a valid interpreter of native views, one whose textual account can be trusted to represent "natural" behavior truthfully, or at least authentically.

For example, recall the way in which Kondo (1990), a Japanese American studying a family-owned business in Japan, described the day she saw someone reflected in the shiny metal surface of a butcher's display case walking in the shuffling style of a typical young Japanese housewife. To her horror, she recognized this person as herself. Later in her stay, others too began to see her as acceptably socialized, and once again she reacted with an ambivalence that perhaps might generate empathy in her readers:

> At a tea ceremony class, I performed a basic "thin tea" ceremony flawlessly, without need for prompting or correcting my movements. My teacher said in tones of approval, "You know, when you first started, I was so worried. The way you moved, the way you walked, was so clumsy! But now, you're just like an *ojosan*, a nice young lady." Part of me was inordinately pleased that my awkward, exaggerated Western movements had *finally* been replaced by the disciplined grace that makes the tea ceremony so seemingly natural and beautiful to watch. But another voice cried out in considerable alarm, "Let me escape before I'm completely transformed." (pp. 23-24)

Whether she is pleased or not with her new skills, this passage, among others, establishes Kondo's credibility as an emic participant in the culture she is studying.

In a quantitative study, confessional material is usually relegated to prefaces, footnotes, and appendices. For example, as Hofstede (1991) explained in his preface to a book on cultures and organizations written for the general public,

> In the late 1960s I accidentally became interested in cultural differences— and gained access to rich data for studying them. This study resulted in the publication in 1980 of a book on the subject, *Culture's Consequences*. It was written for a scholarly public; it had to be, because it cast doubts on the universal validity of established theories in psychology, organizational sociology, and management theory: so I had to show the theoretical reasoning, base data, and statistical treatments used to reach the conclusions. . . . As far as differences among nations were concerned [this] book certainly provided much information, but maybe too much of it at once. Many readers evidently only read parts of the message.

Although this confession is hardly a full-blown narrative tale with characters, plot, and dramatic structure, it does have a confessional tone: that the author's interest in culture was "accidental"—driven by the availability of a large data set—and that few read all of his first scholarly book. Nevertheless, for the general public audience of this later book, such small confessions might well add to the author's rapport with his readers.

In contrast, consider how Bartunek (1984, p. 357) introduces a massive cultural change and restructuring process undertaken in the order of nuns of which she is a member. She says, "My interpretation is based in part on my experience as a member of the order since 1966 and as a consultant for the restructuring after the decision was made to do it." This is the only time in the text that she uses the pronoun I (except for one footnote). Membership in an order of nuns requires a lengthy, formalized, and elaborate initiation process; on a less emotional and spiritual level, success as a consultant often entails a brief but important period in which the consultant proves his or her competence to the client. Bartunek, however, gives no further confessional details about these entrée processes, and after this one sentence the "I" disappears from her text. This impersonality is characteristic of a realist tale and stands in stark contrast to the repeated use of "I" in a confessional tale such as Kondo's (1990).

Van Maanen (1996) labels the third kind of ethnography an impressionist tale. Such a tale is often an extended anecdote included within a longer ethnography or a tale told over drinks after an official research presentation is completed. The author (or oral historian) describes a special event or scene from a personal perspective. The author is an actor in the event and offers a believable (not completely flattering) self-portrayal. Both the "I" and the "other" (one or more cultural members) are kept in view as the tale unfolds. You—the spectator, listener, or reader—feel as if you are there, in a ringside seat, as the action happens. The drama is vivid, details are exact and vibrant, and the course of events is unique and unexpected. The author of an impressionist tale is a master storyteller, one who builds dramatic suspense and does not give the ending away until the very last minute. Impressionist tales, as Czarniawska (1997) explained, are told with a dramatic flair, with some of the plot characteristics of a good story or novel.

Examples of impressionist tales are rare in the literature but, fortunately, not in the bars and parties after formal research presentations. Perhaps the best example comes from Van Maanen, although in this context only a brief excerpt can be given (the whole is well worth reading). He tells the story of riding one night in a patrol car as part of his well-known study of police work. That night, Van Maanen and his police informant give chase to a "roll'n stolen"—that is, a possibly stolen car that refused to stop when hailed. The patrol car carrying Van Maanen and his police companion, David, careens around corners at high speeds. Van Maanen (1988) describes his reactions in terms that make it easy for a reader to identify with him:

> My knuckles are pale from gripping the shotgun jiggling in its cradle before me and I am hanging on to the handhold of the door. I can barely manage the appearance of even limited self-control. Blood is throbbing in my ears. My powers of speech have vanished. I am scared. . . . [a few minutes later, when Van Maanen is asked drive the patrol car by himself]. The radio seems to be screeching at me to do something. The lights and siren, to my astonishment, somehow come on. The demonic shotgun is no longer secure and bounces around the front seat. The power brakes feel awkward and almost toss me through the windscreen at the first stop sign. To complicate matters, I have no idea where I am going. As I round a corner near the interstate, the ticket book, the clipboard, the logbook, the portable radio, David's hat, and God knows what else go sliding out the passenger door I'd forgotten to fully close and onto the street. The shotgun would have gone too had I not grasped the stock of the weapon with a last-second, panic-stricken lunge. Shamefully, I pull to the side of the road to gather up my litter. (pp. 109-115)

Such a description lends authenticity to the author's description of police work. The story shows him in an unflattering light (scared, not in charge, and unclear about what is happening). This lends credibility to his account (after all, if he is willing to describe himself in an unflattering way, he must be telling the truth about what he sees). At the same time, under the surface the author's description of himself is attractive in some ways. He is brave, if a bit foolhardy, to ride in the speeding car, with the shotgun sliding around; if he is willing to take these risks to learn about police work, which most readers expect to entail some danger, then his account might well be credible. Part of this tale's credibility, however, comes from Van Maanen's obvious rhetorical skill. He tells a gripping tale, and that gives persuasive power and the appearance of accuracy to other, more mundane or abstract parts of his text. Thus, skillfully told impressionist tales, like their confessional and realist counterparts, are all ways of writing that enhance the ability of texts to convince us that they are truthfully portraying what is real. Impressionist tales, however, are risky because the author is strengthening his or her credibility by undermining his or her omniscient stature.

Many researchers (especially but not exclusively those using qualitative methods) could use all three kinds of tales in a single account. A confessional tale of the difficulties of entering a cultural setting, or a confessional account of the long and discouraging process of social-ization and, finally, initiation, might give credibility at the start of a cultural description. Also, if the eye/I of the author subsequently dis-appeared into the supposed objectivity of a realistic account, when credibility lagged or the account began to be boring, a vivid impression-ist tale might remind readers of what a brave, dynamic, and perhaps foolishly risky researcher was serving as their eyes and ears on the scene.

Although confessional and impressionist tales serve the purpose of establishing an author's credibility, they also offer information about the author. Such information is an asset for a reader, who can use it to decipher where the biases and interests of an author might lie. Given the emphasis, particularly in realist accounts, on objectivity and trying to write in the (supposedly neutral) descriptive interest, such clues can be of great value to a reader. If you believe, as I do, that it is difficult, if not impossible, to write strictly in the descriptive interest, then the incorpo-ration of confessional and impressionist tales in both qualitative and quantitative research would provide useful information for readers, who might otherwise know even less about who the author is and why or how he or she is studying a given culture. Nevertheless, we as readers should never lose sight of the fact that these tales are told by crafty au-thors who want to make a good impression on their readers.

In the following sections, I dissect what authors do to enhance the credibility of their scholarly writing. In some cases, these writing strate-gies are used primarily in qualitative studies, whereas other strategies are also used in quantitative studies. I discuss these writing techniques so that you will become more aware of their effect on your evaluations of the quality and credibility of a study. Whether you decide to use these strategies more frequently in your own writing is a judgment call, although I suspect we all use some of these strategies some of the time, whether we are aware of it or not.

Writing to Convince

Authenticity

Many cultural researchers have an appropriate modesty about their ability to perceive or convey absolute truth with perfect accuracy. Therefore, Golden-Biddle and Locke (1993; for a fuller exposition, see

Golden-Biddle & Locke, 1997) prefer the use of the term *authenticity* rather than accuracy to describe the ability of a text to describe everyday life in a field setting in a way that seems to genuinely reflect having "been there." The word "authenticity" is useful because, unlike "accuracy," it does not make an implicit truth claim; an authentic account simply tries to represent as best the author can what he or she observed, without any assertion that those observations were objective, accurate, or exactly like what another observer might have seen. Golden-Biddle and Locke delineate several rhetorical strategies that authors use to convey authenticity in a convincing fashion. A text that seems authentic is filled with details of everyday life. Quotations include colloquial phrases such as jargon unique to the particular context. Descriptions of events include details that expose cultural members in intimate or embarrassing moments. Quotations of frank conversations among cultural members may suggest that the presence of the researcher did not inhibit "normal" behavior. Finally, often the author describes what cultural members were thinking or feeling, as when Geertz (1973) begins a sentence with "The Balinese feel...." Such inferences about what cannot be observed can contribute to an impression of authenticity.

Because qualitative studies are evaluated, in part, by the length of time the researcher spent in the field setting, ideally living and working beside cultural members, a credible ethnography includes details about these aspects of the researcher's efforts. Readers are told about a researcher's efforts to collect data in a variety of settings and conditions, transcribing field notes, filming, keeping records, developing close relationships with informants, and so on. Such information enhances the author's credibility as a careful qualitative methodologist. This package of rhetorical strategies enhances authenticity by strengthening the impression that the author has "been there" and has thoroughly and carefully represented in the text what he or she observed. When they are well told, realist, confessional, and impressionist tales often incorporate these kinds of writing strategies.

Plausibility

Golden-Biddle and Locke (1993) also outline some writing strategies that increase the plausibility of an account. Whereas authenticity focuses on the setting studied, plausibility focuses on the relationship between the community of readers (their professional identities and preconceptions, the literature they have read, and the professional context in which they work) and the world portrayed in the author's account. For example, Firth (1936/1967) enhanced the plausibility of his account when he explained how Casuarina trees were like a pine avenue, which was familiar to his readers. An account can fail to achieve plausibility either by being too familiar ("What is new here?") or by being so unfamiliar that no connection with the reader is established. Familiarity is a particular problem in organizational culture research, in which the cultures being studied are familiar to both readers and researchers; such studies share none of the exotic appeal of headhunters and witches. It is difficult to capture the interest of a reader with the mundane details of quality circle meetings and drab, uniform office furnishings.[1]

Golden-Biddle and Locke (1993) discuss the ways in which authors enhance plausibility by justifying whatever is atypical about their study. For example, qualitative researchers tend to select organizations that are exceptional in some way. Although qualitative studies often seek only context-specific knowledge, mainstream journal editors often assume that a study should produce generalizable findings. In response, many qualitative researchers attempt to legitimate their choice of what might appear to be an atypical organizational context, claiming it is representative of a larger sample so that generalizations can legitimately be drawn. For example, as Golden-Biddle and Locke note, Adler and Adler (1988) draw parallels between the basketball teams they studied and other high-commitment organizations, such as the Jonestown mission, astronaut work groups, surgical teams, and combat units. Barley (1983) attempts to justify his study of the semiotics used by funeral directors by briefly describing the use of semiotics in a marketing department and an airplane manufacturing plant. In addition, he uses everyday examples and figures of speech, such as sleeping, to make the obscure and arcane practices of funeral directors seem more familiar and therefore more representative of other, more common occupational categories. Martin et al. (1998) justify their choice of The Body Shop, a cosmetics company with an unusual social change and environmental agenda, by describing the company as admittedly an "outlier," appropriate for examining the limits of the possible in a competitive capitalist marketplace. Golden-Biddle and Locke observe that Bartunek (1984) justifies her choice of a Roman Catholic order of nuns with more subtlety. First, she acknowledges the order's distinctiveness and the resulting limits to generalizability. Then she claims that a focus on this organization "allows certain features of the process of change in interpretive schemes to stand out more sharply than they otherwise might" (1984, p. 370; quoted in Golden-Biddle & Locke, 1993, p. 608). These examples illustrate a variety of ways in which atypical cultural contexts can be justified in an attempt to increase the plausibility (and the relevance) of a cultural portrait.

Many of Golden-Biddle and Locke's (1993) plausibility-enhancing writing techniques are more commonly used by quantitative researchers and may therefore be less appropriate for qualitative researchers. Golden-Biddle and Locke also argue that plausibility of qualitative research is enhanced by the use of schematic diagrams of words that describe conceptual relationships. (Whereas quantitative researchers seem to me to prefer boxes and arrows to represent causal relationships, qualitative researchers often rely on nested, overlapping circles, sometimes with dotted lines to indicate boundary permeability.) Plausibility is also sometimes enhanced when researchers do hybrid studies using systematic coding procedures, such as content analysis, for classifying qualitative observations (e.g., Rafaeli & Sutton, 1987). It is perhaps no accident that studies that adopt these plausibility-enhancing strategies (e.g., Adler & Adler, 1988; Barley, 1983; Bartunek, 1984) tend to be published in mainstream, primarily quantitative journals, such as *Administrative Science Quarterly* and the *Academy of Management Journal*. It is important to note, however, that some ethnographers find these kinds of schematic diagrams and figures unnecessary or even misleading.

Another plausibility-enhancing rhetorical strategy involves inviting the reader to join the royal "we" of the authors, implying that the reader is a member of the authors' community—a fellow scholar who agrees with the authors' conclusions. For example, this book uses the pronoun "we" sometimes to include me as author and you as reader and sometimes to encompass a broader community of scholars. As Golden-Biddle and Locke (1993, p. 606) observe, Barley (1983) also uses a floating "we" or "us" to draw the reader into his text with such phrases as "invites us to see similarities" (p. 397), "Let us consider the distinction" (p. 397), and "In everyday life we have all had occasion to wonder if someone is asleep" (p. 403). He also drafts the reader into participation by referring to the reader directly as you: "As you drive toward me in your speeding car" (p. 396). I have used this same strategy in this book, sometimes referring to the reader directly as "you." Each of these pronoun uses represents an attempt to establish rapport between the reader and the author, thereby enhancing the plausibility of the text.

When a study is written like a story, with a plot that builds to a dramatic crescendo, plausibility is enhanced (Czarniawska, 1998, 1999; Golden-Biddle & Locke, 1993; Jeffcutt, 1994), as Van Maanen stressed in his description of impressionist tales. Unfortunately (for those who enjoy dramatic writing) or fortunately (for those who consider such deliberate use of rhetorical power as unscientific, playing on "irrational" emotions), effective use of dramatic plot structure is rare in academic writing. Kondo (1990) does it well, particularly when she describes going on a retreat with fellow employees of a Japanese family-owned business. The retreat, held at a mountain resort, required an unexpected series of ritualized hardships and team-building activities, including calisthenics and floor scrubbing. Kondo stresses the physical difficulty and humility required in these exercises. Would Kondo be able to survive this ordeal? What would be required next? Would she be able to, or would she even continue to want to, keep up with the other members of her team? Would there be a happy ending and perhaps some rewarding pleasures at the end of this ordeal? Or would it end in her being singled out as a failure or a misfit? The suspense builds with each new activity, and when the end of the retreat is reached, it is described in the dramatic terms of an effectively scripted ritual. Kondo describes her participation in a way that makes us, the readers, feel her pain, stress, and embarrassment, lending plausibility to her account. Although the dramatic intensity of Kondo's account of her company's retreat is exceptional, even a journal article written in a standard style can and often does have some dramatic impact, as Van Maanen argues (1996):

> Even the standardized plots and formats that characterize many objectivist narratives—laying out the goal, specifying the enormous difficulties of achieving it, proposing a means for overcoming the difficulties based on the author's sensible theorizing, and announcing the success of the ideas and methods put forth—can be skillfully orchestrated to produce much applause and recognition for even the most self-effacing author. (p. 379)

A different kind of rhetorical strategy surfaces when an author is making a debatable claim. To enhance the plausibility of his or her arguments, the author will try to smooth over the difficulty by minimizing the validity of contesting claims, citing well-known others who apparently agree with the author, making subtle claims to superior knowledge of the issue, and so on. Often, these kinds of contests are relegated to the margins of a text—in an appendix or a footnote. Sometimes in such marginalized comments, an author can agree with critics; at the same time, the placement of these remarks in the margin of a text communicates that the issue is not of central importance to the main body of the text. For example, when I coedited a book on organizational culture (Frost, Moore, Louis, Lundberg, & Martin, 1991), I made a suggestion to Michael Rosen, the author of one of the book's chapters. He was contributing an analysis of the symbolic significance of Hermes ties in the investment banking industry. I wrote to him that the paper had an unacknowledged, stereotypically masculine focus—for example, phallic metaphors used in explaining the ties' symbolism and references to "we" included only men. In these and other ways, Rosen's text tacitly assumed that all investment bankers were men; the only women given voice in this text were their wives. Rosen (1991) responded to my editor's comment in a footnote, saying that these criticisms were "correct" and explaining that

> speaking toward this silence would require more space than provided by the editors here and perhaps would head in a direction other than they intended. Further, the silk tie is integrally part of the male business uniform in contemporary Western society. It is not uniformly part of the female's. (p. 284, footnote 3)

Rosen's response in the footnote was characteristically open-minded, but I was saddened that, as is often the case, an organizational study relegated concerns about its unspoken masculine orientation to a marginal place in the text. Such a writing strategy is understandable, however, in that it leaves the plausibility of the masculine account intact, whereas a more critical account would deconstruct it and offer an alternative, as described in the following section.

Criticality

In addition to the authenticity and plausibility writing strategies, Golden-Biddle and Locke (1993) suggest a third kind of writing strategy, criticality, which is used only rarely by organizational culture scholars. Criticality strategies are useful to consider because they provide practical guidelines for those who would like to do emancipatory cultural research in the critical interest. Criticality writing strategies prompt readers to reexamine ideas, beliefs, and assumptions that underlie their own work. The reader is encouraged to step back and reflect on what he or she has taken for granted, disrupting usual or conventional ways of doing research and questioning whether alternate approaches might be more appropriate or insightful. This stepping-back process encourages scholars to engage in a cultural critique (Marcus & Fischer, 1986/1999) of the theories and preconceptions of their field of research. This could involve challenging mainstream theories and methods, creating more critical approaches to studying everyday life in organizations, which is in accord with the differentiation perspective on cultural research.

Golden-Biddle and Locke (1993) describe three writing strategies that foster criticality. The first involves carving out room to reflect—an explicit pause. At various places in a text, the reader is encouraged to stop and reflect. For example, Barley (1983, p. 393; as quoted in Golden-Biddle & Locke, 1993, p. 610) encourages readers to stop and consider how organizational culture researchers have begun to make integrationist assumptions about consensually shared meanings: "That so many organizational theorists suddenly have begun to bandy about what suspiciously appears to resemble an interest in contextually shared meaning should give one pause." Another example is provided by Gherardi (1995b), who argues for the study of the cultural functions of emotions as follows:

> This is also a promising perspective for organizational studies should they wish to study, not a purported cold and abstract rationality which identifies the emotions with the devil, but an emotional rationality where reason is coloured by sentiment and is part of everyday reasonableness. (p. 153)

Criticality pauses enrich a cultural study. They offer an opportunity, for a qualitative researcher who refrains from making many theoretical generalizations, to explain the theoretical relevance of whatever contextually specific data are being discussed.

A second criticality strategy involves drawing a distinction between a commonly accepted theory or method (which may be held by the reader) and the theory or method advocated by the author. This distinction can be drawn bluntly, with assertions and contrasting dichotomous conceptual categories, or it can be drawn more gently, with a series of questions. A well-known example of the first dichotomous strategy is Smircich's (1983b) distinction between two kinds of cultural research: culture-as-variable and culture-as-metaphor, introduced in Chapter 1 and summarized in a note to this chapter.[2] In drawing this distinction in a clear and dichotomous way, Smircich effectively challenges the reader's preconceptions, particularly if that reader had been assuming that culture was simply yet another variable that could be added to existing ways of thinking about organizations, like another predictor variable in an equation.

The third criticality strategy that Golden-Biddle and Locke (1993) discuss is encouraging the reader to imagine different ways of approaching research. There are a variety of ways to accomplish this objective: direct exhortation, role modeling the desired behavior, or providing a variety of possible alternatives that the reader could adopt. For example, in this book, I have used the approaches of direct exhortation (e.g., when I urged researchers to use a three-perspective approach in Chapter 5), role modeling (e.g., in my perhaps too rare reflexivity), and providing alternatives (alternative writing styles in this chapter and undone research projects in Chapter 11).

Reflexivity:
Letting the "I" Back In

An author seeking to create an impression of objectivity will describe events as if the author's personal presence did not alter what happened or how events were observed or interpreted. As the ethnographer Crapanzano (1986, p. 57) explains, "His aim is to impress his experience of what he has *seen* so strongly, so vividly, on his readers that they cannot doubt its veracity." In this kind of writing, an author is deliberately heightening the rhetorical power of his or her prose. Many authors of quantitative research achieve the same objective with an opposite writing strategy. They deliberately use the bland and predictable format and language of a standard journal article so that the plausibility-distorting effects of vivid language will not affect the reader. Whether authors increase or decrease the vividness of their word choices, they do so to enhance their tacit claims that they are authentically portraying the cultural "realities" they have observed (e.g., Alvesson, 1998; Chia, 1996).

Many researchers counterbalance tacit claims to objectivity by admitting their own potential for bias. For example, they engage in some self-reflexive analysis of how their own cultural background and demographic characteristics (sex, age, class, etc.) may have influenced their access to cultural informants, their effects on cultural members, and their interpretations of the meanings of events. Chia (1996, p. 42) argues that reflexivity is essential for any author: "The researcher/theorist plays an active role in constructing the very reality he/she is attempting to investigate." This rationale for reflexivity is congruent with becoming-realism, as Law (1994; as quoted in Chia, 1996) explains:

> There is no question of standing apart and observing from a distance. We are participating in ordering too. We're unavoidably involved in the modern reflexive and self-reflexive project of monitoring, sense-making, and control. But since we participate in this project, we're also, and necessarily, caught up in its uncertainty, its incompleteness, its plurality, a sense of fragmentation. (p. 47)

Such reflexivity is difficult for those, such as myself, who were trained to delete all mention of "I," even to the extent of referring to one's self impersonally as "the researcher" or even as "E" (experimenter). The insightfulness of a reflexive analysis can range from the deeper analysis to the minimal and minimally revealing. For example, as illustrated in the previous description of a company retreat, Kondo (1990) does a superb job of describing how her presence, and her identity as a Japanese American young woman of upper-middle-class background, affects her interactions with coworkers from varying kinds of Japanese backgrounds. She frequently uses self-reflexivity to enrich and deepen the reader's understanding of the context she is studying. As a reader, I was left with an impression not of the author's selfish self-absorption but of her selfless willingness to expose her own feelings and thoughts as a way of helping me to deepen my understanding of what she observed and interpreted. At the same time, it was clear that Kondo's account was not seeking or attaining the objective, impersonal, detached tone usually associated with scholarly accounts.

Sometimes, reflexive analysis can take the form of a confessional tale. For example, Whyte (1991) was a student at Harvard University during the time he studied the men in "Cornerville," a working-class neighborhood in which underemployed youth gathered in gangs on the corners of the streets:

> On several afternoons and evenings at Harvard, I found myself considering a trip to Cornerville and then rationalizing my way out of it. How did I know I would find the people whom I meant to see? Even if I did so, how could I be sure that I would learn anything today? Instead of going off on a wild goose chase to Cornerville, I could profitably spend my time reading books and articles to fill in my woeful ignorance of sociology and social anthropology. Then, too, I had to admit I felt more comfortable among these familiar surroundings than I did wandering around Cornerville and spending time with people in whose presence I felt distinctly uncomfortable at first. (p. 178)

Although examples of self-reflexivity by a researcher can seem self-serving and self-absorbed, there is more here than navel-gazing. Confessional tales, such as the more orthodox reflexive analysis of Kondo (1990), have an ironic effect. They reveal the subjectivity, and the potential for bias, of authors. At the same time, because of their putative honesty, confessional tales reinforce an author's implicit or explicit claim to have presented an honest (implying authentic and perhaps even accurate) representation of the culture. This is a form of representationalism. Tacit claims to accuracy and objectivity inescapably resurface, even in parts of a text, such as reflexive analysis, that ostensibly work to undermine and minimize them.

When reflexive analysis is a major part of a text, it can establish greater rapport with readers; simultaneously, it often has the effect of distancing a researcher from those people he or she is studying. For example, when Firth (1936/1967) described his arrival at the island, he used language designed to make the reader identify with himself. He did this at the cost of distancing himself from the chief waiting under a palm tree, the other "natives" on the beach, and the "boy" on the author's boat. In a similar fashion, readers may identify more easily with Whyte (1991) when he describes himself as a student more eager to read his books than to hang out in Cornerville. This admission, however, distances Whyte from the men he studied. Authors are constantly involved in making these kinds of trade-offs because their closeness to their readers is often purchased by a reflexivity that admits a distance between the researcher and the people being studied.

Many authors react to these trade-offs by restricting reflexivity to a single part of the text (sometimes the introduction) and writing the rest in a objectivist or realist style. Other authors place their reflexive observations in the footnotes of their texts, implying that whatever potential biases are revealed are unimportant enough to be marginalized. For example, Van Maanen (1991) reveals in a footnote to his study of the "Smile Factory" at Disneyland that he had been an employee of the company. Furthermore, he was fired using a process of status degradation that he describes in some detail in footnote 3:

> I was fired for what I still consider a Mickey Mouse offense. The specific violation—one of many possible—involved hair growing over my ears, an offense I had been warned about more than once before the final cut was made. . . . All these little steps of status degradation in the Magic Kingdom were quite public and, as the reader might guess, the process still irks. This may provide the reader with an account for the tone of this narrative, although it shouldn't since I would also claim I was ready to quit anyway since I had been there far too long. At any rate, it may just be possible that I now derive as much a part of my identity from being fired from Disneyland as I gained from being employed there in the first place. (p. 76)

These details of personal history (and the puns, irony, and sarcasm with which they are communicated) illuminate why Van Maanen could recount such detailed "behind-the-scenes" knowledge of the Magic Kingdom and why he brought such a critical perspective to this study.

Other cagey authors refrain from all reflexive analysis until the main body of the argument is complete, placing the reflexive material in a final chapter (e.g., Martin, 1992a) or an appendix (e.g., Kunda, 1992; Whyte, 1991). This strategy avoids undermining the author's authority until the reader has completed the text, leaving the reader to do the work of reexamining the text to see where the personal ideology and background of the author may have affected events and interpretations described by the author. Although this latter writing strategy is better than refraining from any reflexivity, many would consider it a cop-out.

Deconstruction

Postmodern theory is particularly insightful about how writing strategies reflect assumptions about what is known. Deconstruction is a mode of postmodern textual analysis that reveals silences and circumlocutions that hide what an author does not want to reveal. Because an

introduction to postmodernism is difficult to do briefly and well, I rely
here primarily on references to additional readings. (Accessible introductions to postmodernism and deconstruction, based on the work of
literary critics, include Moi [1985] and Weedon [1987]. Alvesson and
Deetz [1996] offer a clear, short introduction to the relevance of this
work for organizational studies.)[3]

To show the relevance of deconstruction to cultural studies, and to
provide examples of some deconstructive techniques, I summarize the
results of my (Martin, 1990a) deconstruction of a speech by a high-
ranking executive. He claimed that his company was deeply responsive
to the needs of its female employees, citing with pride how the company
put a computer in the hospital room in which an employee, who was a
new mother, was recuperating from a cesarean section. Deconstruction
revealed a myriad of ways in which the high-ranking executive's language concealed the ways that the company's interests were given precedence over this woman's family life. Deconstructive techniques used in
this analysis included

- dismantling a dichotomy, exposing it as a false distinction (e.g., the public sphere
  of work and the private sphere of the family);
- examining silences—what was not said;
- attending to disruptions and contradictions—places where the speech text did
  not make sense;
- focusing on the elements most alien to the text as a means of deciphering taboos;
- revealing the hidden meanings and associations introduced by the use of metaphors (such as launching a product);
- analyzing double entendres that point to an unconscious, often sexual subtext
  (such as having a woman); and
- reconstructing the text repeatedly with iterative substitution of phrases—what
  could have been said but was not (e.g., by assuming the employee is having a heart
  bypass rather than a cesarean birth).

As the author of the deconstruction of the executive's speech (unlike
the authors of many literary deconstructions), I had an explicit policy-
relevant agenda: to show how this company's policies, ostensibly bene-
fiting women, in fact achieved the opposite. I did this by exploring with
careful "reconstructions" the effects of minor policy change. For example, when heart bypass surgery was substituted for the cesarean section,
other, ostensibly unrelated parts of the executive's speech had to be

altered. This deconstruction revealed ways in which the private and the public spheres unavoidably intersect, despite corporate language that attempts to keep the responsibility for difficulties in the hands of individual employees. I used these reconstructions to explain how this company's policies strengthened gender inequalities, and I used this analysis to show the need for a more ambitious change program if this organization is to become more deeply responsive to the needs of their female employees.[4]

Alternative Writing Styles

Postmodern critics offer deeply unsettling observations about the shortcomings of realist tales. For example, Crapanzano (1986) objects to Geertz's (1973) use of homogenizing language, such as "The Balinese feel . . ." Crapanzano asks,

> Who told Geertz? How can a whole people share a subjectivity? . . . [Geertz's] constructions seem to be little more than projections, or at least blurrings, of his point of view, his subjectivity, with that of the native, or more accurately, the constructed native. (p. 74)

Crapanzano also objects to using a generalized, prototypical description (e.g., of a cockfight), ostensibly based on multiple observations of identical or similar incidents. According to Crapanzano, such generalized descriptions fail to capture the unique characteristics of each incident and do not reflect differing reactions at different times.

To some extent, these criticisms of realist tales are overdrawn. Most realist ethnographers, particularly those who write today, have moved from integrationist language that implies shared worldviews (such as "The Balinese feel . . ." and "Members of this organization believe . . .") to language that acknowledges variation of opinion or interpretation. Because most qualitative studies are not based on random or systematic sampling procedures, if authors of realist tales want to capture variations in cultural members' views, they usually use vague adjectives (such as "some," "a few," and "many") to signal proportions of cultural members sharing a particular viewpoint. Also, rather than creating a generalized, prototypical description of a cockfight or a board meeting, for example, realist authors often describe a single, specific incident, although some go on to claim that incident is somehow prototypical.

Many scholars would generally find these writing strategies to be an incomplete and insufficient response to postmodern criticisms. For example, Putnam (1996, p. 386) argues that "organizational researchers need ways to open up texts for multiple readings; to decenter authors as authority figures; and to involve participants, readers, and audiences in the production of research." Crapanzano (1986) suggests that an author should not distance himself or herself from the people being studied; rather than an "us-them" relationship, authors and cultural members should have a more egalitarian, "I-you" relationship. This implies that the author, rather than disappearing from the text, should practice self-reflexivity throughout the text (in the main body and not just in the footnotes or appendices) using the pronoun "I." The reader also has a responsibility to resist any attempt by the author to tell the readers what they would have experienced had they been a "native" or, better yet, a particular individual "native."

There are a variety of ways to write texts that are responsive to these suggestions. Imagine a writing style continuum anchored on one end by cultural accounts written in the familiar, standard "scientific" style. At the other end of the continuum is the most experimental, radical style that you can imagine. In between are a variety of alternative ways of writing about culture that are responsive to some of the ideas and criticisms described previously. For example, near the more traditional end of this imaginary continuum, a realist tale can acknowledge that cultural members have a variety of perceptions and interpretations of events. If reflexive or deconstructive observations are made in such a realist account, they can be marginalized in footnotes and appendices. Later, I describe an example of this kind of writing (Kunda, 1992), in which reflexive observations are relegated to an insightful appendix and some ironic and provocative footnotes. Somewhere in the middle of this imaginary writing style continuum belongs the last chapter of my book *Cultures in Organizations* (Martin, 1992a). This final chapter took a postmodern view of the three-perspective theory (undermining its implicit claim to tell the truth, the whole truth, and nothing but the truth) and showed a dialogue between researchers and cultural members that added a layer of complex insight to the conclusions of the OZCO study. This chapter, and the fact that it is only one chapter of a book that otherwise tells what is largely a realist tale, is also critically analyzed later.

The best known exemplars of alternative styles of writing about cultures are multivocal accounts that capture the multiple, conflicting views of multiple authors and various disagreeing cultural members. Multivocal styles offer a way to capture in a text the reciprocal, participative roles of ethnographer and informant, advocated by those who practice reflexive ethnography (e.g., Bruni & Gherardi, in press; Linstead, 1993). The third study summarized later is a multivocal account, with cultural members who serve as coauthors, contradicting the conclusions of the academic who initiated this study of the education of working-class men in Britain (Willis, 1977/1981). Finally, at the other end of the imaginary continuum of writing styles, the most radical alternative to be discussed is a double story by Jermier (1985) about a worker with either "false consciousness" or dawning awareness of his cultural position. This account crosses a line of great importance to social scientists, blurring the distinction between science and fiction (see also Calás, 1987). These four alternative ways of writing illustrate the implications of the ideas presented previously so that you, the reader, can move from thinking about the purposes of a phrase or a paragraph to how an entire study might be reframed.

Engineering Culture (Kunda, 1992)

This is a book-length ethnography based on a year of observation in two areas of a high-tech company. A brief summary of the book's contents, before its writing styles are analyzed, may be helpful. Kunda (1992) focuses primarily on engineers and managers but also spends some time with lower-level staff and temporary workers at a technology company (its pseudonym is "Tech"). The book begins by describing the official ideology of the firm and explains how the management of this company tries to "engineer" a culture that expresses thoughts and feelings that employees are supposed to share. Kunda describes the rituals, such as formal training programs, managerial speeches, and group interactions, that are designed to enhance and enact commitment to these competitive, hard-driving, and sometimes aggressive values. The remainder of the book follows employees' internal reactions as they express these values in public, as required for career advancement, whereas in more private or off-stage moments (Goffman [1961] features prominently in the theoretical analysis here) their ambivalence becomes evident. The employees skillfully use irony, try various methods of emotional distancing, and focus on ambiguities to avoid becoming men "without qualities" (apt quotations from Musil's book of this title are scattered throughout). Kunda completes his tale by contrasting the relatively privileged, albeit soul-draining lives of these engineers and managers to the working lives of support staff and temporary workers, who face different problems with fewer rewards. The book concludes with a cautiously worded but nonetheless biting indictment of corporate attempts to control the values and emotions of employees.

This single-authored book, based on a doctoral thesis, is composed of two parts: an ethnography followed by a methodological appendix that contains more reflexive and critical material. In Van Maanen's terms, most of the main body of the text is a realist tale. The main body of Kunda's (1992) text contains a relatively short review of cultural scholarship (not focusing on a single perspective), straightforward reporting of data, and minimal discussion of the author and his relationship to the people studied. The "I" and eye of the author are made invisible, thus enhancing the impression of his trustworthy omniscience. Such attempts to build authenticity and plausibility are familiar tactics that enhance the credibility of this realist tale, in accord with the assumptions of being-realism and representationalism. For example, Kunda does not hesitate to label a specific incident as prototypical:

> Dave Carpenter's presentation at Lyndsville is an example of perhaps the most common encounter between a senior manager and a large group of members. As in most such presentations, the speaker focuses on technical and business issues but uses the occasion to make ideological points as well. (p. 95)

Also, as one would expect in a realist tale, Kunda sometimes seems comfortable making generalizations about shared perceptions that echo Geertz's (1973) "The Balinese feel . . ." For example,

> Members of this group believe generally that "Tech has never encouraged stable groups" and that "it is a Tech tradition not to let any group get too large or too powerful." . . . There is an accepted tendency to frown on simple mappings of the complex network of activities, to be vague about or fashionably dismissive of mechanistic structure. It is conventional wisdom that charts are always outdated and that current ones are at best an invitation to tampering. (p. 30)

This, however, is not an integrationist cultural portrait. Kunda is careful to acknowledge differences among cultural members, using the usual vague adjectives ("some" or "a few") to suggest proportions of people sharing and not sharing these various views; for example, "Members of the audience exchange knowing looks; some whisper to each other; others turn and stare at Ron" (p. 100) and "Some petitioners approach the speaker. A few ask for copies of his transparencies. A group of young engineers address Rick Danko. One says excitedly, seemingly awaiting his approval . . ." (p. 195).

Throughout this realist text, Kunda (1992) is attentive to the inconsistencies, conflicts, contradictions, paradoxes, ironies, and ambiguities that are the focus of differentiation and fragmentation research. This is most notable in his discussion of how employees join in company-mandated rituals that require public expressions of commitment to management's "official" view of the culture. During these rituals, Kunda describes how employees go through their paces with ambivalence, both accepting the "official" view, sometimes with pride, and then mocking it and themselves in more private, backstage moments:

> A commonsense point of view that is sometimes at odds with the official one is expressed. It includes less sanguine views of managerial ideology ("the bullshit that comes from above") and behavior ("the song and dance"), as well as a different view of member attributes: colorfully labeled behavioral scenarios ("setting up," "finger pointing," "midnight phone calls," "pissing contests," "backstabbing," "crucifying") and experiences ("hanging from shoestrings," "pain," "the fear of God," "burn-out"), a cynical awareness of manipulative intents and disguised meanings (giving "Tech strokes," managing and exposing "hidden agendas," doing "rah-rah stuff"), or dispassionate "Tech watching." Expressed differently in various ritual forms—subtle and controlled in top management presentations, aggressive and critical in training workshops, widespread and playful in work group meetings—the liminal mode provides an alternative reality: Participants temporarily detach themselves from their performance of the member role, comment on it, and share with others the awareness, either cheerful or disdainful, of the theatrical nature of the proceedings. (p. 158)

These ambivalent, fragmented selves are far more complex, critical, and self-aware than the dark-suited "company men" that might endorse the official ideology without ambivalence. Kunda's portrait of this culture ultimately contains elements congruent with the integration, differentiation, and fragmentation perspectives, all coexisting in tension with each other. In his conclusion, Kunda points out discrepancies between the management's official, integrated view of the idealized culture and conflicts, ambiguities, and contradictions experienced by the company's employees:

> It is a culture riddled with contradictions between ideological depictions and alternative realities: where democratization is claimed, there are also subtle forms of domination; where clarity of meaning and purpose is attempted, there is intentional and deeply ingrained ambiguity; where an overarching morality is preached, there is also opportunistic cynicism; and where fervent commitment is demanded, there is pervasive irony. (p. 222)

This is a highly complex realistic tale, one that encompasses a wide range of interpretations, theoretical orientations, and interests.

Even in the main body of the text, there are breaks in the flat tone of a realist account. Interspersed within the straight reportage of "facts" and dialogue, Kunda (1992) makes sly jokes. For example, when he offers pseudonyms for people and places, he makes witty asides, some of which would be meaningful only to academic readers well versed in the classics of qualitative sociological research. In addition, his prose is laced with dramatic metaphors and pointed ironies. For example,

> On the one hand, burnout is considered both demeaning and difficult, evidence of a personal failure and dramatic proof that despite their promised benefits, the sirens' call for identification with the organizational demands may have dangerous, painful, and potentially disruptive consequences. On the other hand, many members feel some pride in surviving burnout or living with its threat. It is a battle scar, a purple heart, a call for respect, a sign of belonging and of willing self-sacrifice, an indication one's heart is in the right place. (p. 204)

Jokes, metaphors, and irony are indirect ways an author can signal his or her discomfort with the writing conventions and ontological and epistemological assumptions of a realist tale.

There is more to this realist tale than first meets the eye of the reader. For example, in the footnotes to the main body of the text, Kunda

(1992) is more open about his disdain for cultural work written in the managerial interest:

> 5. Some of the theoretical issues raised by the concept of culture have in the past been addressed by such notions as "organizational climate" and "organizational character" (Ott, 1989). Those who cater to the managerial mind are, it seems, forever looking for innovative formulations. . . .
>
> 11. See for example Ouchi's (1981) glorification of Hewlett-Packard, Peters and Waterman's discussion of excellent companies, and Deal and Kennedy's (1982) conceptually similar analysis of corporate cultures. (p. 242)

In the margins, the conclusion, and the appendix to the main body of the text, Kunda makes his critical view even more visible. At the end of the book, he changes his "just the facts" realist tone and briefly but powerfully indicts this culture as "a rather subtle form of domination, a 'culture trap' combining normative pressure with a delicate balance of seductiveness and coercion" (p. 224). Furthermore, because Kunda has studied not just engineers and managers, he can conclude that staff members (Wage Class 2 employees) and the company's temporary workers were working "under conditions closer to what Etzioni (1961) referred to as coercive control: They are subject to immediate termination and possess no rights as employees" (p. 221). These concluding remarks are congruent with critical theory and with the differentiation perspective. They make it clear that this book represents an emancipatory project. By deliberately relegating this material to the margins of his text (the appendix follows the concluding chapter), Kunda maintains a traditionally authoritative position as omniscient teller of a realist tale throughout the main body of the text. Only at the end does he "show his colors."

Kunda's (1992) appendix offers a more radical departure from the tone of the rest of his text, a change in direction signaled by its title, "Methods: A Confessional Tale of Sorts." Here, despite a first sentence that claims the book represents "ethnographic realism," Kunda undermines his own authority in both conventional and unexpected ways. This is a confessional tale told by a private person. Kunda offers a limited self-reflexive analysis of his relationship to the context and people he studied. This constrained self-reflexivity is offered with an ironic detachment, some reluctance, and not a little modesty—a far cry from the apparently more open and emotionally revealing self-disclosure of

some other ethnographers. Kunda begins with an acknowledgment
that such confessionals ironically can have the effect of increasing an
author's credibility:

> A methods confessional serves to establish a kind of ethnographic credibil-
> ity; here self-criticism not only exposes weaknesses and qualifies assertions,
> but allows a demonstration of the breadth, depth, indeed the relentlessness,
> of an ethnographic incisiveness seemingly so powerful that it is applied most
> scathingly to oneself. Thus, although it reads like a confessional, it is in fact a
> self-application of one's scientific tools, a "realist ethnography" of the re-
> search process. (p. 230)

Kunda goes on to describe a few elements of his background, such as the
fact he is Israeli, revealing only that which has direct and obvious relevance to his book:

> For many Israelis, moreover, "America" is both a dream and a threat, repre-
> senting an option not taken by one's grandparents, and always posing the
> dangerous temptation either to "Americanize" Israel or, more drastically, to
> commit the ultimate betrayal and emigrate. As a resident alien in the United
> States, I was already suspect on both counts. Ethnographic exploration of
> corporate America was an excuse to follow the sirens, examine them up
> close, and in the process turn the tables on the historically one-sided anthro-
> pological enterprise. (p. 231)

This limited self-disclosure is as close as Kunda gets to revealing private
aspects of himself insofar as that private self is relevant to his work as a
scholar.

Kunda (1992) acknowledges methodological issues that made it difficult for him to see all aspects of the culture fully. For example, he found
it easier to gain access to middle- and low-ranking employees, especially
those who believed they did not fit into the company's culture:

> Those who were somewhat different, or marginal, seemed to find their way
> to me: Minorities, especially those with an interest in my Israeli background,
> those who were failing, unhappy, or "burnt out," and those who wanted to
> distance themselves from the "nerd" and "Techie" images. (pp. 236-237)

Kunda also acknowledges discomfort with moving from concrete data
to the abstract generalizations and theoretical discussions demanded

by the norms of his academic discipline. He briefly mentions his discomfort with "standard presentational requirements and forms" (p. 239) as he explains why he has refrained from the use of some of the plausibility and authenticity strategies outlined by Golden-Biddle and Locke (1993). This is neither the standard scientific writing style expected in quantitative studies nor an experimental variant of a realist tale. Although Kunda's book, like most qualitative studies, does include quotations from employees, it does not include their reactions to the text in any detail:

> Responses to the thesis from Tech were limited—largely, I believe, because of my preference for a low-key withdrawal from the field and my decision to reduce my general discomfort with my role and its implications by severing contact with the company. My promised feedback session never materialized, forgotten or considered unnecessary by management and gladly ignored by me. There were no responses to the copy I sent by mail 1 year after I left, and I did not stay in touch with any of the people I had worked with in the field. (p. 239)

This, therefore, is not a multivocal account, with cultural members sharing coauthorship.

This book does, however, in its conclusion, footnotes, and appendix, frame the realist main body of the text with confessional and critical material that encourages the reader to read between the lines to find the hints and outlines of another, very different text. This writing strategy effectively seduces a managerially oriented reader who might be put off by a different text that had begun with critical theory citations of Marx and Foucault, for example, and had used critical terminology, such as "exploitation," "oppression," and "domination." Instead, Kunda draws the reader in. Only at the end of the book does Kunda let critical and confessional material begin to emerge, after the reader has accepted his authority for many pages. This writing strategy permits readers to hear Kunda's criticisms with a mind that may have been slowly opened. It does entail some difficulties, however. It passes the responsibility for rethinking the main body of the text, in light of the critical material at the end, to the reader. The problem here is that the reader is probably less able to perform this rethinking task than the author, who knows himself and the company better than the reader ever could. A similar writing strategy, which relegates nonrealist material to the end of a book and leaves the reader with the responsibility of rethinking the text, is found in my work, as described next.

Cultures in Organizations:
Three Perspectives (Martin, 1992a)

In this 1992 book, I used innovative writing styles in several chapters that deal with the OZCO case study and also in the last chapter, which steps back and critiques the entire volume. The reasons for these writing strategies are analyzed here (and explained in detail in Martin, 1995). OZCO is a three-part case study of the culture of a large, multinational, high-tech company, summarized in this book and described in more detail in my 1992 book. This case, which is coauthored with Meyerson, has three parts, examining the company from the integration, differentiation, and fragmentation perspectives, respectively. Described at more length than in this book, the OZCO case study both illustrates the single theoretical perspectives and shows what can be learned by viewing a culture from all three viewpoints.

In the OZCO case study, we use an unusual writing strategy. In an attempt to make the case study more "realistic," we wanted to minimize our own influence as authors, letting the cultural members "speak for themselves." Whereas most qualitative researchers precede and follow quotations from cultural members with extensive interpretation, we do not do so. Instead, we simply quote cultural members with very little editorial commentary. In an important departure from most ethnographic accounts, we make no inferences about cultural members' thoughts or beliefs, only quoting what could be seen or heard. The result is a case study that sticks, precisely, to what was said, reducing the author's role to primarily that of a quote editor. In this way, the reader can feel confident that we were only minimally imposing our views on the data reported. Therefore, the readers are free to decide for themselves what interpretations are valid.

Despite these efforts, the writing style in the OZCO case has important disadvantages. Also, because the case is organized with minimal elaboration or interpretation from the authors, from an aesthetic point of view it is an ungraceful compendium of quotations from company employees. Although we wanted to reduce our impact as authors to a minimum, we were forced to impose some kind of organizing structure to make the case read coherently. Therefore, we classify quotations from employees into three content theme categories (egalitarianism, innovation, and concern for employee well-being). As explained previously, we also split the case into three parts, or chapters, by sorting quotations into three theoretical classifications (reflecting the integration, differentiation, and fragmentation views of the company's culture). The result is an effective teaching case for use with MBAs and executives, one that illustrates clearly the three-perspective framework. An editorial role, however, gives an author important sources of information control (what abstractions are and are not used, which quotations are chosen, etc.). Despite our efforts to erase our influence as authors of the text of the OZCO case, that influence is unavoidably present. We define the three theoretical perspectives, and we choose quotations that fit these conceptual categories, eliminating those that do not. We choose the three content themes, eliminating material that focuses on other issues. Furthermore, we describe the methods used in the OZCO study in terms that maximize its apparent authenticity and plausibility, using many of the strategies described by Golden-Biddle and Locke (1993), as summarized previously.

The book chapters containing the OZCO case include virtually no reflexivity by us as authors or by our informants. Although the OZCO case is full of quotations from cultural members, we include no opportunity for our informants to respond in writing to what we wrote. Although these writing strategies are commonly used to enhance the authority of authors, postmodern and critical scholarship suggests that this is inadequate. The idea that informants should be given a space to respond, in print, to the text we had written seems especially germane. As one postmodern critic, Tyler (1986), observes,

> No amount of invoking the "other" can establish him as the agent of the words or deeds attributed to him in a record of a dialogue unless he too is free to reinterpret it and flesh it out with caveats, apologies, footnotes, and explanatory detail. (p. 44)

A better book might have encouraged our informants to read the OZCO cases and comment critically on what was said and what we as editors omitted.

To respond to these issues, I added a chapter to this 1992 book. Like Kunda (1992), I placed this critical material at the end of the book, marginalizing it so that the main body of the text could be read before I undermined my authority as an author. In this final chapter, I critique the three-perspective framework presented in the rest of the book, in accord with Golden-Biddle and Locke's (1993) call for criticality. In this last chapter, I summarize a variety of cultural theories that cannot be encompassed by the three perspectives. I take seriously the postmodern critique (e.g., Gagliardi, 1990) that the three-perspective theory is a "totalizing" or imperialistic attempt to build a metatheory that encompasses the work of other cultural researchers by moving to a higher level of abstraction. I agree that this particular metatheory reifies culture, as if it were an objectified variable "out there" that can be precisely codified. By critiquing the three-perspective approach in this way, I reveal the omissions in my own work and pinpoint my uncertainties.

In this final chapter of the book, I also engage in a little personal reflexivity. For example, I give personal reasons for my preference for critical theory and the differentiation perspective and describe my affinities to the multiple views and ambiguities of the fragmentation viewpoint. I state that as a woman who has worked in organizations dominated mostly by men, I have often felt silenced by bosses, deans, and department chairs who made homogenizing statements about "shared" assumptions and convictions that I, in fact, did not share. For this reason, I tend to bristle at integration accounts of culture, believing that they silence dissent and deliberately ignore conflict. In addition, and perhaps more important, I quote and discuss a transcript of a group interview in which OZCO informants listened to and then challenged an important part of the OZCO material, claiming that their remarks during interviews had been accurately quoted but had been taken out of context and misunderstood. At the end of this final chapter, drawing on reader response theory, I explain how readers could each interpret the text for themselves, judging the worth of its interpretations according to their own standards and experiences. In this way, I hope to open the door to even more variation in interpretation and different kinds of critical views.

This summary may make the last chapter of the 1992 book seem harshly critical of my own work. Some readers thought it was harsh and told me they were sorry I had written it: "It undermined what you had done." Others, however, thought the last chapter was not critical enough. It is that last view I explore next. Any attempt to respond fully to criticisms of a realist tale will fall short in some way, and my attempts in this final chapter, however well motivated, were no exception. As in other instances in which reflexivity has been attempted, I may have enhanced my own credibility as an author by only partially undermining my authority. Furthermore, the main body of the text, with its emphasis on the three perspectives, is presented intact as a metatheory; I undermined my authority only in the last chapter (as in Kunda's [1992] appendix). Also, that undermining is partial. For example, self-reflexivity is still minimal due to my own preference for privacy and my training in the need for writing in an impersonal style; too much "I" still sounds egotistic to me (although in this book I am trying to do more). The OZCO employees' critique of the text is restricted to only one small part of the case material; the rest goes unchallenged in this final chapter. Turning over responsibility for interpretation to the reader is inevitable, according to reader response theory, but the move can also be interpreted as passing the buck to the reader rather than trying to respond more critically, and more fully, myself.

For all these reasons, even this last chapter of the 1992 book falls short of a full response to critics of realist ethnographies and "totalitarian" (domination-seeking) metatheories. (A more detailed analysis by Smircich, contrasting the writing strategies of my book, Kunda's ethnography, and a culture review by Trice & Beyer [1993], was published in *Organizational Science, 6,* 1995.) Therefore, my book falls far short of being a multivocal account. The study described in the following section, however, explores this writing strategy fully.

Learning to Labour: How Working Class Kids Get Working Class Jobs (Willis, 1977/1981)

This innovative ethnography (Willis, 1977/1981) is a study of how high schools prepare working-class male students in Britain for their lives as blue-collar workers. In the first and longest part of the book, the results of the author's interviews and observations of these students are presented. In a departure from conventional scholarly writing style, the author's questions and his informants' answers are included in the text. In addition, the author reports apparently verbatim discussions among his informants, as they discuss the schools' rules and practices, as well as their own reactions, preferences, and plans. The author also describes the people and the school's "atmosphere." His theoretical analysis of these data posits that the school's practices socialize the students to take working-class positions in the British class structure. He describes how the students disdain the "boring" class material, with its emphasis on abstraction and mental effort. Willis notes that this reaction blocks their access to a college education, dooming them to the manual labor their parents rely on to pay the bills. The students also adopt leisure habits, interpersonal patterns of behavior, and attitudes toward the law and the government that mimic those of their parents, again preparing themselves to take their expected place in the class structure. Willis concludes that the students come to adopt the class-ridden, hegemonic ideology that justifies their own lack of mobility and access to prosperity.

Next, Willis (1977/1981) gives the "lads" a chance to react to his text and to his interpretation of their behavior. They can relate easily to the quotations and transcripts of dialogue, which they consider as transcribed accurately, for the most part. They disagree, however, with Willis's determinist and class-bound view of their current behavior and future options. They view their behaviors and attitudes as freely chosen and refuse to rely exclusively on the class lens that Willis finds useful. In some ways, they find his views condescending and disrespectful of their autonomy and values. In the final part of the text, the author reserves the last word for himself, explaining and eventually dismissing as defensive the students' reactions to his interpretations of their behavior. This text's construction, with the "lads" being given the opportunity to react to the author in print so that readers can read their reactions, is an important innovation. The fact that the author gives himself the last word is not an innovation, but it is understandable given the discrepancy between his view and theirs.

Of course, a more critical view of this text is possible. First, the "lads'" reactions make it clear that the author failed to achieve an emic or insiders' view of the culture. In an attempt to establish rapport with readers at the expense of distancing himself from the "lads," the author continually makes references and allusions that would not be understood by his working-class subjects but would be accessible and informative for his middle-class audience. Second, although the work is clearly written by an author with left-wing sympathies, it is not clear that this is emancipatory research in the sense that this term is defined by Habermas. For example, where are the opportunities for effective resistance in this account? How might this system of socialization-for-oppression be transformed? Finally, in this book, as in the OZCO case, the "verbatim" dialogue is the product of some heavy editorial work by the author, as is the case in any ethnography.[5] Willis selected which dialogues to quote (and which not to quote). Willis organized those quotations by topics he chose and he ordered, and he decided when to shift the description from one locale to another and from one group of students to another. The author also choreographed the text's changes in focus—for example, when to quote specific individuals and when to bring the larger system into focus. In these ways, this text's innovative structure cannot escape the fact that this is a text written by an author who preserves his right to control what is in his book, albeit this is an author who, more than most, permits the people he studies to speak relatively freely. In contrast, not only do the protagonists in the final piece of writing to be discussed in this chapter speak freely but also readers are allowed to get into their minds and to overhear their thoughts and feelings. This is accomplished by breaking a social science taboo.

"When the Sleeper Wakes: A Short Story Extending Themes in Radical Organizational Theory" (Jermier, 1985)

When Jermier wrote "When the Sleeper Awakes" (1985), he bravely broke the taboo that forbids a social scientist from including fictional material in a research report. This paper is clearly labeled, by the author, as a fictional account. Jermier offers a theoretical justification for his merging of social scientific and fictional writing standards. The critical theories that Jermier wants to use rely heavily on assumptions about what is going on in the mind of an exploited worker, and to illustrate these theories he believed that he had to go beyond what could be observed by a social scientist. Jermier offers two fictionalized descriptions of the private thoughts, unexpressed emotions, and actions of a prototypical worker during a prototypical day. This person is employed by a company that treats its workers with disregard for their economic, physical, and emotional well-being. In the first description of this worker, he is a "sleeper"—that is, a worker with "false consciousness"—who accepts the hegemonic ideology and self-serving explanations of his "superiors." This worker is passive and docile. In his private thoughts, he rationalizes and naturalizes observations, for example, about pollution or exploitation, which initially disturb him. He accepts the consumer orientation of the surrounding society, lusting after new possessions without deeply considering the personal costs of the work required to earn enough money to make these purchases. His lack of awareness contributes to his own exploitation. In a sense, this worker, like the high school students studied by Willis (1977/1981), adopts ideologies and rationalizations that justify his own oppression.

Jermier's (1985) second version of this worker's day presents a more complex picture. This "awake" worker switches in and out of awareness. When he is aware, he is actively but selectively militant, objecting to and seeking to change a system he views as oppressive and flawed. He engages in individual arguments, verbally protesting current conditions. Occasionally, he engages in acts of protest—for example, individual work slowdowns or transient acts of individual defiance. When he switches out of awareness, we see his unconscious conflicts, negative emotions, and willingness to reinterpret and rationalize events. This worker experiences individual deprivation, but he has little well-developed class consciousness. Even in this second description, the worker does not engage in the militant collective protest a neo-Marxist might prefer.

In his conclusion, Jermier (1985) draws out the theoretical analogs of his descriptive material and justifies his use of fictional methods in theoretical terms. Theories of false consciousness and neo-Marxism, like many other critical theories, are rife with assumptions about what is going on in the unconscious mind, including the unexpressed thoughts and emotions of working-class people. Unfortunately, but understandably, empirical research in the critical tradition has seldom collected data about these private aspects of human thoughts and feeling, leaving a large gap in the empirical critical literature. Although fiction is not the only way to fill this gap (e.g., experimental psychologists have found some physiological measures of certain emotions), Jermier argues persuasively that fictional writing is an effective means of doing so. In contrast to most empirical studies that by definition must examine some aspect of the status quo, Jermier's fiction approach may be particularly useful for critical theorists because it offers a way to portray an emancipatory ideal that does not yet exist (Martin, 1992b). (Jermier's study is discussed as one of a few "exemplary" pieces of research by Frost & Stablein [1992], with reviews and critiques by several scholars.)

Calás (1987) addresses similar issues from a broader framework in her dissertation, provocatively titled "Organizational Science/Fiction." Calás delineates the variety of ways in which these two diametrically opposed traditions—science and fiction—are, in fact, more closely related than either cares to admit; ostensibly, scientific work is in many ways, according to Calás, a fiction. Calás argues this point by deconstructing the work of several well-known scholars. Czarniawska (1997, 1998, 1999) makes a related point as she reveals the blurry boundary between narrative and scientific writing. In contrast to Calás and Czarniawska, most social scientists take pride in the difference between their nonfiction approach, based on the scientific method, and that of fiction writers and other denizens of the netherworld of nonscientific writing. To make up the material one writes about is a mortal sin in the eyes of all but a very few social scientists. (Journalists are also forbidden to use fictional techniques to create prototypical characters or incidents, even if they can credibly claim to have observed dozens of similar instances.) For all these reasons, Jermier's (1985) work has been strongly criticized or even worse—ignored—particularly by those who view fiction as "faking data"—an inappropriate and even unethical activity for a social scientist. Those who do not object to Jermier's use of fictional writing strategies, however, have nonetheless criticized his paper as inferior fiction, claiming that the abstract and "dry" theoretical material saps its impact on the reader and the prototypical worker lacks (of course) individuating characteristics and motivations. Sometimes, you just cannot win.

Undermining Realist Representation by Experimenting With Innovative Writing Styles

Clifford and Marcus (1986) are two of the most articulate advocates of experimenting with new writing styles to undermine the norms of realistic representation and acknowledge the ambiguities of meanings and the uncertainties of contemporary life. Clifford and Marcus urge ethnographic writers, and by implication other social scientists, to show the multiplicity of views that informants hold; make visible, in a text, the researcher's contribution to a dialogue with informants; permit multiple, differing authorial voices to be heard, both in quotations and in interpretations of the meanings of those quotations; and disturb—intentionally—the complacency of readers. They argue that such writing strategies are particularly suitable for contemporary times, in which paradigms are in disarray, problems seem intractable, and phenomena are only partially understood. To Clifford and Marcus, the pseudocertainty of a realist tale seems to be unsuitable for our times.

Now, of course, the burden shifts to you and me because we must decide how to react to these variations from realist tales and the usual social scientific writing styles. Referring to the paradigm debates in organizational studies, it is easy to imagine how the protagonists might react to the more innovative, or critical, material summarized previously. Pfeffer, given his desire to create fieldwide consensus about progress in a few research topics selected by an elite body of researchers, would presumably prefer the standardized social scientific writing style. Such a style makes it easier to conduct statistical or theoretical meta-analysis using common standards to assess the quality of results and combine findings across studies. On this issue, Van de Ven might agree with Pfeffer because Van de Ven is concerned with using triangulation of different studies, using different methods, to reach empirically based agreement on disputed questions. The usual realist writing style makes it easier to triangulate the results of different studies, and the ethos of a realist style supports attempts to resolve theoretical disputes through empirical hypothesis testing. In contrast, I suspect Van Maanen would welcome the innovative writing strategies described previously because they include and elaborate many of the ideas in his book, *Tales of the Field* (1988). This range of presumed reactions probably mirrors the reactions of our colleagues to the innovative writing styles described in these chapters.

Given what I have said about reflexivity, it is unfair to conclude this topic of writing styles without stating where I stand on these contentious issues, if it is not already obvious. I, like Van Maanen, welcome these innovative writing strategies because I believe they reflect, with some candor, the uncertainties inherent in doing any kind of research. They are particularly well suited for representing the conflicts of interest captured by the differentiation view and the ambiguities and paradoxes that are the focus of the fragmentation perspective. Therefore, I have begun to explore the use of innovative writing styles in my own work, such as the OZCO case, the final chapter in my 1992 book, the war games review of the cultural literature (Martin & Frost, 1996), and the deconstruction of the executive's speech (Martin, 1990a). I hope to do more experimentation in the future because I find that these innovative writing strategies yield insights from informants and from self-reflexivity that would otherwise not emerge in my thinking and writing.

Nevertheless, when writing quantitative studies, I confess I fall back on standardized writing formats. I rationalize this to myself by saying that it is what journals expect. This rationalization may be unjustified because increasingly some journals (such as *Organization, Organizational Science, The Journal of Management Inquiry,* and most European journals) are open to more innovative writing styles. In addition, the authors of the references cited in this chapter and I are all working to encourage editors and reviewers to be more open in this regard. I am planning to "push the envelope" by experimenting with some of these innovative writing strategies in most new papers that I write. At the same time, I expect I will retreat to realist writing strategies occasionally when I have quantitative data and when I believe I have "gone too far" and want to try to reestablish credibility with more traditional organizational scholars.

Where do you, the reader, stand on the writing dilemma questions with which this chapter began? Some of the innovative writing styles described and illustrated in this chapter (such as the multivocal account and extensive use of reflexivity) are appropriate primarily for qualitative data, whereas other style innovations (such as some of the plausibility enhancing techniques) might be applicable to quantitative studies as well. Which of these styles will you use in your own research? What might you learn from experimenting with styles that are new to you? What new theoretical insights might emerge if you used an innovative approach to writing up the results of a particular study? How much will you be willing to reveal, reflexively, about yourself and your relationships to people and organizations you study? How were you affected by what happened and what you saw, and how did this affect what you wrote and and did not write? How are these issues of author reflexivity affected when two or more people collect and analyze data and when they collaborate on writing a manuscript? When will coauthors use a collective voice in a text, and when will they speak as individuals whose reactions differ? Obviously, these are questions that you must begin answering in your own research, with each new study you conduct. I hope this chapter has exposed you to some approaches that at some time you may find useful to try. If not, at least you know more about why other researchers have chosen to experiment with these ways of writing.

Notes

1. This is a good place to introduce the idea of reader response theory (e.g., Iser, 1978). Whereas the emic-etic distinction sets up a tension between the cultural insider ("native") and the outsider (researcher), reader response theory adds the reader as the third corner of a triangle. Reading is viewed as a subjective response to a text, one that can vary across different readings by the same reader and across different readers. Thus, the author cannot control what is made of the text; that is up to the reader. In this way, reader response theory deprivileges the author. Putnam (1996) contrasts traditional views of authorship, which portray the author as an expert who controls how the text is understood, with reader response theories that emphasize the reader's role in constructing the text's meanings: The narrator is the one who has the power to "position the research, write the text, and select the voice" (p. 384). According to reader response theory, a reader has the ability to interpret and resist the narrator. Furthermore, because readers do not have integrated, stable selves, a reader may read a text differently at other times or in other contexts. Given that texts (it is hoped) have multiple readers, a plethora of interpretations are possible. According to reader response theory, a text becomes a living document constructed, repeatedly, in a kind of vicarious collaboration among cultural natives, authors, and readers, in accord with becoming-realism. Reader response theory is directly relevant to Golden-Biddle and Locke's (1993) ideas about plausibility. Czarniawska (1998) notes that readers are members of communities, and those communities have shared standards regarding what is appropriate in any given kind of text. The meanings of cultural studies, like other texts, are therefore socially constructed. Drawing on Rorty's pragmatist philosophy, Czarniawska concludes, "There is a limited repertoire of texts and responses at any given time and place, there are more legitimate and less legitimate responses, and there is fashion as a selection mechanism" (p. 70). For all the reasons Czarniawska mentions, communities of readers may share some responses to a text; anticipating these responses, an author may choose to write in ways that will increase the text's chances of being viewed as plausible.

2. When culture is treated as a variable and used to predict other variables, such as organizational performance, it fits easily into the mainstream organizational assumptions about the superiority of quantitative methods and the importance of doing research with functional implications, such as improving productivity and performance. Culture-as-variable research is easily congruent with the managerial interest and with Habermas's characterization of technical research. In contrast, culture-as-metaphor posits that culture is not a variable. Instead, it is a metaphor for examining everyday organizational life. Culture-as-metaphor highlights aspects of organizational functioning that have been ignored by the field's emphasis on variables, such as organizational size and structure, that can be measured relatively easily using quantitative methods.

3. See also Boje and Dennehy (1993), Clegg (1990), Cooper (1989), Cooper and Burrell (1988), Czarniawska-Joerges (1992), and Hassard and Parker (1993). It would be important to follow up such introductions with reading less introductory materials, such as Baudrillard (1983), Derrida (1976), and Lyotard (1984). Accessible feminist versions of postmodernism, with some reference to organizational and psychological issues, include Ferguson (1993) and Flax (1990). Deconstructions of organizational-relevant texts have been done, including studies by Kilduff (1993) on March and Simon's *Organizations,* Mumby and Putnam (1992) on bounded rationality, Martin and Knopoff (1997) on Weber's theory of bureaucracy, Knights (1992) on strategic management, Townley (1993) on human resource management, Calás and Smircich (1991) on leadership, and Calás (1987) on Minzberg's work.

4. My (Martin, 1990a) deconstruction stops at this point, refraining from deconstructing the feminist ideology that was the reason for its having been written. This refusal is unjustifiable, according to postmodern theory. Linstead and Grafton-Small (1991, pp. 13-14) note this position and cogently state its shortcomings: "Postmodern ethnography asks of every representation 'is

this fact?' and refuses to come to any final conclusions (Birth, 1990, p. 55). It throws into question its own authority as an account, and whether or not it introduces the device of coauthorship or multiple voices, it nevertheless points to the possibility of an infinitude of interpretations and accounts. With no claim to factual superiority, how can it contest the accuracy of other accounts? How can it avoid the charge of nihilism if it recognizes no absolute authority and all facts, values, and assumptions are undecidable? How can it enable choice between accounts if all are substitutable and none have priority? How can it deal with nonepistemological issues (Morgan, 1983, p. 403; Jackson & Willmott, 1987, p. 364)—ideology, politics, ethics, morality . . . ?" Many other scholars, particularly those who are interested in the practical implications of scholarship, have shared these misgivings about postmodernism's supposed relativism, its potential for serving as a justification for nihilism, and its ability to undermine any commitment to a political or moral agenda (e.g., Okin, 1995; Reed, 1990). Although some postmodernists believe that any position can and should be deconstructed, other versions of postmodernism are more temperate. For example, some postmodern scholars argue that postmodernism is not relativist in the sense that anything goes. Instead, conclusions can still be drawn, but they must be acknowledged as historically contingent and situationally specific. Calás and Smircich (1999; see also Yeatman, 1994), for example, speak approvingly of postmodern studies, including the study described previously, that retain a political agenda throughout the analysis. For example, some recent feminist postmodern work has retained a clear advocacy for change in gender relationships (e.g., Butler, 1989; Collinson & Hearn, 1994; Gherardi, 1995b; Shallenberger, 1994). Feminist postmodern theory has also, in work directly relevant to the study of cultures in organizations, delineated the fragmentation of the self because identity is distributed across a variety of cultural identities. This work attends to the ways in which sex and gender intersect with race, ethnicity, and national identities (e.g., Bell, Denton, & Nkomo, 1993; Calás & Smircich, 1993; Calvert & Ramsey, 1992; Hurtado, 1989; Nkomo, 1992). Calás and Smircich also note that postcolonial work has brought an international perspective to postmodern cultural research, again retaining a political agenda (focused on overcoming the oppressive history of colonial relationships among nations) (e.g., Anzaldua, 1987; Gupta & Ferguson, 1997; Said, 1989; Spivak, 1988). Similar observations are made by Calás and Smircich regarding postmodern organizational scholarship in such traditions as "actor-network theory" (e.g., Latour, 1987; Law, 1994) and the narrative approaches to knowledge discussed in this chapter (e.g., Czarniawska, 1997, 1998; Deetz, 1992; Hatch, 1996; Putnam, 1996; Van Maanen, 1996). This recent scholarship may not adhere to strict postmodern standards of endless deconstruction, but it also has avoided the action paralysis of navel-gazing scholars uninterested in praxis or social change.

   5. See Morley (1992) for a critique of this and other innovative writing strategies.

III
Exploring the
Edges of Cultural Theory

10

Cultural Boundaries

MOVEABLE, FLUCTUATING, PERMEABLE, BLURRED, AND DANGEROUS

Some doubt whether there is a common culture now at all, whether it is right to imagine that "the West" retains any resonance of worthy meaning; or even that it should. To claim commonality is, paradoxically, to be written off as elitist. . . . The round earth, like an hourglass, is turned upside down these days, spilling variegated populations-in-motion into static homogeneous populations, south into north, east into west; the village mentality, with its comfortable reliance on the familiar, is eroded by the polychrome and polyglot. . . . While the kaleidoscope rattles and spins, and tribe assaults tribe, no can predict how this will shake itself out; but the village mentality is certainly dead. The airplane cooked its goose.
—Ozick (1996, p. 284)

A t this point, this book shifts from research that has been done to research that might be done. This chapter introduces a theoretical problem, one that has the potential to make us rethink the ways culture

315

has been defined and studied. That problem is an aspect of the cultural kaleidoscope that Ozick (1996) described previously: How do we draw a boundary around a culture? This apparently simple question raises a host of other issues: "How do I know who is inside that boundary and who is outside the boundary?" "Who exactly am I studying?" "What makes them participants in a culture?" "Can I trust my answer to this last question?" "How do I know?" "Are there degrees of cultural involvement?" "Are there multiple ways to define the boundary of a culture?" "If culture is, at least partly, a subjectively perceived ideational system, how do the boundaries of that system relate to the boundaries of a collectivity, such as an organization or a work group?"

Every boundary creates an inside and an outside, whether that boundary is defined by an etic researcher or by participants in the culture in an emic study. In this chapter, we will move from who is inside or outside a cultural boundary to what ideas are inside or outside. Rather than viewing cultural boundaries as fixed, impermeable, and clearly defined—safe territory for cultural theorists—we will come to view those boundaries as fluctuating, permeable, blurred, and even dangerous. By the end of this chapter, I hope, boundaries will have become a leverage point from which you can see how all cultural theory might be shifted and viewed in a different and useful way.

A Mosaic of Separate and Unique Cultures?

In many ways, organizational culture researchers have reinvented some of the wheels invented, some time ago, by anthropologists (see also sociological work on culture: e.g., Swidler, 1986; Wuthnow, Hunter, Bergesen, & Kurzweil, 1984). Early anthropological studies focused on isolated communities, such as tribes, often located on islands and/or deep in jungles (e.g., Bateson & Mead, 1942; Malinowski, 1922/1961). These were often hunter-gatherer agricultural economies, sometimes linked by hostile or friendly trading relations, having some similarities across cultures in kinship structures, religious beliefs, and living arrangements. Despite these linkages among the societies studied, early anthropology produced a series of ethnographies of isolated cultures— a state of the discipline that Keesing (1981) described as a mosaic:

> In this view, small-scale tribal societies . . . constitute a kind of mosaic of cultures. Each culture is seen as a separate and unique experiment in human possibility—as if each were a differently colored separate piece in a mosaic of

human diversity to be studied, and valued, in its own right. . . . If we look at the tribal world as a mosaic of cultural variation . . . we are led to attribute a spurious separateness and self-containment to these "cultures," to overlook the way peoples were tied into regional systems to trade, exchange, and politics, through which ideas as well as objects flowed. (pp. 111-113)

In a mosaic, a channel of grout (a kind of cement) separates one tile from the next, with no blurring of colors or overlapping of tiles. According to this kind of anthropology, each culture is viewed as separate and unique.

Contemporary anthropology has come a long way from the mosaic view of cultures. Since Keesing used the mosaic metaphor in 1981, contemporary anthropology has become more like an impressionist painting—hard edges and colors blurred, processes of change acknowledged, and linkages and mutual influences explored. Sahlins (1985) argued that cultures cannot be conceptualized as "islands of history"—that is, as isolated entities immune from outside influences, frozen in time. Ethnographies that might, at one time, have been written as if they were snapshots frozen in time now document a process of cultural interpenetration and adjustment (e.g., Clifford, 1988; Kondo, 1990; Marcus & Fischer, 1986/1999). Contemporary anthropologists have also begun to decouple culture from geographical location (Clifford, 1997; Gupta & Ferguson, 1997), exploring, for example, the government of a modern nation-state—a decentralized organization, of sorts, defused across diverse locations, adjusting to regional differences. Thus, contemporary anthropology offers not a mosaic but an impressionist portrait of nested, overlapping cultures that interpenetrate, blurring boundaries.

Those who study organizations from a cultural point of view usually focus on one or more organizations within a nation-state, and as a result those organizations have much in common. Despite these commonalities, organizational scholars often study cultures of organizations as if they were clearly delineated tiles in a mosaic, isolated from each other, frozen in time, with clearly defined boundaries. In contrast, other organizational scholars have sought evidence of similarities across organizational cultures, such as when Peters and Waterman (1982), Ouchi (1981), Ebers (1995), and Porras and Collins (1994) focused on best cultural practices within a small group of profitable firms in the United States. Very few organizational culture studies, however, have sought or attained the complexity of contemporary anthropologists, who view cultures as nested, overlapping, and interpenetrating, as described in the nexus view of cultures in organizations outlined in Chapter 5.

Studies of cultures in organizations have not adequately reflected the rapidly changing environment of contemporary organizations (e.g., Boyacigiller & Adler, 1991; Roberts & Boyacigiller, 1984). In Western industrialized societies, interorganizational alliances, international markets, and multinational corporate structures are commonplace. Air travel and information technology cross international boundaries with ease. International alliances, such as the European common market, the Organization of Petroleum Exporting Countries, and the International Monetary Fund, blur national boundaries. This is indeed a global economy, albeit not a monolithic one free of differences, decouplings, and conflicts of interest. Organizational theories of culture need to reflect this rapidly changing environment (e.g., Hermans & Kempen, 1998; Kreiner & Schultz, 1995; Mills & Hatfield, 1997; Schneider & Barsoux, 1997; Willmott & Knights, 1995), in which clear, stable boundaries between one culture and another may seldom exist.

Today, as Western, industrial influences affect even relatively "undeveloped" societies, anthropological and organizational studies of culture face similar theoretical questions, sometimes in similar bureaucratic settings. For example, to what extent can an organization have a culture that is different from the surrounding societal culture? How should the boundaries of a culture be conceptualized in ways that reflect issues of cultural interpenetration and the process of cultural change? (see Hernes, 1998, 1999). In a complex industrialized society, in which people belong to many different cultural groupings, what does it mean to be a member of a culture? Where does one culture begin and another end? As cross-national contacts increase, answers to these questions will become increasingly important. We all need a theoretical language to describe the complexity of contemporary cultures without the oversimplifications inherent in terminology, such as "global," that denies rather than explores sources of difference.

The Edges of Cultural Theory

The term *organizational culture* is used to describe something we think we can recognize; it is cited in textbooks, included in the titles of books, and is a topic on which I, like many others, do research. Despite its ubiquity, the term organizational culture is problematic because, as I argue later, the boundaries of a culture and the boundaries of an organization are not identical, conceptually or empirically. Nevertheless, most cultural studies simply focus on a context and assume that all people in that context are participants in the culture. Specifically, organizational culture studies almost always assume that cultural participation coincides with a physical location or with a collection of bodies, perhaps people who share a job or work at the same organization. Shortcomings of each of these assumptions are discussed later. Gradually, this discussion will raise a series of major theoretical issues, the resolution of which will require a new language for talking about cultures in organizations (e.g., Gupta & Ferguson, 1997; Hernes, 1999). To acknowledge these boundary-drawing difficulties, and to provide an alternate way to speak about cultural issues, the phrase "cultural member" will be abandoned at this point and "cultural participant" will be used in its place. The first part of the following discussion shows why we need to separate collectivities from cultures, and the second argues that culture needs to be defined, at least in part, subjectively as an ideational system. I begin with a discussion of why it is problematic to assume that the edges of a culture are coincident with physical locations, bodies, or jobs.

Physical Location

Studies often assume that the boundaries of a culture are coincident with the physical location of a context, as indicated by such phrases as "the manufacturing plant's culture" and "the shop-floor culture" or reference to an office or a department as a "cultural context." Such language is used, for example, throughout the first two parts of this book. Usually, the physical location approach to cultural boundary drawing is premised on the idea that physical location promotes cultural development because of the opportunity for interpersonal contact (e.g., Louis, 1985, pp. 75-79; Trice & Beyer, 1993; Van Maanen & Barley, 1985).

It is easy to think of reasons why this conceptual approach is oversimplified and, in some cases, misleading. Even in an organization that has only one physical location, such as a small manufacturing company, some employees will rarely lay eyes on each other; people working graveyard shifts may seldom speak with daytime workers, and lower-level employees may rarely see, not to mention interact with, high-ranking executives (e.g., Burowoy, 1979; Young, 1991). In larger organizations, these interpersonal distances will be exacerbated, even when some communication takes place in written form, over the Internet, or in videos. In multinational corporations with dispersed regional offices, corporate identity and geographic location are radically decoupled, and these separations may be reinforced by language differences (e.g., Globokar, 1997; Hernes, 1998; Koot, 1997; Kreiner & Schultz, 1995). In such multinational corporations, regional bosses may get together or communicate regularly, but lower-level employees of different regions may rarely meet and seldom communicate, even by e-mail or letter (e.g., Kreiner & Tyggestad, 1997). Under such conditions, without even minimal contact or shared experience, it is unlikely that physical location of an organization and the borders of a culture are identical (e.g., Koene, Boone, & Soeters, 1997; Sharpe, 1997). There is no easy or universally applicable way to equate a physical place with a culture (e.g., Clifford, 1997; Gupta & Ferguson, 1997; Passaro, 1997).

Bodies

Cultural studies often assume that culture is embodied—that is, that people are the carriers of culture. To some extent, this kind of language is unavoidable because culture is usually described in terms of what people do, say, and, sometimes, think and feel. It is problematic, however, to assume that culture is embodied in any straightforward way. Such problems become visible if we consider that people can have an effect on others, even if their bodies are seldom seen and their voices rarely heard.[1] For example, Kreiner and Schultz (1995) described a culture that was partially disembodied. EUREKA was "the pan-European programme for the promotion of cross-border and cross-institutional collaboration on technological development" (p. 64). The group spawned a variety of ventures and partnerships. Many of these projects were "geographically dispersed over most of Europe. Thus, face-to-face encounters occurred only occasionally" (p. 78). Despite this lack of geographical proximity, bodily presence, and face-to-face communication, the EUREKA project generated a variety of symbols and beliefs that, haphazardly and incompletely, were adopted, interpreted, and adapted, producing a "soft" culture that facilitated the collaboration process in important ways.

The possibility of disembodied culture is made more visible, and extreme, in the virtual world of the Internet, in which communications
are sometimes signed with pseudonyms and falsified self-descriptions
can disguise a person's identity. On the Internet, in written communication, in "chat rooms," and e-mail, lower-level employees can mas-
querade as professionals; men can pass as women and vice versa; and
races, ethnicity, interests, and opinions can all be disguised. Despite
these decouplings between what is said and who is saying it, and a near-
total lack of face-to-face contact, some ongoing Internet chat rooms
and e-mail groups can become communities that share many of the
attributes that have come to be associated with the word "culture." For
example, Hafner (1997) noted that The Well was an online community
and business that began in 1985

> as a VAX computer and a rack of modems in a ramshackle set of offices in
> Sausalito, California. . . . 10 years later, The Well had grown into a veritable
> Saint Mark's square, with thousands of postings every day on topics ranging
> from the circumcision of newborns to the Gulf War. Despite this growth and
> a conspicuous attempt, at least in principle, to be accessible to anyone with a
> modem, in reality The Well attracted a certain group of people: baby boom-
> ers in their late 30s and early 40s, smart and left-leaning without being self-
> consciously [politically correct], mostly male, many with postgraduate
> degrees. They had come of age in the '60's, and in The Well they found some-
> thing of a club. In the process, The Well became one of those cultural phe-
> nomena that spring up now and again, a salon of creative, thoughtful, and
> articulate participants who are interested in one another's stories in a self-
> absorbed, cabalistic way. (p. 100)

The Well became extraordinarily central to the lives of its contributors.
Tom Mandel was "one of the most visible participants in the club, and
although he had actually laid eyes on only a handful of the other people,
this was the place he wanted to go to die" (p. 100). On March 25, 1995,
on the eve of his death, he wrote the following farewell to The Well (as
quoted in Hafner, 1997):

> I could start off by thanking you all, individually and collectively, for a
> remarkable experience, this past decade on The Well. For better and .for
> worse—there was a lot of both—it has been the time of my life and especially
> a great comfort during these difficult past 6 months. I'm sad, terribly sad I

cannot tell you how sad and grief-stricken I am that I cannot stay to play and argue with you much longer. (p. 100)

The story of The Well is as complex as any cultural story, but the depth of the emotional involvement of its participants was striking given that few of them had ever met and that the "visibility" of cultural carriers such as Tom Mandel was achieved without the usual kinds of face-to-face contact.

Such erasures and replacements of bodies, made more visible on the Internet and in geographically dispersed organizations such as EUREKA, are also present in more conventional organizational contexts. For example, people can speak for and even "pass" for other people, particularly in written communication. For example, a lower-level administrator may draft a memo or a speech for a high-ranking executive. As a result, when a communication from such an executive is received, it is not clear who is doing the communicating or, in cultural terms, which particular body (or bodies) is carrying the culture. To some extent, culture can be expressed and transmitted without bodily contact.

Another way to approach the disjunction between bodies and cultures is to acknowledge that characteristics of our bodies (e.g., race and sex) do not accurately predict our beliefs, cognitions, values, and interests and therefore cannot be used to predict participation in one subculture or another (e.g., Fernandez, 1982; Hernes, 1997; Rosaldo, 1989). These kinds of complications illustrate why culture could, and perhaps should, be conceptualized without assuming embodiment. This issue is more complicated than it first might appear, however. For example, inhabiting, or claiming to inhabit, a female or a male body can influence communication patterns and thereby affect how people treat each other and therefore what they think and feel (e.g., Burrus, 1997; Ferguson, 1984; Flax, 1990). In the previously mentioned Internet example, a person pretending to be a person of the opposite sex does not escape embodiment; he or she enacts its subjective complexities. For example, a woman using a man's name on the Internet can experience, partially, what it is like to be treated like a man (e.g., Hafner, 1997, p. 109). Similarly, racial and ethnic stereotypes may affect interactions with stereotyped people, making it difficult for the stereotyped to elude the effects of their embodiment (e.g., Nkomo, 1992). Therefore, bodies—or, more accurately, assumptions about bodies—still affect what is said and not said, even (e.g., in the case of written communication) when those bodies cannot be seen (e.g., Calás & Smircich, 1996).[2]

Jobs

Organizational studies of culture often assume that all holders of a given type of job are participants in a culture or an occupational subculture. This is a variant of the embodied view of culture, one that focuses specifically on the jobs people hold rather than on any other personal characteristics. These studies assume that which particular individuals hold these jobs is unimportant. For example, some studies focus on occupational cultures. Deindividuated cultural participants are referred to in terms of their jobs, such as programmers, assembly line workers, or funeral directors (e.g., Barley, 1983; Gregory, 1983). Some of these cultures may be occupational (e.g., marketers vs. engineers) or hierarchical (e.g., salaried managers vs. hourly workers) (e.g., Louis, 1983). Others may span levels of a hierarchy and include a variety of jobs, such as when a division or a work group is said to have a culture (e.g., Martin & Siehl, 1983; Van Maanen, 1991; Young, 1991). In each of these examples, cultural boundaries are assumed to be coincident with explicit, apparently objectively measurable variables, such as hierarchical status or divisional, job, or task group assignment.

Boundary-drawing strategies that equate cultural participation with objectively measurable variables are demonstrably too simple, but they are the most common way of defining subcultural boundaries. Problems with this approach become visible if we examine a series of difficulties that a cultural researcher using this approach might have to resolve. For example, how should a researcher deal with people whose jobs require crossing boundaries, such as externally oriented salespeople, public relations staff, top federal government executives with interagency linking responsibilities, and managers working in multinational contexts (e.g., Globokar, 1997; Jang & Chung, 1997)? What about individuals who keep the same job but work in a series of different companies, such as programmers who company hop in a mobile labor market (Gregory, 1983)? Have these individuals changed organizational cultures while keeping their occupational culture? When a person's job changes, such as when a technical person becomes a manager of technical people or a Disneyland ride operator becomes a supervisor, does their subculture change as well (e.g., Van Maanen, 1991)?

What about layoff survivors or temporary workers who have an ambivalent relationship to an employing company, both attached and detached? In all these examples, job assignment is not easily or completely equated with participation in a culture.

There is another particularly important objection to this approach. Jobs refer to instrumental functions within an organization, but there is more to culture than simply those activities that serve an instrumental function. For example, culture can serve expressive, aesthetic, or noninstrumental symbolic purposes (e.g., Gagliardi, 1996; Jelinek, Smircich, & Hirsch, 1983; Schultz & Hatch, 1996; Strati, 1992). For all these reasons, a straightforward identification of culture with a particular set of jobs or occupations is incomplete. We need a more complex theory.

Organizational Stakeholders

Many cultural studies assume that all employees of an organization are participants in its culture. Again, this approach assumes that bodies carry culture; in this case, bodies who are organizational employees are assumed to be cultural participants. The problems with this approach become evident when we ask who is and who is not included within a culture's boundaries. Are part-time employees participants in the culture? Does a culture include people who are stakeholders but not employees, such as shareholders, residents of the surrounding community, or family members (e.g., Deetz, 1992; Kanter, 1977)? Cultural researchers need to consider whether to include these kinds of stakeholders when cultural boundaries are drawn. Such boundary drawing decisions shape what theories and whose interests will be represented in a given cultural study. These implications become visible when we consider, in more depth, whether or under what conditions community and family participants should be included as cultural participants.

When residents in a surrounding community are defined as "outside" the culture, a researcher may be, in effect, taking the position that the focal organization has little moral responsibility for caring about its effects on that community (Egri & Pinfield, 1996; Shrivastava, 1994). If the company has polluted the environment, made its neighbors ill, or put a substantial portion of a community out of work, these issues would be "not part" of this particular cultural study. As this example illustrates, when a researcher draws a boundary line around a culture, he or she also may be drawing a line regarding some controversial political issues. In this way, a cultural theory aligns itself with some interests in an organization, and if (or when) a conflict of interests occurs a theory will favor some viewpoints at the expense of others. In this theoretical arena, as in others, power and theory are inextricably intertwined.

A second example may clarify this point. Suppose an organizational culture researcher focuses on employees and excludes consideration of the views of employees' family members. If a study is focused in this way, the researcher will probably be less likely to consider how what happens at work affects what happens at home and vice versa. Some researchers and employees justify the exclusion of family participants from cultural studies by drawing a sharp distinction between the public world of work and the private sphere of family life, hoping this stance will protect the privacy and autonomy of life at home. Advocates of this viewpoint might argue that the organization does not usually have direct responsibility for the welfare of an employee's family. There is another point of view regarding these matters, however—one that views the public and private domains as inextricably intertwined (e.g., Frug, 1986; Olsen, 1983). For example, if a company expects employees to work more than 60 hours a week on a regular basis, this will affect family relationships and divisions of labor within the home (e.g., Bailyn, 1993; Hochschild, 1989; Kunda, 1996; Okin, 1989). From this point of view, an employee's family members should be included in a cultural study because organizational policies affect the physical and emotional well-being of the families of employees and vice versa. Without consideration of these issues, I have argued (Martin, 1990a) that a study of organizational culture would, in an important way, be incomplete.

A cultural researcher has to decide which categories of potential organizational stakeholders will be conceptualized as cultural participants and included in a cultural study. There is good reason to presume that some stakeholders will have differing views and experiences (e.g., Alvesson, 1996; Jermier et al., 1991; Martin, 1992a, pp. 83-114; Reed, 1985; Van Maanen & Kunda, 1989; Young, 1991). Therefore, who is included or excluded will determine to a considerable extent the content of a cultural portrait. As each category of stakeholder is included or excluded, the researcher implicitly takes a stand on controversial issues. At the very least, the rationale for including and excluding various groups of stakeholders merits discussion and perhaps reconsideration. Neutrality on these boundary-drawing issues is impossible.

Boundary Questions at Higher
Levels of Analysis

The introduction to this chapter stressed the cross-national contacts that characterize contemporary organizational life. For this reason, it is important to explore the relevance of the previously discussed issues for higher levels of analysis, such as nation-states and international organizational alliances. For example, some studies focus on the culture of organizations in a particular nation-state (e.g., Kondo, 1990; Rohlene, 1974; Shenkar & von Glinow, 1994). Others contrast the cultures of different nation-states (e.g., Adler, 1991; Roberts & Boyacigiller, 1984). For example, Hofstede (1991) contrasts the questionnaire responses of employees of a single multinational company, located in different countries, drawing conclusions about national differences in value orientations. Other studies focus on similar organizations in different nation-states, contrasting, for example, the cultures of Japanese and U.S. corporations in a particular industry (e.g., Lincoln & Kahlberg, 1985; Ouchi, 1981; Pascale & Athos, 1981; see Kleinberg, 1989, for a less optimistic view). In these cross-national organizational studies, cultural participation is usually defined in terms of ties to a physical location, usually a nation, and sometimes also in terms of job or task assignment as a full-time employee of a particular firm.

These cross-national studies exhibit variants of all the difficulties discussed previously. For example, should definitions of cultural participation include nonemployee stakeholders, such as shareholders, family participants, neighbors from the same communities, or part-time employees (see Kondo, 1990)?[3] What is the cultural participation of an employee who is from one country and works in another, perhaps temporarily (e.g., Kleinberg, 1989)? Are participants in minority groups or residents of outlying parts of a country, perhaps from island colonies, fully participants in a national culture (e.g., de Vries, 1997)? Can a cultural member be an immigrant? If so, does that immigrant status have to be legal? Once that status is legal, does cultural participation ensue instantly, or does it take time to develop? What about mixed ethnicity, racial, or religious identities that cross national borders (e.g., Hernes, 1997; Rosaldo, 1989)? What does it mean to speak of national cultures in the context of cross-national entities, such as a multinational corporation or the common market in Europe (e.g., Koot, 1997)? Such questions expose the difficulties of equating participation in a legal entity, such as an organization or a nation, with participation in a culture.

The Case for a Subjective Approach
to the Boundary-Drawing Process

The approaches previously described define cultural participation using an objectively measurable criterion, such as job title, employing organization, national citizenship, or a demographic characteristic. Individuals belonging to the same category may react differently, however, having varied subjective reactions to similar experiences and working contexts. For example, an ambitious salesperson may think more like a vice president than like his or her peers—a process labeled "anticipatory socialization" (Schein, 1978). Most funeral directors may use "life-like" approaches to embalming and funeral arrangements (Barley, 1983), but others may prefer to let death show itself without disguise. Because category identity and subjective experiences may be decoupled in these and other ways discussed previously, I argue that these varied subjective experiences must be incorporated into an understanding of culture; objective criteria for assessing participation need to be supplemented with more subjective assessments. Thus, the boundary-drawing process is far more complex than it usually appears. Once we adopt a subjective approach, the nature of culture has to be rethought.

One way to respond to the complications of a subjective viewpoint is to allow for variations in intensity of participation in a culture so that some people (bodies) are more fully participants in a culture than others. For example, a researcher could determine if part-time workers have less self-identification with a culture than full-time employees. Would all part-time workers, however, react to a culture with the same degree of distancing? Once intensity of participation in a culture is a possibility, culture becomes a subjectively defined concept, and it becomes possible to think of an individual being, to varying degrees, a member of several partially overlapping or nested cultures (e.g., Calás & Smircich, 1993; Hernes, 1997; Martin, 1992a). For example, Anzaldua (1987) describes "mestizas" (women of mixed ancestry with multiple cultural identities) who learn to be Indian in some Mexican contexts and to be Mexican in some Anglo contexts. Bell (1990) describes the complex identity of some upwardly mobile black women who work in an organization dominated by white men, feel limited affinities with white women, and retain an enduring but complex relationship to the black communities in which they were raised. A subjective approach forces recognition of disjunctions between category membership and cultural participation, such as when individuals with similar demographic characteristics, hierarchical status, and task assignments have different reactions to a culture or consider themselves to be participants in different cultures. These complex self-identities find their mirror on the organizational and national levels of analysis, in which subjective multicultural commitments are enacted (e.g., Czarniawska, 2000; Kymlicka, 1995) to the detriment of some subgroups (e.g., de Vries, 1997; Okin, 1996).

Furthermore, intensity of an individual's cultural participation can change subjectively over time (e.g., Greenwood & Hinings, 1988; Hatch, 1993; Mills & Hatfield, 1997; Pettigrew, 1985a). For example, an alienated employee may slowly disengage or even develop an antagonism to a culture, and a new employee may become gradually socialized into a culture (Schein, 1978). A marginalized or deviant person who moves to the edge of a culture may be a crucially important cultural member because he or she defines what is "in" by being "out" or "almost out" (e.g., Meyerson & Scully, 1995). For example, Martin and Siehl (1983) describe how DeLorean, in his role as division manager at General Motors, skillfully calibrated the degree to which his division could deviate from the conformity-oriented culture of the rest of the firm. Van Maanen (1991) describes his increasing alienation as an employee of Disneyland. These examples show individuals moving subjectively in and out of participation in a culture, working at the edges of what is permitted and condoned (Swidler, 1986). The movement from objective to subjective criteria for boundary drawing is crucially important because it moves away from the implicit assumption that culture is a unitary phenomenon, shared equally and similarly by all bodies in a particular context.

Etic (Outsider) and Emic (Insider) Research Strategies

At this point, the etic versus emic distinction becomes relevant. An etic research strategy takes an outsider stance toward a culture, for example, by deciding who is and is not a cultural participant based on analysis of some "objective" criteria, such as years of employment, hours worked per work week, or job assignment. An emic approach would use a more subjective criterion and would focus on participation as a culturally defined product, relying on the subjective assessments of potential cultural participants with regard to who is in and who is out. Although there is a possibility that both etic and emic conceptualizations might agree about who is a participant in a culture and who is not, they might well disagree about the participation status of more than a few types of people.

If cultural participation is subjectively defined, it lies in the eye of the beholder; therefore, one person may define it differently than another. Whose word on the participation question is an emic or etic researcher to believe? Even researchers studying the same context may come up with different answers, in part because they may have differing power orientations and political ideologies (e.g., contrast the views of Hewlett-Packard Corporation in Ouchi [1981] and McGovern & Hope-Hailey [1997]). A labor relations scholar or a critical theorist might think it essential to consider the views of lower-level workers and more powerful individuals, whereas a top executive or a management teacher from a business school might think it important only to focus on the views of top executives. Thus, both etic and emic approaches entail judgment calls. This complexity does not make cultural research impossible or inherently sloppy. It is essential, however, to be explicit and detailed about the uncertainties inherent in the subjective process of deciding who to include and who to exclude from cultural participation. A researcher's introspection about his or her own ideological preferences, followed by a frank and full description of the other subjective factors discussed previously, would help readers to see the strengths and limitations of any choices made. Because any boundary-drawing choice has power implications, this approach would make the workings of power in theory more visible and thus more open to understanding and challenge.

Separating a Collectivity
of Bodies From a Culture of Ideas

Instead of asking where a boundary should be placed or "Who is in or out of a culture?" we can ask "What is in and out of a culture?" Shifting the question in this way disembodies culture. To maintain this orientation, it helps to make a distinction between a collectivity and a culture. A *collectivity* is a collection of bodies bound together by interdependence, such as a nation-state, an organization, an interorganizational alliance, a level of a hierarchy, or a profession. People in a collectivity can be bound together by kinship, employment status, similar training, shared fate (e.g., those whose jobs were threatened by downsizing), or even coercion (e.g., imprisonment). A collectivity—for example, an organization—is a structure, with jobs held by bodies, arranged in space, over time. A collectivity includes people in relationships, around whom borders (albeit debatable borders) can be drawn so that the people within can be counted. When people exist in relationship with each other in collectivities, they create cultures. Thus, cultures are an aspect of collectivities. *Culture* can be defined as patterns of interpretation composed of the meanings associated with various cultural manifestations, such as stories, rituals, formal and informal practices, jargon, and physical arrangements. If culture is defined in this subjective way, culture is an ideational system (composed of subjectively construed ideas). Using this approach, culture would be studied by following ideas rather than simply assuming that participation is determined by bodily presence within a boundary.[4] Therefore, participation in such an ideational system could be defined with an emic or etic research strategy.

To examine this conceptual issue from another vantage point, culture has been defined as aspects of people's collective lives that represent their attempts to comprehend and make sense of their experiences. In this regard, people belong to multiple, overlapping collectivities, some but not all of which are reflected in overlapping, nested cultural identities. The content of these cultural identities—the "what" in the question presented previously—is subjectively experienced and to some extent socially constructed. A cultural researcher's job is to understand and communicate these overlapping, issue-specific subjective orientations, preserving the complexities of their commonalities, overlaps, and differences.

This distinction between a collectivity and a culture provides conceptual leverage without assuming that culture is located in a particular physical context. In a culture, bodies can be present or absent, lied about, or disguised. Even the Internet, in which communication can take place by e-mail and identities can be disguised and distorted with pseudonyms, can be examined with this approach to culture. An individual's complexity is not equated with the instrumental activities of a job description or a task assignment, so the full range and power of a cultural approach are not reduced to its instrumental component. When culture is conceptually distinguished from participation in a collectivity, cultural research cannot be brushed aside as "old wine in new bottles." Studies of collectivities may entail familiar tasks, such as counting employees, describing jobs, and assessing performance, but studies of culture must also map the subjective, socially constructed aspects of working life, which is a different and very difficult task.

This subjective approach should not be misconstrued as an overly idealistic or universalistic approach to the study of culture. Culture is more than ideas, feelings, and talk; therefore, it is essential, as argued in Chapter 3, to study a full range of cultural manifestations. Culture is enacted in behavior, moment by moment. For example, people may enact participation in a professional group by expressing concern for professional standards. Furthermore, such behavior, thought, and talk take place in a material world. A subjective cultural approach can, and I argue should, encompass the study of material conditions, such as pay, working conditions, and dress norms—not as objective facts but as subjectively perceived, understood, and enacted. Thus, two people exposed to the same material conditions of work can react differently, in effect having different experiences (e.g., Larsen & Schultz, 1990). For example, people may react differently to a particularly luxurious office space. A secretary working in that space may find the luxury a distasteful waste of money, whereas a would-be top executive may be pleased with the prospect of enjoying such a space someday. Workers confined to a filthy working area may, to some extent, become acclimated so that they no longer notice smells or dirt with acuity, whereas visiting managers may be more sensitive to these aspects of a work environment (e.g., Jermier, 1985). Thus, culture lies in the eye of the beholder, although most observers might agree that the carpeted luxury of an executive suite is a far cry from the grit and noise of many assembly lines.

The Cultural Production of Boundaries

Once cultural participation is defined subjectively, even cultural boundaries can be seen as subjectively created products of the culture (e.g., Czarniawska-Joerges, 1992; Kreiner & Schultz, 1995). Cultures create their own boundaries using initiation and retirement rituals, for example, to argue about where boundaries should be drawn or whether they should be moved (Trice & Beyer, 1984). With a subjective approach, the edges of a culture are viewed as socially constructed, but it is important to remember that those social constructions will usually not be the product of consensus; instead, many social constructions will co-exist. To translate this idea into research terms, a researcher might find it informative to ask a cultural participant, "From your vantage point, does the culture of (naming a collectivity) include this idea or this inter-pretation?" Alternatively, a researcher might attend to what cultural participants do and do not mention or interact with as they go about their working lives. When boundaries are examined in these indirect ways, some aspects of boundaries will generate collectivity-wide consensus, others subcultural consensus only, and still others great variation with no clarity and no consensus.

The nature of the boundary can also be conceptualized differently. When cultural researchers define cultural participation traditionally, in terms of physical location, bodies, jobs, or organizational employment status, we write about culture as if, on a map of cultural terrain, boundaries could be drawn with firm, clear lines. This hope for clearly defined cultural boundaries is unlikely to be fulfilled. As recognized in old European maps that marked the boundaries of the known world with dotted or blurred lines, sprinkling the map edges with wind-blowing gods and warning signs such as "Dragons lurk here," the edges of cultures are not stable, impenetrable, clearly defined, or even safe. In discussing cultural edges, we need to develop a cultural theory that acknowledges these boundary-drawing difficulties and reconceptualizes boundaries as moveable, fluctuating, permeable, blurred, and dangerous. The lesson here is not that we must have clear, precise ways to define the boundaries of a culture. Cultural boundary definitions are inevitably judgment calls that are, in a sense, arbitrary. Judgment calls need justification (although that justification will always be incomplete).

Before proceeding, a note about language may be useful. As I describe boundaries in the following sections, I use the word "collectivities" to stress that these ideas apply at varying levels of analysis (e.g., nation-states, organizations, and work groups) and to distinguish such collectivities from cultures. I use words such as cultural "participant" rather than "member" to acknowledge that people in a collectivity vary in the extent to which and in the intensity with which they are involved in a culture. In this way, categories of people who belong to a collectivity, such as employees, are not automatically assumed to be cultural participants. Furthermore, in discussing culture, I try to follow ideas rather than people (the "what" rather than the "who") in determining where the edges of a culture lie. I have tried to say what I mean using these terms in an attempt to develop a way of speaking about culture that is sensitive to the boundary-drawing difficulties discussed in this chapter.

Moveable

If culture is an ideational system subjectively perceived, there are still physical correlates of its boundaries. We might think that the physical location of a cultural boundary would be relatively easy to define, such as an office, a building, or a collection of office spaces. Cultural participants, however, may temporarily move a physical boundary. For example, they may work online or stage a retreat off-site, away from daily distractions at work, so that long-range plans or controversial decisions can be made. What can be said online (e.g., in an e-mail), at an off-site retreat, or in a parking lot is different from what can be said face-to-face in an office, even if that office is private. Therefore, conflict-reduction rituals are often held off-site in bars (e.g., Van Maanen, 1986), restaurants, and parks. In a sense, a change to an off-site location gives cultural participants a kind of permission to express emotions that would usually be hidden or controlled under normal working conditions (Douglas, 1975; Trice & Beyer, 1984). More permanent changes in physical boundary location are also possible, such as when cultural participants regularly telecommute from home or work away from the home office on a regular basis. Thus, culture is a moveable feast.

Fluctuating

The edges of a culture also change over time, alternately expanding and collapsing inward, like a person breathing in and out (e.g., Czarniawska-Joerges, 1992; Pettigrew, 1985b). Cultures and collectivities are loosely coupled so that a change in one may sometimes, over time, create a change in the other. For example, a collectivity such as an organization may downsize, expelling long-term employees. Assuming these employees have been enculturated, it is unlikely that they instantly cease to be participants in the culture when they are no longer employees of the firm. Like people who retire, they have a kind of "emeritus" cultural status, which is activated when they see old friends from work or muse about the past. Culture survives in their memories, in addition to being enacted on a daily basis, so that the culture at the time of their departure, presumably recalled without a daily updating, exists as long as they remember it. Suppose an organization then expands, hiring new full-time and temporary employees, merging or acquiring other firms, and building interorganizational alliances that might, in time, fail or expand. Many of the employees of these new parts of the organization might in time, to varying extents, become cultural participants. If the boundaries of a collectivity fluctuate over time, they may create, with informative lags and exceptions, changes in the boundaries of a culture. This raises a theoretically important research question: Under what conditions do cultural boundaries eventually coincide with organizational boundaries, and when and why do they not?

Boundary fluctuation raises the specter of constant cultural flux. Any cultural "snapshot" that in effect freezes time is a gross distortion. It takes time to study a culture, and even in a short time period, as any cultural researcher knows, the boundaries of a culture can fluctuate dramatically (e.g., Geertz, 1995; Pettigrew, 1985a; Sahlins, 1985). Particularly if culture is defined as a subjective phenomenon, a cultural study ideally is less like a single snapshot and more like a collection of rarely ending videos, with each video camera aimed differently, seeing different events, and having different "voice-over" interpretations (Martin & Frost, 1996). Some video cameras might be aimed at the community surrounding the organization or at an employee's family, whereas others would focus on physical manifestations, such as conveyer belts, computer screens, or the flip chart at a meeting. Researchers would control some cameras, and cultural participants would control others. Both researchers and cultural participants would be filmed in interaction. Thus, culture could be described as the ever-changing juxtapositions of these ongoing films on multiple projection screens, giving the audience participants enough information to add their own interpretations to those of cultural participants.

Permeable

The edges of a culture are permeable (e.g., Kreiner & Schultz, 1995; Marcus & Fischer, 1986/1999; Swidler, 1986). Here, the distinction between a collectivity and a culture becomes critical. Some individuals regularly cross collectivity boundaries as part of their jobs, such as when salespeople reach out to customers, executives join the boards of directors at other companies, and financial officers plan mergers and acquisitions. A consultant or other temporary worker may enter the organization for a time, offer important assistance, and then leave. To what extent do these collectivity boundary crossings entail crossing cultural boundaries as well? When a cultural member speaks of difficult company matters during pillow talk with a spouse, where are the edges of the culture? As these examples illustrate, the boundaries of a collectivity such as an organization are rarely impermeable, and the subjectively defined borders of a culture are even less so. Here, a useful metaphor might be the membranes of a cell, which permit the exchange of materials by a process of osmosis that is possible because the membranes are permeable.

Blurred

Just as employees self-consciously use physical location to legitimate different kinds of emotional expression and behavior, so too they self-consciously negotiate the subjective placement of a cultural boundary to enhance the achievement of their own goals (e.g., Clifford, 1997; Gupta & Ferguson, 1997; Passaro, 1997). For example, a whistle-blower may expose a corporation's fraud or pollution, or a government employee may draw attention to waste or bribery. In the eyes of some cultural participants, this may be disloyalty, a cultural transgression. The whistle-blower, however, may view himself or herself as a member preserving the culture, exhibiting a superior kind of loyalty (e.g., Graham, 1986). From this perspective, whistle-blowing is the act of the ultimate cultural insider. In this instance, a boundary is being negotiated, drawing attention to the fact that its location is not objectively definable and clear in the same way to all.

Subcultural boundaries are also deliberately blurred (e.g., Kondo, 1990; Kunda, 1992). Participants have an investment in keeping some subcultural boundaries intact and in destroying or undermining others. For example, a high-ranking executive who is a participant in an egalitarian culture may go out of his or her way to show kindness, personal vulnerability, or a lack of snobbishness to a lower-level employee. Such actions do not usually go unnoticed, and they may have the effect of bringing a lower-level employee into the cultural fold by making high-ranking executives seem more appealing. For example, one of the most common types of organizational stories (Martin et al., 1983) focuses on the age-old question, "Is the big boss human?" In these stories, a high-ranking executive goes out of his or her way to show egalitarianism, for example, by obeying safety rules designed for assembly line workers. Such actions undermine status differences in a minor way that leaves the formal structure of the hierarchy intact. Examples of such apparent egalitarianism include abolishing designated parking spaces, executive dining rooms, and executive-only elevators. Such apparently egalitarian cultural artifacts paradoxically increase acceptance of other kinds of inequality. For example, showering lower-level employees with interpersonal attention from higher-ranking executives makes those lower-level employees more accepting of large pay inequalities between themselves and management (Martin & Harder, 1994). In these ways, some apparently egalitarian practices can undermine egalitarianism by making high-ranking employees seem more attractive and more deserving of their high status; the distinction between keeping intact and undermining subcultural boundaries is blurred.

Physical arrangements can also be used to reify and exaggerate culturally defined boundaries between high- and low-ranking employees (e.g., Gagliardi, 1990; Larsen & Schultz, 1990; Pfeffer, 1992). For example, the bodily functions of executives (eating and elimination) draw attention to what they have in common with lower-ranking employees. In hierarchical cultures, these functions are often hidden by the use of separate executive toilets and dining rooms. Plush offices, softly carpeted halls, and beautiful artwork create a separate executive world vastly different from the dirt and noise of manufacturing facilities or the repetitive drone of data processing centers. In some cultures, status distinctions may be important even after working hours, thus tacitly extending cultural boundaries. For example, high-ranking cultural participants may feel constrained to wear ties or dresses to the grocery store and the airport, avoid downscale bars and entertainment, and otherwise act in accord with the dignity and decorum expected of someone in their position. As in the previous example, it is unclear whether these practices are always successful at reinforcing hierarchy. Marked hierarchical differentiation, ostensibly aimed at reinforcing and legitimating status differences, may undermine them by making high-ranking executives seem distant, snobbish, and uncaring. In each of these instances, boundaries are blurred, and their meanings are unclear.

Dangerous

Edges are dangerous places, and when cultural boundaries are blurred rather than reinforced it can make people uncomfortable. For example, photographs of President Clinton dressed in a baseball cap and jogging clothes and eating a Big Mac sandwich caused a stir. Presidents in a democracy are to represent every man (and woman), but not at the expense of a second cultural requirement—to be a dignified embodiment of national pride. When the president behaved in this culturally inconsistent way, he was operating in a danger zone—not for the first or last time. Such taboo behavior breaks a boundary, exposing the fragility of a cultural edifice (e.g., Douglas, 1975; Turner, 1969).

For example, one obvious taboo is sexuality in the workplace (e.g., Hearn & Parkin, 1987; Martin, 1990a), particularly in the United States, in which controversies regarding sexual harassment have recently proliferated. Opinions vary about the inevitability of sexual attractions at work and their desirability (e.g., contrast Gherardi [1995b] and Gutek & Morasch [1982]), and many employees have found it difficult to know where to draw the line. Sexual approaches at work, particularly from high-ranking executives, arouse controversy precisely because they threaten culturally accepted boundaries of power and sexuality, work and pleasure, and sexuality inside and outside of marriage. Pushing these boundaries is a form of living dangerously, on the edge of culturally inappropriate behavior, although who defines what is inappropriate varies. Because sexuality is such a controversial arena, in which deep taboos are frequently and none too secretly violated, this is a particularly fertile (seminal?) area for cultural research.

Cultural participants reinforce and reify boundaries in an attempt to make them seem immovable, stable, impermeable, and clear—and therefore a source of security and safety (Douglas, 1975). At the same time, cultural participants undermine boundaries in ways that show boundaries to be moveable, fluctuating, permeable, blurred, and sometimes dangerous (e.g., Geertz, 1995). In these ways, boundaries are culturally produced. Cultural participants have it both ways, reinforcing and undermining boundaries; thus, as cultural researchers, our theories need to reflect these tensions and complexities.

Liminality: Managing Boundary Crossing

Because of the danger and discomfort inherent in boundary crossing, even the mildest of these transitions can be difficult. Turner's (1969) notion of liminality is important here. There is a moment in a transition when a person enters a liminal state, belonging neither to the category of the past nor to the category of the future. Such liminal states are disorienting and sometimes even frightening, and thus they must be handled with care. It is for this reason that so many of the rituals described in Chapter 3 dealt with liminal periods of individual transition, in which cultural participants celebrated promotions, demoted leaders, retired with grace, or otherwise transitioned from one role or position to another (Trice & Beyer, 1984). Similarly, cultures have less individualized liminal experiences that focus on transitions for the collectivity. These transitions are also marked with ceremonies, such as celebrations of an initial public stock offering or a wake mourning a company's demise. The subjectively defined boundaries of a culture are also zones of liminality. Swidler (1986) argues that it is at the edges, where new cultural habits are being formed and old ones are being rejected or modified, that it is easiest to see a culture and understand its workings. Even here, or especially here, it is clear that cultural boundaries are seldom clearly defined edges. These are contested terrains, where boundaries are moved, changed, penetrated, and blurred.

Beyond a Mosaic View
of Organizational Cultures

The ideas in this chapter build on and go beyond ideas introduced in the first and second parts of this book. Just as early anthropological studies produced a mosaic view of isolated tribal societies, functioning without interaction with each other or the larger society, many studies of organizational cultures assume cultural uniqueness and "stress the internal, rather than to look to the external, societal, cultural context in which organizations are embedded" (Jelinek et al., 1983, p. 338). Because organizational research, in contrast to many early anthropological studies, does not focus on geographically isolated, nonindustrialized cultures, organizational researchers do not have the advantages (and disadvantages) that come with studying a drastically different culture located far away. A collectivity, such as an organization, is a microcosm of, not separate from, surrounding cultural influences. Therefore, in Chapter 3 I argued that claims of cultural uniqueness should be taken with a grain of salt: Culture is composed of elements, some of which are truly unique, others are falsely believed to be unique, and still others are commonly understood to be not unique. For example, in Chapter 5, Figure 5.4 showed in objectivist terms how a programmer's subculture was common to three high-tech companies in Silicon Valley, despite claims of cultural uniqueness (Gregory, 1983). This figure is revised in

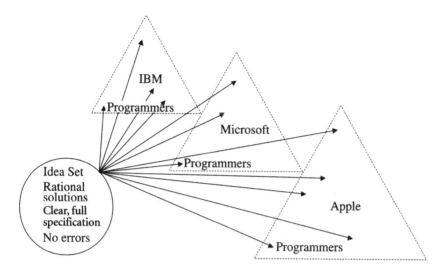

Figure 10.1. Adaptation of Gregory's (1983) Model of Occupational Cultures, With Permeable Boundaries

Figure 10.1 to show the subjectivist view of cultures with permeable boundaries (idea centered rather that people centered) introduced in this chapter.

In contrast to the mosaic view of isolated and unique cultures, the nexus approach brings the society surrounding a collectivity—its external environment—into the forefront of cultural studies. As outlined at the end of Chapter 5, the nexus approach to the study of culture posits that a collectivity such as an organization is a nexus, in which a variety of internal and external cultural influences come together. In Chapter 5, these ideas were illustrated using objectivist terms in Figure 5.5, which depicted the effects of feeder cultures on the organizational subcultures of the Trust for Public Land. The ideas about a subjective approach to the definition of cultural boundaries presented in this chapter take the nexus argument several steps further. First, the boundaries of a collectivity and a culture are not assumed to be or treated as if they were the same. What is unique about a culture is the way in which a particular mix of internal and external cultural influences (ideas, not people) combines and interacts within boundaries that are moveable, fluctuating, permeable, blurred, and dangerous. This can be illustrated with a subjectivist revision, as shown in Figure 10.2.

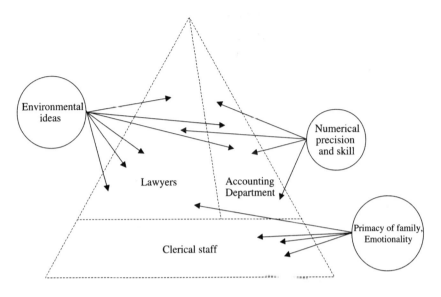

Figure 10.2. Adaptation of "Feeder" Cultures at the Trust for Public Land, With Permeable Boundaries

The nexus approach and these ideas about boundaries of cultures are congruent with contemporary organizational developments, in which buzz words such as "multinational" and "global" capture the increasing frequency and depth of cross-national exchanges. These ideas also make it easier to encompass the changing demographics in many industrialized countries, in which an organization's "multicultural" workforce is often composed of people from a variety of racial, ethnic, national, and other different backgrounds. These ideas easily accommodate an expansion of focus to include organizational stakeholders who are not employees, such as families and community residents. In all these ways, by conceptualizing the boundaries of a culture as permeable, moveable, and fluctuating, we allow for intercultural penetration and cultural change. Such an approach explicitly acknowledges the difficulty of determining where one culture ends and another begins. Instead, this theoretical approach allows for cultures and subcultures in organizations to be nested, overlapping, and multiple, with blurred edges. In this way, redefining culture boundaries offers a theoretical leverage point, opening the door to new ways of thinking about culture.

In the next and (good news) final chapter of this book, this focus on the future of cultural theory and research is maintained, but the emphasis is shifted to specific studies of theoretical importance that have not yet been done.

Notes

1. Yvette Hartmann of the University of British Columbia (personal communication, 2000) suggests we explore the relationship between population ecology theory and cultural inertia (e.g., Baron, Burton, & Hannan, 1996; Baron, Hannan, & Burton, 1999; Baron, Hannan, Hsu, & Koczak, in press; Hannan, Burton, & Baron, 1996). Individual bodies enter organizations ("birth" within a population) and leave organizations ("death" within a population). She argues that if we define an organization's culture in terms of the embodied individuals that participate in it, the entering and leaving of those individuals results in a permanently changing culture. When culture is embodied in this way, there is no cultural stability that transcends the entering and leaving of bodies. If culture is not embodied, however, culture may be transmitted with distortion and variation to new participants; there may be life cycles of culture or elements of culture that do not coincide with the lengths of time individuals are employed by an organization.

2. These complexities are reinforced by the structure of language. As will later become evident, as I try to find a language that does not presume culture is embodied, such a language is nearly impossible to sustain. Nevertheless, the problem of embodiment remains crucially important because we need to sustain awareness of ideas that are difficult to express.

3. A related issue is the part-whole problem associated with inadequate sampling procedures. For example, the responses of employees of a single multinational company (usually male managers and professionals) should not be taken to represent all the men and women of an entire country, including children, the aged, the unemployed, and rural residents (e.g., Hofstede, 1991).

4. This is a version of a mind-body split. This is obviously an oversimplification, but deconstructing this dichotomy raises issues beyond the scope of this chapter. Exploring the ramifications of such complexities for cultural theory would be a worthy endeavor.

11

Terra Incognita

IDEAS FOR FUTURE RESEARCH

The map is not the territory.
—Van Maanen (1979, p. 9)

This book offers a map of the terrain of organizational culture theory and research, a map that is like those old maps from before the days of Mercator projections and satellite photographs. So far, we have reviewed carefully the parts of the map that seem to be well traveled, where territories, roads, and boundaries are well-defined. We have also examined ill-defined, fuzzy borderlines, forks in the road of theory development, and edges of the known marked with signs such as "Dragons lurk here." This chapter begins by asking "How far have we come?" and it then addresses the question "Where do we need to go next?"—into areas that on those old maps would be marked as "terra incognita" (unknown territory). Rather than outlining future research ideas with generalities, a few theoretically important, as yet undone studies will be described. I hope these ideas for future research may

342

prove useful either as road maps or as a stimulant for you to go on an independent trip of your own into uncharted territory.

How Far Have We Come?

Chapter 2 provided a review of the major, fundamental disputes that have provoked bitter disagreements and misunderstandings among organizational culture researchers. These disputes concern

- objective and subjective approaches to the study of culture;
- etic and emic methods;
- whether a researcher seeks theoretical generalizations or context-specific cultural understandings or both;
- whether a study chooses a narrow focus (on one or a few cultural manifestations) or breadth (the full range of cultural manifestations); and
- the depth of cultural understanding sought.

Sufficient information was given about each of these disputes so that readers could determine where their preferences, as consumers or producers of cultural research, lie on each of these dimensions.

In Chapter 3, many different definitions of culture were quoted, contrasted, and critically analyzed. Ideational and materialistic definitions were distinguished. A series of controversial assumptions were discussed using contradictory definitions of culture: Is culture best defined narrowly (one or a few cultural manifestations) or broadly? Is an organization's culture unique? Is culture necessarily shared? Is culture that which is clear, or does it include ambiguity? Given the proliferation of contradictory cultural definitions, the rest of the chapter focused on what cultural researchers actually study when they claim to be studying culture. These cultural manifestations include

- rituals;
- organizational stories;
- jargon;
- humor;
- physical arrangements (architecture, dress, and decor);
- formal and informal practices; and
- espoused and inferred content themes, such as values and basic assumptions.

I then offered my own definition of culture—one that stresses the patterns of interpretation (the meanings) underlying these manifestations.

Moving from definitions and operationalizations of culture to theories of culture, Chapter 4 reviewed much of the cultural literature, finding that most studies use one of three theoretical approaches:

- The integration perspective assumes consistency across manifestations, organization-wide consensus, and clarity. According to this view of culture, if something is ambiguous it is not part of the culture.

- The differentiation perspective offers interpretations of manifestations that are inconsistent with each other, finds consensus only within subcultural boundaries, and allows for ambiguity—only within the interstices between subcultures, which are therefore islands of clarity. Subcultures can reinforce, conflict with, or exist independently of each other.

- The fragmentation perspective focuses on interpretations of manifestations that are not clearly consistent or clearly inconsistent with each other. Although particular issues may generate interest, these issues do not create clusters of people who feel the same way about more than one issue, so little organization-wide or subculture-specific consensus is found. Ambiguity, rather than clarity, is the heart of a culture.

This chapter concluded with an argument among hypothetical proponents of each of the three perspectives so that readers could see, in action, the clash among these theoretical views.

Chapter 5 offered my view of culture, which argues that any culture is understood more fully if it is studied from all three theoretical perspectives. One of these perspectives is likely to be easy to determine (the "home" perspective) by researchers and by cultural participants. The other two perspectives will be more hidden but an important source of insight nonetheless. A perspective that is hidden today may become a home perspective tomorrow. In this way, hidden perspectives offer a preview of an organization's cultural future. Three-perspective views of a variety of cultures in both cross-sectional and longitudinal studies were summarized in this chapter. Common misunderstandings, characteristics, and limitations of the three-perspective view were discussed. Finally, the nexus view of a culture's environment was described, with case studies showing how external cultural influences affect cultural development within an organization.

In Chapter 6, I challenged the idea that theory and research can be purely descriptive. Such claims of neutrality mask the ways in which research is written in a managerial or critical interest. An argument among hypothetical advocates of these three kinds of interests was used to show how interest assumptions can create theoretical misunderstandings and bitter disagreement. Examples of single-perspective studies written in the managerial, critical, and apparently descriptive interests were analyzed to show how these interests have affected and limited organizational culture research.

Part I, encompassing Chapters 1 through 6, reviewed much of the organizational culture literature. Each of these first six chapters began and ended with a discussion of dilemmas that readers of cultural research must recognize and cultural researchers must resolve; for example, How is culture being defined? What manifestations of culture are being studied? In a particular study, does the definition of culture agree with its operationalization? What theoretical perspectives are most useful? In whose interests is the study written?

In Part II, the focus shifts from what has been done to the process of doing research. Chapter 7 addressed methodological disputes in the cultural arena and included a discussion of quantitative, qualitative, and innovative hybrid approaches. In this chapter, as in all the others, my objective as author was to encourage readers to appreciate and to be able to evaluate knowledgeably approaches that may be unfamiliar. Given the range of theories, interests, methods, and writing styles in the organizational culture literature, such a broad-minded approach is essential if we collectively are to move beyond culture wars and learn to appreciate, with critical discernment, the full range of cultural studies that have been done.

Chapter 8 continued this emphasis on appreciation of multiple approaches, showing how the lack of appreciation for theories, interests, and methods other than one's own can distort the review process and make it less than constructive. This chapter included positive and negative hypothetical reviews of real organizational culture studies; my own evaluations of these studies tied together all the material presented so far. Chapter 9 offered several innovative approaches to writing, with examples taken from the organizational culture literature.

Part III turned attention from the past to the future of organizational culture research. In Chapter 10, one deep theoretical problem—how to draw a boundary around the edges of a culture—was used as a lever to open up a series of important theoretical issues. A different way of speaking about cultures (as having participants rather than members, distinguishing collectivities from cultures, etc.) followed from this discussion of boundaries as moveable, fluctuating, permeable, blurred, and dangerous.

Although the dilemmas and potential solutions in the organizational culture arena are not limited to the options discussed in this book, this book is already long. The ideas discussed so far and also later simply offer a map, and as Van Maanen (1979, p. 9) reminds us, "A map is not the territory." Where the territory seems different from the map or where the map labels the territory terra incognita—these poorly understood places are precisely where future research is most likely to reveal important and new insights.

Where Next?

The study ideas discussed in the following sections are arranged in an order, beginning with the ideas that are most closely aligned with prior theory and research and ending with those that stake out new territory. Some of these study suggestions are tacitly or explicitly related to the ideas about cultural boundaries and the edges of cultural theory presented in Chapter 10. For each study suggestion, I present the basic theoretical motivation, supplemented with specific hypotheses phrased as questions. In some cases, I suggest a method of studying the issue and offer criticisms that may be helpful to anticipate. In some of these study suggestions, I do not attempt to apply and integrate the ideas presented in Chapter 10 because doing so would require a complex rethinking of cultural theory and the development of a new conceptual language, which are too much to attempt in a chapter such as this.

Understanding and Predicting Cultural Change

Longitudinal studies of organizational cultures are very rare (for exceptions, see Baron, Burton, & Hannan, 1996; Baron, Hannan, Hsu, & Kozak, in press; Greenwood & Hinings, 1988; Hannan, Burton, & Baron, 1996; Pettigrew, 1985b). Instead, cultural research on change has frequently offered oversimplified generalizations about cultural inertia or the ease of value engineering. Few attempts have been made to reconcile these opposing views of cultural change. Few cultural theorists have tried to integrate what is known about organizational change more generally with cultural change in particular. As a result, ideas that have been generally discredited, such as stage theories of change, surface in cultural change research with insufficient critical examination. Therefore, our understanding of cultural change—particularly change that is not top-down, anticipated, and controlled by management—is spotty at best. One study that shares none of these faults and offers a careful view of top-down, bottom-up, and environmentally caused cultural changes is Pettigrew's *The Awakening Giant: Continuity and Change in ICI* (1985b). This longitudinal case study of a large corporation required the involvement of many researchers throughout many years, resulting in a long book (longer even than this one). The insights that derive from this kind of study (particularly regarding management's abilities to react to unexpected environmental jolts) are exceptionally valuable.

A longitudinal study (of one or many organizations) could address a variety of questions. Some hypotheses could come from the three-perspective view of cultural change, which posits that hidden rather than home perspectives may carry the keys to understanding the next period in a firm's development. Thus, for example, if the integration view of a culture seems to be the home perspective in a given organization, will the differentiation and fragmentation views offer useful hints about the issues and conflicts that will be more important at a later time? If fragmentation is dominant, will the rudimentary subcultures of the differentiation view or whatever is shared in an organization-wide consensus hold clues to what the future will hold? How can a researcher determine which of two suppressed perspectives will become the next home view? These hypotheses, which lie at the heart of the three-perspective framework, have yet to be fully explored.

To date, little research has explored whether a three-perspective approach can be useful to practitioners hoping to control the cultural change process. For example, a study could determine if subcultural differences could be used to help implement a top-down cultural change effort (see Bartunek & Moch, 1991). Some subcultures might respond to the proposed change with enthusiasm. Other subcultures might be pockets of resistance, and still others are pockets of indifference, ignorant of or not caring about whatever change is proposed. It seems reasonable to hypothesize that an effective cultural change intervention might start with "test case" experimentation with a couple of enthusiastic subcultures to determine if modifications in the planned change process are needed. Resistant subcultures might be studied (without trying to change them at this point) to determine why their resistance is occurring. Would changing some aspects of the planned cultural change reduce this resistance? Whatever is learned from these pockets of enthusiasm and resistance could be used to modify a cultural change program before attempting to implement it more broadly across those subcultures that were initially indifferent to the change effort.

Finally, it would be interesting to follow over time organizations that are faced with competing value demands to determine how these competing pressures can be reconciled effectively. For example, market pressures for efficiency and profitability may cause tension when a for-profit organization is also committed to nonmarket objectives, such as a commitment to "social responsibility" or religious goals (for a description of the dilemmas faced by such organizations, see Whetten, 2001). What do these kinds of organizations learn about cultural change as they attempt to balance these competing value demands? What cultural changes are outside managerial control? How do poor economic conditions affect noneconomic value commitments? Of course, there are other cultural change questions worth addressing, but these ideas sug gest the range of issues that merit attention.

Longitudinal studies of cultural change, however, are rare for good reason. Retrospective cultural accounts, whether collected in interviews or by relying on organizational archives, are inevitably oversimplified and biased. Individual memories fade and get distorted. Archives (what to save and not save, whose views are preserved, and what is and is not said in writing or official film records) are selected and maintained by managers. Official corporate histories and videos are usually paid for and controlled by the management of the firm and usually present a rose-colored, leader-centered view of the past. For all these reasons, it is better to study cultural changes as they occur rather than relying on a biased view of the past. If retrospective accounts must be relied on, all the skills of a trained historian will be needed.

Whether a researcher chooses to study a single organization for a long time or many organizations for a shorter time, the time investment in a longitudinal study, for both researchers and organizational employees can be enormous. It is difficult to sustain such a commitment for a long time. In addition, longitudinal studies entail a career risk. A longitudinal researcher has to invest a huge amount of time and effort into a single study; as in any study, the results may be disappointing. If the study uses qualitative methods, the only way to present the full scope and complexity of the results may be in a single, book-length publication. Such risks are greater for the younger scholar, whose reputation is not yet established and who may not yet have tenure. Longitudinal studies may be more feasible for established scholars or those who do not mind a risk. The amount to be learned, however, is great, particularly given the rarity of such studies.

Multinational Corporations: Balancing Centralization and Localization

As described in Chapter 7, multinational corporations, to capitalize on the benefits of size, have a need to homogenize policies on an international level. At the same time, experienced international employees often stress the need to be sensitive to local cultural differences, for example, in norms about the importance of promptness, close interpersonal relationships, and the morality (or lack thereof) of bribery. Studies that have examined this tension between homogeneity and sensitivity to local difference are rare (see Jaeger, 1979; Sackmann, 1997; van Reine, 1996), and further research would be useful, particularly as international contacts become more common.

One kind of multinational corporation that faces such tensions in a clearly visible form is an advertising agency. Increasingly, such agencies have merged and acquired international affiliates to service large clients on a worldwide basis and take advantage of the economies of scale. At the same time, work practices, consumer expectations, media reach, and interpersonal norms differ across countries. One rationale for international expansion in the advertising industry was that local agencies would have different—and effective—ideas about how to reach local consumers. It has been difficult, however, for international advertising agencies to decide when to require cross-national uniformity in advertising content, brand image, types of media outlets, or even agency personnel practices. Should these policies be controlled by headquarters or a lead agency, or should local agencies be given autonomy? It is difficult, if not paradoxical, to try and reap the advantages of both centralization and decentralization at once (e.g., Lawrence & Lorsch, 1967). (Consider, for example, the collapse of the once bally-hooed merger of Publicus and True North.)

An in-depth study of these issues in an advertising multinational could address a wide range of questions of both theoretical and practical importance. The difficulties involved in such a study would not be unusual. For example, to the extent that cross-national misunderstandings were happening, the company's employees might be interested in hiding these difficulties to protect themselves from headquarters retaliation, to preserve remnants of local autonomy, or to protect the company's (or their own) reputation. Of course, the cost of an international study would be great. Such a study might require or at least benefit from a multiperson research team with different international identities or at least different language skills. Such skill and identity differences may well make it more difficult to coordinate the work of such a team and produce a mutually satisfactory, coauthored research publication. Researchers from different countries, for example, may have different criteria for assessing the worth of a study and different ideas about how and where to publish the results. Such difficulties are a partial explanation for the scarcity of cross-national research that attempts to understand in-depth the dilemmas of working in an international context in which some boundaries become blurred, other boundaries move, and still others become intensified.

International Cultural Issues
That Do Not Coincide With National Boundaries

As detailed in some of the previous chapters, much international research has simply reified national stereotypes. Often, studies have taken an exclusively integration point of view, portraying national cultures in clear and homogeneous terms. (This tendency to view other cultures as homogeneous may be a specific instance of a fundamental cognitive bias—the tendency to view one's own membership group as complex and internally differentiated, whereas the "other" group is viewed as homogeneous.) As in other domains of research, this heuristic has political implications, serving some interests more than others. If national cultures are conceived of as homogeneous, this theoretical choice tacitly denies the existence of, for example, religious, ethnic, class, and gender differences within a country. Such a bias is strengthened if only members of a mostly male, managerial or professional elite are studied, as is often the case in cross-national studies. In effect, such an integration portrait of a national culture silences the views of a majority of its members.

Of course, exceptions to this pattern of cross-national research do exist, but such studies are rare and valuable. For example, Kondo's (1990) study of a family-owned business in Japan revealed, with great care and in detail, ways in which members of this firm acknowledged and lived with differences due to age, class, and sex. This cultural portrait blends ideas from all three theoretical perspectives without using this theoretical language. In a study with similar strengths, Rofel (1989) lived and worked in a silk factory in China, where changing political circumstances challenged the plant's old commitments to an "iron rice bowl" (guaranteed subsistence wages for all), irrespective of pressures for productivity or profitability. Such in-depth studies of particular organizations offer views of national cultures that contain elements of all three theoretical perspectives but do not draw explicitly on the organizational cultural literature cited in this book.

A three-perspective approach to the study of national cultures would avoid homogenizing stereotypes, allow for differences within a nation state, and could incorporate ambiguities as well as clarities within a portrait of a complex culture. These attributes are particularly important given the changes in global relations mentioned in previous chapters. Technological developments such as the Internet and the frequency of air travel have given people the opportunity to cross national borders. Political developments, such as the North America Free Trade Agreement, and the policies of the International Monetary Fund, the World Bank, and the European Common Market have fostered international boundary crossing. Ironically, in the process some national differences have been heightened. Also, some regional identities that cross national boundaries, such as Alsace-Lorraine, may have been intensified.

This changing pattern of cross-national, cross-cultural contact raises many questions. What does the word "global" (as in "global economy") mean, and what are the implications for cultural studies? Does "global" imply cultural homogenization, with the dominance of Western industrial or U.S. priorities, for example, in the International Monetary Fund or the World Bank? In some domains, is the goal a more efficient exchange of goods, ideas, and services, keeping the cultural distinctiveness of these inputs intact, for example, in the exchange of food products in the European Common Market? Is cultural homogenization occurring in some locales or some industries and not in others? How does a small country such as Denmark keep its national commitments (e.g., to a social safety net, gender equality, and egalitarianism more generally)? Under what conditions does homogenization, or its threat, create a cultural backlash, for example, in fundamental Islamic countries? How do the roles of women in different countries differ, and how does intercultural contact affect these differences? You can imagine dozens more questions that are raised by the issue of cross-national boundary blurring.

For all such studies, the primary difficulty is an empirical one: How can a researcher investigate such large questions over such a large expanse of people, issues, and geography? It would be important not to rely on archival data, such as news accounts in the media or opinion polls designed for other purposes, if the full complexity and diversity of cultural phenomena are to be explored. Difficulties in these kinds of studies are familiar to anthropologists entering other cultures: a language to be learned, entrée to be gained not only as a researcher but also ultimately as some kind of cultural insider, the loneliness and difficulty of long-term, participant-observation research, and so on. A multinational research team might offer useful insights; problems sharing insights and producing a jointly authored account could be acute but theoretically interesting and worthy of reflexive analysis. Use of some of the less representational writing styles would enrich such a study. The inherent limitations of such a study, particularly regarding generalization, have been discussed in this book. Alternatively, a researcher could do a quantitative study using a random, stratified sampling procedure to tap a wide range of ideas in a variety of locales. The difficulties of doing such a study, and the shortcomings inherent in trading off breadth and depth, should be familiar by now.

New Media for Studying Cultures: Videos and Hypertext

To date, organizational culture research has almost always relied on methods that produce data that can be described in words, such as observations by a researcher or questionnaire data. Although most social sciences rely on the written word (anthropologists and historians have been more willing to use other media), this may be particularly inappropriate for cultural research. Reliance on the written word limits the kinds of cultural manifestations that can be studied. The sounds and images in a video, for example, can capture tone of voice, nonverbal communication patterns, the faces and dress of cultural members, and more detail about the physical layouts in which they work. These kinds of cultural manifestations add greater breadth, and perhaps depth, to a cultural portrait. Visual media are particularly suitable for communicating emotional aspects of organizational cultures in which verbal expression of emotions is limited by workplace norms. In addition, a camera literally represents a point of view; different kinds of camera shots could represent different points of view of cultural members or different theoretical perspectives on a culture.

Studies presented using nonwritten media could be used, as is, in the classroom for teaching purposes. In addition, insights derived from media such as videos could be described in words in a traditional scholarly article. More important, the results of studies might (in an ideal world, in which such products would be included in a vita and considered as a "publication") be presented in nonwritten formats, such as videos, photos, CD-ROMs, and Web pages. On a Web page, written text could be accompanied by click-video access to elaborate a point previously made in words. Informants could be seen and heard speaking. Such media might well appeal to younger audiences, whose sensitivity to the visual has been enhanced by their collective neglect, compared to older audiences, of written sources of information.

Taking this multimedia approach a step further, hypertext makes it possible to include new kinds of information, with new kinds of user control, in a cultural portrait. Presenting a qualitative case study using hypertext, for example, could give a "reader" control over what aspects of a culture he or she wants to learn about (Krug [1999] did a cultural dissertation on CD-ROM using hypertext). A reader could click on an image of a face to hear that person speak. A reader could follow cues, pictures, video clips, and text to learn more about a particular subculture. Conflicting cultural viewpoints, perhaps corresponding with the three theoretical perspectives, could be color coded so that a reader of hypertext could learn how these perspectives offer internally coherent but externally conflicting views of a culture. If many people "read" a hypertext description of a culture, the computer could track which aspects of the culture they wanted to see, in what order they requested information, how long they studied each bit of information, and what kinds of information they ignored. If some of these readers' characteristics were known (e.g., sex, occupation, and relation to the culture being described), the researcher could determine if people in different categories read the hypertext differently. A reader could be given feedback on his or her click-through patterns, suggesting, for example, what the reader's "home" perspective might be and what kinds of information were repeatedly missed.

There are good reasons why alternative media are seldom used to study cultures (for exceptions, see Gagliardi, 1990; Harper, 1987; Van Maanen, Dabbs, & Faulkner, 1982). Obviously, the researcher would need to master the medium to be used, whether it be film editing or hypertext. Less obvious but more important, there needs to be a way in which an alternative-media study engages with and contributes to the written literature. For example, researchers who eschew generalizations and theory building could argue that such a cultural portrait offers a different kind of insight, perhaps deeper, because it can tap a wider range of cultural manifestations than can a study that relies on traditional media. Furthermore, through the use of different camera vantage points or different color codings in hypertext, it may also be possible to signal to the reader that certain data are congruent with certain theoretical perspectives, operationalizing such concepts with a new kind of acuity. At the very least, supplementing traditional kinds of word-dependent presentations with data presented using alternative media will make classrooms, colloquia, and Web pages more interesting and differently informative.

Virtual Organizations:
New Organizational Forms Created by the Internet

Technological innovations have created new kinds of organizations, many of which are likely to have odd and theoretically interesting kinds of cultures. For example, an organization is responsible for laying the cables that cross the globe, linking people in different countries through the Internet. These cables are laid by groups of temporary workers drawn from throughout the world. They come together in a jungle to dig a ditch for the cable, or they go in ships to lay cables across the seafloor, dodging the mountains and canyons of an underwater world.

Although parts of these cable-laying teams travel from country to country, they do not speak the same language. They work together only for a short time before regrouping, in a different mix, on the other side of the globe. Contact between cable-laying groups and with headquarters is minimal and seldom face-to-face. What does organizational culture mean in such a context?

Also, consider a virtual online community such as The Well. As described in Chapter 10, this was a community that grew up in the form of a "chat room" on the Internet. Initially, one person was responsible for coordination in the The Well, including the maintenance of membership lists and other technical tasks. Over time, contributors to the conversation at The Well developed rules for behavior, sanctioned deviants, and became in many ways a community. When one long-term contributor learned he had a mortal illness, he relied on his friends at The Well to work through his feelings about dying. This was not a superficial set of relationships, although some members were closer than others. As the community grew, it encountered the problems common to most communities. For example, some members wanted to change customary patterns of behavior. Others felt a need for new rules or a desire to avoid the overcontrol of behavior through explicit rules. Many members of The Well never met each other, and for all members face-to-face meetings were relatively rare. On the Internet, it was possible to set up a false identity.

To some extent, this was a disembodied culture or, more precisely, a culture in which one could, to some extent, experience what it would be like to have a different body or a different occupation—in other words, to be someone else. Under these unusual and attenuated conditions, what does it mean to say that The Well has a culture? What is the relationship between this culture, the "self" of an online contributor, and the self-image that contributor projects online? Is such a culture really disembodied, or do bodily images (even if unseen) affect what is said and done? Is misrepresenting one's body (sex, race, etc.) acceptable in some online cultures but not in others? At what point does online community become a culture? If it is when contributors return to a Web site often and develop multifaceted relations with many other site visitors, this transformation of an online community into a culture bears a striking resemblance to the mythical variable of "site stickiness" that so many Web-based companies want to maximize to increase revenues. Relatively esoteric questions about online cultures have direct relevance to practical questions of great interest to e-commerce practitioners.

Studies of unusual cultures, such as The Well and the global cable-laying company, may well require unusual data collection methods. To study the cable-laying company using participant observation would require unusual research, with great personal stamina, some unusual skills for an academic, and quite a bankroll. To study an online community such as The Well, it might be possible to obtain records of saved e-mail conversations, bulletin boards, and other communication. The cooperation of the now-dispersed community would probably be required, however, at least that of those whose names were on the communications one wanted to study. Such a study raises ethical issues of great difficulty, but their resolution might well be of interest to a wide range of people coping with similar issues. It seems likely that the technological changes associated with the Internet will create a wide range of new organizational forms that are not considered in our theories. It will be found for cultural studies, like other domains of research, that the results of such studies raise questions we have not yet contemplated. Therefore, this is an exceptionally fertile territory for exploration. As old pirate maps used to note, "Treasure may be buried here."

Deconstructing the Work: Family Boundary

Organizational cultures are gendered in obvious and nonobvious ways (e.g., Mills, 1988, 1995, 1997; Schein, 1998). Although all kinds of research are well suited for investigating obvious pay and promotion inequalities, many gender inequalities persist because of unintentional discrimination and institutionalized sexism that is often invisible to its perpetrators. Culture research is well suited to discern the subtle, ostensibly gender-neutral practices that disadvantage women (e.g., Mills, 1988, 1995; Mills & Hatfield, 1997). For example, the requirement that all professional employees work exceptionally long hours is particularly difficult for women, who bear the bulk of child care responsibilities, even in dual-career couples. This example is prototypical in that most of the practices that appear gender neutral, but in fact disadvantage women, concern the blurred and permeable boundary between work life and home life. This is particularly germane in family-owned businesses (Yanagisako, 2000).

Organizational theorists have generally taken the position that the public sphere of work is separate from the private sphere of the family and the home. (It is important to note that "family" here need not be the traditional nuclear family; indeed, most households in the United States do not consist of a mother, a father, and a child or children.) There are good reasons for reifying a separation between a public and a private sphere. Individuals may desire privacy and autonomy, for example. Companies, too, have a reason for reifying this separation; for example, if an employee encounters difficulties at home in caring for a dependent, those problems are the responsibility of the individual and not the company.

Despite these attempts to separate the public and the private spheres, these two spheres are inextricably interlocked (e.g., Frug, 1986; Olsen, 1983). What happens at home affects what happens at work. For example, suppose a sick child requires care all night. This leaves an employee with a difficult choice: stay at home with the child when the employee is expected and perhaps needed at work or go to work, exhausted from the long night of child care, and worry about the sick child all day while trying to work effectively. What happens at work also affects what happens at home. For example, consider the 80-hour workweeks that are the norm in some high-tech companies in Silicon Valley (also among untenured professors at some universities). This work policy affects home life, often by so attenuating home time that family relations are deeply troubled. In such a context, the oft-heard advice "Get a life" seems apt but difficult for many to respond to given the prevalence of the workaholic norms. These examples are negative, but sometimes the interaction between work and family can be positive. I remember what a joy it was to come home from a difficult day teaching MBAs and to play with my infant son.

Cultural studies are uniquely situated to study the ways in which work and family issues influence each other, particularly in contexts in which official rhetoric claims the two domains are separate. For example, Meyerson and Kolb (in press) helped The Body Shop institute a series of gender-equity culture change projects, some of which touched on the work-family intersection. Drawing on feminist theory to design those cultural interventions, structure the researchers' own interactions, and analyze what succeeded, what failed, and why, these co-authors modeled an innovative, feminist approach to designing a planned intervention process.

Research such as this suggests that the work-family intersection could be a fruitful domain for cultural researchers. Other studies might focus on the effects of long working hours (see Bailyn, 1993; Collinson, 1992; Kunda, 1996; Perlow, 1997), alternative ways of dividing home responsibilities between members of a couple, the effects of working at home (e.g., telecommuting), and the advantages and disadvantages of part-time or temporary work. Such studies would help deconstruct the separation between public and private responsibilities and help us all better understand how what happens in one of these domains affects the other. This is a research topic for which it would be particularly helpful to have a policy focus (e.g., overtime laws, child care norms, and corporate "flex-time" practices) and to contrast international cultures with different policies and practices.

There are a few difficulties that can be expected in this kind of research. First, there is a pragmatic career concern. Family concerns are all too often seen as women's concerns, although men are certainly affected too. I argue that full opportunities at work will never be open to women until men's responsibilities at home change. It is the case, however, that some scholars, and even some academic departments, value research on such "women's issues" less than traditional organizational scholarship. Second, when studying families, it is important to study families of differing income and class levels because resources available for purchasing cleaning and child care services as well as social norms about the appropriateness of such purchases will differ. Third, in this domain, organizations may have very progressive policies, but it is essential to determine how many women and men are actually taking advantage of these policies. If they do so (e.g., use a flex-time schedule or take a parental leave), does this affect their subsequent career trajectory? Finally, by examining the intersection of work and family and delineating the ways in which the two domains are not separate, you would be challenging a presumption that many people have never questioned. Furthermore, it may be in their interest to portray work and family as separate. As in any research domain, if you can challenge this preconception successfully, your work will be labeled innovative and groundbreaking—"an original contribution to the literature." It will be difficult to convince those who have a vested interest in thinking differently, however. The payoffs and the risks of innovative research are greater.

An Enlightenment Tale of Progress
or a Recapitulation of the Culture Wars?

It has been my goal in this book to explore a broad range of cultural theories, interests, methods, writing styles, and research questions. It is my hope that the presentation of all these issues has been detailed enough so that you can decide which of these you want to learn more about and perhaps try. I hope you will learn to read, and assess knowledgeably, cultural work that represents a wide range of views on these issues. Also, if a few of us experiment with new approaches, all the better. The map may not be the territory, but it could be a better map to a larger world of cultural research.

I may have mapped this terrain, but it is less than clear what you will choose to do with this map. There are at least two very different ways to read this book. It can be read as an enlightenment tale of progress, delineating what has been learned so far about culture. This is the way most literature reviews are written, including most of the volumes in Sage's **Foundations for Organizational Science** series, of which this book is a part. From this vantage point, many conclusions can be drawn from this book. These conclusions are phrased here in the being-realism, representational language of an enlightenment tale of progress:

> There is ample empirical evidence in single-perspective studies supporting the integration, differentiation, and fragmentation viewpoints. In addition, many studies using all three theoretical perspectives have been conducted in a wide variety of organizations (and countries), and all of these studies produced evidence congruent with all three perspectives. If a reader endorses neopositivist assumptions about empirically based theoretical generalizations, this empirical evidence simply cannot be ignored. Thus, any study that relies on a single perspective is examining only a small part of a culture, with predictable blind spots regarding the unstudied perspectives. Therefore, it is better to see what can be learned about any cultural setting by using all three perspectives. Furthermore, it is better to read cultural theory and research conducted from a wide variety of theoretical perspectives, interest orientations, and methods. This broad approach will help ensure that the full range of what is known is, in fact, known to you. In this way, it is hoped, you will not end up reinventing the wheel by doing a study that someone else has already done.

This book can also be read more modestly, with a postmodern twist, as a tale not of progress but of "culture wars" among advocates of competing viewpoints. This "culture wars" reading of the book is congruent with being-realism and does not endorse the certainties of representationalism:

> The organizational culture literature is a battleground, with advocates of competing viewpoints struggling for intellectual dominance (Martin & Frost, 1996). Some of these viewpoints are theoretical (integration, differentiation, fragmentation, and other frameworks), some are focused on issues of power and control (labeled as interests here), and some are methodological (e.g., the struggle between advocates of qualitative and quantitative methods in cultural studies). The three-perspective approach is simply yet another move on this battlefield, an attempt to build a metatheory that dominates other theoretical approaches by encompassing them in a higher level of abstraction (e.g., Gagliardi, 1991).

If you regard the field of cultural studies as a struggle for intellectual dominance, then you have some options. You could critique those who buy into the enlightenment model. You could vary, across studies, your choices of theories, interests, and methods, with a self-critical eye pointing out the shortcomings of each. You could, with self-awareness of the shortcomings of any one choice, join the culture wars, doing work congruent with the theory, interest, and method you find most useful, perhaps with the goal of furthering some political cause, ideology, moral stance (e.g., Okin, 1995; Yeatman, 1994), or your own career.

Most researchers do not study organizational culture; if they do, they may not rely primarily on the theoretical perspectives reviewed in this book. Even so, they will be faced with choices about what interest or interests to represent, what methods to use (or to read about), and what kinds of writing styles could best express the insights and limitations of a particular study. It is my hope that this book, whether it is read as an enlightenment tale or a guide to a battlefield, may offer some useful insights to all sorts of scholars, cultural and noncultural, and therefore become a map worth unfolding occasionally.

References

Abolafia, M., & Kilduff, M. (1988). Enacting a market crisis: The social construction of a speculative bubble. *Administrative Science Quarterly, 33,* 177-193.

Abratt, R. (1989). A new approach to the corporate image management process. *Journal of Marketing Management, 5,* 63-76.

Adler, N. (1991). *International dimensions of organizational behavior.* Boston: Kent.

Adler, P., & Adler, P. (1988). Intense loyalty in organizations: A case study of college athletics. *Administrative Science Quarterly, 33,* 401-417.

Agar, M. (1980). *An informal introduction to ethnography.* New York: Academic Press.

Agar, M. (1986). *Speaking of ethnography.* Beverly Hills, CA: Sage.

Albert, S., & Whetten, D. (1985). Organizational identity. In L. Cummings & R. Staw (Eds.), *Research in organizational behavior, Vol. 7* (pp. 263-295). Greenwich, CT: JAI.

Aldrich, H. (1992). Understanding, not interpretation: Vital signs from three perspectives in organizations. In M. Reed & M. Hughes (Eds.), *Rethinking organizations: New directions in organizational theory and analysis.* Newbury Park, CA: Sage.

Altman, Y., & Baruch, Y. (1998). Cultural theory and organizations: Analytical method and cases. *Organization Studies, 19,* 769-785.

Alvesson, M. (1993a). *Cultural perspectives on organizations.* Cambridge, UK: Cambridge University Press.

Alvesson, M. (1993b). Organizations as rhetoric: Knowledge-intensive firms and the struggle with ambiguity. *Journal of Management Studies, 30,* 997-1015.

Alvesson, M. (1996). *Communication, power and organization.* Berlin: de Gruyter.

Alvesson, M. (1998). *The local and the grandiose: Method, micro and macro in comparative studies of culture and organizations.* Unpublished manuscript, Lund University, Sweden.

Alvesson, M., & Berg, P. (1992). *Corporate culture and organizational symbolism.* Berlin: de Gruyter.

Alvesson, M., & Billing, Y. (1997). *Understanding gender and organizations.* Thousand Oaks, CA: Sage.

Alvesson, M., & Deetz, S. (1996). Critical theory and postmodern approaches to organization studies. In S. Clegg, C. Hardy, & W. Nord (Eds.), *Handbook of organization studies* (pp. 191-217). London: Sage.

Alvesson, M., & Melin, L. (1987). *Major discrepancies and contradictions in organizational culture: Both in the phenomenon of culture itself and in cultural studies.* Paper presented at the International Conference on Organizational Symbolism and Corporate Culture, Milan.

Alvesson, M., & Willmott, H. (Eds.). (1992). *Critical management studies.* London: Sage.

Alvesson, M., & Willmott, H. (1995). Strategic management as domination and emancipation: From planning and process to communication and praxis. In C. Stubbart & P. Shrivastava (Eds.), *Advances in strategic management, 11.* Greenwich, CT: JAI.

Alvesson, M., & Willmott, H. (1996). *Making sense of management: A critical analysis.* London: Sage.

Anzaldua, G. (1987). *Borderlands/La Frontera: The new Mestiza.* San Francisco: Spinsters/Aunt Lute.

Aurelio, J. (1995). Using Jungian archetypes to explore deeper levels of organizational culture. *Journal of Management Inquiry, 4,* 347-368.

Baburoglu, O., & Göcer, A. (1994). Whither organizational culture? Privatization of the oldest state-owned enterprise in Turkey. *Industrial & Environmental Crisis Quarterly, 8,* 41-54.

Bailyn, L. (1993). *Breaking the mold: Women, men and time in the new corporate world.* New York: Free Press.

Barley, S. (1983). Semiotics and the study of occupational and organizational cultures. *Administrative Science Quarterly, 28,* 393-414.

Barley, S. (1986). Technology as an occasion for structuring: Evidence from observations of CT scanners and the social order of radiology departments. *Administrative Science Quarterly, 31,* 78-108.

Barley, S., Meyer, G., & Gash, D. (1988). Cultures of culture: Academics, practitioners, and the pragmatics of normative control. *Administrative Science Quarterly, 33,* 24-61.

Baron, J., Burton, M., & Hannan, M. (1996). The road taken: Origins and evolution of employment systems in emerging companies. *Industrial and Corporate Change, 5,* 239-275.

Baron, J., Hannan, M., & Burton, D. (1999). Building the iron cage: Determinants of managerial intensity in the early years of organizations. *American Sociological Review, 64,* 527-547.

Baron, J., Hannan, M., Hsu, G., & Kozak, O. (in press). In the company of women: Gender and the organization-building process in start-up firms. In M. Guillén,

R. Collins, P. England, & M. Meyer (Eds.), *Economic sociology at the millennium.* New York: Russell Sage.

Bartunek, J. (1984). Changing interpretive schemes and organizational restructuring: The example of a religious order. *Administrative Science Quarterly, 29,* 355-372.

Bartunek, J., & Moch, M. (1991). Multiple constituencies and the quality of working life intervention at FoodCom. In P. Frost, L. Moore, M. Louis, C. Lundberg, & J. Martin (Eds.), *Reframing organizational culture* (pp. 104-114). Newbury Park, CA: Sage.

Bateson, G., & Mead, M. (1942). *Balinese character: A photographic analysis.* New York: New York Academy of Science.

Baudrillard, J. (1983). *Simulations.* New York: Semiotext(e).

Becker, H. (1982). Culture: A sociological view. *Yale Review, 71,* 513-527.

Befu, H. (1963). Patrilineal descent and personal kindred in Japan. *American Anthropologist, 65,* 1328-1341.

Bell, E. (1990). The bicultural life experience of career-oriented black women. *Journal of Organizational Behavior, 11,* 459-478.

Bell, E., Denton, T., & Nkomo, S. (1993). Women of color: Toward an inclusive analysis. In E. Fagenson (Ed.), *Women in management: Trends, issues and challenges in managerial diversity* (pp. 105-130). Newbury Park, CA: Sage.

Benghozi, P. (Ed.). (1987). Art and organization [Special issue]. *Dragon, 2.*

Berg, P. (1989). Postmodern management? From facts to fiction in theory and practice. *Scandinavian Journal of Management, 5,* 201-217.

Berger, P. (1967). *The sacred canopy.* Garden City, NY: Doubleday.

Berger, P., & Luckmann, T. (1967). *The social construction of reality.* Garden City, NY: Doubleday.

Bernstein, D. (1992). *Company image and reality: A critique of corporate communications.* London: Cassell.

Birth, K. (1990). Reading and the righting of writing ethnographies. *American Ethnologist, 17,* 549-557.

Blake, W. (2000). Auguries of innocence I. In D. Fuller (Ed.), *Selected poetry and prose.* Harlow, UK: Longman. (Original work published 1863)

Blau, P. (1965). The comparative study of organizations. *Industrial and Labour Relations Review, 28,* 323-338.

Boas, F. (1901). The Eskimo of Balin Land and Hudson Bay. *Bulletin of the American Museum of Natural History, 15*(Part 1).

Bockus, S. (1983). *Corporate values: A refutation of uniqueness theory.* Unpublished manuscript, Stanford University, Stanford, CA.

Bogdan, R., & Taylor, S. (1975). *Introduction to qualitative research methods.* New York: John Wiley.

Boje, D., & Dennehy, R. (1993). *Managing in the postmodern world.* Dubuque, IA: Kendall/Hunt.

Boland, R., & Hoffman, R. (1983). Humor in a machine shop: An interpretation of symbolic action. In L. Pondy, P. Frost, G. Morgan, & T. Dandridge (Eds.), *Organizational symbolism.* Greenwich, CT: JAI.

Botti, H. (1995). Misunderstandings: A Japanese transplant in Italy strives for lean production. *Organization, 2,* 55-86.

Boyacigiller, N., & Adler, N. (1991). The parochial dinosaur: Organizational science in a global context. *Academy of Management Review, 16*, 262-290.

Brown, J., & Duguid, P. (1991). Organizational learning and communities-of-practice: Toward a unified view of working, learning, and innovation. *Organizational Science, 2*, 40-57.

Bruner, J., Goodnow, J., & Austin, G. (1956). *A study of thinking.* New York: John Wiley.

Bruni, A., & Gherardi, S. (in press). Omega's story: The heterogeneous engineering of a gendered professional self. In M. Dent & S. Whitehead (Eds.), *Managing professional identities.* New York: Routledge.

Brunsson, N. (1985). *The irrational organization.* New York: John Wiley.

Brunsson, N. (1986). Organizing for inconsistencies: On organizational conflicts, depression, and hypocrisy as substitutes for action. *Scandinavian Journal of Management Studies, 2*, 165-185.

Brunsson, N. (1988). *Organizational reforms.* Paper presented at the SCANCOR conference on organizations, Hemsedal, Norway.

Brunsson, N. (1989). *The organization of hypocrisy: Talk, decisions and actions in organizations* (N. Adler, Trans.). New York: John Wiley.

Brunsson, N. (1995). Ideas and actions: Justification and hypocrisy as alternatives to control. *Research in the Sociology of Organizations, 13*, 211-235.

Bryman, A., Gillingwater, D., & McGuinness, I. (1996). Industry culture and strategic response: The case of the British bus industry. *Studies in Cultures, Organizations and Societies, 2*, 191-208.

Buell, B. (1997, December 4). "Ambidextrous" organizations judged most likely to succeed. *Stanford Report*, 10.

Burowoy, M. (1979). *Manufacturing consent: Changes in the labor process under monopoly capitalism.* Chicago: University of Chicago Press.

Burrell, G., & Morgan, G. (1979). *Sociological paradigms and organizational analysis.* London: Heinemann.

Burrus, K. (1997). National culture and gender diversity within one of the universal Swiss banks: An experimental description of a professional woman officer and president of the Women Managers' Association. In S. Sackmann (Ed.), *Cultural complexity in organizations* (pp. 209-227). Thousand Oaks, CA: Sage.

Butler, J. (1989). *Gender trouble: Feminism and the subversion of identity.* New York: Routledge.

Calás, M. (1987). *Organizational science/fiction: The postmodern in the management disciplines.* Unpublished doctoral dissertation, University of Massachusetts, Amherst.

Calás, M., & Smircich, L. (1987). *Post-culture: Is the organizational culture literature dominant but dead?* Paper presented at the International Conference on Organizational Symbolism and Corporate Culture, Milan.

Calás, M., & Smircich, L. (1991). Voicing seduction to silence leadership. *Organization Studies, 12*, 567-602.

Calás, M., & Smircich, L. (1993, March/April). Dangerous liaisons: The "feminine-in-management" meets globalization. *Business Horizons*, 71-81.

Calás, M., & Smircich, L. (1996). From "the woman's" point of view: Feminist approaches to organization studies. In S. Clegg, C. Hardy, & W. Nord (Eds.), *Handbook of organization studies* (pp. 218-257). London: Sage.

Calás, M., & Smircich, L. (1999). *Past-postmodernism? Reflections and tentative directions.* Unpublished manuscript, University of Massachusetts, Amherst.

Calvert, L., & Ramsey, J. (1992). Bringing women's voice to research on women in management: A feminist perspective. *Journal of Management Inquiry, 1*, 79-88.

Campbell, D., & Fiske, D. (1959). Convergent and discriminant validation by the multitrait-multimethod matrix. *Psychological Bulletin, 56*, 81-105.

Campbell, D., & Stanley, J. (1966). *Experimental and quasi-experimental designs for research.* Chicago: Rand McNally.

Chalmers, A. (1982). *What is this thing called science?* (2nd ed.). Brisbane, Australia: University of Queensland Press.

Chatman, J. (1991). Matching people and organizations: Selection and socialization in public accounting firms. *Administrative Science Quarterly, 36*, 459-484.

Chia, R. (1996). The problem of reflexivity in organizational research: Towards a postmodern science of organization. *Organization, 3*, 31-59.

Christensen, S., & Kreiner, K. (1984). *On the origin of organizational cultures.* Paper presented at the International Conference on Organizational Symbolism and Corporate Culture, Lund, Sweden.

Clark, B. (1972). The organizational saga in higher education. *Administrative Science Quarterly, 17*, 178-184.

Clark, H. (1998). Communal lexicons. In K. Malmkjaer & J. Williams (Eds.), *Context in language learning and language understanding* (pp. 63-87). Cambridge, UK: Cambridge University Press.

Clegg, S. (1990). *Modern organization: Organization studies in the postmodern world.* London: Sage.

Clegg, S., & Dunkerley, D. (Eds.). (1977). *Critical issues in organizations.* New York: Routledge Kegan Paul.

Clegg, S., & Hardy, C. (1996). Organizations, organization and organizing. In S. Clegg, C. Hardy, & W. Nord (Eds.), *Handbook of organization studies* (pp. 1-28). London: Sage.

Clifford, J. (1988). *The predicament of culture: Twentieth-century ethnography, literature, and art.* Cambridge, MA: Harvard University Press.

Clifford, J. (1997). Spatial practices: Fieldwork, travel, and the disciplining of anthropology. In A. Gupta & J. Ferguson (Eds.), *Anthropological locations* (pp. 185-222). Berkeley: University of California Press.

Clifford, J., & Marcus, G. (1986). *Writing culture: The poetics and politics of ethnography.* Berkeley: University of California Press.

Cohen, M., & March, J. (1974). *Leadership and ambiguity: The American college president.* New York: McGraw-Hill.

Cohen, M., March, J., & Olsen, J. (1972). A garbage can model of organizational choice. *Administrative Science Quarterly, 17*, 1-25.

Collinson, D. (1992). *Managing the shop floor: Subjectivity, masculinity and workplace culture.* New York: de Gruyter.

Collinson, D., & Hearn, J. (1994). Naming men as men: Implications for work, organization and management. *Gender, Work and Organization, 1,* 2-22.

Collinson, D., Knights, D., & Collinson, M. (1990). *Managing to discriminate.* London: Routledge.

Cook, T., & Campbell, D. (1979). *Quasi-experimentation.* Chicago: Rand McNally.

Cook, T., & Reichardt, C. (1979). Beyond qualitative versus quantitative methods. In T. Cook & C. Reichardt (Eds.), *Qualitative and quantitative methods in evaluation research* (pp. 7-32). Beverly Hills, CA: Sage.

Cooke, R., & Rousseau, D. (1988). Behavioral norms and expectations: A quantitative approach to the assessment of culture. *Group and Organizational Studies, 13,* 245-273.

Cooper, R. (1989). Modernism, postmodernism and organizational analysis. The contribution of Jacques Derrida. *Organizational Studies, 10,* 479-502.

Cooper, R., & Burrell, G. (1988). Modernism, postmodernism and organizational analysis: An introduction. *Organization Studies, 9,* 91-112.

Cox, T. (1993). *Cultural diversity in organizations: Theory, research, and practice.* San Francisco: Barrett-Koehler.

Cox, T., Jr., & Nkomo, S. (1990). Invisible men and women: A status report on race as a variable in organizational behavior and research. *Journal of Organization Behavior, 11,* 419-431.

Crapanzano, V. (1986). Hermes' dilemma: The masking of subversion in ethnographic description. In J. Clifford & C. Marcus (Eds.), *Writing culture* (pp. 51-76). Berkeley: University of California Press.

Czarniawska, B. (1997). *Narrating the organization: Dramas of institutional identity.* Chicago: University of Chicago Press.

Czarniawska, B. (1998). *A narrative approach to organization studies* (Qualitative Research Methods Series). Thousand Oaks, CA: Sage.

Czarniawska, B. (1999). *Writing management: Organization theory as a literary genre.* Oxford, UK: Oxford University Press.

Czarniawska, B. (2000). Identity lost or identity found? Celebration and lamentation over the postmodern view of identity in social science and fiction. In M. Schultz, M. Hatch, & M. Larsen (Eds.), *The expressive organization.* Oxford, UK: Oxford University Press.

Czarniawska-Joerges, B. (1988). *Ideological control in non-ideological organizations.* New York: Praeger.

Czarniawska-Joerges, B. (1992). *Exploring complex organizations: A cultural perspective.* Newbury Park, CA: Sage.

Daft, R. (1980). The evolution of organizational analysis in ASQ: 1959-1979. *Administrative Science Quarterly, 25,* 623-636.

Daft, R., & Weick, K. (1984). Toward a model of organizations as interpretation systems. *Academy of Management Review, 9,* 284-295.

Damon, C. (1997). *Making sense of Meridian. A cultural analysis of organizational life in a new television station.* Unpublished manuscript, University of Kent at Canterbury, UK.

Davis, S. (1984). *Managing corporate culture.* Cambridge, MA: Ballinger.

Deacon, D., Bryman, A., & Fenton, N. (1998). Collision or collusion? A discussion and case study of the unplanned triangulation of quantitative and qualitative research methods. *Social Research Methodology, 1,* 47-63.

Deal, T., & Kennedy, A. (1982). *Corporate cultures: The rites and rituals of corporate life.* Reading, MA: Addison-Wesley.

Deetz, S. (1992). *Democracy in an age of corporate colonization: Developments in communication and the politics of everyday life.* New York: State University of New York Press.

Degot, V. (1987). Portrait of the manager as an artist. *Dragon, 2,* 13-50.

Dellheim, C. (1987). The creation of a company culture: Cadburys, 1861-1931. *American Historical Review, 92,* 13-44.

Denison, D. (1990). *Corporate culture and organizational effectiveness.* New York: John Wiley.

Denzin, N., & Lincoln, Y. (Eds.). (1994). *Handbook of qualitative research.* Thousand Oaks, CA: Sage.

Derrida, J. (1976). *Of grammatology.* Baltimore: Johns Hopkins University Press.

de Vries, S. (1997). Ethnic diversity in organizations: A Dutch experience. In S. Sackmann (Ed.), *Cultural complexity in organizations* (pp. 297-314). Thousand Oaks, CA: Sage.

DiMaggio, P. (1997). Culture and cognition. *Annual Review of Sociology, 23,* 263-287.

Doi, T. (1973). *The anatomy of dependence.* Tokyo: Kodansha.

Donaldson, L. (1985). *In defense of organization theory: A reply to the critics.* New York: Cambridge University Press.

Douglas, M. (1975). *Implicit meanings.* London: Routledge Kegan Paul.

Dutton, J., & Dukerich, J. (1991). Keeping an eye on the mirror: Image and identity in organizational adaptation. *Academy of Management Review, 34,* 517-554.

Early, P. (1995). Of culture, quagmires, and perspectives. *Contemporary Psychology, 40,* 578-579.

Ebers, M. (1995). The framing of organizational cultures. *Research in the Sociology of Organizations, 13,* 129-170.

Egri, C., & Pinfield, L. (1996). Organizations and the biosphere: Ecologies and environments. In S. Clegg, C. Hardy, & W. Nord (Eds.), *Handbook of organization studies* (pp. 459-483). London: Sage.

Eisenberg, E. (1984). Ambiguity as strategy in organizational communication. *Communication Monographs, 51,* 227-242.

Enomoto, E. (1993). In-school truancy in a multiethnic urban high school examined through organizational culture lenses (Doctoral dissertation, University of Michigan, 1993). *UMI Dissertation Services,* 9331999.

Etzioni, A. (1961). *A comparative analysis of complex organizations.* New York: Free Press.

Evans-Pritchard, E. (1937). *Witchcraft, oracles and magic among the Azande.* Oxford, UK: Clarendon.

Evered, R. (1983). The language of organizations: The case of the Navy. In L. Pondy, M. Luis, P. Frost, & T. Dandridge (Eds.), *Organizational symbolism.* Greenwich, CT: JAI.

Feldman, M. (1989). *Order without design: Information processing and policy making.* Palo Alto, CA: Stanford University Press.

Feldman, M. (1991). The meanings of ambiguity: Learning from stories and metaphors. In P. Frost, L. Moore, M. Louis, C. Lundberg, & J. Martin (Eds.), *Reframing organizational culture* (pp. 145-156). Newbury Park, CA: Sage.

Ferguson, K. (1984). *The feminist case against bureaucracy.* Philadelphia: Temple University Press.

Ferguson, K. (1993). *The man question.* Berkeley: University of California Press.

Fernandez, J. (1982). *Racism and sexism in corporate life: Changing values in American business.* Lexington, MA: Lexington Books.

Firth, R. (1967). *We, the Tikopia.* London: Allen and Unwin. (Original work published 1936)

Flax, J. (1990). *Thinking fragments: Psychoanalysis, feminism, and postmodernism in the contemporary west.* Berkeley: University of California Press.

Fleming, P., & Stablein, R. E. (1997). *Normative control in organization and management theory* (Working Paper Series 97/01). Dunedin, New Zealand: University of Otago, Department of Management.

Foucault, M. (1977). *Discipline and punishment: The birth of prison.* London: Lane.

Foucault, M. (1980). *Power/knowledge.* New York: Pantheon.

Frederick, T. (1985). *A theory of culture development and methodology for analysis.* Unpublished manuscript, Stanford University, Stanford, CA.

Friedman, S. (1983). *Cultures within cultures? An empirical assessment of an organization's subcultures using projective measures.* Paper presented at the annual meeting of the Academy of Management, Dallas.

Frost, P., Moore, L., Louis, M., Lundberg, C., & Martin, J. (Eds.). (1991). *Organizational culture.* Newbury Park, CA: Sage.

Frost, P., & Stablein, R. (Eds.). (1992). *Doing exemplary research.* Newbury Park, CA: Sage.

Frug, G. (1986). The ideology of bureaucracy in American law. *Harvard Law Review, 97,* 1276-1388.

Gagliardi, P. (Ed.). (1990). *Symbols and artifacts: Views of the corporate landscape.* Berlin: de Gruyter.

Gagliardi, P. (1991). *Reflections on reframing organizational culture.* Invited presentation at the International Conference on Organizational Symbolism and Corporate Culture, Copenhagen.

Gagliardi, P. (1996). Exploring the aesthetic side of organizational life. In S. Clegg, C. Hardy, & W. Nord (Eds.), *Handbook of organization studies* (pp. 565-580). London: Sage.

Geertz, C. (1973). *The interpretation of cultures.* New York: Basic Books.

Geertz, C. (1980). *Negara: The theater state in nineteenth century Bali.* Princeton, NJ: Princeton University Press.

Geertz, C. (1983). *Local knowledge: Further essays in interpretive anthropology.* New York: Basic Books.

Geertz, C. (1988). *Works and lives: The anthropologist as author.* Stanford, CA: Stanford University Press.

Geertz, C. (1995). *After the fact: Two countries, four decades, one anthropologist.* Cambridge, MA: Harvard University Press.

Gephart, R. (1978). Status degradation and organizational succession: An ethnomethodological approach. *Administrative Science Quarterly, 23,* 553-581.

Gephart, R. (1988). *Ethnostatistics: Qualitative foundations for quantitative research.* Newbury Park, CA: Sage.

Gherardi, S. (1995a). When will he say "Today the plates are soft?": The management of ambiguity and situated decision-making. *Studies in Cultures, Organizations and Societies, 1,* 9-27.

Gherardi, S. (1995b). *Gender, symbolism and organizational culture.* London: Sage.

Glaser, B., & Strauss, A. (1967). *The discovery of grounded theory.* Chicago: Aldine.

Globokar, T. (1997). Eastern Europe meets west: An empirical study on French management in a Slovenian plant. In S. Sackmann (Ed.), *Cultural complexity in organizations* (pp. 72-86). Thousand Oaks, CA: Sage.

Goffman, E. (1961). *Asylums: Essays on the social structure of mental patients and other inmates.* Chicago: Aldine.

Golden, K. (1992). The individual and organizational culture: Strategies for action in highly-ordered contexts. *Journal of Management Studies, 29,* 1-21.

Golden-Biddle, K., & Locke, K. (1993). Appealing work: An investigation of how ethnographic texts convince. *Organization Science, 4,* 595-616.

Golden-Biddle, K., & Locke, K. (1997). *Composing qualitative research.* Thousand Oaks, CA: Sage.

Goodhead, G. (1985). *What do corporations believe?* Unpublished manuscript, Stanford University, Stanford, CA.

Gottfredson, S. (1978, October). Evaluating psychological research reports: Dimensions, reliability, and correlates of quality judgments. *American Psychologist, 33,* 920-934.

Grafton-Small, B., & Linstead, S. (1995). *Bricks and bricolage: Deconstructing corporate images in stone and story.* Paper presented at the Antibes Conference Workshop on Organizational Symbolism and Corporate Culture, Antibes, France.

Grafton-Small, R., & Linstead, S. (1987). *Theory as artifact.* Paper presented at the International Conference on Organizational Symbolism and Corporate Culture, Milan.

Graham, J. (1986). Principled organizational dissent: A theoretical essay. *Research in organizational behavior, 8,* 1-52.

Greenwood, R., & Hinings, C. (1988). Organizational design types, tracks and the dynamics of strategic change. *Organization Studies, 9,* 293-316.

Gregory, K. (1983). Native-view paradigms: Multiple cultures and culture conflicts in organizations. *Administrative Science Quarterly, 28,* 359-376.

Greiner, L. (1972). Evolution and revolution as organizations grow. *Harvard Business Review, 50,* 37-46.

Gundry, L., & Rousseau, D. (1994). Communicating culture to newcomers. *Human Relations, 47,* 1065-1088.

Gupta, A., & Ferguson, J. (Eds.). (1997). *Anthropological locations.* Berkeley: University of California Press.

Gutek, B., & Morasch, B. (1982). Sex-ratios, sex role spillover, and sexual harassment of women at work. *Journal of Social Issues, 38,* 55-74.

Habermas, J. (1971). *Knowledge and human interests* (J. Shapiro, Trans.). London: Heinemann.

Hafner, K. (1997, May). The epic saga of The Well: The world's most influential online community. *Wired,* 98-142.

Hannan, M., Burton, D., & Baron, J. (1996). Inertia and change in the early years: Employment relations in young, high technology firms. *Industrial and Corporate Change, 5,* 503-536.

Hardy, C., & Clegg, S. (1996). Some dare call it power. In S. Clegg, C. Hardy, & W. Nord (Eds.), *Handbook of organization studies* (pp. 622-641). London: Sage.

Harper, D. (1987). *Working knowledge: Skill and community in a small shop.* Chicago: University of Chicago Press.

Harré, R. (1986). *Varieties of realism: A rationale for the natural sciences.* Oxford, UK: Blackwell.

Harris, S., & Sutton, R. (1986). Functions of parting ceremonies in dying organizations. *Academy of Management Journal, 19,* 5-30.

Hassard, J. (1988). Overcoming hermeticism in organization theory. *Human Relations, 41,* 247-259.

Hassard, J., & Parker, M. (Eds.). (1993). *Postmodernism and organizations.* London: Sage.

Hassard, J., & Pym, D. (Eds.). (1990). *The theory and philosophy of organizations: Critical issues and new perspectives.* London: Routledge.

Hatch, E. (1973). *Theories of man and culture.* New York: Columbia University Press.

Hatch, M. (1990). The symbolics of office design. In P. Gagliardi (Ed.), *Symbols and artifacts: Views of the corporate landscape* (pp. 129-146). Hawthorne, NY: de Gruyter.

Hatch, M. (1993). The dynamics of organization culture. *Academy of Management Review, 18,* 657-693.

Hatch, M. (1996). The role of the researcher: An analysis of narrative position in organization theory. *Journal of Management Inquiry, 5,* 359-374.

Hatch, M. (1997). Irony and the social construction of contradiction in the humor of a management team. *Organization Science, 8,* 275-288.

Hatch, M. (1999). Exploring the empty spaces of organizing: How improvisational jazz helps redescribe organizational structure. *Organizational Studies, 20,* 75-100.

Hatch, M., & Ehrlich, S. (1993). Spontaneous humour as an indicator of paradox and ambiguity. *Organization Studies, 14,* 505-526.

Hatch, M., & Jones, M. (1996). Photocopy lore at work: Aesthetics, collective creativity and the social construction of organizations. *Studies in Culture, Organizations and Societies, 3,* 1-25.

Hatch, M., & Schultz, M. (1997). Relations between organizational culture, identity and image. *European Journal of Marketing, 31,* 356-365.

Hearn, J., & Parkin, P. (1987). *"Sex" at "work."* New York: St. Martin's.

Hedberg, B. (1981). How organizations learn and unlearn. In P. Nystrom & W. Starbuck (Eds.), *Handbook of organizational design: Adapting organizations to their environments, 1* (pp. 3-27). Oxford, UK: Oxford University Press.

Hermans, H., & Kempen, H. (1998). Moving cultures: The perilous problems of cultural dichotomies in a globalizing society. *American Psychologist, 53,* 1111-1120.

Hernes, H. (1997). Cross-cutting identifications in organizations. In S. Sackmann (Ed.), *Cultural complexity in organizations* (pp. 343-366). Thousand Oaks, CA: Sage.

Hernes, T. (1998). *Exploring the fringes of organizations.* Unpublished manuscript, TromsØ University, TromsØ, Norway.

Hernes, T. (1999). *Organizational boundaries: A dynamic perspective. Exploring the fringes of organizations.* Unpublished manuscript, Tromsø University, Tromsø, Norway.

Hirsch, P., & Andrews, A. (1983). Ambushes, shootouts, and knights of the roundtable: The language of corporate takeovers. In L. Pondy, M. Luis, P. Frost, & T. Dandridge (Eds.), *Organizational symbolism.* Greenwich, CT: JAI.

Hochschild, A. (1989). *The second shift: Working parents and the revolution at home.* New York: John Wiley.

Hodson, R. (1998). Organizational ethnographies: An underutilized resource in the sociology of work. *Social Forces, 76,* 1173-1208.

Hofstede, G. (1980). *Culture's consequences: International differences in work-related values.* Beverly Hills, CA: Sage.

Hofstede, G. (1991). *Cultures and organizations: Software of the mind.* New York: McGraw-Hill.

Hofstede, G., Neuijen, B., Ohayv, D., & Sanders, G. (1990). Measuring organizational cultures. *Administrative Science Quarterly, 35,* 286-316.

Hong, Y., Morris, M., Chiu, C., & Benet-Martinez, V. (2000). Multicultural minds: A dynamic constructivist approach to culture and cognition. *American Psychologist, 55,* 709-720.

Hurtado, A. (1989). Relating to privilege: Seduction and rejection in the subordination of white women and women of color. *Signs, 14,* 833-855.

Iacocca, L. (1984). *Iacocca: An autobiography.* New York: Bantam.

Ignatow, G., & Jost, J. (2000). *"Idea hamsters" on the "bleeding edge": Metaphors of life and death in Silicon Valley* (Research Paper No. 1628). Stanford, CA: Stanford University, Graduate School of Business.

Iser, W. (1978). *The act of reading: A theory of aesthetic response.* Baltimore: Johns Hopkins University Press.

Ishida, T. (1984). Conflict and its accommodation: Omote-Ura and Uchi-soto relations. In E. Krauss, T. Rohlen, & P. Steinhoff (Eds.), *Conflict in Japan.* Honolulu: University Press of Hawaii.

Jackson, N., & Willmott, H. (1987). Beyond epistemology and reflective conversation: Towards human relations. *Human Relations, 40,* 361-380.

Jaeger, A. (1979). *An investigation of organizational culture in a multinational context.* Unpublished doctoral dissertation, Stanford University, Stanford, CA.

Jaggar, A. (1983). *Feminist politics and human nature.* Totowa, NJ: Rowman & Allanheld.

Jamison, M. (1985). The joys of gardening: Collectivist and bureaucratic cultures in conflict. *Sociological Quarterly, 26,* 473-490.

Jang, S., & Chung, M. (1997). Discursive contradiction of tradition and modernity in Korean management practices: A case study of Samsung's new management. In S. Sackmann (Ed.), *Cultural complexity in organizations* (pp. 51-71). Thousand Oaks, CA: Sage.

Jeffcutt, P. (1991). *Styles of representation in organizational analysis: Heroism, happy endings and the carnivalesque in the organizational symbolism literature.* Paper presented at the International Conference on Organizational Symbolism and Corporate Culture, Copenhagen.

Jeffcutt, P. (1994). From interpretation to representation in organisational analysis: Postmodernism, ethnography and organisational symbolism. *Organisation Studies, 15,* 241-274.

Jeffcutt, P. (in press). *Culture and symbolism in organizational analysis.* Thousand Oaks, CA: Sage.

Jelinek, M., Smircich, L., & Hirsch, P. (1983). Introduction: A code of many colors. *Administrative Science Quarterly, 28,* 331-338.

Jermier, J. (1985). When the sleeper wakes: A short story extending themes in radical organization theory. *Journal of Management, 11,* 67-80.

Jermier, J., Slocum, J., Fry, L., & Gaines, J. (1991). Organizational subcultures in a soft bureaucracy: Resistance behind the myth and facade of an official culture. *Organizational Science, 2,* 170-194.

Jick, T. (1979). Mixing qualitative and quantitative methods: Triangulation in action. *Administrative Science Quarterly, 24,* 602-611.

Jones, M., Moore, M., & Snyder, R. (1988). *Inside organizations: Understanding the human dimension.* Newbury Park, CA: Sage.

Jonsson, S., & Lundin, R. (1977). Myths and wishful thinking as management tools. In P. Nystrom & W. Starbuck (Eds.), *Studies in Management Sciences: Prescriptive Models of Organizations* (Vol. 5, pp. 157-170). Amsterdam: North Holland.

Kanter, R. (1977). *Men and women of the corporation.* New York: Anchor.

Katz, D., & Kahn, R. (1978). *The social psychology of organizations* (2nd ed.). New York: John Wiley.

Keesing, R. (1981). *Cultural anthropology: A contemporary perspective.* New York: Holt, Rinehart & Winston.

Kilduff, M. (1993). Deconstructing organizations. *Academy of Management Review, 18,* 13-31.

Kilduff, M., & Corley, K. (2000). *Organizational culture from a network perspective.* Unpublished manuscript, Pennsylvania State University, University Park.

Kilmann, R. (1985). *Beyond the quick fix: Managing five tracks to organizational success.* San Francisco: Jossey-Bass.

Kilmann, R., Saxton, M., Serpa, R., & Associates. (1985). *Gaining control of the corporate culture.* San Francisco: Jossey-Bass.

Kimberly, J. (1979). Issues in the creation of organizations: Initiation, innovation, and institutionalization. *Academy of Management Journal, 22,* 437-457.

Kimberly, J., & Miles, R. (1980). *The organizational life cycle.* San Francisco: Jossey-Bass.

Kimberly, J., & Quinn, R. (Eds.). (1984). *Organizational transitions.* Homewood, IL: Irwin.

Kitayama, S., & Markus, H. (Eds.). (1994). *Emotion and culture: Empirical studies of mutual influence.* Washington, DC: American Psychological Association.

Kleinberg, J. (1989). Cultural clash between managers: America's Japanese firms. In S. Prasad (Ed.), *Advances in international comparative management* (Vol. 4, pp. 221-244). Greenwich, CT: JAI.

Knights, D. (1992). Changing spaces: The disruptive impact of a new epistemological location for the study of management. *Academy of Management Review, 17,* 514-536.

Knights, D., & Willmott, H. (1987). Organizational culture as management strategy. *International Studies of Management and Organization, 17,* 40-63.

Koene, B., Boone, C., & Soeters, J. (1997). Organizational factors influencing homogeneity and heterogeneity of organizational cultures. In S. Sackmann (Ed.), *Cultural complexity in organizations* (pp. 273-293). Thousand Oaks, CA: Sage.

Kondo, D. (1990). *Crafting selves: Power, gender, and discourses of identity in a Japanese workplace.* Chicago: University of Chicago Press.

Koot, W. (1997). Strategic utilization of ethnicity in contemporary organizations. In S. Sackmann (Ed.), *Cultural complexity in organizations* (pp. 315-339). Thousand Oaks, CA: Sage.

Koot, W., Sabelis, I., & Ybema, S. (1996). *Contradictions in context.* Amsterdam: University Press.

Kotter, J., & Heskett, J. (1992). *Corporate culture and performance.* New York: Free Press.

Kreiner, K., & Schultz, M. (1995). Soft cultures: The symbolism of cross-border organizing. *Studies in Culture, Organizations and Societies, 1,* 63-81.

Kreiner, K., & Tyggestad, K. (1997). *The coproduction of chip and society.* Unpublished manuscript, Lund University, Lund, Sweden.

Krug, K. (1999). *A hypermediated ethnography of organizational change: Conversations in the Museum of Anthropology.* Interdisciplinary PhD dissertation, University of British Columbia, Vancouver, Canada.

Kunda, G. (1992). *Engineering culture: Control and commitment in a high-tech corporation.* Philadelphia: Temple University Press.

Kunda, G. (1996). *Scenes from a marriage: Work and family in corporate drama.* Paper presented at the Academy of Management Meetings, Cincinnati, OH.

Kunda, G., & Van Maanen, J. (1999). Changing scripts at work: Managers and professionals. *Annals of the American Academy, 561,* 64-80.

Kymlicka, W. (1995). *Multicultural citizenship: A liberal theory of minority rights.* Oxford, UK: Oxford University Press.

Larsen, J., & Schultz, M. (1990). Artifacts in a bureaucratic monastery. In P. Gagliardi (Ed.), *Symbols and artifacts: Views of the corporate landscape* (pp. 282-302). Berlin: de Gruyter.

Latour, B. (1987). *Science in action.* Cambridge, MA: Harvard University Press.

Law, J. (1994). *Organizing modernity.* Oxford, UK: Blackwell.

Lawrence, P., & Lorsch, J. (1967). *Organization and environment: Managing differentiation and integration.* Boston: Harvard University, Graduate School of Business Administration.

Letiche, H. (1991). *Postmodernism goes practical.* Paper presented at the International Conference on Organizational Symbolism and Corporate Culture, Copenhagen.

Levitt, B., & Nass, C. (1989). The lid on the garbage can: Institutional constraints on decision making in the technical core of college-text publishers. *Administrative Science Quarterly, 34,* 190-207.

Lincoln, J., & Kahlberg, A. (1985). Work organization and workforce commitment: A study of plants and employees in the U.S. and Japan. *American Sociological Review, 50,* 738-760.

Linstead, S. (1991). *The text of culture: Implications of post-modern thought for the analysis of culture in organizations.* Paper presented at the European Group for Organizational Studies conference, Vienna.

Linstead, S. (1993). From postmodern anthropology to deconstructive ethnography. *Human Relations, 46,* 97-120.

Linstead, S., & Grafton-Small, R. (1991). *No visible means of support: Ethnography and the end of deconstruction.* Paper presented at the International Conference on Organizational Symbolism and Corporate Culture, Copenhagen.

Louis, M. (1983). Sourcing workplace cultures: Why, when, and how? In R. Kilmann (Ed.), *Managing corporate cultures* (pp. 126-136). San Francisco: Jossey-Bass.

Louis, M. (1985). An investigator's guide to workplace culture. In P. Frost, L. Moore, M. Louis, C. Lundberg, & J. Martin (Eds.), *Organizational culture* (pp. 73-94). Beverly Hills, CA: Sage.

Lucas, R. (1987). Political-cultural analysis of organizations. *Academy of Management Review, 12,* 144-156.

Lundberg, C. (in press). Working with cultures in organizations: A social rules perspective. In C. Cooper, S. Cartwright, & C. Early (Eds.), *Handbook of organization culture (and climate).* Chichester, UK: Wiley.

Lyotard, J. F. (1984). *The postmodern condition: A report on knowledge* (G. Bennington & B. Massumi, Trans.). Minneapolis: University of Minnesota Press.

Mahoney, M. (1977). Publication prejudices: An experimental study of confirmatory bias on the peer review system. *Cognitive Theory and Research, 1,* 161-175.

Malinowski, B. (1961). *Argonauts of the Western Pacific.* New York: E. P. Dutton. (Original work published 1922)

March, J., & Olsen, J. (Eds.). (1976). *Ambiguity and choice in organizations.* Bergen, Norway: Universitetsforlagert.

Marcus, G., & Fischer, M. (1999). *Anthropology as cultural critique: An experimental moment in the human sciences.* Chicago: University of Chicago Press. (Original work published 1986)

Markus, H., & Kitayama, S. (1991). Culture and the self: Implications for cognition, emotion, and motivation. *Psychological Review, 98,* 224-253.

Markus, H., & Kitayama, S. (1994). A collective fear of the collective: Implications for the selves and theories of selves. *Personality and Social Psychology Bulletin, 20,* 568-579.

Marshall, J. (1984). *Women managers: Travelers in a male world.* London: Wiley.

Martin, J. (1982). Stories and scripts in organizational settings. In A. Hastorf & A. Isen (Eds.), *Cognitive social psychology* (pp. 255-305). London: Routledge.

Martin, J. (1990a). Deconstructing organizational taboos: The suppression of gender conflict in organizations. *Organizational Science, 1,* 339-359.

Martin, J. (1990b). Breaking up the mono-method monopolies in organizational research. In J. Hassard & D. Pym (Eds.), *Theory and philosophy of organizations* (pp. 30-43). London: Routledge.

Martin, J. (1992a). *Cultures in organizations.* New York: Oxford University Press.

Martin, J. (1992b). Escaping the inherent conservatism of empirical organizational research. In R. Stablein & P. Frost (Eds.), *Doing exemplary research* (pp. 233-239). Newbury Park, CA: Sage.

Martin, J. (1994). The organization of exclusion: The institutionalization of sex inequality, gendered faculty jobs, and gendered knowledge in organizational theory and research. *Organization, 1,* 401-431.

Martin, J. (1995). The style and structure of cultures in organizations: Three perspectives. *Organizational Science, 6,* 230-232.

Martin, J. (in press). Swimming against the tide: Aligning values and work. In R. Stablein & P. Frost (Eds.), *Renewing research practice.* Thousand Oaks, CA: Sage.

Martin, J., Brickman, P., & Murray, A. (1984). A moral outrage and pragmatism: Explanations for collective action. *Journal of Experimental Social Psychology, 20,* 484-496.

Martin, J., & Casscells, A. (1985). *Companies where women succeed or fail.* Unpublished manuscript, Stanford University, Stanford, CA.

Martin, J., Feldman, M., Hatch, M., & Sitkin, S. (1983). The uniqueness paradox in organizational stories. *Administrative Science Quarterly, 28,* 438-453.

Martin, J., & Frost, P. (1996). The organizational culture war games: A struggle for intellectual dominance. In S. Clegg, C. Hardy, & W. Nord (Eds.), *Handbook of organization studies* (pp. 599-621). London: Sage.

Martin, J., & Harder, J. (1994). Bread and roses: Justice and the distribution of financial and socio-emotional rewards in organizations. *Social Justice Research, 7,* 241-264.

Martin, J., & Knopoff, K. (1997). The gendered implications of apparently gender-neutral organizational theory: Re-reading Weber. In A. Larson & E. Freeman (Eds.), *Ruffin lecture series. Vol. 3: Business ethics and women's studies* (pp. 30-49). Oxford, UK: Oxford University Press.

Martin, J., Knopoff, K., & Beckman, C. (1998). An alternative to bureaucratic impersonality and emotional labor: Bounded emotionality at The Body Shop. *Administrative Science Quarterly, 43,* 429-469.

Martin, J., & Meyerson, D. (1988). Organizational culture and the denial, channeling and acknowledgment of ambiguity. In L. Pondy, R. Boland, Jr., & H. Thomas (Eds.), *Managing ambiguity and change* (pp. 93-125). New York: John Wiley.

Martin, J., & Meyerson, D. (1997). *Executive women at Link.Com* [A set of eight teaching cases, with instructor's notes]. Boston: Harvard University Press.

Martin, J., & Meyerson, D. (1998). Women and power: Conformity, resistance, and disorganized co-action. In R. Kramer & M. Neale (Eds.), *Power and influence in organizations* (pp. 311-348). Thousand Oaks, CA: Sage.

Martin, J., & Powers, M. (1983). Truth or corporate propaganda: The value of a good war story. In L. Pondy, P. Frost, G. Morgan, & T. Dandridge (Eds.), *Organizational symbolism.* Greenwich, CT: JAI.

Martin, J., & Siehl, C. (1983). Organizational culture and counterculture: An uneasy symbiosis. *Organizational Dynamics, 12,* 52-64.

Martin, J., Sitkin, S., & Boehm, M. (1985). Founders and the elusiveness of a cultural legacy. In P. Frost, L. Moore, M. Louis, C. Lundberg, & J. Martin (Eds.), *Organizational culture* (pp. 99-124). Beverly Hills, CA: Sage.

Martin, J., Su, S., & Beckman, C. (1997). *Enacting shared values—Myth or reality? A context-specific values audit.* Manuscript in preparation.

Maslach, C. (1974). Social and personal bases of individuation. *Journal of Personality and Social Psychology, 29,* 411-425.

McCaskey, M. (1988). The challenge of managing ambiguity and change. In L. Pondy, R. Boland, Jr., & H. Thomas (Eds.), *Managing ambiguity and change* (pp. 1-18). New York: John Wiley.

McDonald, P. (1991). The Los Angeles Olympic Organizing Committee: Developing organizational culture in the short run. In P. Frost, L. Moore, M. Louis, C. Lundberg, & J. Martin (Eds.), *Reframing organizational culture* (pp. 26-38). Newbury Park, CA: Sage.

McGovern, P., & Hope-Hailey, V. (1997). Inside Hewlett-Packard: Corporate culture and bureaucratic control. In S. Sackmann (Ed.), *Cultural complexity in organizations* (pp. 187-206). Thousand Oaks, CA: Sage.

McGrath, J. (1982). Dilemmatics: The study of research choices. In J. McGrath, J. Martin, & R. Kulka (Eds.), *Judgment calls in research: An unorthodox view of the research process* (pp. 69-102). Beverly Hills, CA: Sage.

McGrath, J., Martin, J., & Kulka, R. (1982). *Judgment calls in research: An unorthodox view of the research process.* Beverly Hills, CA: Sage.

Meyer, A. (1982). Adapting to environmental jolts. *Administrative Science Quarterly, 27,* 515-537.

Meyer, J., & Rowan, B. (1977). Institutionalized organizations: Formal structures as a myth and ceremony. *American Journal of Sociology, 83,* 340-363.

Meyerson, D. (1991a). "Normal" ambiguity? A glimpse of an occupational culture. In P. Frost, L. Moore, M. Louis, C. Lundberg, & J. Martin (Eds.), *Reframing organizational culture* (pp. 131-144). Newbury Park, CA: Sage.

Meyerson, D. (1991b). Acknowledging and uncovering ambiguities in cultures. In P. Frost, L. Moore, M. Louis, C. Lundberg, & J. Martin (Eds.), *Reframing organizational culture* (pp. 254-270). Newbury Park, CA: Sage.

Meyerson, D. (1994). Interpretations of stress in institutions: The cultural production of ambiguity and burnout. *Administrative Science Quarterly, 39,* 628-653.

Meyerson, D., & Kolb, D. (in press). Moving out of the "armchair": Developing a framework to bridge the gap between feminist theory and practice. *Organization.*

Meyerson, D., & Martin, J. (1987). Cultural change: An integration of three different views. *Journal of Management Studies, 24,* 623-647.

Meyerson, D., & Scully, M. (1995). Tempered radicalism and the politics of ambivalence and change. *Organizational Science, 6,* 565-600.

Miller, D., & Friesen, P. (1983). Successful and unsuccessful phases of the corporate life cycle. *Organization Studies, 4,* 339-356.

Mills, A. (1988). Organization, gender, and culture. *Organization Studies, 9,* 351-370.

Mills, A. (1995). Man/aging subjectivity, silencing diversity: Organizational imagery in the airline industry. The case of British Airways. *Organization, 2,* 243-269.

Mills, A. (1997). Practice makes perfect: Corporate practices, bureaucratization and the idealized gendered self. *Administrative Studies, 4,* 272-288.

Mills, A., & Hatfield, J. (1997). Air Canada vs. Canadian: Competition and merger in the framing of airline culture. *Studies in Culture, Organizations and Societies, 4*(1), 1-32.

Moi, T. (1985). *Sexual/textual politics: Feminist literary theory.* London: Methuen.

Morgan, G. (Ed.). (1983). *Beyond method.* London: Sage.

Morgan, G., & Ramirez, R. (1984). Action learning: A holographic metaphor for guiding social change. *Human Relations, 37,* 1-28.

Morley, D. (1992). *Television, audiences, and cultural studies.* London: Routledge.

Morrill, C., & Fine, G. (1997). Ethnographic contributions to organizational sociology. *Sociological Methods & Research, 25,* 424-451.

Morris, M., Leung, K., Ames, D., & Lickel, B. (1999). Views from inside and outside: Integrating emic and etic insights about culture and justice judgment. *Academy of Management Review, 24,* 781-796.

Morris, M., & Peng, K. (1994). Culture and cause: American and Chinese attributions for social physical events. *Journal of Personality and Social Psychology, 7,* 949-971.

Mumby, D. (1987). The political function of narrative in organizations. *Communication Monographs, 54,* 113-127.

Mumby, D. (1988). *Communication and power in organizations: Discourse, ideology and domination.* Norwood, NJ: Ablex.

Mumby, D. (1994). Cultures in organizations: Three perspectives, by Joanne Martin. *Academy of Management Review, 19,* 156-159.

Mumby, D., & Putnam, L. (1992). The politics of emotion: A feminist reading of bounded rationality. *Academy of Management Review, 17,* 465-486.

Nakane, C. (1970). *Japanese society.* Berkeley: University of California Press.

Nkomo, S. (1992). The emperor has no clothes: Rewriting "race in organizations." *Academy of Management Review, 17,* 487-513.

Nord, W., & Connell, A. (1996). The bloodless coup: The infiltration of organization science by uncertainty and values. *Journal of Applied Behavioral Science, 32,* 407-427.

Nord, W., & Connell, A. (1998). *Criteria for good theory in organization studies 2000 A.D.* Unpublished manuscript, University of South Florida, Tampa.

Okin, S. (1989). *Justice, gender, and the family.* New York: Basic Books.

Okin, S. (1995). Gender and relativism in recent historical scholarship. *New Zealand Journal of History, 29,* 211-225.

Okin, S. (1996). Is multiculturalism bad for women? *Boston Review, 22,* 25-40.

Olsen, F. (1983). The family and the market: A study of ideology and legal reform. *Harvard Law Review, 96,* 1497-1578.

O'Reilly, C. (1989). Corporations, culture, and commitment: Motivation and social control in organizations. In M. Tushman, C. O'Reilly, & D. Nadler (Eds.), *Management of organizations: Strategies, tactics, and analyses* (pp. 285-303). Cambridge, MA: Ballinger.

O'Reilly, C., Chatman, J., & Caldwell, D. (1991). People and organizational culture: A profile comparison approach to assessing person-organization fit. *Academy of Management Journal, 34,* 487-516.

O'Reilly, C., & Tushman, M. (1997). *Winning through innovation: A practical guide to leading organizational change and renewal.* Boston: Harvard Business School Press.

Ott, J. (1989). *The organizational culture perspective.* Pacific Grove, CA: Brooks/Cole.

Ouchi, W. (1981). *Theory Z: How American business can meet the Japanese challenge.* Reading, MA: Addison-Wesley.

Ouchi, W., & Jaeger, A. (1978). Type Z organization: Stability in the midst of mobility. *Academy of Management Review, 3,* 305-314.

Ouchi, W., & Wilkins, A. (1985). Organizational culture. *Annual Review of Sociology, 11,* 457-483.

Ozick, C. (1996). *Fame and folly.* New York: Knopf.

Pascale, R., & Athos, A. (1981). *The art of Japanese management: Applications for American executives.* New York: Simon & Schuster.

Passaro, J. (1997). "You can't take the subway to the field!" "Village" epistemologies in the global village. In A. Gupta & J. Ferguson (Eds.), *Anthropological locations* (pp. 147-162). Berkeley: University of California Press.

Pedersen, J., & Dobbin, F. (1997). *Constructing organizations: Neo-institutionalism and organizational culture* (Papers in Organization No. 21). Copenhagen: Copenhagen Business School, Institute of Organization and Industrial Sociology.

Perlow, L. (1997). *Finding time: How corporations, individuals, and families can benefit from new work practices.* Ithaca, NY: Cornell University Press.

Perrow, C. (1984). *Normal accidents.* New York: Basic Books.

Peters, T., & Waterman, R. (1982). *In search of excellence: Lessons from America's best-run companies.* New York: Harper & Row.

Pettigrew, A. (1979). On studying organizational culture. *Administrative Science Quarterly, 24,* 570-581.

Pettigrew, A. (1985a). Examining change in the long-term context of culture and politics. In J. Pennings & Associates (Eds.), *Organizational strategy and change* (pp. 269-318). San Francisco: Jossey-Bass.

Pettigrew, A. (1985b). *The awakening giant: Continuity and change in ICI.* Oxford, UK: Blackwell.

Pfeffer, J. (1992). *Managing with power: Politics and influence in organizations.* Cambridge, MA: Harvard Business School Press.

Pfeffer, J. (1993). Barriers to the advance of organizational science: Paradigm development as a dependent variable. *Academy of Management Review, 17,* 599-620.

Podsakoff, P., & Dalton, D. (1987). Research methodology in organizational studies. *Journal of Management, 13,* 419-441.

Pondy, L., Frost, P., Morgan, G., & Dandridge, T. (Eds.). (1983). *Organizational symbolism.* Greenwich, CT: JAI.

Porras, J. (1987). *Stream analysis: A powerful way to diagnose and manage organizational change.* Reading, MA: Addison-Wesley.

Porras, J., & Collins, J. (1994). *Built to last.* New York: HarperBusiness.

Pratt, M. (1986). Fieldwork in common places. In J. Clifford & G. Marcus (Eds.), *Writing culture: The poetics and politics of ethnography* (pp. 35-37). Berkeley: University of California Press.

Putnam, L. (1996). Situating the author and the text. *Journal of Management Inquiry, 5,* 382-386.

Pye, L. (1991). The state and the individual: An overview interpretation. *China Quarterly, 127*, 443-446.

Rafaeli, A., & Sutton, R. (1987). Expression of emotion as part of the work role. *Academy of Management Review, 12*, 23-37.

Ramirez, R. (1987). An aesthetic theory of social organization. *Dragon, 2*, 51-63.

Reed, M. (1985). *Redirections in organizational analysis.* London: Tavistock.

Reed, M. (1990). From paradigms to images: The paradigm warrior turns postmodern guru. *Personnel Review, 19*, 35-40.

Reed, M. (1996). Organizational theorizing: A historically contested terrain. In S. Clegg, C. Hardy, & W. Nord (Eds.), *Handbook of organization studies* (pp. 31-56). London: Sage.

Rifkin, C. (1985). *Rituals in organizations.* Unpublished manuscript, Stanford University, Stanford, CA.

Riley, P. (1983). A structurationist account of political cultures. *Administrative Science Quarterly, 28*, 414-437.

Risberg, A. (1999). *Ambiguities thereafter.* Lund, Sweden: Lund University Press.

Roberts, K., & Boyacigiller, N. (1984). Cross-national organizational research: The grasp of the blind men. In B. Staw & L. Cummings (Eds.), *Research in organizational behavior* (Vol. 6, pp. 423-475). Greenwich, CT: JAI.

Roberts, K., Rousseau, D., & LaPorte, T. (1994). The cultures of high reliability: Quantitative and qualitative assessment aboard nuclear powered aircraft carriers. *Journal of High Technology Management, 5*, 141-161.

Rodgers, W. (1969). *Think.* New York: Stein & Day.

Rofel, L. (1989). *Eating out of one big pot: Hegemony and resistance in a Chinese factory.* Unpublished doctoral dissertation, Stanford University, Stanford, CA.

Rohlene, T. (1974). *For harmony and strength: Japanese white-collar organizations in anthropological perspective.* Berkeley: University of California Press.

Rosaldo, M., & Lamphere, L. (Eds.). (1974). *Woman, culture, and society.* Stanford, CA: Stanford University Press.

Rosaldo, R. (1989). *Culture & truth: The remaking of social analysis.* Boston: Beacon.

Rosen, M. (1985). Breakfast at Spiro's: Dramaturgy and dominance. *Journal of Management, 11*, 31-48.

Rosen, M. (1991). Breakfast at Spiro's: Dramaturgy and dominance. In P. Frost, L. Moore, M. Louis, C. Lundberg, & J. Martin (Eds.), *Reframing organizational culture* (pp. 77-89). Newbury Park, CA: Sage.

Rourke, F. (1972). *Bureaucracy and foreign policy.* Baltimore: Johns Hopkins University Press.

Rousseau, D. (1990a). Assessing organizational culture: The case for multiple methods. In B. Schneider (Ed.), *Frontiers of industrial and organizational psychology* (Vol. 3, pp. 153-192). San Francisco: Jossey-Bass.

Rousseau, D. (1990b). Normative beliefs in high and low fund raising organizations. *Group and Organization Studies, 15*, 448-460.

Runkel, P., & McGrath, J. (1972). *Research on human behavior: A systematic guide to method.* New York: Holt, Rinehart & Winston.

Rusted, B. (1987). "It's not called show art!" Aesthetic decisions as organizational practice. *Dragon, 2*, 127-136.

Sabelis, I. (1996). Temporal paradoxes: Working with cultural diversity in organizations. In W. Koot, I. Sabelis, & S. Ybema (Eds.), *Contradictions in context* (pp. 171-192). Amsterdam: VU University Press.

Sabrosky, A., Thompson, J., & McPherson, K. (1982). Organized anarchies: Military bureaucracy in the 1980s. *Journal of Applied Behavioral Science, 18,* 137-153.

Sackmann, S. (Ed.). (1997). *Cultural complexity in organizations.* Thousand Oaks, CA: Sage.

Sahlins, M. (1985). *Islands of history.* Chicago: University of Chicago Press.

Sahlins, M. (1995). *How "natives" think about Captain Cook, for example.* Chicago: University of Chicago Press.

Said, E. (1989). Representing the colonized: Anthropology's interlocutors. *Critical Inquiry, 15,* 205-225.

Sales, A., & Mirvis, P. (1984). When cultures collide: Issues of acquisition. In J. Kimberly & R. Quinn (Eds.), *Managing organizational transition* (pp. 107-133). Homewood, IL: Irwin.

Sathe, V. (1985). *Culture and related corporate realities: Text, cases, and readings on organizational entry, establishment, and change.* Homewood, IL: Irwin.

Schall, M. (1983). A communication rules approach to organizational culture. *Administrative Science Quarterly, 28,* 557-581.

Schank, R., & Abelson, R. (1977). *Scripts, plans, and knowledge.* Hillsdale, NJ: Lawrence Erlbaum.

Schein, E. (1978). *Career dynamics: Matching individual and organizational needs.* Reading, MA: Addison-Wesley.

Schein, E. (1985). *Organizational culture and leadership.* San Francisco: Jossey-Bass.

Schein, E. (1987). *The clinical perspective in field work.* Newbury Park, CA: Sage.

Schein, E. (1991a). The role of the founder in the creation of organizational culture. In P. Frost, L. Moore, M. Louis, C. Lundberg, & J. Martin (Eds.), *Reframing organizational culture* (pp. 14-25). Newbury Park, CA: Sage.

Schein, E. (1991b). What is culture? In P. Frost, L. Moore, M. Louis, C. Lundberg, & J. Martin (Eds.), *Reframing organizational culture* (pp. 243-253). Newbury Park, CA: Sage.

Schein, E. (1996). Three cultures of management: The key to organizational learning. *Sloan Management Review, 38,* 9-21.

Schein, E. (1999). *The corporate culture survival guide: Sense & nonsense about culture change.* San Francisco: Jossey-Bass.

Schein, L. (1998). The other goes to market: Gender, sexuality, and unruliness in post-Mao China. In M. Diamond (Ed.), *Women and revolution: Global expressions* (pp. 363-393). Amsterdam: Kluwer.

Schneider, B. (Ed.). (1990). *Organizational climate and culture.* San Francisco: Jossey-Bass.

Schneider, S., & Barsoux, J. (1997). *Managing across cultures.* New York: Prentice Hall.

Schultz, M. (1991). Transitions between symbolic domains in organizations. *Organization Studies, 12,* 489-506.

Schultz, M. (1992). Postmodern pictures of culture. *International Studies of Management & Organization, 22,* 15-35.

Schultz, M. (1995). *On studying organizational cultures: Diagnosis and understanding.* Berlin: de Gruyter.

Schultz, M., & Hatch, M. (1996). Living with multiple paradigms: The case of paradigm interplay in organizational culture studies. *Academy of Management Review, 21,* 529-557.

Schwartz, H., & Davis, S. (1981). Matching corporate culture and business strategy. *Organizational Dynamics, 10,* 30-48.

Sebag, L. (1964). *Marxisme et structuralisme.* Paris: Payot.

Selznick, P. (1957). *Leadership and administration.* Evanston, IL: Row & Peterson.

Sergiovanni, T., & Corbally, J. (Eds.). (1984). *Leadership and organizational culture.* Urbana: University of Illinois Press.

Sewell, G., & Wilkinson, B. (1992). Someone to watch over me: Surveillance, discipline, and the just-in-time labour process. *Sociology, 26,* 271-289.

Sewell, G., & Wilkinson, B. (1998). Empowerment or emasculation: Shop floor surveillance in a total quality organisation. In P. Blyton & P. Turnbull (Eds.), *Reassessing human resource management* (pp. 97-115). London: Sage.

Shallenberger, D. (1994). Professional and openly gay: A narrative study of the experience. *Journal of Management Inquiry, 3,* 119-142.

Sharpe, D. (1997). Managerial control strategies and subcultural processes: On the shop floor in a Japanese manufacturing organization in the United Kingdom. In S. Sackmann (Ed.), *Cultural complexity in organizations* (pp. 228-251). Thousand Oaks, CA: Sage.

Shenkar, O., & von Glinow, M. (1994). Paradoxes of organizational theory and research: Using the case of China to illustrate national contingency. *Management Science, 40,* 56-71.

Shrivastava, P. (1994). *Greening business: Towards sustainable corporations.* Cincinnati, OH: Thompson Executive Press.

Shriver, S. (1986). The vision. In M. Viorst (Ed.), *Making a difference: The Peace Corps at twenty five* (pp. 15-29). New York: Weidenfeld & Nicolson.

Shweder, R. (1991). *Thinking through cultures: Expeditions in cultural psychology.* Cambridge, MA: Harvard University Press.

Siehl, C. (1984). *Cultural sleight-of-hand: The illusion of consistency.* Unpublished doctoral dissertation, Stanford University, Stanford, CA.

Siehl, C., & Martin, J. (1984). The role of symbolic management: How can managers effectively transmit organizational culture? In J. Hunt, D. Hosking, C. Schriesheim, & R. Stewart (Eds.), *Leaders and managers: International perspectives on managerial behavior and leadership* (Vol. 7, pp. 227-239). Elmsford, NY: Pergamon.

Siehl, C., & Martin, J. (1988). Measuring organizational culture: Mixing qualitative and quantitative methods. In M. Jones, M. Moore, & R. Snyder (Eds.), *Inside organizations: Understanding the human dimension* (pp. 79-104). Newbury Park, CA: Sage.

Siehl, C., & Martin, J. (1990). Organizational culture: A key to financial performance? In B. Schneider (Ed.), *Organizational climate and culture* (pp. 241-281). San Francisco: Jossey-Bass.

Silverman, D. (1970). *The theory of organizations.* New York: Basic Books.

Sims, H., & Gioia, D. (1986). *The thinking organization.* San Francisco: Jossey-Bass.

Smircich, L. (1983a). Concepts of culture and organizational analysis. *Administrative Science Quarterly, 28,* 339-358.

Smircich, L. (1983b). Organizations as shared meanings. In L. Pondy, P. Frost, G. Morgan, & T. Dandridge (Eds.), *Organizational symbolism* (pp. 55-65). Greenwich, CT: JAI.

Smircich, L., & Calás, M. (1987). Organizational culture: A critical assessment. In F. Jablin, L. Putnam, K. Roberts, & L. Porter (Eds.), *Handbook of organizational communication* (pp. 228-263). Newbury Park, CA: Sage.

Smircich, L., Calás, M., & Morgan, G. (Eds.). (1992). Theory development forum [Special issue]. *Academy of Management Review, 17.*

Smircich, L., & Morgan, G. (1982). Leadership: The management of meaning. *Journal of Applied Behavioral Science, 18,* 257-273.

Smith, V. (1993). Cultures in organizations: Three perspectives by Joanne Martin. *Contemporary Sociology, 22,* 418-421.

Snyder, C., & Fromkin, H. (1980). *Uniqueness: The human pursuit of difference.* New York: Plenum.

Spivak, G. (1988). Can the subaltern speak? In C. Nelson & L. Grossberg (Eds.), *Marxism and the interpretation of culture* (pp. 271-313). Chicago: University of Chicago Press.

Sproull, L. (1981). Beliefs in organizations. In P. Nystrom & W. Starbuck (Eds.), *Handbook of organizational design: Vol. 2. Remodeling organizations and their environments* (pp. 203-244). Oxford, UK: Oxford University Press.

Stablein, R. (1996). Data in organization studies. In S. Clegg, C. Hardy, & W. Nord (Eds.), *Handbook of organization studies* (pp. 509-525). London: Sage.

Stablein, R., & Nord, W. (1985). Practical and emancipatory interests in organizational symbolism: A review and evaluation. *Journal of Management, 11,* 13-28.

Starbuck, W. (1983). Organizations as action generators. *American Sociological Review, 48,* 91-102.

Starbuck, W. (2000). *Taking stock of the publication process.* Paper presented at the ASAC-IFSAM 2000 conference, July 8-11, Montreal.

Stephenson, W. (1953). *The study of behavior: Q-technique and its methodology.* Chicago: University of Chicago Press.

Stevenson, W., & Bartunek, J. (1996). Power, interaction, position, and the generation of cultural agreement in organizations. *Human Relations, 49,* 75-104.

Strati, A. (1992). Aesthetic understanding of organizational life. *Academy of Management Review, 17,* 568-581.

Strati, A. (1999). *Organization and aesthetics.* London: Sage.

Strober, M. (1990). Human capital theory: Implications for HR managers. *Industrial Relations, 29,* 214-239.

Sunesson, S. (1985). Outside the goal paradigm: Power and structured patterns of nonrationality. *Organization Studies, 6,* 229-246.

Sutton, R. (1994). *The virtues of closet qualitative research.* Unpublished manuscript, Stanford University, Stanford, CA.

Swidler, A. (1986). A culture in action: Symbols and strategies. *American Sociological Review, 51,* 237-286.

Takashi, S. (1997). Organizational culture and innovation: Theoretical modeling and statistical testing. *Journal of Economics, 62*, 27-67.

Tedlock, B. (1991). From participation observation to observation of participation: The emergence of narrative ethnography. *Journal of Anthropological Research, 47*, 69-94.

Tobias, A. (1976). *Fire and ice*. New York: William Morrow.

Tom, A. (1986). *To make a life for myself: An ethnography of a job training program*. Unpublished doctoral dissertation, Stanford University, Stanford, CA.

Torbert, W. (1976). *Creating a community of inquiry*. London: Wiley.

Townley, B. (1993). Foucault, power/knowledge, and its relevance for human resource management. *Academy of Management Review, 18*, 518-545.

Triandis, H. (1989). The self and social behavior in differing cultural contexts. *Psychological Review, 90*, 506-520.

Trice, H., & Beyer, J. (1984). Studying organizational cultures through rites and ceremonials. *Academy of Management Review, 9*, 653-669.

Trice, H., & Beyer, J. (1985). Using six organizational rites to change cultures. In R. Kilmann, M. Saxton, & R. Serpa (Eds.), *Gaining control of the corporate culture* (pp. 370-399). San Francisco: Jossey-Bass.

Trice, H., & Beyer, J. (1993). *The cultures of work organizations*. Englewood Cliffs, NJ: Prentice Hall.

Tulin, M. (1997). Talking organization: Possibilities for conversation analysis in organizational behavior research. *Journal of Management Inquiry, 6*, 101-119.

Turner, B. (1971). *Exploring the industrial subculture*. London: Macmillan.

Turner, B. (1986). Sociological aspects of organizational symbolism. *Organizational Studies, 7*, 101-115.

Turner, B. (1990). The rise of organizational symbolism. In J. Hassard & D. Pym (Eds.), *The theory and philosophy of organizations: Critical issues and new perspectives* (pp. 83-96). London: Routledge.

Turner, V. (1969). *The ritual process: Structure and anti-structure*. Chicago: Aldine.

Tushman, M., & Romanelli, E. (1985). Organizational evolution: A metamorphosis model of convergence and reorientation. In L. Cummings & B. Staw (Eds.), *Research in organizational behavior* (Vol. 7, pp. 171-222). Greenwich, CT: JAI.

Tyler, S. (1986). Post-modern ethnography: From document of the occult to occult document. In J. Clifford & C. Marcus (Eds.), *Writing culture* (pp. 122-140). Berkeley: University of California Press.

U.S. General Accounting Office. (1992). *Organizational culture: Techniques companies use to perpetuate or change beliefs and values* (GAO/NSLAD-91-105). Washington, DC: Government Printing Office.

Uttal, B. (1983, October 17). The corporate culture vultures. *Fortune, 180*, 66-72.

Van de Ven, A. (1997). *The buzzing, blooming, confusing world of organization and management theory: A view from Lake Wobegon University*. Paper presented at the Academy of Management conference, Boston.

Van Maanen, J. (1976). Breaking-in: Socialization to work. In R. Dubin (Ed.), *Handbook of work, organization, and society* (pp. 67-130). Chicago: Rand McNally.

Van Maanen, J. (Ed.). (1979). *Qualitative methodology*. Beverly Hills, CA: Sage.

Van Maanen, J. (1986). Power in the bottle. In S. Srivasta (Ed.), *Executive power.* San Francisco: Jossey-Bass.

Van Maanen, J. (1988). *Tales of the field: On writing ethnography.* Chicago: University of Chicago Press.

Van Maanen, J. (1991). The smile factory: Work at Disneyland. In P. Frost, L. Moore, M. Louis, C. Lundberg, & J. Martin (Eds.), *Reframing organizational culture* (pp. 58-76). Newbury Park, CA: Sage.

Van Maanen, J. (1995a). Style as theory. *Organizational Science, 1,* 133-143.

Van Maanen, J. (1995b). Fear and loathing in organization studies. *Organization Science, 6,* 687-692.

Van Maanen, J. (1996). On the matter of voice. *Journal of Management Inquiry, 5,* 375-381.

Van Maanen, J., & Barley, S. (1984). Occupational communities: Culture and control in organizations. In B. Staw & L. Cummings (Eds.), *Research in organizational behavior* (Vol. 6, pp. 287-366). Greenwich, CT: JAI.

Van Maanen, J., & Barley, S. (1985). Cultural organization: Fragments of a theory. In P. Frost, L. Moore, M. Louis, C. Lundberg, & J. Martin (Eds.), *Organizational culture* (pp. 31-54). Beverly Hills, CA: Sage.

Van Maanen, J., Dabbs, J., Jr., & Faulkner, R. (1982). *Varieties of qualitative research.* Beverly Hills, CA: Sage.

Van Maanen, J., & Kunda, G. (1989). "Real feelings": Emotional expression and organizational culture. In L. Cummings & B. Staw (Eds.), *Research in organizational behavior* (Vol. 11, pp. 43-103). Greenwich, CT: JAI.

van Marrewijk, A. (1996). The paradox of dependency: Cross-cultural relations of three Dutch development organizations and their Bolivian counterparts. In W. Koot, I. Sabelis, & S. Ybema (Eds.), *Contradictions in context* (pp. 113-131). Amsterdam: VU University Press.

van Reine, P. (1996). Globalization and the local development of models for management and organization: The periphery talks back. In W. Koot, I. Sabelis, & S. Ybema (Eds.), *Contradictions in context* (pp. 87-111). Amsterdam: VU University Press.

Weaver, G., & Gioia, D. (1994). Paradigms lost: Incommensurability vs. structurationist inquiry. *Organization Studies, 15,* 565-589.

Webb, E., Campbell, D., Schwartz, R., & Sechrest, L. (1972). *Unobtrusive measures: Non-reactive research in the social sciences.* Skokie, IL: Rand McNally. (Original work published 1966)

Weedon, C. (1987). *Feminist practice and post-structuralist theory.* Cambridge, UK: Basil Blackwell.

Weick, K. (1979). *The social psychology of organizing.* Reading, MA: Addison-Wesley.

Weick, K. (1983). Contradictions in a community of scholars: The cohesion-accuracy tradeoff. *Review of Higher Education, 6,* 253-267.

Weick, K. (1991). The vulnerable system: An analysis of the Tenerife air disaster. In P. Frost, L. Moore, M. Louis, C. Lundberg, & J. Martin (Eds.), *Reframing organizational culture* (pp. 117-130). Newbury Park, CA: Sage.

Weick, K. (1999). Theory construction as disciplined reflexivity: Tradeoffs in the 90s. *Academy of Management Review, 24,* 797-806.

Wels, H. (1996). Strategy as paradox and paradox as strategy. Images of and paradoxes in Chinese culture: Expatriate managers in Sino-Western joint ventures. In W. Koot, I. Sabelis, & S. Ybema (Eds.), *Contradictions in context* (pp. 113-131). Amsterdam: VU University Press.

Westra, A. (1996). Between contrariness and complaisance: The paradox of power—About tools of upward influence in the Netherlands. In W. Koot, I. Sabelis, & S. Ybema (Eds.), *Contradictions in context* (pp. 151-169). Amsterdam: VU University Press.

Whetten, D. (2001). *Hybrids as a special case of organizational identity.* Unpublished manuscript, Brigham Young University, Marriott School, Provo, UT.

Whitehead, A. (1985). *Science and the modern world.* London: Free Association Books. (Original work published 1926)

Who's excellent now? (1984, November 5). *Business Week*, 76-88.

Whyte, W. (1991). Street corner society: Excerpts from the appendix to the 1955 edition. In P. Frost, L. Moore, M. Louis, C. Lundberg, & J. Martin (Eds.), *Reframing organizational culture* (pp. 173-191). Newbury Park, CA: Sage.

Wilkins, A. (1979). *Organizational stories as an expression of management philosophy: Implications for social control in organizations.* Unpublished doctoral dissertation, Stanford University, Stanford, CA.

Willis, P. (1981). *Learning to labour.* London: Routledge Kegan Paul. (Original work published 1977)

Willmott, H. (1987). Studying managerial work: A critique and a proposal. *Journal of Management Studies, 24,* 248-270.

Willmott, H. (1990). Strength is ignorance, slavery is freedom: Managing culture in modern organizations. *Journal of Management Studies, 30,* 515-552.

Willmott, H. (1994). Theorizing human agency: Responding to the crises of (post)-modernity. In J. Hassard & M. Parker (Eds.), *Towards a new theory of organizations.* London: Routledge.

Willmott, H., & Knights, D. (1995). Culture and control in a life insurance company. *Studies in Culture, Organizations and Societies, 1,* 1-18.

Wright, J. (1979). *On a clear day you can see General Motors.* Grosse Point, MI: Wright.

Wuthnow, R., Hunter, J., Bergesen, A., & Kurzweil, E. (1984). *Cultural analysis.* Boston: Routledge Kegan Paul.

Xenikou, A., & Furnham, A. (1996). A correlational and factor analytic study of four questionnaire measures of organizational behavior. *Human Relations, 49,* 349-371.

Yanagisako, S. (2000). *Capital and kinship: An ethnography of Italian family capitalism.* Unpublished manuscript, Stanford University, Stanford, CA.

Yarmey, A., & Yarmey, M. (1997). Eyewitness recall and duration estimates in field settings. *Journal of Applied Social Psychology, 27,* 330-344.

Ybema, S. (1996). The duck-billed platypus in the theory and analysis of organizations: Combinations of consensus and dissensus. In W. Koot, I. Sabelis, & S. Ybema (Eds.), *Contradictions in context* (pp. 39-61). Amsterdam: VU University Press.

Ybema, S. (1997). Telling tales: Contrasts and commonalities within the organization of an amusement park-confronting and combining different perspectives. In S. Sackmann (Ed.), *Cultural complexity in organizations* (pp. 160-186). Thousand Oaks, CA: Sage.

Yeatman, A. (1994). *Postmodern revisionings of the political.* London: Routledge.

Young, E. (1989). On the naming of the rose: Interests and multiple meanings as elements of organizational culture. *Organization Studies, 10,* 187-206.

Young, E. (1991). On the naming of the rose: Interests and multiple meanings as elements of organizational culture. In P. Frost, L. Moore, M. Louis, C. Lundberg, & J. Martin (Eds.), *Reframing organizational culture* (pp. 90-103). Newbury Park, CA: Sage.

Zimbardo, P. (1969). The human choice: Individuation, reason, and order versus deindividuation, impulse and chaos. In W. Arnold & D. Levine (Eds.), *Nebraska symposium on motivation* (pp. 237-308). Lincoln: University of Nebraska Press.

Zucker, L. (1977). The role of institutionalization in cultural persistence. *American Sociological Review, 42,* 726-743.

Name Index

Subject Index

About the Author

Joanne Martin is the Fred H. Merrill Professor of Organizational Behavior at the Graduate School of Business, Stanford University, where she also holds a courtesy appointment in the Department of Sociology. She received a PhD in social psychology from Harvard University. She has served in various positions, including as a member of the Board of Governors of the Academy of Management. In August 2000, she received the Academy's Distinguished Educator of the Year award. She also serves on the board of directors of Consulting Psychologist Press and on various advisory boards. She is author of more than 60 articles and five books, including *Cultures in Organizations: Three Perspectives* (1992) and *Reframing Organizational Culture* (coedited with P. Frost, L. Moore, M. Louis, & C. Lundberg; Sage, 1991). Her current research interests include both culture and gender.